Dram Theati .ıts

R A Banks MA PhD

Hodder & Stoughton

A MEMBER OF THE HODDER HEADLINE GROUP

British Library Cataloguing in Publication Data

Banks, R.A.
  Drama and theatre arts
  1. Drama – History
  1. Title
  809-fi   PN1721
ISBN 0 340 3716 25

First published 1991
Impression number 16 15 14 13 12 11 10 9
Year 1998 1997 1996 1995

Printed in Great Britain for Hodder & Stoughton Educational, a division of Hodder Headline Plc, 338 Euston Road, London NW1 3BH by Athenæum Press Ltd, Gateshead, Tyne & Wear.

Contents

Part Four Criticism

For Mary-Lou

Acknowledgments

For permission to quote copyright material the author and publishers wish to thank: Methuen London for an extract from *The Dumb Waiter* by Harold Pinter; Haskell House Publishers, New York for an extract from *Life in Shakespeare's England* by J. Dover Wilson; J. M. Dent & Sons Ltd for an extract from *An Apology for the Life of Mr Colley* by C. Cibber; J. M. Dent & Sons Ltd for an extract from a translation by Michael Oakley of The Art of Poetry from the *Collected Works of Horace*; Oxford University Press for an extract from *The Poetics* by Hamilton Fyfe, based on Aristotle: *The Poetics* translated by Ingram Bywater (1920); Penguin Books Ltd for quotations from *Euripides: The Bacchae and other Plays* © Philip Vellacott 1954, 1972; Chatto & Windus for an extract from *Greek Drama for the Common Reader* by F. L. Lucas; Penguin Books Ltd for the introduction from *Plautius: The Rope and Other Plays* translated by E. F. Watling, © E. F. Watling, and for short extracts from *Seneca: Four Tragedies and Octavia* translated by E. F. Watling © E. F. Watling; Oxford University Press for an extract from *The Drama of the Medieval Church* translated by K. Young (1933) and for an extract from *The Development of English Drama in the Late Seventeenth Century* by R. D. Hume (1976); Cambridge University Press for an extract from *A History of English Drama II* by Allardyce Nicoll; Methuen London for extracts from *Brief Chronicles* by Martin Esslin and for extracts from *The Absurd* by A. P. Hinchcliffe; the translation of *Rhinoceros* used here is by Derek Prouse in *Eugene Ionesco, Plays Volume 4*, 1960, John Calder (Publishers) Ltd; translations of Artaud by Victor Corti are taken from Antonin Artaud, *The Theatre and its Double*, John Calder (Publishers) Ltd, 1970; Mrs Eva Reichmann for a review by Max Beerbohm of *Justice*; *The Observer* for a criticism of J. B. Priestley's *An Inspector Calls* by J. C. Trewin; the *Daily Mail* for a criticism of J. B. Priestley's *An Inspector Calls* by Lionel Hale; Deborah Rogers Ltd Literary Agency for Kenneth Tynan's review of John Osborne's *Look Back in Anger* in *Curtains*; *The Times* for a review of Tom Stoppard's *Rozencrantz and Guildenstern are Dead* by Irving Wardle (*The Times* 12.4.67); the *Evening Standard* for a review of *Romeo and Juliet* by Milton Schulmann (*Standard* 24.2.77); the *Sunday Telegraph* for *Length and Brecht*, a review of Bertold Brecht's *Mother Courage and Her Children* by Francis King (*Sunday Telegraph* 11.11.84); the University of London for a report of the GCE examiners of the University of London, 1981 © University of London Schools Examinations Board; Methuen London for an extract from *The Caucasian Chalk Circle* by Bertold Brecht and for an extract from *The Cherry Orchard* by Chekov translated by M. Frayn, 1978; Faber and Faber for an extract from *Murder in the Cathedral*, 3rd edition, by T. S. Eliot © Faber and Faber 1937 and for an extract from *Waiting for Godot* by S. Beckett © Faber and Faber 1955; The Society of Authors on behalf of the Bernard Shaw estate for an extract from *Androcles and the Lion* by Bernard Shaw; Methuen London for an extract from *Pirandello: Six Characters in Search of an Author*, translated by John Linstrum; David Higham Associates Ltd for an extract from *Under Milkwood* by Dylan Thomas; Penguin Books for an extract from *Journey's End* by R. C. Sherriff. First published 1929. Published by Penguin 1983 © 1929 by the estate of R C Sherriff.

For permission to reproduce the illustrations in this book the author and publishers would like to thank: The Victoria and Albert Museum (The Roman Theatre at Orange, Scenery designed by Louthenbourg for use in Covent Garden, The Destruction of the Second Covent Garden Theatre, a playbill for the Theatre Royal Drury Lane and a playbill for Astley's Theatre); Flashbacks (Jean Louis Barrault in *Les Enfants du Paradis*); The National Theatre (*Venice Preserv'd*); The Chichester Festival Theatre Productions Co. Ltd (print of Chichester Festival Theatre); Barbara Lanning (Estragon and Vladimir in Borough Road College English Department's production of *Waiting for Godot*, 1973).

Introduction

This book is primarily intended for those studying Drama and Theatre Arts for examinations such as GCE A and O Levels of the Associated Examining Board and the University of London, and the new GCSE/16 + examinations. Students on Drama courses at colleges and the general reader interested in Drama and the Theatre should also find it a useful and comprehensive survey. It includes not only a very detailed examination of the notion of 'text' and the way stage and theatre developed, but also a close examination of the history of Drama as one of the Performing Arts from Greek times to the 1980s. Dramatic theory is discussed in its own period alongside developments in history, science, society, art, music, and theatre architecture. The theory is closely related to the study of individual authors and texts, many of which are specified set topics in examination syllabuses. The contributions of theatrical craftsmen such as Artaud, Brecht, Craig and Stanislavski receive special attention.

Drama, however, is not a subject to be tackled principally through books. It is one which has at its heart a live production, a sensitive re-creation of an experience shaped between playwright, director, actors, audience and all the others associated with this central 'performing art'. The approach used in this book has borne this fact in mind throughout; it is thorough and comprehensive but it is not a literary history. Theory is related to practice and a chapter on the way modern theatre critics writing about actual performances approach their own special art has been included, together with examples of reviews of productions in the theatre.

Drama has always been related to its own historical and social times; it mirrors and helps give direction to contemporary manners, thought, and attitudes. Drama and the Theatre cannot be studied in isolation from their own ages but require a context. Genres, fashions, philosophical movements, legislation, changing audiences, and new scientific developments that alter the lighting, sets, machinery and auditorium – all are part of the development of the Performing Arts. Religion and politics have left their indelible marks too. These are some of the features and areas considered in this book. Each chapter carries its own questions, exercises, and suggestions for project-work.

All writers on Drama and the Theatre today (and this author is no exception) are deeply indebted to works by scholars such as Allardyce Nicoll, E. K. Chambers, Stephen Josephs, H. D. F. Kitto, M. C. Bradbook, Eric Bentley and many more referred to in the text and in the selected bibliography. Phyllis Hartnoll's revised edition of *The Oxford Companion to the Theatre* is a fundamental aid to all students studying the subject. The modern student has a host of scholarly, well-researched works to help him or her establish basic facts on which to form attitudes and approaches to the subject, as well as to follow up specific areas of interest in great detail.

I am also personally grateful to Miss B. C. Lanning who helped me in selecting photographs and especially to Mrs Daphne Meeking, who, once again, has borne with my handwriting to produce her customary immaculate, well set-out typescript. Mary-Lou, my wife, has encouraged me throughout with her suggestions and constant support; without her this book would not have been possible.

Sunbury-on-Thames, 1985   R A Banks

PART ONE

Towards an Understanding of Drama

1
The Nature of Drama

1.1

There is no single definition of the word 'drama' which covers all the richness of its many forms, its multi-faceted nature, and its readiness to change and adapt itself. There have been some serious attempts to define the meaning, however:

> **Drama**: a story of life and action for representation by actors: a composition intended to be represented on the stage: dramatic literature: theatrical entertainment: a dramatic situation, or series of absorbing events.
> *adjs.* dramatic, -al, belonging to the drama: appropriate to or in the form of drama: with the force and vividness of drama.
> *ns.* dramatics, dramaticism, the acting, production, study of plays: show of excessive, exaggerated emotion.
> *v. i* dramatise, -ize, to compose in, or turn into, the form of a drama or play: to exaggerate the importance or emotional nature of.
> (Chambers Twentieth Century Dictionary, new edition, 1972)

The origin of the word in English has its source in the Greek word *dráein* ($\partial\rho\acute{\alpha}\epsilon\iota\nu$): to do.

1.2

The definition in the *Oxford English Dictionary* (corrected edition, 1933) adds a further dimension, that of verisimilitude, 'as in real life':

> **Drama**: composition in prose or verse, adapted to be acted upon a stage, in which a story is related by means of dialogue and action, and is represented with accompanying gesture, costume, and scenery, as in real life: a play.

1.3

Some elements of the meaning of the word 'drama' in Modern English usage begin to emerge from such dictionary definitions. Drama includes some or all of the following:

- (*a*) a *representation* (or a *re-presentation*) of some aspects of life;
- (*b*) a *composition* (*i.e.* something 'put together'. It will have a form, therefore, and involve *selection*, and an *arrangement* of material);
- (*c*) an *interpretation* of an action, usually on a stage. This implies an *audience*, a *point of view* from which the action is interpreted, a *context*, and a *production* (including gesture, costume, and scenery);
- (*d*) *entertainment*; (this may be linked with *literature* or a literary 'text');
- (*e*) *impact, force,* and *vividness*. It may also include *exaggeration*.

1.4

Some attempts to define 'drama' or 'play' emerge from the use of the words by critics, playwrights, and literary writers throughout the centuries:

(*i*)   A tragedy, then, is the imitation of an action that is serious, has magnitude, and is complete in itself; in *language* with pleasurable accessories, each kind brought in separately in the various parts of the work; in a dramatic, not in a narrative form . . . Here by 'language with pleasurable accessories' I mean that with *rhythm* or *song* superadded.

As they act the stories, it follows that in the first place the *Spectacle* (or stage-appearance of the actors) must be some part of the whole.

There are in the natural order of things two causes – Character and Thought . . . Now the action (that which is done) is represented in the play by the Fable or Plot. The *Plot* is simply this, the combination of the incidents of things done in the story; whereas *Character* is what makes us ascribe certain moral qualities to the agents and *Thought* is shown in all they say. There are six points consequently of every tragedy which determine its quality: Plot, Character, Diction, Thought, Spectacle and Melody.

(Aristotle, 384–322 BC, *Poetics*, translated by W. Hamilton Fyfe, Oxford, 1940)

(*ii*)   Comedy is an imitation of the common errors of our life, which he (the poet) *represented* in the most ridiculous and scornful sort that may be; so as it is impossible that any beholder can be content to be such a one . . . Tragedy . . . showeth forth the ulcers that are covered with tissue . . . that, with stirring the effects of admiration and commiseration, *teacheth* the uncertainty of this world.

(Sir P. Sidney, *An Apologie for Poetry*, 1580–1)

(*iii*)   A play is: A *just and lively image of human nature*, representing its passions and humours, and the changes in fortune to which it is subject, for the *delight* and *instruction* of mankind.

(J. Dryden, *Essay on Dramatick Poesie*, 1668)

(*iv*)   *The stage but echoes back the public's voice.*
The drama's laws the drama's patrons give,
For we that live to please, must please to give.

(S. Johnson, at the Opening of the Drury Lane Theatre, 1747)

(*v*)   The Athenians employed *language, action, music, painting*, the *dance*, and *religious institutions* to produce a common effect in the representation of the highest idealisms of *passion* and of *power* . . . The tragedies of the Athenian poets are as mirrors in which *the spectator beholds himself* . . . In the drama of the highest order there is little food for censure or hatred; it *teaches* rather *self-knowledge* and *self-respect* . . . The drama is a prismatic and many-sided mirror, which

collects the brightest rays of human nature and divides and reproduces them . . . and touches them with majesty and beauty. *But in periods of the decay of social life, the drama sympathises with that decay.*
(Shelley, *A Defence of Poetry*, 1821)

(*vi*) NINA   Your play's hard to act; there are no living people in it.
      TREPLER Living people! *We should show life neither as it is nor as it ought to be, but as we see it in our dreams.*
(Anton Chekhov, *The Seagull*, 1896)

(*vii*) You don't expect me to know what to say about a play when I don't know who the author is, do you? If it's by a good author, it's a good play, naturally. That stands to reason.
(G. B. Shaw, *Fanny's First Play*, Epilogue, 1911)

1.5

The definition of drama changes according to writer, period, and context, but some further aspects of drama emerge from these excerpts:

Drama may:
(*a*) include *plot, character, thought, rhythmical language*;
(*b*) *imitate and represent life as it is* and *instruct*;
(*c*) *reflect what the audience demands*;
(*d*) include *music* (songs), *painting, dance, idealistic representations*, and *allow the spectator to see himself or herself*;
(*e*) *portray life* neither realistically nor idealistically '*but as we see it in our dreams*'.

1.6

Any definition of drama is, therefore, complex. Even to discuss what a play is raises complicated issues, since there is a marked difference between what may be called **the text** of a play and what a spectator takes away from a **performance** or **realisation** of the 'text'. The interpretation of a play results from a strange alchemy which changes the words on a page through direction, acting, and realisation into an experience within every individual watching a 'performance'.

1.7 What is the 'Text' of a Play?

The 'text' begins with the dramatist or group of dramatists setting down the words on a page. Birth, origins, family background, education, experiences, attitudes to life, and relationships will all help condition what is written. Equally important will be the context in which the text is produced: 'What was happening around the writers when they were setting down the text – personally, socially, politically, economically, as well as in the theatre?' 'Why did they write at all?' 'Why choose a particular form or style of writing?' 'How was the text to be produced?' These are merely a few of the questions that help to determine the shape of a dramatic work.

1.8

At some periods in the history of the theatre such questions are of great importance in understanding the origin of a 'text'. Galsworthy's views on the injustices in society, where there seemed one law for the rich and another for the poor, help to explain the nature of *Strife* (1909) or *The Silver Box* (1906). The aftermath of the First World War, with its conflicting emotions of patriotism and sense of waste, helps to account for the form, style, and effect of R. C. Sherriff's play, *Journey's End*, which had a successful run on the London stage at the Savoy Theatre in 1929 and 1930, although some of the dialogue ('simply topping', 'jolly bucked', and 'thanks most awfully') has worn badly across the years. To understand John Osborne, the frustration of the young in the 1950s, and the flatness of the theatre in London at the time help to explain the immediate success of *Look Back in Anger* at the Royal Court in 1956.

1.9

Ironically, however, very little is known of the personal life of William Shakespeare, other than that he was born in Stratford-upon-Avon, was the son of a tanner and dealer in wool and hides, married Anne Hathaway, had three children including a set of twins, worked as a member of the Lord Chamberlain's Men, and for twenty years or so was a successful playwright. More is known about the historical context in which he wrote and, occasionally, from the plays themselves a careful reader can uncover the background within the London theatre which helped determine what he wrote. Consider, for example, the following passage from *Hamlet*:

Enter Hamlet and three of the Players

HAM Speak the speech, I pray you, as I pronounced it to you, trippingly on the tongue; but if you mouth it as many of your players do, I had as lief the town-crier spoke my lines. Nor do not saw the air too much with your hand, thus, but use all gently; for in the very torrent, tempest, and, as I may say, whirlwind of your passion, you must acquire and beget a temperance that may give it smoothness. O, it offends me to the soul to hear a robustious periwig-pated fellow tear a passion to tatters, to very rags, to split the ears of the groundlings, who for the most part are capable of nothing but inexplicable dumb-shows and noise. I would have such a fellow whipped for o'erdoing Termagant. It out-Herods Herod. Pray you avoid it.

(III, ii, 1–14)

This set of instructions is given by Hamlet to a group of actors visiting the court at Elsinore asking them to put on a play, *The Murder of Gonzago*, before the King. The very device of using **a play within the play** is one well-known to Elizabethan playwrights (see 'Pyramus and Thisby' in *A Midsummer Night's Dream* where the whole convention is guyed). Plays were enacted on the dais of halls from the time of Sir Thomas More (1478–1535) onwards (see E. K. Chambers, *The Elizabethan Stage*, 1, 229) by groups of players visiting the great houses of England and Shakespeare uses the practice to good effect in a play put on in the professional theatre. Shakespeare's mocking of **dumb shows**, a device he himself is about to use in the play, reminds his audience of the clumsiness of the device to fore-shadow the contents of a play or a scene by using a symbolical or historical tableau (see *The Spanish Tragedy*, acted in 1592) or to save the dramatist the bother of composing dialogue by presenting an incident in pantomime instead. Shakespeare uses the dumb show differently in *Hamlet*, however, by anticipating what would be played out in full later. So that his audience would understand this change in the conventional use, Shakespeare makes Ophelia explain it: 'Belike this show imports the argument of the play' (III, ii, 136). The same technique of using a dumb show had been employed by Shakespeare in *A Midsummer Night's Dream* (1595/6) where the 'show'which precedes the Pyramus and Thisby play probably had actors miming the action whilst the Prologue was laboriously explaining it (V, i, 126–50)*.

The exaggerated acting-styles used in earlier pageant plays and well-known in the popular theatre of England in the sixteenth century are referred to in the simple sentence, 'it out-Herods Herod'. In the Coventry *Pageant of the Shearmen and Taylors* Herod said, 'I stampe! I stare! . . . I rent! (rant) I rawe! (rave) and now run I wode (*mad*)!' and his speech was followed by the stage direction: '*Erode ragis in the pagond and in the strete also*'.

Exaggerated acting-styles were also known in the Elizabethan theatre itself. Earlier in *Hamlet* (II, ii, 430–40) the Prince had spoken of an earlier play on the subject of Dido and Aeneas: ' . . . an excellent play, well-digested in the scenes, set down with as much modesty as cunning. I remember one said there was no sallots (*ribald comments*) in the lines to make the matter savoury . . . an honest method'. In 1612 Thomas Heywood, an actor and playwright himself had given in his *An Apology for Actors* a similar counsel to Hamlet's for sound acting:

> This is the action behooveful in any . . . not to use any impudent or forced motion in any part of the body, no rough, or other violent gestures, nor on the contrary, to stand like a stiff starched man, but to qualify everything according to the nature of the person personated: for in overacting tricks, and toiling too much in the antic habit of humours, men of the ripest desert, greatest opinions, and best reputations, may break into the most violent absurdities.

1.10

The text, therefore, of Hamlet's opening remarks to the players consists of much more than a set of instructions on how to act. Within its own play it carries a special significance; within its historical theatrical and dramatic context it carries a richness of meaning that a contemporary audience, both the informed and the uneducated, would have understood. The speech itself is in prose and follows a scene which contained the poetry of the soliloquy 'To be or not to be' and is just before the confessional scene where the King declares his offence to heaven itself and Hamlet misses a much more real and immediate opportunity to avenge his father than that of putting on a play within a play.

The **text**, then, is clearly much more than words within the immediate

---

* For the use of the dumb-show in *Hamlet* see J. Dover Wilson, *What Happens in Hamlet*, third edition, 1951, 144–53 and Harold Jenkins (ed.), Arden edition of *Hamlet*, 1981, 501–5.

setting of the play and within a historical or contemporary context. Consider, for example, the following extract from Pinter's *The Dumb Waiter*.

The play was first produced by the Hampstead Theatre Club on 21st January, 1960, and later the same year at the Royal Court Theatre. It has only two characters. Ben (played originally by Nicholas Selby) and Gus (played originally by George Tovey). The action of the play is the present and the scene consists of a basement room somewhere in Birmingham on an autumn evening. In the basement there are doors off the back wall, right and left. In the centre of the back wall is a service lift (the Dumb Waiter). The play is concerned, amongst other things, with the relationship of the two men as they await messages, via the lift, from someone in a room above. The title of the play is not without significance.

This extract forms the conclusion to the play:

> (GUS *exits by the door* L. BEN *remains sitting on the bed, still. The lavatory chain is pulled once off* L, *but the lavatory does not flush. Silence.*
> GUS *re-enters and stops inside the door, deep in thought. He looks at* BEN, *then walks slowly across to his own bed. He is troubled. He stands, thinking. He turns and looks at* BEN. *He moves a few paces towards him*)

GUS (*Slowly in a low, tense voice*) Why did he send us matches if he knew there was no gas? (*Silence.* BEN *stares in front of him.* GUS *crosses to the* L *side of* BEN, *to the foot of his bed, to get to his other ear*) Ben. Why did he send us matches if he knew there was no gas? (BEN *looks up*) Why did he do that?

BEN Who?

GUS Who sent us those matches?

BEN What are you talking about?
(GUS *stares down at him*)

GUS (*thickly*) Who is it upstairs?

BEN (*nervously*) What's one thing to do with another?

GUS Who is it, though?

BEN What's one thing to do with another? (*He fumbles for his paper on the bed*)

GUS I asked you a question.

BEN Enough!

GUS (*with growing agitation*) I asked you before. Who moved in? I asked you. You said the people who had it before moved out. Well, who moved in?

BEN (*hunched*) Shut up.

GUS I told you, didn't I?

BEN (*standing*) Shut up!

GUS (*feverishly*) I told you before who owned this place, didn't I? I told you.
(BEN *hits him viciously on the shoulder*)
I told you who ran this place, didn't I?
(BEN *hits him again viciously on the shoulder*)
(*Violently*) Well, what's he playing all these games for? That's what I want to know. What's he doing it for?

BEN What game?

GUS (*passionately, advancing*) What's he doing it for? We've been through our tests, haven't we? We got right through our tests, years ago, didn't we? We took them together, don't you remember, didn't we? We've proved ourselves before now, haven't we? We've always done our job. What's he doing all this for? What's the idea? What's he playing these games for?

(*The box in the shaft comes down behind them. The noise is this time accompanied by a shrill whistle, as it falls.* GUS *rushes to the hatch and seizes the note*)

(*Reading*) "Scampi!" (*He crumples the note, picks up the tube, takes out the whistle, blows and speaks*) We've got nothing left! Nothing! Do you understand? (BEN *seizes the tube and flings Gus away. He follows Gus and slaps him hard back-handed across the chest*)

BEN   Stop it! You maniac!

GUS   But you heard!

BEN   (*savagely*) That's enough! I'm warning you!

(*Silence.* BEN *hangs up the tube. He goes to his bed and lies down. He picks up his paper and reads. Silence. The box goes up. They turn quickly, their eyes meet.* BEN *turns to his paper. Slowly* GUS *goes back to the* R *side of his bed, and sits. Silence. The hatch falls back into place. They turn quickly, their eyes meet.* BEN *turns back to his paper. Silence.* BEN *throws his paper down*)

Kaw! (*He picks up the paper and looks at it*) Listen to this! (*Pause*) What about that, eh? (*Pause*) Kaw! (*Pause*) Have you ever heard such a thing?

GUS   (*dully*) Go on!

BEN   It's true.

GUS   Get away.

BEN   It's down here in black and white.

GUS   (*very low*) Is that a fact?

BEN   Can you imagine it?

GUS   It's unbelievable.

BEN   It's enough to make you want to puke, isn't it?

GUS   (*almost inaudible*) Incredible.

(BEN *shakes his head. He puts the paper down and rises. He fixes the revolver in his holster.* GUS *stands up. He goes towards the door* L)

BEN   Where are you going?

GUS   I'm going to have a glass of water.

(GUS *exits* L. BEN *brushes the dust off his clothes and off his shoes. The whistle in the speaking tube blows. He goes to it, takes the whistle out and puts the tube to his ear. He listens. He puts it to his mouth*)

BEN   Yes. (*To his ear; he listens. To his mouth*) Straight away. Right. (*To his ear, he listens. To his mouth*) Sure we're ready. (*To his ear; he listens. To his mouth*) Understood. Repeat. He has arrived and will be coming in straight away. The normal method to be employed. Understood. (*To his ear; he listens. To his mouth*) Sure we're ready. (*To his ear; he listens. To his mouth*) Right. (*He hangs up the tube*) Gus! (*He takes out his comb and combs his hair, adjusts his jacket to diminish the bulge of the revolver. The lavatory flushes off* L. BEN *goes quickly to the door* L) Gus! *The door* R *opens sharply.* BEN *turns.* GUS *stumbles in. He is stripped of his jacket, waistcoat, tie, holster and revolver. He stops, body stooping, his arms at his sides, he raises his head and looks at Ben. A long silence follows and they stare at each other as* —

the CURTAIN *falls*

H. Pinter, *The Dumb Waiter*

At the heart of the extract is conflict – conflict between the two men and someone outside the room, the two men and their environment, the two men and themselves. The dramatic tension is indicated not only by the dialogue but by the moods and attitudes shown in the stage directions. The pauses, the movements on and off the stage, the repetitive actions, the one-sided conversation with someone unseen above, the unanswered questions, the noises from outside the basement, the physical attitudes and stances of the two men – all build up the sense of growing conflict. The falling of the curtain marks the end of the play, but the dash after the final word 'as' leaves the audience to resolve the conflict for itself in the light of their own interpretation of the action.

The drama is occurring inside the minds and emotions of the audience. The interpretation or realisation on the stage or by the actors is the intermediary vehicle encapsulating meaning, and links those watching and the play itself. The text consists of the words, their representation by actors, the production, and their interpretation by the individual within the audience; all these elements have in them the essential quality of drama – **conflict**.

1.11

A play cannot portray life exactly as it is, detail by detail, but it can portray the essential human predicaments, choices, emotions, values, relationships, experiences, and judgements by making an audience weep or laugh, feel shock, identify with the action, or even stand back and observe. To show life in all its details would require more time, space, and implicit concentration by an audience than are available. The 'text' must rely, therefore, on the **selection** of an attitude and plot by the playwright, the **selection** of an interpretation of the text by the actor, director and producer, and the **selection** of a response by an audience. All these forms of 'selection' depend one on the other and are inter-active. The exciting thing about drama is that the 'text' of a play allows this selection to adapt to new performances, new situations, new contexts, and new audiences, since the transformation of plot into meaning takes place in the imagination.

1.12

Selection, in its turn, depends on **condensation**, the distilling of events, experiences, and attitudes into recognisable moments of some significance. The 'To be or not to be' soliloquy of Hamlet, for example, expresses not only Hamlet's immediate predicament but also that of all men and women faced with the choice of one action or another. The *particular* moment focuses the *universal* problem of mankind. Such a distillation, represented from the words, through the actor, to the imagination of the audience, concentrates human experience into a span. Such a concentration in itself leads to an intensification of the experience.

> . . . . the world's riches, which dispersed lie,
> Contract into a span.

(G. Herbert)

Later, it will be shown how some of the conventions of the theatre concerned with the so-called 'Unities' of Action, Time, and Place have tried to come to grips with these matters of **selection**, **condensation**, and **intensification** of particular and universal experiences (see pages 183–185).

1.13

Just as 'All the world's a stage And all the men and women merely players', so every stage, in its turn, represents the world or some aspect of it. Significantly, the very earliest diagram of a 'set' in the history of British drama represents the World; it gives in detail the setting to be used for *The Castell of Perseverance* (*c.* 1405). In the production a number of scaffolds or rostra were to be erected within a circle, with the Castle itself at the centre. The 'scaffolds' were the seats of the Flesh, Worldly Pleasure, the Devil, Covetousness and God. Humanum Genus (Mankind) was assailed by the Bad Angel, Worldly Pleasure, Belial, Caro (the Flesh), and the Seven Deadly Sins; on the other side were found the Good Angel, Confession, Shrift, Penitence, and the Seven Divine Virtues. God sat on his throne and the play ended with a debate involving Misericordia (Mercy), Iustitia (Justice), Pax (Peace) and Veritas (Truth). Again conflict was at the heart of the drama but here the Universal Virtues and Vices and Man himself were represented by individual characters (see pages 22–23).

1.14

The **text** itself on which modern productions are based has not always been clear-cut, an easy thing to establish. Even the words themselves, at the heart of the text, have caused problems. Before the arrival of printing in England (Caxton produced his first printed book in England in 1477), the plays were copied by hand. The manuscripts were long and costly to produce and presumably only those approved for duplication on religious and political grounds were copied. Such manuscripts were vulnerable and throughout the period since 1477 there have been systematic attempts to destroy religious artefacts which presented doctrines not currently favoured. There has been, therefore, a censorship exercised both in the production and the survival of manuscripts. Add to this both accident and human inaccuracy in the copying of one hand by another, and loss, and it is surprising that we have as much of the pre-1477 texts as we have. Allardyce Nicoll (*British Drama*, fifth edition, 1962) remarks that 'Those which have come down to us are unquestionably merely an infinitesimal portion of a literary activity once far-reaching in its extent'.

Even after the arrival of printing in England, the preservation of the words produced by a dramatist as the basis of his play remained uncertain. The first English Copyright Act was the statute of 1709 during the reign of Queen Anne, but the Crown established its rights to the printing of books very soon after Caxton (when Henry VIII in 1533 repealed an earlier act (1483) which gave aliens the right to import books). It was common for the Crown to grant the sole privilege to an individual to print new books. The Crown often licensed printers and, in 1557, Queen Mary incorporated 97 named persons to constitute the Company of Stationers; no-one was allowed to exercise the art of printing unless he was a freeman of the Company. *Prohibited* books were to be destroyed. The charter was confirmed by Queen Elizabeth in 1559. From 1557 the Stationers' Company began to keep registers of the owners of 'copy'. Any piratical printer could be stopped and his press destroyed. By 1600, therefore, the sole right of printing a book was protected first by the Crown, which gave sole rights for a number of years and secondly, by the Stationers' Company.

Thanks to these developments we can find the dates on which Shakespeare's plays were registered, but even here there was no guarantee that the texts were those actually written by the playwright himself. By 1623, seven years after Shakespeare's death, two of his friends in the theatre, John Heminges (possibly the first actor to depict Falstaff) and Henry Condell, had decided that it was important to collect all of Shakespeare's works together in a single volume. In that year they published the so-called *First Folio* but it seems that many of the companies which had first produced the plays of the time looked upon them as their own. Apart from Ben Jonson, who had his own *Works* printed in 1616, many of the plays of the Elizabethan period (*e.g.* those of Beaumont and Fletcher) had to wait until the Commonwealth period to be released for publication. Nevertheless, there were pirated versions of Shakespeare's plays produced during his life-time. After all, he was a 'box-office' success. Once a work was published and registered with the Stationers' Company, the writer lost legal control of it; the new right lay with the publisher. Elizabethan printing, too, was prone to error; English spelling was by no means stable; punctuation was intended as an aid to speakers reading aloud, rather than to readers; uneducated compositors found it hard to interpret some of the difficult words used by University-educated playwrights: for example, in the first quarto edition of Marlowe's *Dr Faustus* the word *oncaymaeon* – Greek ον καιμὴ ον, being or not being – should have occurred but it was amended to 'economy' variously spelt. Elizabethan handwriting was difficult to decipher, especially differences between *d* and *e*, *p* and *x*, *-st* and *-se*, *b* and *t* (*e.g.* Falstaff's last words reported by Mistress Quickley in *Henry V* included 'and *a'babbled* of green fields' but this was printed, because of a misreading, as 'and *a'tabled* of green fields' or '*on a table* of green field' until 1904; the misreading even attracted hundreds of words by editors determined to make sense of the word *tabled!*). Heminges and Condell referred to pirate editions as 'those stolen and surreptitious texts' when they came to put together the *First Folio.*

Difficulty in establishing what a playwright might have really written persisted into the nineteenth century. Even as late as this plays carried the words 'Authentic Copy' on their title pages in order to lay claim to reliability of the copy itself.

Very strict copyright laws today, however, make it unnecessary for playwrights to have any hesitation in producing definitive editions of their work. Not only are the words of the play protected but the rights to perform the play are similarly protected. Such rights are rigorously enforced for works still in copyright. A typical reminder might well appear in the form of:

It is an infringement of the copyright laws of the British Commonwealth of Nations, the United States of America, and all other countries of the Universal Copyright Convention to give any public performance or reading of this play either in its entirety or in the form of excerpts without the prior consent of the copyright owners; or to copy any part of it by manuscript, typescript, photography or any other means of reproduction.

A producer and a director of a play written before such rigorous laws were enforced have the problem of establishing the 'authentic' copy to use; such a process often involves hours spent in libraries in some scholarly research.

1.15   Conclusion

Drama includes, therefore, some or all of the following elements: the 'authentic' words printed on the page; the presentation or re-presentation of some aspects of life; a 'composition', dependent on selection and arrangement; an interpretation for an audience; a point of view – or several points of view, from which the action is seen; vividness; impact; enhancement and intensification of emotion and language; spectacle; thought; plot; a reflection of what an audience expects; performance; a context; the audience's response to, and involvement with, the action.

Drama begins with the words on the page, but it rapidly moves off the page, through the imaginations of those who 'realise' the words in performance and those who share the dramatic experience as audience and participants, into a new creation.

Questions

1. How far do you find the definition of 'drama' summarised in Section **1.15** of this chapter appropriate to describe a play you are currently studying? What would you add or take away from it to make it appropriate?
2. Where does the *conflict* lie in one play you know well?
3. What do you understand by the term 'context' when you apply it to a play you are studying?
4. What areas would you need to research thoroughly in order to understand in more detail a play you are interested in?
5. By commenting on a play you have seen recently, show how the director's interpretation of the text affected what happened on the stage.
6. If you were to direct a play you are studying, where would you place the emphasis in interpreting it for an audience? How would you 'realise' this interpretation?
7. Explain how your direction of a play might vary according to two kinds of audience you had in mind: a group of drama students and the general public.
8. Find out what you can from a library about the laws of copyright with particular reference to the forthcoming production of a play you are planning or hope to share in.
9. Describe the relative importance of both *plot* and *character* in a play you know well.
10. Show how *one* scene in a play you are studying could be made to have a strong imaginative impact on an audience in a theatre.

PART TWO

The Historical Context

2
The Stage

2.1

The shape of the stage and the auditorium where a piece of drama is to be enacted will clearly influence very strongly the *text* of a play. It will help to determine the conventions of dramatic production at any period, and the devices available to the playwright and actors to exploit the limitations and opportunities of such conventions to the full. The shape of the stage and its auditorium will also affect the relationship between actors and spectators and dictate the extent to which an audience can participate in the drama itself.

Sometimes in the past the actors had to leave their acting area and go amongst the audience to create direct audience participation; this sometimes happened in the medieval period (see pages 21–22). Sometimes the audience clambered up on to the stage and interrupted the action of the plot as part of the play itself. In Beaumont and Fletcher's *The Knight of the Burning Pestle* (printed 1613), a grocer and his wife in the audience insist that their apprentice, Ralph, should have a part in the play. He becomes a Grocer Errant and takes part in the absurd adventures of the sub-plot.

The Elizabethan public theatre had little scenery but some properties and the stage was surrounded on three sides by the audience who could eavesdrop on soliloquies or be addressed by the actors at very close quarters. The platform stage of the period allowed also the flexibility of 'continuous staging', as it is sometimes known, where, as in *Arden of Faversham* (1592), all the actors remained on the stage whilst the dialogue continued and the imaginary setting changed from inside a house to outside a house, from one place to another in an attempt to depict 'the great malice and dissimulation of a wicked woman, the unsatiable desire of filthy lust and the shameful end of all murderers'. In the period when the 'proscenium arch' flourished (late nineteenth and the first part of the twentieth century) the audience was effectively separated from the stage, relegated to playing the role of spectators watching an action which could close in on itself as an entity and move into fantasy (as in James Barrie's *Peter Pan*) or into the intimate and stylised form of verse-drama (as in T. S. Eliot's *The Cocktail Party*). More recently drama has moved into, and through, attempts to break down the 'proscenium arch' barrier such as are found in 'theatre-in-the-round' movements and the newly designed, Elizabethan-inspired theatres at Stratford, Chichester, and Minneapolis.

This *inter-action* between, and *inter-relation* with players and audience is important to any discussion of the fundamental nature of drama and to the distinction, which is sometimes made, between 'theatre' and 'drama'. Where, for example, does the real action of a play take place? Is it on the stage (or acting platform) *or* is it in the minds and imaginations of the audience? The answers to such questions will determine the kind of 'text' a playwright will produce and the kinds of devices (*e.g.* soliloquies, asides, disguises, lighting, entrances and exits) that he or she will use.

A survey of the way 'the stage' has been viewed at different times in the history of drama will show some of the ways playwrights have attempted to solve the problems of players-audience relationships.

2.2   The Greek Stage

The Greek theatre consisted essentially of three parts: the *orchestra* (from the Greek word *orcheesthai*, to dance) which was a complete circle of space where the chorus chanted and danced, as with their voices and gestures they played out the dramatic action; the *auditorium* (from the Latin word *audire*, to hear) which rose in tiers of seats cut out from the rock and sometimes faced with marble, and which encircled about two thirds of the orchestra; and the *stage* (or the *logeion*, the speaking-place) which consisted of a long, narrow platform backed by a permanent architectural structure connected to the booth or the dressing-room behind it. This booth was known as the *skene* (which meant in Greek 'a tent or a stage building', but now means in English either the stage performance itself or the place where the plot is enacted: *scene*).

It is not known just how high this platform, or stage, was raised above ground level in its earliest form. It has been suggested that initially it might have been merely an altar-table, possibly of the god Dionysus, on which an actor climbed and held a dialogue with the chorus. On some early vases from southern Italy such a basic table-stage is represented. Later, perhaps by the fifth century BC, a wooden stage evolved and was connected by steps to the *orchestra*. Architectural evidence dating from the fourth century BC at Megalopolis indicates that the *stage* was made of wood, was about four feet high, and had a stone colonnade as a background. Vitruvius, a Roman architect who served as a military engineer under Julius Caesar in the African war of 46 BC, describes the stage of the Greek theatre as being between ten and twelve feet high, and there are surviving examples of Greek buildings which support this statement.

The best preserved of Greek theatres, built about 350 BC, is found at Epidauros, a town in Argolis on the Saronic Gulf. The circle of the *orchestra* there is about 66 feet across and the theatre itself is 373 feet in diameter. The lower tiers of seats are thirty-two in number and these are separated from the twenty tiers above them by a wide passage (or *diazoma*). There are twenty-four flights of steps which radiate out from the centre of the orchestra and allow easy access to every part of the theatre.

Another theatre (completed about 330 BC) was that of Dionysus in Athens. It was huge and accommodated about thirty thousand people. Other Greek theatres, altered later by the Romans, have survived at Egesta, Syracuse, Argos, and Ephesus.

The Chorus in Greek drama was originally seen as representing the audience; it was made up of about fifteen people or so, and spoke at strategic points in a play to question a leader or to provide answers to questions the spectators might be posing. The leader (the first of whom was probably *Thespis*, who often took several parts in a play and disguised himself in dramatic masks, the invention of which is ascribed to him) stood at the centre of the 'orchestra', on the *thymele* or altar. All the actors and members of the Chorus were men; women never performed in the Greek theatre.

The huge distance which separated the players from the audience en-couraged the use of the Chorus, where concerted voices could carry a summary of the plot so far or underline the important features of the play more easily to those listening in the open air. The role of the Chorus has later been adapted in the English theatre, where one or more of the actors will comment on the action of the play; (see, for example, the Prologue in Shakespeare's *Henry V*, the Chorus in Milton's *Samson Agonistes* (1671), the Women of Canterbury in T. S. Eliot's *Murder in the Cathedral* (1935), or The Manager in Thornton Wilder's *Our Town* (1938)).

The actors were often padded out to increase their size and wore special shoes (*cothurni*) with thick soles which could raise their height by as much as nine inches. They moved about the stage very little and wore masks which made them quickly recognisable, almost as type-figures, from a distance. A feature of the drama, conditioned by the circumstances of the stage and its auditorium quickly established itself – that of adapting itself rapidly to involve the audience in the play.

2.3   The Roman Stage

The Romans adapted the Greek theatre to meet their special needs. The auditorium, with its tiers of seats, became more of a semicircle and the area, once occupied by the Chorus, became part of the spectator area and was used by senators and other dignitaries.

The stage became important and was raised. At the same time it was brought nearer the audience. An excellent example of a Roman theatre, which has survived, occurs at Orange in France. There the auditorium could hold as many as 7000 people and has been partly hollowed out from the landscape. It is enclosed by walls and has a diameter of 340 feet. The stage was 203 feet wide and 45 feet deep. Other Roman theatres which have survived are found at Rome (the theatre of Marcellus, BC 23–13), at Athens (the Odeion of Herodes Atticus, AD 161), at Ostia and at Pompeii, at Syracuse, and at Verulamium (second century AD) in England.

Amphitheatres were unknown to the Greeks. They were oval and the central arena (287 feet by 180 feet in the Colosseum at Rome) was surrounded by rising tiers of seats. The word 'arena' means 'sand' or 'beach' in Latin, since the space was strewn with sand. Amphitheatres were used for gladiatorial combats and some were even used for naval exhibitions; water pipes beneath some of the arenas suggest that the spaces could be flooded. Amphitheatres dating from Roman times have been found at Verona, Pompeii, Pozzuoli, Capua, Syracuse, Pola, Nîmes, Arles, El Djem (near Carthage), and at Caerleon (Monmouth).

The Roman theatre at Orange, France.

2.4   The Medieval Stage

Much of British drama owes its origins to the Church. A church building is, in itself, well-designed to act as a theatre. It has an auditorium (in the nave), a space, often raised, beyond the nave in the eastern part of the building where the rituals of the liturgy and the miracle of the Mass are enacted (the sanctuary), and an arch which separates the nave from the sanctuary (the chancel arch). Chancel arches were increasingly filled with screens made up of mullions, open tracery, and sculptured statues and sometimes surmounted by crosses (rood-screens) from the Tudor period onwards. The choir, often installed beyond the chancel arch, acted as the link between the clergy and the congregation, part of the ritual itself and yet expressing the thoughts and emotions of the congregation.

However, the audience was better influenced when the actors in a performance faced the audience directly and were in immediate touch with them. This could be easily managed by substituting what might be called the 'open stage' for the earlier 'arena stage'. Then the audience could sit or stand at the foot of a raised platform and surround it on three sides. It was during the Middle Ages that such a development in the stage began.

About 1264, Pope Urban IV instituted by papal decree the Feast of Corpus Christi on the Thursday after Trinity Sunday. The office was composed by none other than St. Thomas Aquinas (*c.* 1225–74). In 1311 the office was formally placed in the Church calendar by the Council of Vienne. As part of the festival Pope John XXII ordered a procession of those taking part but left it to the participants to decide the nature of the procession for themselves. We know that the festival became very popular in England and in 1325 the Merchants' Guild at Ipswich organised such a procession and from 1327 the Skinners' Guild organised processions in London. The guilds began to assume responsibility, too, for the plays known as **miracles** or **mysteries** which were arranged in cycles and based on Biblical incidents. The festival of Corpus Christi became the time when such 'mysteries' were performed. The earliest Corpus Christi plays were performed at Chester and by 1327–8 a cycle of 'mysteries' had been established. The earliest *actual* record of the performance of a Corpus Christi play comes from Beverley in Yorkshire in 1220 where *The Resurrection of Our Lord* was performed in a churchyard. Further cycles of plays ranging from the Creation to the Last Judgement followed elsewhere, at York in 1378 and in Coventry in 1392.

At first, liturgical plays were acted out in special locations, variously called *sedes* (seats), *loci* (places), or *domus* (houses). Within a church itself such stations or locations were set up and remained in full view of the audience in what is described as 'a simultaneous setting', where the actors could move from one station to the next to continue the story and to take the attention of the congregation with them. The distance between the locations became part of the setting for such liturgical plays, the few yards between them representing a journey or surrounding countryside. The 'mystery' plays elaborated these locations into *mansions*, little rooms curtained off at both sides and at the back, often with decorations of carved or painted scenery; around each 'mansion' remained a space (the *platea*) for the actors to use. Sometimes these 'mansions' were arranged in a stationary set, placed in a curving row facing the audience, or in a circle or in a rectangle. Often in the Corpus Christi cycles of mystery plays, the locations became *pageants*, set on platforms on wheels and drawn from place to place; one contemporary writer described such a 'pageant' at Chester as being 'a high scaffold with two rooms, a higher and a lower, upon four wheels. In the lower they apparelled themselves and in the higher room they played, being all open on the top, that all beholders might hear and see them'. In the lower room, in a curtained-off area to hide the wheels and linked to the upper room by a trap-door, the actors could dress themselves. The 'pageants' moved about the town with specific guilds being responsible for specific plays, each of which dealt with a simple incident or related incidents. The actors were paid for their work.

The effect of this particular development of *the stage* was primarily to bring the audience into intimate contact with the actors, who would address the spectators directly and sometimes leave the platform to move amongst them. It allowed for both intimacy and immediacy in the action; it also gave scope for individual characters to be developed – such as Noah's wife, Mak the sheep-stealer, Herod the tyrant, or even the lazy, good-for-nothing third shepherd of the early fifteenth century *The Second Shepherds' Pageant* written at Wakefield. Such close performances allowed emphasis to be placed on the actor and his role and encouraged stylised performances, playing to the audience, subtleties in speaking dialogue, and awareness of rapidly changing moods and attitudes. Pageants, however, and any form of 'open stage' discouraged scenic elaboration or moving from one incident to another with any rapidity.

However, in the play *Processus Noe cum Filiis*, written by a brilliant playwright at Wakefield and certainly performed there in 1554, Noah actually sets about building an ark in front of the audience but its finishing is left to the audience's imagination:

> To begin of this tree my bones will I bend;
> I trow from the Trinity succour will be sent.
> It fares full fair, think me, this work to my hand;
> Now blessed be he that this can amend.
> Lo, here the length,   (*Takes measurements*)
> Three hundred cubits exactly;
> Of breadth, lo, it is fifty;
> The height is even thirty
> Cubits in full measure.

Nevertheless, the 'arena stage' was not dead and the 'platform stage' was sometimes combined with it. In Cornwall, just east of Perranporth, an old earthwork might well have formed a natural theatre. There are many such earthworks in Cornwall dating from very early times; they are circular (and known as 'rounds') and seem to have originally been defensive works. A deep ditch was dug round the fortification with one gap left in it to act as an entrance. The earth from the ditch was piled up inside the circle and the hill so formed was often levelled off. Here was a natural 'theatre' for medieval people. Several manuscripts of Cornish plays give circular diagrams to show where the 'mansions' or 'scaffolds' were to be set up. The mansions in turn could be the scene of the dramatic action and the centre of the circle provided a further acting area. The spectators could move round the circle to follow the play as the plot moved from centre to centre; scene changes could occur, therefore, as new characters on fresh mansions became the centre of attention.

The most elaborate stage diagram of a circular stage is given in the manuscript (folio 191^v) of *The Castle of Perseverance*, written about 1440. It is a 'Morality' play (see pages 84–90), contains more than 3600 lines of verse, and tells the story of man's progress from birth to final judgement. He is persuaded by good and bad angels to resist or yield to the delights of the World but is rescued and brought to the Castle of Perseverance by the Seven Virtues, to be protected against the assaults of the World, the Flesh, and the Devil. He is drawn back to sin, however, and dies. His body, in the best medieval tradition, is chided by his soul but at the final judgement man is defended by the Four Daughters of God who plead for mercy and justice.

The diagram shows a circular playing area, round which runs a ditch. In the

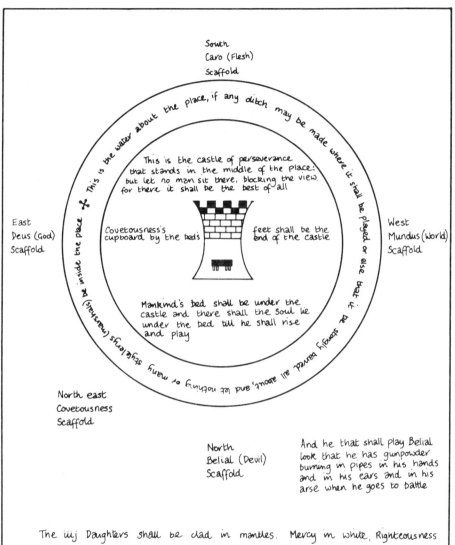

South
Caro (Flesh)
Scaffold

This is the water about the place, if any ditch may be made where it shall be played or else that it be strongly barred all about, and let nothing but ground be inside the place (marsh steering) be inside the place

This is the castle of perseverance
that stands in the middle of the place:
but let no man sit there, blocking the view,
for there it shall be the best of all

Covetousness's
cupboard by the bed's

feet shall be the
end of the castle

Mankind's bed shall be under the
castle and there shall the Soul lie
under the bed till he shall rise
and play

East
Deus (God)
Scaffold

West
Mundus (World)
Scaffold

North east
Covetousness
Scaffold

North
Belial (Devil)
Scaffold

And he that shall play Belial
look that he has gunpowder
burning in pipes in his hands
and in his ears and in his
arse when he goes to battle

The iiij Daughters shall be clad in mantles. Mercy in white, Righteousness in red altogether. Truth in sad green and Peace all in black — and they shall play in the place — altogether till they bring up the Soul.

centre of the circle there is a tower, beneath which man's bed is set up. Mansions are set up around the outside of the ditch with God in his traditional place in the east and the Devil in his traditional place in the north. The diagram is accompanied by elaborate descriptions of such an 'arena stage'.

2.5   The Renaissance

It was the 'platform stage', however, which continued to be developed and which would dominate the British theatre for centuries to come. The medieval hall had at one end a raised platform or dais; a minstrel's gallery became a feature of many great houses. Penshurst Place in Kent (AD 1341) and Hatfield House in Hertfordshire (AD 1607–11) are good examples of such houses.

There is evidence that plays were performed in large houses with these features. Allardyce Nicoll (*British Drama*, fifth edition 1962, 42) has suggested that perhaps groups of minstrels

> attached to the houses of the gentry . . . gradually proceeded to engage in theatrical activities, so that in many districts small companies, most of them including no more than some four players, sprang into being; some of their members no doubt were already professionals, drawn from the minstrel class; others were carpenters and weavers . . . In order to protect themselves, most of these put themselves under the patronage of prominent lords; at these lords' mansions they presented their Christmas shows and for many months of the year they wandered round from place to place as strolling actors.

By the 1480s there already existed the King's players and other groups patronised by the Earl of Essex, and Richard, Duke of Gloucester. Members of the Universities of Oxford and Cambridge and of the Inns of Court, as well as boys of the Chapel Royal and St. Paul's, put on plays early in the sixteenth century. In *Hamlet* there is a reference to bands of child players:

> an eyrie of children, little eyases, that cry out on the top of question, and are most tyrannically clapp'd for't. These are now the fashion, and so berattle the common stages – so they call them – that many wearing rapiers are afraid of goose-quills.
>
> (II, ii)

It is, of course, a band of strolling players that Hamlet uses to prove the guilt of his uncle in the castle at Elsinore.

There is an interesting passage in *The Life of Sir Thomas More* written by his son-in-law, William Roper, which refers to groups of players which visited the great house of Cardinal Morton, Henry VII's chancellor. More (1478–1535) spent his early years in Morton's household:

> Sir Thomas Moore . . . was by his Father's procurement receaved into the house of the right reverend, wise and learned prelat Cardinall Mourton, where (thoughe hee was yonge of yeares, yet) would he at Christmas tyd sodenly sometymes stepp in among the players, and never stud[y]inge for the matter, make a parte of his owne there presently amonge them, which made the lookers on more sport than all the players besid.

2.6   The Elizabethan Period

By the time Elizabeth came to the throne in 1558 the experiments in stage-development were far advanced. During her reign the design of specially built playhouses emerged and at the time of her death in 1603 the English theatre was well established.

Before the first theatre was built, players frequently made use of inn-yards for their performances. These enclosed yards would have had galleries running round all four sides, were open to the air, and could easily accommodate an erected platform, round which on three sides an audience could assemble, and from which on the fourth side actors could make their way into the inn's living accommodation to change and seek new properties. The audience was close to the action and it is possible that some of its members also sat round the edge of the platform itself. Such a custom continued into the eighteenth century, when David Garrick stopped the practice. This proximity of the audience allowed the *aside* to be effectively used and allowed an actor to express his thoughts aloud to himself in a soliloquy in a very effective manner.

It is arguable whether the inn-yard was the sole model for the development of theatres in the Elizabethan period. In Italy and elsewhere in Europe experiments in drama were leading to an open-air structure with an acting platform and the audience in close proximity to the players.

The first permanent playhouse in England was probably that erected at Shoreditch in 1576. It was conveniently near to the City of London but it lay outside the jurisdiction of the City, where many of those in civic authority regarded the playhouse as potentially morally and medically dangerous. It was alleged that the plays and the crowds could spread plague, encourage thieves and ungodly behaviour, and lead people to neglect their work, especially apprentices. The Lord Mayor of London and his advisers made it clear that continued production of plays in the City itself would be unacceptable.

James Burbage*, the actor-manager of the Earl of Leicester's Company, opened *The Theatre*, therefore, in 1576 in Shoreditch. The money was provided by John Brayne, who had already converted an inn, the Red Lion, into a playhouse. Another theatre, the *Curtain*, was built very soon after. John Stow referred to them in *A Survey of London* (1598):

> And near thereunto (the former priory of Holywell) are builded two public houses for the acting and shew of comedies, tragedies and histories, for recreation. Whereof the one is called the Curtain, the other the Theater: both standing on the south-west side towards the field.

A year after Stow's book, 1599, James Burbage dismantled the *Theatre* and took the material south of the River Thames to Southwark, where he set it up as the *Globe*, which became the theatre where Shakespeare, who had a share in it, acted and presented many of his plays. In 1613 a peal of ordnance at the entry

---

* Not to be confused with his son, Richard Burbage (1567?–1619) the famous actor who began his career in *The Theatre* and went on to play the major parts in plays by Shakespeare, Jonson, and Beaumont and Fletcher.

of the King in the play *Henry VIII* caught the thatch of the theatre on fire and the *Globe* burnt down.* It was rebuilt a year later.

Fortunately, we have a description of the *Globe*, within the very detailed contract for another theatre, the *Fortune*, dated January 8, 1600 and quoted in John Dover Wilson, *Life in Shakespeare's England*, second edition, 1913, 208–10:

> . . . The frame of the said house to be set square and to contain four score foot of lawful assize every way square without, and fifty-five foot of like assize square every way within, with a good, sure and strong foundation of piles, brick, lime and sand both without and within to be wrought one foot of assize at the least above the ground.
>
> And the said frame to contain three storeys in height, the first or lower storey to contain twelve foot of lawful assize in height, the second storey eleven foot of lawful assize in height, and the third or upper storey to contain nine foot of lawful assize in height. All which storeys shall contain twelve foot and a half of lawful assize in breadth throughout, besides a jutty forwards in either of the said two upper storeys of ten inches of lawful assize, with four convenient divisions for gentlemen's rooms and other sufficient and convenient divisions for two-penny rooms, with necessary seats to be placed and set as well in those rooms as throughout the rest of the galleries of the said house and with such-like stairs, conveyances and divisions without and within as are made and contrived in and to the late erected playhouse on the Bank, in the said parish of St. Saviour's, called the *Globe*; with a stage and tiring-house (dressing-house) to be made, erected and set up within the said frame with a shadow or cover on the said stage . . .
>
> And which stage shall contain in length forty and three foot of lawful assize and in breadth to extend to the middle of the yard to the said house. The same stage to be paled in below with good, strong and sufficient new oaken boards, and likewise the lower storey of the said frame withinside; and the same lower storey to be also laid over and fenced with strong iron pikes. And the said stage to be in all other proportions contrived and fashioned like unto the stage of the said playhouse called the *Globe*, with convenient windows and lights glazed to the said tiring-house, and the said frame, stage and staircases to be covered with tile and to have a sufficient gutter of lead to convey the water from the covering of the said stage to fall backwards. And also the said frame and the staircases thereof to be sufficiently enclosed without with lath, lime and hair, and the gentlemen's rooms and two-penny rooms to be sealed with lath, lime and hair, and all the floors of the said galleries, storeys and stage to be boarded with good and sufficient new deal boards of whole thickness where needed shall be. And the said house, and other things before-mentioned, to be made and done, to be in all other contrivitions, conveyances, fashions, thing and things effected, finished and done, according to the manner and fashion of the said house called the *Globe*, saving only that all the principal and main posts of the said frame and stage forward shall be square and wrought pilaster-wise with carved proportions called satyrs to be placed and set on top of every of the same posts . . .

* 'One man had his breeches set on fire that would perhaps have broiled him, if he had not by the benefit of a provident wit put it out with bottle ale.' Sir Henry Wotton, *Reliquae Wottonianae*, London, 1651.

The raised stage, then, might have originated from the platforms, scaffolds, or 'mansions' of medieval drama, the raised dais of large houses, or the platforms erected in inn-yards, but by Elizabethan times it was firmly established. The audience was arranged around three sides of the stage or even on it, standing in an open central space or seated in galleries with divisions into 'boxes' for gentlemen and those who could pay two-pence. The stage was at least partially covered but the 'wooden O', to which Shakespeare refers in the Prologue to *Henry V*, was open to the skies. The actors had a dressing-room or tiring-room at the back of the stage. The plays themselves suggest that the roof over the stage might have contained a trap-door. In *Cymbeline* 'Jupiter descends in thunder and lightning sitting upon an eagle' and the boards of the stage itself might have had a trap-door, too, as the earlier *pageants* had, to allow for Ophelia's grave in *Hamlet*, the cries of the old murdered king ('old mole') beneath the stage in *Hamlet* (II, v), and the stage directions in *Macbeth* (where each of the three apparitions, an armed head, a bloody child, and a child crowned with a tree in his hand, descends (IV, i).

Performances took place in the afternoon to make use of the natural light and the action moved on from scene to scene without intervals. The setting of day or night, one country or another, had to emerge from the language of the play itself. The acts and scene divisions with their stage directions giving the settings and time were not always given in the 1623 Folio edition of Shakespeare's works. In *Antony and Cleopatra*, for example, the indications of locality in stage directions are not to be found in this earlier edition of Shakespeare's works. There is an astonishing array of scenes in what are usually given as Acts Three and Four in modern editions of the play – thirteen scenes in Act Three and fifteen scenes in Act Four – but the audience is never lost. Shakespeare and his actors had to help them follow the movement of the action of the play across nine days selected across a ten-year period, and from Alexandria to various parts of Rome, Misenum, Syria, Caesar's camp, Antony's camp, and back again. Shakespeare's language transmutes the restrictions of the theatre through an appeal to his audience's imagination. The action takes place in *their* heads rather than on the stage. In another play, *Henry V*, Shakespeare makes his method of working explicit:

> But pardon, gentles all,
> The flat unraised spirits* that hath dar'd
> On this unworthy scaffold to bring forth
> So great an object: can this cockpit hold
> The vasty fields of France? or may we cram
> Into this wooden O the very casques
> That did affright the air at Agincourt?
> O, pardon, since a crooked figure may
> Attest in little place a million,
> And let us, ciphers to this great accompt
> On your imaginary forces work.
> Suppose within the girdle of these walls

* The dull, uninspired actors and playwright (*so* Arden edition)

Are now confin'd two mighty monarchies . . .
Piece out our imperfections with your thoughts.

(*Henry V*, Prologue)

Scene divisions for the Elizabethans did not mean necessarily that the scenery was changed but merely that one group of actors had left the stage and another lot were about to enter. The audiences of the period detected where and when the action of the play was taking place from what was said rather than from stage directions which divided the play into acts and scenes.

The properties used by Elizabethan actors included thrones, rocks, cages, bedsteads, bloody heads, and 'gorgeous and sumptuous apparel'. The productions were visually rich, although most of the plays were enacted in contemporary modern dress, even if a sketch made of a production of *Titus Andronicus* in 1595 shows an actor wearing what seems to have been a replica of a Roman cloak.

Official attitudes of the authorities towards the public theatres began to change towards the troubled end of Elizabeth's reign. At her death the problem of the succession would reassert itself and the Wars of the Roses, so vividly reconstructed by Shakespeare, were not far away historically. The Armada had reminded England that foreign intervention in its affairs could not be ruled out. James I, a Catholic from Scotland, introduced a different, more lavish way of life to the Court after his accession in 1603. In the theatre, plot reasserted itself over character and the action became more and more elaborate. The staging of tragedies of horror and revenge, often set in Italy or somewhere else abroad, the development of so-called 'private' theatres, roofed-in, lit by artificial light, with audiences sitting down, and the practice of charging high admission fees, often six times the amount charged at the public theatres, gathered momentum.

The Puritans, too, had always been suspicious of, and hostile towards, the theatre. Stephen Gosson's *The Schoole of Abuse* (1579) expressed their attitudes:

> In our assemblies at plays in London, you shall see such heaving, and shoving, such itching and shouldering to sit by women . . . such tickling, such toying, such smiling, such winking . . . Not that any filthiness in deed is committed within the compass of that ground, as was done in Rome, but that every wanton and his paramour . . . are there first acquainted.

Stephen Gosson's attack on the licentiousness provoked by the new theatres is all the more interesting since he had tried, unsuccessfully, to be a playwright himself before he took holy orders. An even more astonishing puritanical attack on stage plays came in 1633 when a barrister from Lincoln's Inn, William Prynne (1600–69) published a huge work, *Histriomastix*. Unfortunately for Prynne, the work was seen to have included an attack on Charles I and his Queen. Prynne was sentenced by the Star Chamber in 1634 to life-imprisonment, a fine of £5000, and the loss of both his ears in the pillory. He was slow to learn and continued to write in the Tower of London. In 1637 he was again fined £5000, had the remnants of his ears cut off, and was branded on the cheeks with the letters *SL* (*Seditious Libeller*). He was released by the Long

Parliament in 1640 and found favour with Charles II at the Restoration in 1660.

On September 2, 1642, Parliament issued the *First Ordinance Against Stage Plays and Interludes* which decreed that 'public stage-plays shall cease and be foreborne'. The theatres were closed and England found itself at the start of a bloody civil war.

2.7

Two developments in the theatre had a profound effect on the development of scenery for the stage during the reigns of James I and Charles I. The Elizabethan stage had used many properties, as has been pointed out earlier, but the action of the play was presented representationally rather than realistically. *First*, the development of private theatres, which were roofed-in and had artificial lighting, added new scope for those interested in producing elaborate scenery against which the actors could perform. The admission fee to such theatres effectively excluded the 'groundlings' and lower classes; plays could be aimed more at the court. *Secondly*, the development of the **masque** as a theatrical form became important with the collaboration of Ben Jonson, the playwright, Alfonso Ferrabosco the younger (*c.* 1575–1628), the musician, and Inigo Jones (1573–1652), the architect. Jones also worked with other writers of masques such as Samuel Daniel (1562–1619), who wrote masques for court festivities such as *Tethy's Festival* (1610) and *Hymen's Triumph* (1615), Thomas Heywood (died 1650?), Sir William D'Avenant (1606–68), and others. Many other dramatists of the period, including Francis Beaumont (1584–1616), Thomas Middleton (1570?–1627), and George Chapman (1559?–1634?) wrote masques, too.

It was clearly a popular form of entertainment amongst the court and upper classes. Masques (or masks) were dramatic entertainments which used dances and disguises and introduced spectacular and musical entertainments as well as plot and character. They had some effect on the later plays of Shakespeare. He introduced, for example, an elaborate masque into the fourth act of *The Tempest*, where Iris, Ceres, Juno, and Nymphs combine song, dance, and poetry as part of a magical entertainment conjured up by Prospero.

The work of Inigo Jones made a major contribution to the development of the English theatre. Until about 1625 the stage had remained comparatively bare, except for the sometimes elaborate properties that were brought on or placed about the boards. During the Renaissance in Italy an interest in Roman plays, especially those of Terence and Plautus, was revived. The work of the Roman architect Vitruvius, a military engineer who served with Julius Caesar, was published in AD 1486. The style of the book, *De Architectura*, is somewhat obscure but it is essentially a book on town planning. The fifth section of it dealt with theatre-architecture, but in spite of its scrappiness, Italian designers re-examined Vitruvius's writing to see what he had to say about scenery. Michelangelo, Andrea del Sarto, Raphael, and Leonardo da Vinci, amongst others, turned their artists' skills to designing and painting scenery. They aimed to produce a realistic, three-dimensional representation. By using a device known later as a *camera obscura* (the original device which gave rise much later to the pin-hole camera) it was possible to project an image of, say, a building on to a flat surface. In this way the rules of *perspective* could be studied. On the stage, drawing in perspective on flat pieces of scenery placed one behind the other could create an illusion of space and depth. If the stage were 'raked' (or sloped) a similar illusion could be created.

Castiglione (1478–1529), the author of the famous book *The Courtier* (which is referred to in Sir Philip Sidney's work *An Apologie for Poetry*. This book, published in 1595, was provoked by Stephen Gosson's dedication to him of his *School of Abuse*, and contained the first survey of English drama) described in a letter to a friend a stage designed in perspective by one Giralamo Genga:

> The stage represented a very beautiful city, with streets, palaces, churches and towers. The streets looked as if they were real, and everything was done in relief, and made even more striking through the art of painting and well-conceived perspective.
>
> (Translated by A. M. Nagler in *Source Book in Theatrical History* (Theatre Annual), 1952.)

The first recorded use of perspective in the theatre was for Ariosto's *Cassaria* at Ferrara in 1508. Serlio's *Second Book of Architecture* (1545) contained designs in perspective for stock scenes of comic, tragic, and satirical plays.

The Italians of the Renaissance wanted, however, to produce an illusion of movement as well as perspective in their scenery. In the sixteenth century engineers tried to produce clouds descending with people in them (Shakespeare would have found this useful for the masque in *The Tempest*), a river flowing past, sea monsters swimming and blowing out water, and conflagrations.

The elaborate use of perspective and visual effects meant that they could be appreciated at their best from one position in the theatre only and the noise produced by the machines could destroy the illusion. The first problem was not solved but provided the king or nobleman had the best seat in the house, the rest of the audience would have to endure at best a distortion, and at worst an obscuring, of their view. The noise could be concealed by the introduction of accompanying music.

The play which is usually called 'the first English comedy', Ralph Udall's *Ralph Roister Doister* (printed about 1567), was played by the boys of Westminster School, of which the playwright was headmaster. Scenery was probably used for the production of this play and consisted of canvas stretched over wooden frames which were then painted in perspective to resemble a street. The frames were called 'players' houses'. Entrances at the sides of houses and a passage at the end of the street could be engineered by leaving gaps between the frames. The play's comedy depends to a large extent on the comings and goings of people and so exits and entrances needed to be slickly contrived. (Modern farces, of course, rely even more heavily on this device.) Scenery was evolving alongside plot construction and stage-craft.

However, it was the writers of masques along with Inigo Jones who introduced the extensive use of scenery to the English theatre. Allardyce Nicoll in *British Drama* (fifth edition, 1962, 126–7) quotes a comment on Thomas Nabbes's *Hannibal and Scipio* (1635) which makes clear that the innovation of elaborate scenery and covering music to the English stage had arrived:

> The places sometimes chang'd too for the scene,
> Which is translated as the music plays
> Betwixt the acts.

Nicoll also quotes Heywood's praise of Inigo Jones's work:

> ... to every act, nay almost to every scene, by his excellent inventions (he) gave such an extraordinary lustre, upon every occasion changing the stage to the admiration of all the spectators that, as I must ingeniously confess, it was above my apprehension to conceive, so to their Sacred Majesties and the rest of the auditory it gave so general a content that I presume they never parted from any object, presented in that kind, better pleased.

It was to Inigo Jones, too, that the English theatre owes first the introduction of the painted *drop-curtain*, not common until the nineteenth century when it was used to hide scene changes rather than to leave the audience wondering at the transmutation taking place before their very eyes as in the seventeenth century, and secondly, the *proscenium arch*, originally introduced to conceal the devices needed to change scenery and to provide an ornamental picture-frame for the scene – it was initially changed for every new production.

The elaborate scenes, dances, music, and costumes of the masques emphasised spactacle rather than the dramatic action of the Jacobean theatre or the action and character of Shakespeare's plays. Masques, such as *Comus* written by John Milton and presented at Ludlow Castle before the Earl of Bridgewater, Lord President of Wales, in 1634, was called a masque but it illustrates the way in which such compositions were moving away from drama into pastoral and other forms of entertainment.

Other devices introduced into Renaissance Italian theatre would have to await later technical developments in England. The Teatro Olimpico (completed in 1583) at Vicenza used a set pierced by doorways through which street scenes were seen in perspective. We know that this theatre, filled with statues, a triumphal arch, and sets using perspective, was seen by Inigo Jones on his visit to Italy when he was still in his twenties. The effect of lighting was considered and in 1550 Leone de' Somi in *Dialoghi in materia di rappresentagioni sceniche* (Dialogues on Stage Affairs) argued that natural-looking scenes of day and night could be achieved by lighting the stage naturally from one side only. Changes in scenery were carried out by arranging decorated and painted flats one behind the other and then successively removing them as the play proceeded. In 1638 Nicola Sabbatini in the *Practica di fabricar scene e macchine ne' Teatri* (Manual for Constructing Theatrical Scenes and Machines) set out in detail ways of creating and working devices such as moving flats about the stage in soaped grooves. The idea of *décor simultané*, the scenes for different parts of the action on the stage at the same time, came from Italy but was more popular in France than England. The revolving stage and the method of quick scene-changing by raising scenery through slits on the stage from a basement, by means of a large drum beneath the stage, were found in the *Teatro Novissimo* of Giacomo Torelli (1608–78). Corneille wrote *Androm̀ede* in France, staged in 1650 at the Petit-Bourbon to demonstrate Torelli's innovations. The Italians in the seventeenth century developed *baroque* settings in the theatre, where a painted backcloth and wings, three or more on each side of the stage, parallel to each other, perhaps with a raked stage, gave an impression of depth and natural colour. The main Italian users of this form of set were Bernardo Buontalenti (1536–1608), Bernini (1598–1680), Burnacini (1636–1707) and later on Paranesi (1720–78).

2.8   The Restoration to 1843

Between the closure of the theatres in England in 1642 and the restoration of Charles II to the throne on May 29, 1660, plays in England continued to be printed. The influence of the French court on drama in France was to produce an effect on English drama after the Restoration. The great plays of Corneille (*Medée* in 1635, *Le Cid* in 1636, *Horace, Cinna* and *Polyeucte* in 1640 and *Le Menteur* in 1644) led on to Molière's burst of great dramatic works in the 1660s and Racine's during the next twenty years. Ideas they contained on comedy and tragedy, the unities, and dramatic construction would reverberate through criticism for a long time in England.

Charles II kept a firm hand on the English theatre immediately he returned to London. He awarded patents to only two companies, those led by Thomas Killigrew (1612–83) and Sir William D'Avenant (1606–68). Killigrew's company was known as the King's Men and D'Avenant's as the Duke's Men, the Duke being the King's brother and heir to the throne. The first company played at the various Theatres Royal and the second at the Duke's houses in Lincoln's Inn Fields and in Dorset Gardens. In 1682 the two companies became one.

A new playhouse in Drury Lane was opened in 1663. Colley Cibber (1671–1757) fortunately wrote a description of the original theatre and some of the alterations that had been made to it during his own lifetime. In 1740 the following description appeared in his *An Apology for the Life of Mr Colley Cibber, Comedian.* (It is quoted in Stephen Joseph's *The Story of the Playhouse in England,* Barrie and Rockliff, 1963. The *Apology* gives a valuable account of the theatre and actors at the start of the eighteenth century. It was edited by R. W. Lowe in two volumes published in 1889. It has since been published in Dent's *Everyman's Library*):

> As there are not many spectators who may remember what form the Drury Lane Theatre stood in, about forty years ago, before the old patentee, to make it hold more money, took it in his head to alter it, it were but justice to lay the original figure, which Sir Christopher Wren first gave it, and the alterations of it, now standing, in a fair light; that equal spectators may see, if they were at their choice, which of the structures would incline them to a preference . . .
>
> It must be observed then, that the area, or platform of the old stage, projected about four foot forwarder, in a semi-oval figure, parallel to the benches of the pit;

and that the former lower doors of entrance for the actors were brought down between the two foremost (and then only) pilasters; in the place of which doors, now the two stage boxes are fixed. That where the doors of entrance now are, there formerly stood two additional side-wings, in front to a full set of scenes, which had then almost a double effect, in their loftiness and magnificence. By this original form, the usual station of the actors, in almost every scene, was advanced at least ten foot nearer to the audience, than now they can be; because, not only from the stage's being shortened, in front, but likewise from the additional interposition of those stage boxes, the actors (in respect to the spectators, that fill them) are kept so much more backward from the main audience than they used to be.

But when the actors were in possession of that forwarder space, to advance upon, the voice was then more in the centre of the house, so that the most distant ear had scarce the least doubt, or difficulty in hearing what fell from the weakest utterance: all objects were thus drawn nearer to the sense; every painted scene was stronger, every grand scene and dance more extended; every rich or fine-coloured habit had a more lively lustre: nor was the minutest motion of a feature (properly changing with the passion or humour it suited) ever lost, as they frequently must be in the obscurity of too great a distance; and how valuable an advantage to the facility of hearing distinctly is to every well-acted scene, every common spectator is a judge. A voice scarcer raised above the tone of a whisper, either in tenderness, resignation, innocent distress, or jealousy suppressed, often has as much concern with the heart, as the most clamourous passions; and when on any of these occasions, such affecting speeches are plainly heard, or lost, how wide is the difference, from the great or little satisfaction received from them?

Here, then, is a very detailed account not only of the design and construction of theatres in 1663 and in 1740, but also of the way actors used the stage to affect their audiences. The actors kept to the front of the stage in the earlier period and moved out on the fore-stage into the audience on a long, narrow, projected stage. Scenery was used as well as sumptuous, rich, costume. The actors could also enter this fore-stage from doors in front of the proscenium arch. This account by Colley Cibber also gives some indication of acting-styles, especially that of changing the voice and the face's expression to suit the mood. There was clearly an intimacy possible between actor and audience in the early Restoration theatre.

The back of the stage often had elaborately painted scenery, influenced strongly by Italian and French styles, which was movable across or off the stage along grooves. The stage itself was lit by chandeliers suspended over it.

A major development in the English theatre took place during this Restoration period. Actresses appeared in dramatic productions. Boys continued for a time to play some women's parts but by 1670 the introduction of women into plays was the convention rather than the exception.

Mrs Betterton (died 1711) first known as Mrs Saunderson, was the first important actress on the English stage. She played many of the great female Shakespearean roles, Lady Macbeth, Ophelia, and Juliet. She was the wife of James Betterton, the most famous actor of the period, who joined D'Avenant's company at Lincoln's Inn Fields in 1661, where he opened a little theatre of his own in 1695 to produce Congreve's *Love for Love*. In 1705 he opened a new theatre built by Sir John Vanbrugh in the Haymarket but it became a house for music and opera and the players returned to the Lincoln's Inn Fields Theatre. Other famous actresses followed. Nell (Eleanor) Gwyn (1650–87) was an illiterate orange-seller and the mistress of Charles II; she was particularly renowned on the London stage for her rendering of the fashionable Prologues and Epilogues to the new plays springing up. Elizabeth Barry (1658–1713) played in more than one hundred roles, including Monimia in *The Orphan*, Belvidera in *Venice Preserved*, and Zara in *The Mourning Bride*, three plays by the popular Thomas Otway, who was devoted to her but whose love was unrequited, patronised as she was by the Earl of Rochester. Anne Bracegirdle (1663?–1748) was the friend of Congreve whose comedies she helped to success on the stage; she also excelled in parts such as Portia, Desdemona, Ophelia, Cordelia, and Mrs Ford in the adaptations of Shakespeare which were growing up fast during this period. She was eclipsed by Anne Oldfield (1683–1730), who first impressed London audiences with her performance as Lady Betty Modish in Colley Cibber's *The Careless Husband* (printed in 1715) and went on to play Cleopatra, Calista (in Nicholas Rowe's *The Fair Penitent*, 1703), and Lady Townly (in Cibber's *The Provoked Husband*, 1728).

The introduction of actresses on to the stage added new dimensions to the kinds of dramatic action that could be portrayed. Women's roles could be expanded and the relationships between men and women explored more deeply.

2.9

In 1698 Jeremy Collier had voiced growing misgivings about the increased licentiousness in the theatre in his *Short View of the Immorality and Profaneness of the English Stage*, in which he attacked Vanbrugh and Congreve. In the wake of the official reaction Congreve and D'Urfey were prosecuted and Mrs Betterton and Mrs Bracegirdle were fined. The drama continued to flourish, however, but in 1737 a Licensing Act allowed dramatic performances in London only at Drury Lane and the new theatre at Covent Garden, opened by John Rich in 1732. This act was an attempt to restrict the activities and success in London of dramatic productions outside the so-called 'patent' theatres at Drury Lane and Lincoln's Inn Fields. 'Minor' theatres had helped to meet the growing demand for dramatic entertainment; the famous *Beggar's Opera* by John Gay had been put on in the little Lincoln's Inn Fields Theatre in 1728 *but* it was from a minor provincial theatre that the famous Mrs Sarah Siddons (1755–1831) was to emerge on to the London stage. David Garrick (1717–79) also gave his first performance at a theatre in Ipswich in 1740 in *Oroonoko*, Thomas Southerne's adaptation of Mrs Aphra Behn's novel about a royal slave. Later Garrick joined Lacy to manage the Drury Lane Theatre and made a major impact on the development of English drama. The eighteenth century was struggling on the one hand to regulate performances, and on the other to meet the growing public demand in post-Restoration times for drama.

The increased demand outside London came, therefore, at a time when dramatic performances were officially restricted to two theatres in the capital, and so provincial acting companies moved about the country, first playing in barns and booths, and later in playhouses erected at Bath, Bristol, York, Ipswich, Birmingham and Liverpool.

In London occasional attempts were made to smash the official monopoly by audiences paying to watch a concert but seeing instead a play inserted between two very short musical performances, but the restrictions also had an effect on the development of the stage itself. To meet increased demand the auditorium had to be expanded and the stage pulled back from it behind a proscenium arch. This development in itself led to a number of important changes in English drama, dramatic production and stage design.

First, plays had to take account of the fact that the audience was further removed from the actors than before. Colley Cibber, as was shown earlier (see page 32), regretted the fact that the intimacy between actor and audience, where a dropped voice or a change in facial features could immediately be seen as significant, might be lost. The loss of the fore-stage would demand different dialogue, different voice levels, and different stage devices: for example, there is a world of difference between the delivery of the soliloquy in Shakespearean times and the uttered aside by the mustachio-twirling villain of Victorian melodrama. It was David Garrick who finally banished spectators from sitting on the stage itself by the firm establishment of the proscenium arch (the 'picture frame' arch) in the English theatre. Audiences in Garrick's day did not accept their banishment too readily to begin with, and actors, whose wages depended on the size of audiences, worried about the alienation of the spectators.

Secondly, the need for spectacle asserted itself and could be met when the stage was seen through a picture-frame arch. David Garrick is sometimes described as the manager who introduced footlights into the theatre. This is arguable, but the separation of actors and audience allowed the use of footlights to be developed. Garrick abandoned the chandeliers hanging over the fore-stage and used lights placed behind the proscenium arch to light up the scene on stage. Actors, therefore, kept behind the arch where they would be lit up. On a fore-stage the actor was all-important; behind the proscenium arch the actor became part, albeit the important part, of a scene. On a visit to Paris in 1771, David Garrick, who had managed the Drury Lane Theatre since 1747, met Philippe Jacques de Loutherbourg, renowned for his painting of battle scenes and romantic landscapes. He joined Garrick at Drury Lane as scenic designer. He introduced cut-cloths, backdrops which were cut out to reveal further scenes behind them. He devised a scenic entertainment, called *Eidophusikon*, made up of a landscape of Greenwich stretching away in perspective to Chelsea, Poplar, Hampstead and Greenwich, with the Port of London crammed with shipping in the foreground. Thunder-sheets, and ways of suggesting rain falling and wind blowing added to the excitement. By moving silks and pieces of glass in front of lamps behind the arch, clouds seemed to move, the storm to pass, and the seasons to change. In Fielding's *Tom Jones* (1749), in an account of Tom's visit to see Garrick's *Hamlet*, Tom's

Scenery designed by De Loutherbourg for use in the Covent Garden Theatre
(*c.* 1771–1785).

servant, Partridge, says, 'It was a wonder how so many fiddlers could play at one time, without putting one another out'. Nor could he help observing when all the candles were lighted, 'That there were candles enow burnt in one night, to keep an honest poor family for a whole twelvemonth'. (These details and others are recorded in S. Joseph, *The Story of The Playhouse in England*, 1963.)

Thirdly, the theatre had to show 'order, decency, and decorum', as one contemporary writer said: 'punctuality in attendance at rehearsals was exacted and complied with, and as much due attendance paid to the business of the scene as during the time of acting a play'. Garrick 'dropped' actors who could not learn their lines on time. The actor-manager had asserted himself.

The restrictions on the number of theatres and the steady demand for plays from the public led to further expansion of the existing buildings. In 1787 the Theatre Royal in Covent Garden and in 1792 the Drury Lane Theatre were extended – Drury Lane to hold 3611 people. Without further lighting and because of the distances between actor and audience, subtle interpretations of action must have been increasingly difficult. The use of music (*e.g.* in operas) and exaggerated gestures (*e.g.* in melodrama) would become increasingly important in the theatre. Declamation rather than asides, set speeches rather than subtle exchanges would pragmatically become important in drama.

Charles Lamb's account of visits as a child to 'Garrick's Drury' in 1781–2 (given in *The Essays of Elia*) reveals the magic of the theatre at the end of the eighteenth century:

> . . . the theatrical fruitnesses . . . the green curtain that veiled a heaven to my imagination . . . The boxes at that time, full of well-dressed women of quality, projected over the pit; and the pilasters reaching down were adorned with a glistening substance resembling sugar candy . . . the orchestra lights arose . . . the bell sounded . . . it rang a second time . . . The curtain drew up and the play was *Artaxerxes*. The next play was *The Lady of the Manor* . . . followed by a pantomime, called *Lun's Ghost*. My third play followed in quick succession. It was *The Way of the World**. I think I must have sat at it as grave as a judge . . . I remember the hysteric affectations of good Lady Wishfort . . .

When he revisited the same theatre some years later:

> The same things were there materially . . . The green curtain was no longer a veil drawn between two worlds . . . but a certain quantity of green baize, which was to separate the audience for a given time from certain of their fellow-men who were to come forward and pretend (their) parts. The lights – the orchestra lights – came up a clumsy machinery. The first ring, and the second ring, was now but a trick of the prompter's bell . . . The actors were men and women painted.

The same writer, Charles Lamb, describes his recollections of the actors from Drury Lane in another essay *On Some of the Old Actors*. There he mentions the forgettable Whitfield, Parker, Benson, Burton, Phillimore and Mr Barrymore. Mrs Jordan made more of an impression on Lamb and so did Mrs Powell whose 'fine spacious person filled the scene'. Bensley 'had the true poetic enthusiasm' . . . 'the fine madness'; 'his voice had the dissonance, and at times the inspiring effect, of the trumpet; his gait was uncouth and stiff . . . He seized the moment of passion with greatest truth . . . He was totally destitute of trick and artifice. He seemed come upon the stage to do the poet's message simply . . . He let the passion or the sentiment do its own work without prop or bolstering . . . If few can remember Dodd, many yet living will remember Dickey Suett*'.

Hazlitt's essay on Sarah Siddons (1755–1831), the sister of the famous actor John Kemble (1757–1832) and wife of another actor, William Siddons, gives us a good contemporary insight into the acting-styles of one of the most famous actresses of the English stage at the turn of the eighteenth century. Hazlitt wrote in *The Examiner* of June 15th, 1816:

> The homage she received is greater than that which is paid to queens . . . She was Tragedy personified . . . To have seen Mrs Siddons, was an event in everyone's life . . . Mrs Siddons always spoke as slow as she ought . . . the machinery of the voice seems too ponderous for the power that wields it. There is too long a pause between each sentence, between each word in each sentence. The stage waits for her. At present she acts the part (of Lady Macbeth) more with a view to effect . . . with both hands sawing the air, in the style of parliamentary oratory, the worst of all others. There was none of this weight or energy in the way she did the scene the

---

* Written by William Wycherley in 1700.
* Described by Hazlitt as 'that fine old croaker'!

first time we saw her, twenty years ago. She glided on and off the stage almost like an apparition.

The marked contrast between Mrs Siddon's earlier performance and her later one might have come about because of changing theatrical conditions. Joanna Baillie (1762–1851), one of whose plays was produced by Kemble and Mrs Siddons in 1800, wrote: '. . . the largeness of our two regular theatres, so unfavourable for hearing clearly, has changed in a great measure the character of the pieces exhibited within their walls'. The opportunity grew for scenic artists and machinists, choruses, melodrama, stereotyped characters, and bold plots.

The Drury Lane Theatre built by Killigrew (1612–83) had been rebuilt by Sir Christopher Wren in 1674. When it was extended in 1792 this theatre had an opening for scenery 43 feet wide and 38 feet high.

> The painter and machine contriver will have a large space 85 feet in width, 92 in length and 110 in height. In the roof of the theatre are contained, beside the barrel-loft, ample room for the scene-painters, and four very large reservoirs, from which water is distributed over every part of the house for the purpose of instantly extinguishing fire.'
>
> (Quoted by S. Joseph in *The Story of the Playhouse in England*, 1963, from W. C. Oulton, *History of the Theatres in London*, 1796.)

Nevertheless, the theatre burnt down in 1809 and was rebuilt in an even larger, more elaborate manner to open in 1812. (It was reconstructed in 1921 and the theatre exists today and has housed many famous modern musicals.)

The Covent Garden Theatre (opened by Rich in 1732) was enlarged in 1787, rebuilt in 1792, and burnt down in 1808. (Its successor suffered the same fate in 1856. The rebuilt theatre is now the Royal Opera House.) At each rebuilding the theatres became bigger – and, some would argue, the audiences became more and more uncontrolled. The opening of the rebuilt Covent Garden Theatre after the fire of 1808 saw a protest which lasted sixty-seven nights against the management's attempt to introduce new prices – the audience won! The roughness of the audience in the larger patent theatres also demanded plays with action, declamations and great spectacles (aquatic escapades in specially constructed tanks, horse shows, and dance displays) to keep them amused. 'Minor' playhouses which sprang up were allowed to survive by the authorities provided they avoided dialogue. They used mime, or songs, or display-boards (like the captions for silent films) to explain what was happening on the stage. Gradually they were allowed to introduce dialogue provided music accompanied it.

2.10   The Nineteenth Century

In 1843 an Act for Regulating Theatres revoked the Licensing Act and broke the monopoly of the two patent theatres, but spectacle had become vital for the stage. By 1843 Drury Lane was having to organise shilling concerts to remain solvent and Covent Garden had had to become an opera house. The 'minor' theatres could now come into their own and they turned from the crude melodramas and elaborate spectacles of the early nineteenth century towards new audiences.

The 'pit' of the theatre, which was originally where the audience stood, then sat on rough benches, changed. In the smaller theatres the front rows of the pit had proper seats known as 'stalls' and the back rows were extended to an area below the first tier of 'boxes'. In 1865 there is a record of carpets being laid amongst the stalls, which were cushioned. Matinées were introduced and the representations put on the stage resembled life, with drawing-rooms, cups and saucers, cupboards, and all the paraphernalia of the parlour or best room. At the beginning of the nineteenth century, theatres stayed open many hours, often until midnight and showed farces, tragedies, pantomimes and other entertainments as part of the programme; by the end of the century the programme again consisted of a single play, perhaps with a brief curtain-raiser, and theatres stayed open for much shorter periods.

The court of Queen Victoria and so-called Victorian morality and attitudes affected the theatre. The Queen invited actors and companies to give 'command performances' at Windsor Castle. The theatre reverted to belonging to all classes, not solely to the lower classes of the early nineteenth century or to the upper classes of the Restoration.

A number of other important developments gradually came about following the 1843 Act. The repertory system, where plays were put on for a very short time at one theatre before being moved on to another, became harder to maintain if the expense of putting on a lavish and detailed production was to be recovered. In Shakespeare's day plays rarely ran for more than a night or two before they were replaced. In 1640 Middleton's *The Game of Chess* ran for nine performances, and in 1728 *The Beggar's Opera* ran for a month, but those were exceptions. In the second half of the nineteenth century, with the new theatres, expensive productions, and the new role of actors who were also managers (*e.g.* Henry Irving), long runs became possible and desirable. Actors were increasingly hired to play a part rather than to join a company. This in due course would need an organisation to protect actors and the development of trade unions in other walks of life was looked upon with interest by the players. Equity, the actors' trade union was eventually founded in Britain on September 1, 1929; its predecessor, the earlier First Actors' Association, founded by Henry Irving, had not survived for long.

The improvement in travel, through the development of railways, meant that London plays could go 'on tour' and plays put on in the Theatres Royal up and down the land could be brought to London if they were successful.

Actors felt the need to take their profession seriously enough to warrant proper training and admission to the role of actor. Even as early as 1750 the idea of an acting school had been discussed and this led in 1861 to the founding of the London Academy of Music and Dramatic Art (LAMDA), and in 1904 to the Royal Academy of Dramatic Art (RADA) by Beerbohm Tree, based at Her Majesty's Theatre. The Central School of Speech and Drama, based originally at the Albert Hall in London, followed in 1906, founded by Elsie Fogerby (1866–1945). Not all plays could attract large audiences and, in order to make sure that worthwhile, interesting plays could be put on, the Independent Theatre Club (1891 – but it was short-lived) and the Incorporated Stage Society (1899, lasting for forty years or so) were established. Repertory playhouses specially designed to accommodate short runs were also developed in the provinces.

Technical developments within the theatres themselves continued apace in the nineteenth century. One of the huge problems facing playwrights, actors, producers, and scenic designers once the theatres had been roofed in and the stage had retreated with its elaborate scenery behind the proscenium arch, was that of adequate illumination. Since the Renaissance in Italy oil lamps and candles had been used. Nicola Sabbattini in *A Manual for Constructing Theatrical Scenes and Machines* had described a method of dimming lights and de Loutherbourg, the scenic designer of David Garrick, had experimented with the primitive lighting available to vary light and shade and even to change the colour of sets to produce atmosphere. In 1815 Lord Byron who was on the management committee of the Drury Lane Theatre, thought that the introduction of gas to light the building would bring the risk of poisoning the audience; however, on September 6, 1817, Drury Lane Theatre was lit by gas. By the 1840s nearly all other theatres had followed. The invention of 'limelight', the burning of a stick of lime in a gas jet, allowed other experiments in lighting to follow beyond that of merely varying the amount of light projected on to the stage or used in the auditorium.

The risk of fire led to a whole spate of legislation about safety in the theatres but more significantly, the lights in the auditorium could be dimmed or blacked out easily, leaving the stage brightly illuminated. There was even a famous and very successful Victorian three-act thriller, *Gaslight*, which had at the centre of its plot a gas light which blazed or dimmed in one room according to the activities of a murderer in another part of the house. This development in lighting provided the final break between spectator and actor in a performance; the audience remained passive on-lookers and the stage was set for scrupulous and minute examination, with sets open to very exacting scrutiny. Electric lighting was introduced into the theatre in 1881 providing increased safety and a source of power to operate machinery, and the audience became firmly established in the roles of mere spectators.

In spite of these major developments in acting and theatrical conditions, the nineteenth century does not figure as one of the great periods in the development of English drama. The nineteenth century in both England and France saw the vast expansion of the novel and painting as major art forms instead. In the middle of the century the theatre was held in low esteem by writers. In *Alton Locke*, a novel by Charles Kingsley written in 1850 comes the condemnation:

> We were passing by the door of the Victorian Theatre; it was just half-price time – and the beggary and rascality of London were pouring in to their low amusement, from the neighbouring gin palaces and thieves' cellars.

Twelve years earlier Charles Dickens in *Nicholas Nickleby* had showed his contempt for playwrights:

> 'Do you understand French?'
> 'Perfectly well.'
> 'Very good,' said the manager, opening the table-drawer, and giving a roll of paper from it to Nicholas. 'There! Just turn that into English and put your name on the title page.'

At the end of the century writers such as Oscar Wilde (1854–1900), Bernard Shaw (born 1856 and writing plays and dramatic criticism from 1891 onwards), Sir Arthur Wing Pinero (born 1855 and writing nearly all his plays before 1900, although he died in 1934), John Millington Synge (1871–1909 and working at his plays about the turn of the century) and Henry Arthur Jones (1851–1929 but writing most of his plays in the 1890s) would do something to restore the reputation of drama written in English.

The major developments in dramatic art, however, in the late nineteenth century were taking place on the Continent of Europe. August Strindberg (1849–1912) in Sweden, Henrik Ibsen (1828–1906) in Norway, Anton Chekhov (1860–1904) in Russia, and Emile Zola (1840–1902, primarily a novelist but the author of a short play, *Jacques Damour*, produced in 1887 in Paris by André Antoine and a group of amateurs, the *Théâtre libre*) in France were in the vanguard of a new movement, **naturalism**, which would come to have a marked effect on the theatre.

Antoine was strongly influenced by the theatrical work of the director-designer George II, Duke of Saxe-Meinigen. He experimented with stage design and made different levels on it. He 'designed' backgrounds before going into rehearsal and used lighting to gain realistic effects. Antoine and his group of amateurs tried to show on the stage life as it was. Zola's play, *Jacques Damour*, was set in the backroom of a shop and the furniture used in the set came from Antoine's mother's home. For another production, *Les Bouchers* (1886), real sides of beef were hung up. The stage became a real room, or office, or workshop.

The move towards **naturalism** was given a firm home in the Moscow Art Theatre where **Konstantin Stanislavski** (1865–1938) and **Vladimir Nemirovich-Danchenko** were working in 1897. Stanislavski directed the plays of Chekhov, Turgenev, Tolstoy, and Gorky in a naturalistic way. The actors became the characters they were playing and the sets became the real settings for the action – Ibsen played a major role in the development of the so-called 'Free Theatre' in the 1890s and Strindberg associated himself with the movement, although he rejected it in the last years of his life.

Set against this **naturalism** on the Continent was **symbolism** which was a strong reaction against it. The exponents of this movement aimed at the essential meaning of experience rather than an attempt to reproduce realistic portraits and descriptions of life. In 1891 Paul Fort's *Théâtre d'Art* in Paris and those who followed it wanted their setting to symbolise rather than to recreate realistically the settings of life itself. Colour, light and shade and shapes could symbolise thoughts and emotions. **Adolphe Appia**, a Swiss designer, wanted to help Richard Wagner to project his 'music into visible scenic form'. The relatively recent introduction of electric lighting into the theatre made possible its realisation.

Both the naturalists and the symbolists took another look at the traditional stage and its proscenium arch. The 'picture frame' seemed unnatural and unhelpful symbolically. The new Bayreuth Opera House, designed for Wagner's operas and opened in 1876, put the orchestra into a deep orchestra pit and used *two* proscenium arches between actors and audience.

However, at the start of the twentieth century, the projection of the play's action out into the audience once again seemed to be the only way to break down actor/audience divisions.

2.11 The Twentieth Century

By the start of this century, therefore, the wheel had come full circle. The stage had moved from the audience into the theatres, had retreated from the spectators into its picture-frame, and was now moving back into the auditorium. The major difference, however, was that new, massive developments in scenic design and stage lighting were there to give producers, directors and actors additional help in their interpretations of 'text'.

The commercialisation of the theatres, the growth of repertory companies, the growing interest in amateur dramatics, and the impact first of the cinema, then of television, and then of the video-recorder on the theatre, would affect not only the technical presentation of dramatic action on the stage but also the nature of the dramatic action itself. The music-hall, sketches, revues, pantomimes, and extravagant musicals and ice-shows would develop the theatre and put extra strains on its flexibility to meet public demands.

Additionally, political and social movements, wars, revolt, poetry, feminism, civil rights, and a host of other developments in the life of Britain and the World have had their impact on drama, which has continued to hold the mirror up to nature and to reflect what people are doing, saying, and feeling. Some of these movements affected the concept of 'stage' in the twentieth century.

At the heart of these developments lies the essential implication in the theatre that there is an interaction between 'text' and actor/interpreter *and* actor and audience. The second of these interactions is missing in the cinema and on television where the audience remains cut off from the actor/interpreter.

The raised stage set on the other side of a proscenium arch and fronted by a line of footlights has been a long time dying. It is still the norm in many theatres, merely because most of our buildings set aside specifically for dramatic productions date from an earlier period when these things were new.

However, things were changing fast. *Theatricalism* recognised that the play was enacted in the theatre but wanted to create illusion by means of theatrical devices in as many and varied ways as possible. This might have meant using such devices as projected background (as in New York Theatre Guild's presentation of Shaw's *Back to Methuselah* in 1922) *or* transparencies (as in Simonson's production of Arthur Miller's *Death of a Salesman* in 1949) *or* the frequently changing, lavishly designed sets (as in the London productions of *My Fair Lady* in the 1950s and 1960s where Cecil Beeton's set of the Ascot Races drew astonished gasps and spontaneous applause from audiences night after night).

The stage itself moved about the theatre in an astonishing way. The platform or acting area without platform might move into the centre of the auditorium with the audience set out around it on all four sides. The audience might be centrally placed with the action taking place all around it. Scenic cloths, flats, and backdrops could be dispensed with altogether or could be replaced with columns or arches, or piles of blocks. The stage might be 'open' or 'enclosed'. It might consist of one platform or several or none at all. It might have scenery, flats, lighting or none of these. The theatre will continue to adapt its staging of plays to match social and artistic developments, that is certain.

Some examples of how the stage has been adapted in the twentieth century will show the huge variety of experimentation that has taken place.

The studio theatre at the London Academy of Music and Dramatic Art (LAMDA) was built as an adaptable space, which could be set up as a traditional theatre with a proscenium arch variable between 28 and 44 feet in width with an orchestra pit and auditorium; as an open stage over the pit with the audience set up around it; *or* as a complete theatre-in-the-round with movable tiers of seats and the four sides of the acting area and exits and entrances arranged from around the outside walls of the building.

Bernard Miles converted an old warehouse for his Mermaid Theatre – the stage was slightly raised at one end of the auditorium, without a proscenium arch. At the back there was an inner stage with a gallery above it. The seats in the auditorium faced the stage but rose in tiers away from it in a single bank.

The Festival Theatre at Chichester is a hexagonal building with a slightly raised stage running across one of the angles inside the building. There is a raised acting platform set above the stage itself, reached by flights of steps on each side. Each flight of steps is broken in the middle by smaller acting platforms. The stage juts out into the auditorium and follows the hexagonal shape of the building itself: the area with four sides of the hexagon forms the acting platform and the rest of the hexagon is blanked off by the back wall of the stage. The audience sits in tiered banks of seats set around these four sides of the stage's cut-off hexagonal shape.

Elaborate stage settings used by *Bertolt Brecht* are worth mentioning as further examples of theatrical experimentation and innovation. In the 1928 production of *Die Dreigroschenoper* (*The Threepenny Opera*) an organ picked out in electric lights formed the permanent background to the production along with prison cages and stairways on castors that could be easily moved about the stage. Brecht used screens above the actor's head on which to project captions and illustrations (a device used more recently in the London production of *Oh What a Lovely War!*). In 1949 Brecht's and Erich Engel's production of *Mutter Courage und ihre Kinder* (*Mother Courage and her Children*) used a revolving stage to help depict movement from country to country and year to year, whilst Mother Courage's wagon remained stationary against the changing background.

The building of three new theatres on the South Bank in London (the Olivier, the Lyttelton, and the Cottesloe), as part of Britain's National Theatre marked a major development in the history of the Theatre.

France had a National Theatre as early as 1680 and Denmark, Sweden, and

The stage and auditorium of the Chichester Festival Theatre.

Austria have had theirs for over two hundred years. In 1848 Effingham Wilson proposed a new theatre especially for the production of Shakespeare's plays. The movement gathered some momentum with the visit to London of the Comédie Française in 1879 and Matthew Arnold threw his weight behind it. Henry Irving took up the cause and, after his death in 1904, William Archer and Harley Granville-Barker, one being the translator of Ibsen and the other an actor, director, and critic, took up the cause. James Barrie, Arthur Wing Pinero, Thomas Hardy, Robert Bridges, and John Galsworthy also supported the movement. In 1908 the Shakespeare Memorial National Theatre committee was set up. In 1913 a site was set aside for the National Theatre in Bloomsbury. The campaign, set back by the First World War, rumbled on and by 1938 another site opposite the Victoria and Albert Museum was chosen. Again a world war broke out but in 1942 the London County Council suggested the establishment of the National Theatre on the South Bank of the Thames near Waterloo. After a series of disappointments and periods of economic recession, in July 1962 the South Bank National Theatre and Opera House Board was set up to build theatres on two sites given by the LCC between County Hall and Hungerford Bridge. In August 1962 Laurence Olivier was named as the first artistic director of the National Theatre Company. In 1966 the Government decided that there should be only one theatre built for the moment and plans for an opera house were shelved. The Greater London Council offered another site on the Princess Meadow on King's Reach. In March 1973 Olivier was succeeded by Peter Hall as artistic director and, after more disappointments about the opening date, the National Theatre opened in stages: on 16 March, 1976, the Lyttelton Theatre (still unfinished) opened with a production of Beckett's *Happy Days*; in October, 1976, the Olivier opened with Albert Finney in Marlowe's *Tamburlaine the Great*; in March, 1977, the Science Fiction Theatre of Liverpool put on a production of Ken Campbell and Chris Langham's show *Illuminatus* in the Cottesloe Theatre.

The Olivier Theatre has a fan-shaped auditorium for 1160 people. It has dispensed with the proscenium arch. Its ceiling has angular panels and long tubular light-holders instead of chandeliers. It has two tiers of sharply raked seats with side banks on higher levels sweeping down to the stage, which can reduce its enormous playing area by closing in the back of the scene. The theatre has been carefully designed so that the actor can remain in close contact with any spectator because there is a wide span of vision from stage to auditorium.

The Lyttelton Theatre has a proscenium arch. It accommodates 890 seated in straight tiers of seats without any central aisle. There are no pillars to block the view of the audience and, as in the Olivier Theatre, the lighting, sound, and director's boxes are at the back of the stalls. The proscenium arch can be adapted from the nine metres width used in the Old Vic Theatre to 13.6 metres. Its height, too, can be adapted from 5 metres to 9 metres. Here is a flexibility to the proscenium not seen before.

The Cottesloe Theatre is rectangular, 21 metres by 19 metres. It can hold 400 people but is easily adapted to become a very small and very intimate theatre. Three sides of the room have two tiers of galleries, each of which looks down on a floor space that can very easily be adjusted. This floor space is free of fixed seating or staging and so the theatre is especially useful for experiments in theatre (see *Lark Rise* and *Candleford* by Keith Dewhurst, pages 290–291).

Questions

1   Describe the features of a dramatic production in which you have taken part which were determined by, or exploited, the physical conditions of the stage or theatre in which you were working. (Use *diagrams*, if they will help your description.)

2   *Discuss some of the difficulties you would meet and show how you would solve them, if you were staging a pre-twentieth-century play you know well using either:
   (i)   a conventional theatre with a proscenium arch, *or*
   (ii)   an alternative method of staging. *e.g.* out-of-doors, on a 'pageant' or platform, or in a 'theatre-in-the-round' setting.

3   *Plan the interior of a theatre which would allow you to stage plays in a conventional way but which would also allow you to experiment with other production styles (give a diagram).

4   *Explain how you would use and adapt a building well-known to you, but one not built as a theatre, as a place where you could mount regular drama productions for an audience.

5   Describe the most interesting use(s) of a stage, for a dramatic production, you have seen recently.

6   Imagine that you are about to share in the open-air production of a play using a local natural setting by an amateur theatre group. Argue the case *either* for *or* against using an 'arena' stage in preference to a 'platform' stage. (Say which play you are hoping to produce and relate your argument to the play's demands.)

7   Discuss, with appropriate and detailed examples from plays you know well, the advantages of using an 'apron' stage for producing plays for audiences today.

8   Write a dialogue between an ancient Greek (or Roman), who has been miraculously brought back to life today, and a modern director. The Greek (or Roman) has just witnessed a revival of a Greek (or Roman) tragedy in a modern theatre and has some questions to ask and some points to make.

9   Imagine that you are a director living in *either* medieval *or* Elizabethan *or* Restoration England who, through a 'time-warp' is able to watch a play produced today in a modern theatre. Write a personal commentary on things you would notice in the production under the headings of (a) *scenery*, (b) *lighting*, (c) *other stage effects*. (Make comparisons, where you can, with your own productions.)

10   Describe a production where, in your opinion, the carefully planned use of the stage has brought actors and audience close in various ways.

The questions marked * *could form the basis of project work.*

3
Greek and Graeco-Roman Drama

3.1
You should first read and understand the description of Greek and Roman theatres and amphitheatres given in Sections **2.2** and **2.3** earlier on pages 18–20, since this description sets out in some detail where and how productions were mounted in Greek and Roman times.

3.2 Dramatic Theory
Aristotle was born in 384 BC at Stagira (Stavros) in Chalcidice at the northern end of the Aegean Sea, the son of a doctor at the court of King Amyntas of Macedon. He studied for twenty years in Plato's 'Academy' and, after five years of travelling, was appointed by King Philip of Macedon as tutor to his son Alexander, aged thirteen. Alexander later became known as Alexander the Great. In 335 BC Aristotle returned to Athens and opened the 'Lyceum', a supplement to the Greek educational system founded in the 'Academy'. Fearful of being considered a traitor by the Athenians following Alexander's death, he retired to Chalcis in Euboea and died there at the age of sixty-three.

His main work on drama and poetry, *The Poetics*, has had a major effect on drama and dramatic criticism following the rediscovery of his work in Western Europe at the start of the Middle Ages. Roger Bacon (1214?–1294), the philosopher, mentions a translation into Latin of *The Poetics* by a German and the Arabs clearly knew of it earlier. Chaucer's Clerk of Oxenford, it will be remembered, was so up-to-date with his reading that:

> He preferred having twenty books in red
> And black, of Aristotle's philosophy,
> To having fine clothes, fiddle or psaltery.

The main points of dramatic theory set out in his work may be summarised. (*The Poetics* is incomplete; the book on comedy has not survived and Aristotle deals with tragedy in discussing the epic.)

(*a*)   Dramatists are concerned with the gods and their influence on human lives. In **plot** it is better to have the *probable impossible* (an unlikely event outside real life which nevertheless fits the dramatic context) than the *improbable possible* (an event taken from real life which does not fit the dramatic context). A work of art, including a play, must create its own context within which it must keep. **Character** too must be consistent and in harmony with a play's context.

(b) **Tragedy** is the imitation (representation) of an action that is serious, has magnitude, and is complete in itself. It is set out with ornaments (such as verse and music) in a dramatic rather than a narrative form, with incidents which arouse pity and fear. Such incidents will allow the spectator to be 'purged' or 'purified' of such emotions by **catharsis** (a purification). We do not need to see terrible events arousing horror taking place before our eyes; the mere recital of such events (as in *Oedipus*) will be sufficient to arouse our emotions. 'Spectacle' or the showing of the events is unnecessary and not artistic. Events such as the killing of enemies will not arouse pity unless the enemy suffers badly, but murder within a family can arouse pity and fear (*e.g.* the murder of Clytemnestra by Orestes or of Eriphyle by Alcmeon). The deed may be consciously carried out (*e.g.* Medea's murder of her children in Euripides) or in ignorance (*e.g.* Oedipus's killing of his father in Sophocles). Murder may be contemplated but resisted. The worst situation is when a person is on the point of doing the deed but leaves it undone (*pace* Hamlet), since the absence of suffering leaves an action done, or merely contemplated, untragic.

(c) There are six parts to every tragedy. The first and most important is **plot**: 'the combination of the incidents or things done in the story'. 'It is in our actions – what we do – that we are happy or the reverse'. It is possible to have a tragedy without characters but not one without plot. Plot is the last aspect in which the young dramatist learns to succeed. (Dryden agreed and thought Ben Jonson's *Epicoene* 'the finest piece of plotting'.)

The plot should have 'a beginning, middle, and end'. *A beginning* is that which is not necessarily after anything else and which has naturally something else after it; *an end* is that which is naturally after something else, as its necessary or usual consequence, but has nothing else after it. *A middle* is by nature after one thing and has also another after it. A well-constructed plot cannot, therefore, either begin or end at any point.

The plot must be of some length 'which allows the hero by a series of probable or necessary stages to pass from misfortune to happiness (comedy) or from happiness to misfortune (tragedy)'. Such a transition is known as peripety. Its unity does not consist necessarily in having one man or woman as the hero (such as *The Odyssey*, for example). A plot must not be episodic (*i.e.* where there is neither probability nor necessity in the sequence of the episodes); it may be *simple* (where it occurs without peripety or discovery, a change from ignorance to knowledge or love to hate) or *complex* (where it involves either peripety or discovery or both). Both 'peripety' and 'discovery' must arise from the structure of the plot and not merely be tacked on; they must be necessary. Within these comments on plot lie the essential details of what came to be known in dramatic theory as the Unity of Action.

Three kinds of plot are to be avoided: a good man must not pass from happiness to misery; a bad man must not pass from misery to happiness;

an extremely bad man must not fall from happiness to misery. The best tragic plots show a man who is not outstandingly good or just, whose disasters come to him not by vice and depravity but by an error of judgement (*e.g.* Oedipus, Thyestis, Alcmeon, Orestes, Telephus). Euripides, whose choruses are often irrelevant to his plot, whose character of Iphigenia is inconsistent, whose Menelaus in *Orestes* is depraved, whose Melanippe is too philosophical for a woman, is faultless nevertheless in his conception and execution of plot, Aristotle argues. (Some modern twentieth century views of Euripides might be that his characters are more like human beings than those of Aeschylus and Sophocles!)

(*d*) **Character** is the second of the six points of tragedy. There are four points to aim at: (*i*) characters must be *good*; what a person says or does must reveal a moral purpose and if the purpose is good, 'even in a woman or a slave, though one is perhaps inferior and the other a wholly worthless being' (!), then the character is good; (*ii*) characters must be '*appropriate*' – it is not appropriate in a female character to be manly or clever'; (*iii*) characters must be *real*; (*iv*) characters must be *consistent*. Nevertheless, dramatists writing tragedy may make their characters better than those of ordinary men without losing appropriateness, reality, or consistency.

(*e*) **Diction** is the third of the six points of tragedy: 'the composition of the verses'. This depends on the art of the poet who should be able 'to distinguish in the spoken language command and prayer, simple statement and threat, question and answer, etc.'; it should observe the rules of grammar and be clear. The use of figurative language (metaphor) will ensure the diction is not mean and the use of ordinary words will ensure the diction is not obscure.

(*f*) **Thought** is the fourth of the six parts of tragedy. It must be apparent in all the characters do or say, 'in every effort to prove or disprove, to arouse emotion (pity, fear, anger, and so on), or to exaggerate or minimise things. The thought may be explicit in word or implicit in deed'.

(*g*) **Spectacle** is the fifth of the six parts of tragedy, the stage-appearance of the actors. We do not necessarily need to *see* the horrors; frequently the account of the horrors is more effective. (See, for example, the narration of Samson's destruction of the temple in Milton's *Samson Agonistes* given by a messenger; the spectacle of the temple's collapsing could not be shown effectively on the stage.) To produce the effect of horror by means of spectacle often requires extraneous aid and shows that the dramatist does not understand the nature of tragedy. Spectacle is best reported, therefore.

(*h*) **Melody** is the sixth of the elements making up tragedy. Aristotle hardly touches on this topic again after enumerating the parts of tragedy. It is, however, he says, 'the greatest of the pleasurable accessories of tragedy'. Elsewhere he describes music as being 'a very real factor in the pleasure of drama' (see the discussion of *melodrama* pages 185–187 and 218–222).

Conveniently, in Chapter Four of *The Poetics*, Aristotle traces **the development of Greek tragedy**. Drama, he explains, began in improvisations derived from laudatory hymns to the gods (tragedy) or in improvisations of a scurrilous character spoken by the leader of a 'phallus' song, a ribald hymn in honour of Phales, the god of fertility and the Companion of Dionysus (comedy); (see Aristophanes's *Acharnians*, lines 241 *ff.*).

Then tragedy advanced little by little. The number of actors was first increased by Aeschylus to two (with each actor playing more than one role), who reduced the business of the Chorus, still to be regarded as essential to the action and a major part of the whole play; he made dialogue, or the spoken part of tragedy take the lead over the music of the drama. *Sophocles* added a third actor and used scenery, too. Tragedy began to acquire 'magnitude', that is length and dignity. It discarded short stories, episodic in nature, and changed its metre from trochaic (/U) to iambic (U/) rhythms. A number of unified episodes or acts made up the tragedy. They proceeded through a series of crises to a *dénouement*, or untying of the knots tied in the course of the dramatic action.

Comedy, on the other hand, was worse than tragedy, since it dealt with the ridiculous – a 'blunder or deformity not productive of pain or harm to others'; the mask in comedy, for example, made people laugh, was ugly and distorted, but did not hurt.

Quintus Horatius Flaccus (65 BC–8BC), known usually as **Horace**, was a Roman writer of Odes and Satires, but his *The Art of Poetry* has continued to have a marked influence on British literary critical theory and, to a lesser extent, on British dramatic criticism. As a young man of about twenty he visited Athens and later fought on the side of Brutus against Octavius Caesar at Philippi in 42 BC, as a result of which he was deprived of his inheritance. Later he became a friend of the two poets Virgil and Varius.

The *Art of Poetry* is conversational in style and intentionally casual; it moves from idea to idea without any strictly ordered line of development. Horace was not a dramatist and his work was mainly concerned with poetry, but he did make some comments, too, on drama. His central theme, however, was that of 'decorum', the right words in the right places.

First, Horace pointed out that the style and language of comedy and tragedy must be fitting for the subject:

A comic affair doesn't want to be stated in verse
That goes with tragedy; likewise the feast of Thyestes
Scorns to be told in the rhythms of everyday life,
That almost befit a comedy's slippered ease.
Each of the styles should keep to the fitting place
Allotted it . . .

If the words that uttered go ill with the part played,
I shall either nod off to sleep or burst out laughing.
Sorrowful tones befit an unhappy expression
Those full of threats the look of one who is angry;
Saucy words for the playful, grave for the sober . . .
If a speaker's words are out of tune with his fortunes,
A Roman audience, front seats and back seats alike,
Will hoot with laughter.*

Secondly, he argued that characters should be 'coherent' and consistent:

Should you entrust to the stage
A theme unattempted as yet and dare to create
A new character, let it be kept to the end
Just as it first came forth when the play began,
And be consistent.

This, if closely implemented by a dramatist, would destroy any development in character during the course of the play. Othello, Lear, Hamlet and Macbeth match up sadly against Horace's 'law of character'.

Thirdly, no new themes or incidents should be introduced into well-known plots, such as that of the Trojan War. The dramatist must discriminate carefully between what should be put on the stage in action and what is better narrated:

An event is either acted upon the stage
Or told of there as having occurred. The feelings
Are more reluctantly roused by what comes in
By way of the ears than what lies open before
The trusty eyes and what the man in the audience
Can see for himself; you will not, though, bring on to the stage
What should be enacted off it; many a deed
You will take away from our sight – en eloquent actor
Will presently tell the audience what has been done.
So don't let Medea butcher those boys of hers
In front of the crowd, or impious Atreus cook
Human entrails in full view of the people.

Fourthly, a play should be no longer than five acts and no god should intervene unless it was absolutely necessary to break a knot in the action. Here Horace was referring to the Greek stage convention of the *deus ex machina*, the god who was swung out over the orchestra by a crane-like contraption, from which he directed and, god-like, solved at a stroke the problems that the characters were facing:

And don't have a god intervening, unless there occurs
A knot in the action worthy of being untied

---

* The translations of Horace in this chapter are taken from Lord Dunsany and Michael Oakley, *The Collected Works of Horace*, 1961 (Everyman's Library, J. M. Dent).

By such a deliverer; nor should there be on the stage
A fourth * character, doing his best to speak.

Fifthly, the duties of the Chorus were set out:

The Chorus ought to sustain the part of an actor,
With all his strenuous duties, singing nothing
Between the acts which does not assist the plot
And duly fit in with it. Yes, it should favour the good
And give them friendly advice, should check the angry
And lovingly cherish those who fear to do no wrong;
It should praise the fare that is placed on the frugal board,
Should praise the beneficial justice and law, and peace
With its open gates; should keep secrets and also
Pray to the gods and beseech them that fortune may go
Back to those sick at heart and away from the proud.

Such a clear list of the functions of the Chorus, as seen by a Roman, repays
close consideration: supporting and reinforcing the protagonist; using their
comments economically but relevantly; honouring the good and those who
avoid self-indulgence and love peace; keeping confidences and seeking help for
those in despair; rejecting the proud.

Sixthly, Horace described the development of tragedy and comedy in Greek
times:

Thespis is said to have been the first to discover
The Tragic Muse, a kind unknown hitherto,
And also to have carried his dramas around in tents
To be sung and acted by players whose faces were daubed
With wine-lees. After him *Æschylus* came,
Who invented the mask and the handsome tragic robe,
Set up a stage of simple pieces of wood
And taught the actors to speak in a lofty tone
And add to their height by wearing the tragic boot.
To these succeeded the **Old Comedy**, winning
No little renown; but its freedom gave way to excess
And to violence needing a law to keep it in check.
The law was obeyed; to its own disgrace, the *Chorus*
Lapsed into silence, losing the right to do harm.

Horace felt that Roman dramatists achieved more by breaking free from
Greek models and using their own style, subjects, and language:

There is no style of writing our poets have left unattempted,
And the honour that they have earned has not been least
When they've ventured to leave the steps of the Greeks behind
And tell of events at home, either by training
Their actors in home-bred tragedy or by writing
Of native comedy.

* Thespis sixth century BC introduced the first actor; Aeschylus fifth century BC added a
second; Sophocles fifth century BC a third, although a fourth actor was needed in *Oedipus at
Colonnus*.

3.3   The Chorus

Aristotle said that tragedy sprang from some type of choral lyric, possibly the dithyramb, originally a hymn sung in honour of Bacchus, the god of wine, and Dionysus, who was seen as the god of fertility, the one who gave ecstasy. After being torn limb from limb by the Titans Dionysus rose again from the grave.

The choral lyric associated with Dionysus is first mentioned by Archilochus of Paros (*c.* 700–650 BC), who implies that he improvised words in honour of the god whilst a Chorus answered him. Later in the seventh century BC the Dorians enjoyed choral dance and song. About 600 BC Arion of Corinth developed some kind of tragic lyric; the word *tragedy* is thought by some to have arisen from the Greek word *tragoida* (a goat song, from *tragos*: a goat), because the first tragic Choruses might have worn goatskins or been dressed like goats, or because a goat was sacrificed, or a goat was the prize for the best song.

In the sixth century Thespis is thought to have invented an actor who answered the chorus; he was called *hypocrites*, 'one who plays a part' (from which the Modern English word *hypocrite* is derived). Tragedy, therefore, arose from the Chorus. The actor was not a part of the Chorus and did not stand in the 'orchestra' of the Greek theatre; he probably stood on a raised platform or stage. The role of the Chorus changed; it was no longer simply the body narrating the tragedy–it was also a dramatic character who could *exchange* dialogue with the actor.

The introduction of the actor made drama possible, since conflict could occur between actor and Chorus. Aeschylus's addition of a second actor and Sophocles' introduction of a third (and possibly a fourth in *Oedipus at Colonnus*) allowed the action of the play to become more complex. The actors could, of course, play several parts each. The *Agamemnon* of Aeschylus had six characters. In an early play, Aeschylus's *Suppliant Women*, two actors unfolded the story by addressing and exchanging remarks with the Chorus but not often between themselves; in *Seven Against Thebes* the two actors had a dialogue between themselves without reference to the Chorus. Three actors increased dramatic flexibility further; there could now be exchanges between actors and the Chorus could comment on what was happening. As the role of the actors increased, so the role of the Chorus diminished to a point where its very existence in Greek drama was threatened once it no longer participated in the action of the play. In the *Eumenides* the Chorus had almost ceased to exist. Sophocles made the Chorus essentially dramatic by accepting that it could not control the action in the plot but insisting that it was part of it. The themes of *Antigone* (Creon's edict about the burial of the dead) and *Tyrannus* (the plague in Thebes) by Sophocles are concerned with public attitudes and the Chorus could speak as representatives of the public's attitudes. Only when Greek tragedy left the arena of public concern and began to deal with more private grief, as in *Electra* or the *Medea*, did the Chorus seem unnecessary.

The Chorus in Sophocles was, however, very individual. It took sides and argued its corner. It had its own point of view and was not merely a 'spectator' commenting on the events being narrated. In *Antigone* it both sympathised with her and yet disapproved of what she did. Dramatically it moved within the area of approval and recoil between Creon and Antigone. In *Electra*, however, the Chorus identified with the heroine. Technically, the Chorus broke up speeches and led actors to reply to what they had just been listening to.

The Chorus in Euripides's plays showed further changes. He certainly saw it as a body of ideal spectators commenting on the action, but in the *Medea* he suggested that the group of fifteen women of Corinth might perhaps have tried to stop Medea butchering her children in the house whilst they stood outside commenting. Ideally, perhaps, spectators *ought* to participate in the action, but the tragedy was private rather than public and therefore the outside spectators ought not to interfere. The Chorus, significantly, deliberated on the question of whether or not it should enter the action as participants. In the *Medea*, as in Sophocles's *Antigone*, the chorus changed sides and added to the dramatic conflict in the play.

In *Andromache*, Euripides kept the Chorus to one side of the action and of the tragedy. In *Hecuba, Suppliant Women* and *Troiades*, H. D. F. Kitto (*Greek Tragedy*, third edition, 1961) suggests that the Chorus became 'the representative or the symbol of suffering humanity'.

Wealthy Athenians were often chosen by lot to have the privilege of paying for Choruses in dramatic productions. They became known as *Choregi*, or Chorus-providers, and there was a lot of competition between them to provide the most spectacular display for their Choruses.

The role of the Chorus, therefore, over the period of Greek drama evolved gradually, it has been argued. It began as narrator, assumed the role of an actor with one or more other actors, it commented on the action as ideal spectators, it revealed the emotions of the main characters and judged them, it broke up the action of the play by introducing pauses and times for reflection, it even pushed the plot in one direction or another, it regulated audience's responses, and sadly became by the end of this period the technical means of merely showing that the event or the play was ending. **It is essential, in considering a Greek play to examine the Chorus's part in that play**. No blanket description of the role of the Chorus will necessarily apply to it, since the Chorus was used at different times by different playwrights in different ways.

3.4 Greek Dramatic Performances

The size of the theatre meant that audibility might have proved a problem. Nevertheless, the bowl-shaped arrangement of the seats would throw the sound up towards the top tiers of seats. It is quite possible to hear a single human voice coming from the 'orchestra' at the back of a Greek theatre, as a practical test easily shows, but the voice has to be loud. Even the *skene* at the back of the platform would not have diminished the need for the actor to speak up. However, the excellent acoustic properties of Greek theatres arose from careful architectural design. The same attention was paid to sound in Roman theatres; Vitruvius even suggests that jars placed in theatres at strategic points would reverberate to the human voice and amplify it.

Masks would have helped an audience to recognise quickly the kind of character being portrayed by actors, a king or a priest, a slave, an old man, or a woman. Although the number of actors speaking in the play was limited to two or three (and very rarely four), many others who did not speak might also have appeared masked in the theatre. The Chorus, too, would have worn masks. This use of masks in early drama is still echoed in the use in the modern theatre of the words *Dramatis Personae*, where the word 'personae' is the Latin word for 'masks'; the phrase means 'the masks (characters) of the play'. Masks were worn, too, by the Chorus but they were unlikely to have worn the buskins, or thick-soled shoes (*cothurni*), used by the actors to raise their height.

The devices of a mechanical nature were few in the Greek theatre. The **mechane**, or crane, used to lower a god from the skies to solve problems (*deus ex machina*) or to represent the flight, say, of Pegasus, has already been mentioned (see page 52). In comedy it could be used for humour: flying away to heaven on a huge dung-beetle instead of Pegasus, or stranding an actor above the stage when he needs to be on it to speak some lines. A rolling platform was also used which was pushed out on to the stage, the **ekkyklema**. How it worked in detail is not known, but it could be used dramatically suddenly to reveal an actor; in Aristophanes's *Acharnians*, Euripides is too busy writing to enter the stage to lend a costume to an actor and so has himself rolled out on an 'ekkyklema'. Sometimes, fixed at both ends of the stage were tall, revolving, prism-like structures known as **periaktoi**, used in the changing of scenes.

Costume, sometimes rich and ornate and based on the priests' robes at Eleusis or ragged and torn to indicate beggars, and condemned as reducing the stage's dignity, was used. **Properties** could indicate the nature of particular characters: the king held a sceptre, travellers wore wide-brimmed hats, heralds carried wreaths, the Furies bore lighted torches, death (in Euripides's *Alcestis*) had black wings, and the gods carried their own distinctive emblems – a bow (Artemis, the huntress), a thunderbolt (Zeus, the god of thunder), or a trident (Poseidon, the god of the ocean).

3.5   Greek Tragedy

There was a marked progression during the fifth century BC in Greek tragedy from public or communal themes to those more concerned with the private affairs of the individual. **Aeschylus** (525 BC–456 BC) was, perhaps, the first tragedian in Greece. It is perhaps comic, however, to reflect that he is said to have met his death in Sicily at Gela when an eagle, mistaking the poet's bald head for a stone, dropped a tortoise on it to break its shell and so fulfilled the fateful prophesy that he would die by a blow from heaven. He is said to have written seventy tragedies, but of these only seven have survived: the *Persians*, the *Seven Against Thebes*, the *Suppliants*, *Prometheus*, *Agamemnon*, *Choephori*, and *Eumenides* (the last three making up the trilogy of the *Oresteia*). He is concerned with the moral order governing mankind where sin produces more sin, which produces more suffering, until Justice arrives to set the universe to rights.

Sophocles (495 BC–406 BC), as a young man, was renowned for his skill in music and gymnastics, and his great physical beauty and in 468 BC he managed to wrest the first prize in the dramatic contest from the ageing Aeschylus at the solemnities of the Great Dionysia. He held the first prize until

Euripides rose to oust him. As Sophocles grew older his son, Iophon, brought him before the Phratores, on the charge that he was senile. Sophocles is reported to have replied, 'If I am Sophocles, I am not beside myself; and if I am beside myself, I am not Sophocles'. Iophon lost the case after his father read a passage from his latest play, *Oedipus at Colonnus*.

He is thought to have produced as many as 123 plays but only seven have survived intact: *Antigone, Electra, Maidens of Trachis, Oedipus Rex (Tyrannus), Ajax, Philoctetes,* and *Oedipus at Colonnus.* In his tragedies H. D. F. Kitto, (*Greek Tragedy*, third edition, 1961) has argued that there is a powerful sense of a kind of justice and a rhythm or pattern in human affairs, where the dead seem to be killing the living. In the *Electra* it is said, 'The dead live. Those slain long ago will drain from their slayers blood which flows in another direction'. Justice in Sophocles is moral and inevitable but, although the tragic hero contributes to his own downfall and must be seen to have been at least partly responsible for his own fate, disaster may come inevitably and inexorably without justification, as Shakespeare puts it in *King Lear*:

As flies to wanton boys, are we to the gods;
They kill us for their sport.

The blows of fate will step in and destroy the vulnerable with a relentlessness that will arouse pity and fear. Nevertheless, man stands in Sophocles with his full dignity. Nothing can rob him of that unless he willingly gives it away. Antigone does her duty and will be welcomed by the dead.

The introduction of the third actor by Sophocles was a major innovation in drama since it allowed him to show the character of his main hero from a number of different angles. In many ways, since the hero (or heroine) is static in Greek tragedy, the character does not develop but is progressively revealed more and more clearly. The third actor allows this progressive revelation to become clearer and clearer.

Euripides (480 BC–406 BC) was the successor to Sophocles after gaining first prize from Sophocles in the dramatic contest in 441 BC. Socrates preferred his plays because he dealt in them with the sufferings and fate of ordinary men and women. He was essentially a rationalist and he managed to satirise the religion of his time in many of his plays. Eighteen of his plays have survived (excluding *Rhesus*, whose origins are now doubted): *Alcestis, Medea, Hippolytus, Hecuba, Andromache, Ion, The Suppliants* (the refusal of Creon to bury the Argive Warriors), *The Heracleidae, Heracles, Iphigenia among the Tauri, Trojan Women, Helen, The Phoenician Women, Electra, Orestes, Iphigenia at Aulis, The Bacchae* and *Cyclops*.

Some of his plays have been accused of being badly constructed (*Medea, Hippolytus, The Heracleidae, Heracles, Andromache, Hecuba, The Suppliants* and *Trojan Women*), judged by the criteria laid down by Aristotle, who was highly critical of Euripides. Aristotle argued in *The Poetics* that:

The perfect plot must have a single and not a double issue; the change in the hero's fortunes must be not from misery to happiness, but on the contrary from happiness to misery; and the cause of it must lie not in any depravity, but in some

great error on his part . . . The critics are wrong, therefore, who blame Euripides for taking this line in his tragedies and giving many of them an unhappy ending. On the stage and in public performances such plays, properly worked out, are seen to be the most truly tragic and Euripides, even if his execution be faulty in every other point, is nevertheless seen to be certainly the most tragic of the dramatists.
(Ingram Bywater's translation of *The Poetics*, W. Hamilton Fyfe, Oxford, 1940)

Aristotle criticised Euripides's *Medea* because she killed her children 'knowingly and consciously', Aegeus's timely arrival was highly improbable, and the *deus ex machina* at the end depended on a stage mechanical device rather than arising out of the plot itself. Aristotle also thought that the Choruses in Euripides often had little to do with the plot; in *Iphigenia at Aulis* the character of Iphigenia was inconsistent; and in *Orestes* Menelaus was unnecessarily depraved.

Aristotle's praise of Euripides as 'the most tragic of the poets' needs to be further considered in the light of his critical comments on tragedy (see pages 49–50). He might well have thought that modern approval of Euripides for making his characters more like ordinary men and women would have been a defect in tragedy since, he argued, 'tragedy is an imitation of persons better than the ordinary man'. (Chapter 15 of *The Poetics*).

In *The Phoenician Women* Euripides increased the number of parts to eleven, and in his later plays reduced the role of the Chorus. (Aristotle says that Agathon, Euripides's younger contemporary, introduced choral odes that were unrelated to the main plot and merely served to break up the play into sections and this finally gave rise to Horace's judgement that a play should be split necessarily into 'five acts'.)

Euripides, in spite of Aristotle's criticism, remains a dramatist of considerable force. He writes powerful scenes which are linked to themes concerned with the way the gods behave: 'If human beings behaved in the way the gods behave,' he argued, 'should we not condemn them out of hand?' He is contemptuous of the ways the gods bring misery to mankind. In *The Bacchae* the new cult of Dionysus had spread at Thebes and the god is pursued by adoring, frenzied women. King Pentheus refuses to bow to Dionysus, who then appears in human form to work the destruction of the King, who is lured to watch in secret the maddened women performing the rites of Dionysus. The women mistake him for a wild animal and they tear him apart with their bare hands. Even his own mother, Agavë, is deceived and carries her son's head in triumph. The scene where she gradually recovers her mind and sees what she has done is dramatically overpowering. The triumph of the god Dionysus at the end implicitly comments in a satirical way on the unfeeling attitude of the gods, but the play is not a condemnation of either Dionysus or of religion.

The Bacchae was the last of Euripides's plays except for *Iphigenia among the Tauri*. It provides a comment, therefore, on the point which Euripides had reached in his treatment of tragedy. This is not to suggest that there is a clear line of development in Euripides as a tragic writer; clearly there is not. At the heart of *The Bacchae* lies the struggle inside man of the rational and civilised (represented by Pentheus: the Greek word *'penthis'* means 'suffering') and the instinctive and emotional (represented by Dionysus). Between the two there is a struggle, an 'agon'. In denying the right of the other to exist, each suffers. Dionysus sets out his opposition to Pentheus in his first speech:

> Pentheus . . . he
> Is a fighter against the gods, defies me from
> Libations, never names me in prayers. Therefore I will
> Demonstrate to him, and all Thebes, that I am a god.*

Pentheus, in his turn, denies the right of Dionysus or Bacchus to exist:

> I'll put a stop to this outrageous Bacchism.
>   . . . Once let me
> Get that fellow within my walls – I'll cut his
> Head from his shoulders; that will stop him . . .
>   . . . The truth about Dionysus
> Is that he's dead, burnt to a cinder by lightning.

The vengeance of one intended for the other is terrifying; Dionysus drives people mad, makes them lose their reason:

> Therefore I have driven those same sisters mad, turned them
> All frantic out of doors; their home now is the mountain;
> Their wits are gone.

Pentheus, likewise, mocks Cadmus and Teiresias, who neither 'despise religion' because they are mortal nor deny the Dionysian part of men or women:

>   The Bacchic ecstasy
> And frenzy hold a strong prophetic element.
>   . . . Pentheus, pay heed to my words. You rely
> On force; but it is not force that governs human affairs.
> Do not mistake for wisdom that opinion which
> May rise from a sick mind. Welcome this god to Thebes . . .
>   . . . since, in all matters, self-control
> Resides in our own natures. You should consider this.

Ironically, the 'rational' Pentheus has not considered man's real nature and so is destroyed through *hubris*, an insolence or arrogance that invites disaster in Greek tragedy. It takes a blind man to point this out to Pentheus, whose 'foolish words bespeak a fool' Teiresias prefers to judge people by what they do rather than by what they say: 'I judge his acts'. A later critic, Hegel, saw this as being at the heart of tragedy – the self-wasting in a conflict where two essential features of man's make-up seek to destroy each other and deny the right of the other to exist.

Pentheus is filled with such self-destructive violence; 'He shall be stoned to death':

---

* Quotations are all from Philip Vellacott's *Euripides: The Bacchae and Other Plays*, Penguin, revised 1972.

Go, someone, quickly to his seat of augury,
Smash it with crowbars, topple the walls, throw all his things
In wild confusion, turn the whole place upside down.

The words 'turn upside down' occur, significantly, four times in the play.
Teiresias calls him:

Foolhardy man! You do not know what you have said.
Before you were unbalanced; now you are insane.

Violence has made the rational irrational, the sane insane. Later, Dionysus is
similarly rebuked by Cadmus for his vengeance: 'Gods should not be like
mortals in their vindictiveness'.

At the heart of the play is the debate, the dialectic, between Pentheus and
Dionysus (lines 450–550); the god describes himself but Pentheus fails to
recognise him: 'Where is he, then? Not visible to my eyes'. Dionysus explains:
'You, being a blasphemer, see nothing'.

DIONYSUS   (*to Pentheus*)   I am sane, and you are mad.
PENTHEUS   My word overrules yours.
DIONYSUS   You know not what you are saying, what you do nor who you are.
PENTHEUS   Who? Pentheus, son of Echion and Agavë.

This passage of rapidly exchanged dialogue (known in Greek tragedy as
stichomythia) embodies the dialogue of the blind talking to the blind and the
deaf to the deaf. Destruction must follow.

The destruction comes accompanied by an earthquake. The restrictions of
the Greek theatre to show an earthquake on the stage are more than overcome
by the descriptive detail contained in the Messenger's account of it, in
figurative and symbolic terms. One is reminded of the similarly graphic
account by a messenger of the destruction of the heathen temple by Samson in
Milton's *Samson Agonistes*, a play (with a Chorus) firmly based on Greek
dramatic tradition.

The Bacchae is marked by an unrelenting impetus which carries the plot
inexorably and inevitably on. The plot is extremely well-unified and here,
even at the end of the great period of Greek tragedy, the function of the Chorus
reasserts itself as a central 'actor' in the conflict. The first speech of the Chorus
(lines 63 *ff.*) contrasts the differences between the pure ecstasy of the mountains
and the frenzied ecstasy of the hunt; the idea of 'the hunt', 'the pursuit' is one of
the major themes running through the play. It also stresses 'the brute wildness'
and increases in its intensity as it goes on to herald the entrance of blind
Teiresias and Cadmus who 'see things clearly; all others are perverse'. The
Chorus is the voice of contrast, of what is prescribed, of conflict, of hunting.

The second intrusion of the Chorus into the play (lines 551 *ff.*) comments on
what happened and describes, by contrasting Pentheus and Dionysus, the
anger of the king. The theme of hunting is taken up and the Chorus associates
itself with Dionysus. The Chorus also spans the time gap between the god's
arrest and his release – the playwright uses them technically to suggest time
passing. It also invites Dionysus to present his case and then leads on to the

second personal confrontation between the protagonist and the antagonist (Pentheus and Dionysus).

The third time that the Chorus enters the play (lines 861 *ff.*) it resumes the symbol of the hunt and debates man's nature and his search through time to reach the conclusion:

> . . . he who best
> Enjoys each passing day
> Is truly blest.

It re-enters the play (lines 977 *ff.*) and takes up the theme of Justice, and the hunt of the Bacchic daughters of Cadmus turns on Pentheus. Again, the Chorus acts as a time-span and the death of the King is reported through an exchange of stichomythia with the Messenger who graphically describes the earthquake in symbolic language. The irony is that Pentheus's own mother and life-giver, Agavë, is one of the hunters and she tore her son apart herself.

The Chorus is now firmly in the play and explores repentance and man's sadness in a rapid exchange of conversation with Agavë. It is left to them to explain what has happened in the play:

> Gods manifest themselves in many forms,
> Bring matter to surprising ends;
> The things we thought would happen do not happen;
> The unexpected God makes possible.
> And that is what has happened here to day.

3.6 Greek Comedy

The Greek word **koμos** (*komos*) means a revel. In John Milton's masque *Comus* (1634), the word is the name of a pagan god, invented by the English poet, who is the son of Bacchus and Circe and who waylays travellers and tempts them to drink a magic potion which changes their faces into those of wild beasts. In Greek times the word 'komos' described a procession or dance, a kind of sacred romp through the countryside, a 'Furry' or Flower Dance of the kind still practised even in England at Helston in Cornwall on 8th May. The Greek dance, with a Chorus chanting a lyric, gave rise to tragedy, but linked with a kind of satyr play, used as a humorous relief to a serious lyric, primitive comedy is thought to have emerged. Aeschylus is reputed to have written a satyr play, *Net-fishers*, and Sophocles, *The Searchers*. The only satyr play to survive, however, is Euripedes's *Cyclops*, which tells how Apollo lost his cattle and the satyrs (wood gods with long ears, shown by the Romans as being half-goat) go looking for them with their noses to the ground in a kind of pantomime. Such 'satyr' plays often involved Silenus, the father of the satyrs, a jolly creature riding on an ass, intoxicated and crowned with flowers. There is an elaborate *komos* introduced into what is perhaps the best known of all Greek comedies, *The Frogs* by Aristophanes, where at one point the dancing stops and the play changes to satire, a mock proclamation and lampooning.

The word **comedy** is linked to *komos* (*komoidia*). It is traditional to assign the origin of comedy to a district in Greece called Megara, once part of Attica.

There, a kind of farce grew up which would have become completely lost in history had not Aristophanes parodied it in a scene in his play *Acharnians*: a man of Megara comes to market to sell his two daughters and after a lively exchange about the quality of the 'pigs' he manages to sell them off to the gullible Old Honesty for some garlic and salt.

Later **Epicharmus** (born about 540 BC) went to Sicily and there produced some plays apparently full of social satire and caricature about class. He is thought to have been the originator of two stock comedy characters that still exist in comedy today, the drunkard and the parasite. His works, however, are known to us only from fragments that have survived or from references in other writers' works.

Aristophanes (*c.* 444 BC–*c.* 380 BC) is undoubtedly the most important of Greek comedy writers. His plays contain caricatures of many of the leading men of his day and contain devastating attacks on the Peloponnesian War (431–404 BC) between Athens and Sparta; the Sophists (in *Clouds*) who gave instruction in intellectual and ethical matters for money (the 'Sophists' were often contrasted with the more proper 'Philosophers'); and the excessive love of going to law, which was a feature of Athenian life (satirised in *Wasps*). Eleven of his comedies have survived: *Acharnians* (an attack on those pursuing a war policy); *Knights* (an attack on Cleon who opposed peace; the playwright had already been impeached and fined for attacking Cleon in a lost play, *Babylonians*); *Wasps* (an attack on demagogues and litigants); *Birds* (a general political satire); *Frogs* (a long 'flyting' or argument between Aeschylus and Euripides for the prize for tragedy in the underworld); *Plutus* (an allegory about how the virtuous would become wealthy); *Lysistrata* and *Ecclesiazusae* (on the power women can exert on men to get their own way); *Thesmophoriazusae* (the trial of Euripides who was convicted at the female festival of Thesmophoria); *Clouds* (a criticism of the Sophists); and *Peace* (advocating peace with Sparta). The topics of his plays are remarkably 'modern' for today's reader: contemporary political abuse; war-hysteria; demagogues; the rights and power of women; wealth; pacifism; philosophy and sociology.

Aristophanes's plots usually consist of a series of sketches round a single character or theme. The dialogue is sometimes that of ordinary people, often using broad dialect to drive home their points or becoming laughable as foreigners try to speak Greek, and sometimes the dignified, elegant language of a choral lyric. There were some startling 'theatrical' presentations in Aristophanes. In *Birds* for example, at its entrance, the Chorus is dressed as birds – one a flamingo, another a hoopoe, another a pompous cockerel, and so on. In another play the jurymen are shown as a Chorus of wasps who enter in pantomimic procession preceded by boys holding lamps moving from side to side to imitate the insects' head movements. The Chorus, in becoming comic, becomes almost grotesque. Aristophanes's method is sometimes that of burlesque (reducing the mighty and the powerful to the trivial), such as the attack on Socrates in *Clouds*, and sometimes that of mock-heroic (elevating the trivial to the larger scale of life amongst the epic heroes and gods), where a sausage-seller defeats two slaves, really two well-known generals, in serious debate in *Knights*.

F. L. Lucas (*Greek Drama for the Common Reader* revised edition, 1967), has suggested that the comedy of the time of Aristophanes had the following typical, though variable, form:

1   Some character has a bright idea: a man thinks of stopping the war by flying to heaven on a dung-beetle, or a woman tries to stop it by organising a women's sexual strike.
2   A Chorus, sympathetic or hostile, enters.
3   There follows a set debate about the proposal.
4   The Chorus turns and addresses the audience directly (a *parabasis*), perhaps a relic of the mockeries flung at bystanders by the old phallic mummers.
5   A series of farcical episodes arises from putting the original idea into practice.
6   All ends in a scene of revelling such as a feast or a wedding; a further relic of the primitive merrymaking.

In the Greek comedy which followed Aristophanes (sometimes called The 'New Comedy') the comedy moved from public figures to private individuals, the lyric dwindled, and the Chorus deteriorated to a group that was largely separate from the main plot and intervened only to break up the main plot with diversions. Only a few fragments of these new comedies have survived; the most accomplished of the new school seems to have been **Menander** (*c.* 342 BC– 292 BC), who was drowned while swimming in the harbour of Piraeus. His plays showed the life of contemporary Athens and were adapted by two Roman writers of comedy, **Plautus** (*c.* 254 BC–184 BC) and **Terence** (*c.* 190 BC–159 BC). It is through their work and adaptations of Greek plays that we can see something of Menander's genius.

3.7   Roman Comedy

Little of the work of the 'New Comedy' writers, as they have been called, of the Greek theatre has survived but the Romans have declared their debt to it in their own plays.

Fragments of two of **Menander**'s plays have allowed a reconstruction of them. *The Arbitration* deals with the claims of two parties for the right to possess an abandoned baby and in the *Rape of the Locks* a woman is accused of associating with a strange young man, has her hair cut off as a punishment, only for the identity of the young man to be declared as her brother.

Love-plots, long-lost children, the problems of young love, and the type-casting of many of the characters (angry old man, young lover, etc.) would resound through dramatic history to our own times. The Romans took over such devices, sometimes combining two Greek plots into one (*contaminatio*) played out in Greek costume (*palliata*) and sometimes in Roman dress (*comedia togata*).

The Romans developed their style of theatre from that of the Greeks. The stage was increased in size and the orchestra was made into a semi-circle. There was even a curtain used to hide the stage; it apparently rose from a slot in the ground rather like a blind unwinding. Spectacle was important and the plays themselves were often divided into *diverbia* (spoken dialogue) and *cantica* (sung sections). The presentations, therefore, were kinds of musical comedy, in fact.

The Prologue to Plautus's *Menaechmi* acknowledges the Greek source of the play quite unequivocally:

> Tis the way
> With poets in their comedies to feign
> The business passed at Athens, so that you
> May think it the more Grecian – For our play
> I'll not pretend the incidents to happen
> Where they do not: the argument is Grecian,
> And yet it is not Attic, but Sicilian.

Eleven Roman writers' names have come down through history to us: Livius Andronicus, Naevius, Ennius, Plautus, Pacuvius, Coecilius, Porcius Licinius, Terence, Lucus Lavinius, Accius and Afranius. The main contributions to the development of the drama by the Romans include: the integration of a sub-plot into a play (for example the use of a farcical under-plot, rather than the Grecian interjection of farce and caricature at various points in the play); the development of stock characters such as the parasite; the insistence on the Unity of Place (where the scene remains unchanged throughout the play); the extensive use of dramatic irony (where spontaneous, unconscious clashes between events come about not from character but chance (Plautus's *Captives* is full of examples of dramatic irony); mistaken identity (as in the *Menaechmei*), with confusion between twins or because of impersonation (as in *Pseudolus*); the hiding of characters and their subsequent revelation; (in Plautus's *Mostellaria* a master is kept out of his house on the pretext that it is haunted whilst some outrageous events go on in the building – *cf.* Ben Jonson's *The Alchemist*); the use of types as characters; and the introduction of love-plots, sometimes artificially contrived.

There are two comedy writers from Roman times, whose surviving work includes whole plays. Titus Macchius **Plautus** (*c*. 254 BC–184 BC) was born in Umbria and in his early life apparently knew considerable poverty. He clearly derived much of his plays from Greek drama, but unfortunately his Greek originals have not survived to give us a point of comparison. His characters are 'types' rather than individuals. (Here, the plays of Ben Jonson, 1572–1637, bear comparison with characters such as Subtle, Sir Epicure Mammon, Tribulation Wholesome, Dame Pliant, Mosca (the fly) a parasite, Volpone (the fox), Voltore (the vulture), Corbaccio (the crow).) Oddly enough, the playwright's own name (*Plautus*) means 'the flat- or broad-footed man'. His second name (Macchius) was adapted from the name of a character, Maccus, he was said to have played, a clown in farce.

Twenty of Plautus's plays have survived: *Amphitruo, Asinaria, Aulularia, Bacchides, Captivi, Casina, Cistellaria, Curculio, Epidicus, Menaechmi, Mercator, Miles, Mostellaria* (a Ghost Story), *Persa, Poenulus, Pseudolus, Rudens* (dealing with storm and a shipwreck), *Stichus, Trinummus,* and *Truculentus*. The plots have sometimes been divided into three kinds: (*i*) *fabula Atellana*, a rustic plot based on stock clown figures; (*ii*) *fabula praetextata*, serious plays on legendary or historical themes: (*iii*) *fabula togata*, light domestic comedy of Roman middle-class or village life (see E. F. Watling, *Plautus, The Rope and Other Plays*, 1964, 11).

An examination of *Aulularia* (or *The Pot of Gold*) by Plautus will reveal some of the characteristics of his kind of comedy. The ending of the play has been lost but E. F. Watling in his translated version of the play (*Plautus, The Pot of Gold and Other Plays*, 1965) has reconstructed the final scene of the drama from clues found earlier in the text. There is a central character, Euclio, a miserly old man (*cf.* Molière's Harpagon in *L'Avare*, 1668). The remaining members of the Dramatis Personae are also type-figures: a housekeeper, an elderly bachelor, a young man, a cook, a slave, or flute-girls.

The Prologue to the play, Lar Familiaris (the household god), sees himself as a vital part of the action. He is the development of Chance or Fate and the precursor of characters such as the Manager in Thornton Wilder's *Our Town* or Prospero in *The Tempest*. He acts, too, **as the link between the stage and the audience**. An important part of a play is the *exordium*, or introduction, where the audience is given the information it needs to follow the subsequent action and where issues are raised which can lead to 'complications' of plot and ultimately to its *dénouement*.

The major character, Euclio, has already been drawn as a tetchy, old miser even before he has entered the stage:

> There's the master, shouting as usual. He's turning his old housekeeper out of the house, so that she shan't know what he's up to. I expect he wants to have a look at his money, to make sure it hasn't been stolen.

The language of Euclio is stereotyped, full of abuse, but his first speeches are interesting mixtures of **asides** to the audience, expressions of inner thoughts, and direct dialogue with the housekeeper, Staphyla. Her reaction is also a mixture of inner thoughts, asides, dialogue – and of mime, when she puts herself into the posture of a hanging corpse.

The first **change of scene is skilfully engineered**. As Euclio leaves the stage Eunomia, or the one well-named (Greek εὐ + νομος), is ushered out of a house by Megadorus, a neighbour and an elderly bachelor, just as in the first scene Staphyla had been pushed out by Euclio. The dialogue is pithy, to the point, in the language of **everyday speech**, and varied – question and answer, action and reaction, swift-moving comment and slower thoughtful musing.

The link between the two opening scenes occurs in the next change of scene – the confrontation between Megadorus and Euclio. We are witnessing here a very smooth-running piece of **stage-craft** where exits and entrances are well-engineered. The confrontation develops into a jockeying for position about the proposed marriage; the **crises** and the Aristotelian **peripetes** (significant turning points in the plot) are happening in front of the audience's very eyes.

The minor characters, Strobilus, the significantly-named young cook, Anthrax, and the rude cook, Congrio, bring a **sub-plot** quickly into action. It provides **comic relief**. The characters are really **caricatures** but they act as commentators on the action taking place in the main plot; this was to become one of the traditional uses of the sub-plot in later, particularly in Elizabethan, times on the British stage. Then the sub-plot goes further and actually enters the main plot. There is knock-about comedy, of the kind that Henri Bergson* described as '**the mechanical**' with beatings, threats, chases and attempts at concealment.

The **soliloquy** of Megadorus provides an interlude in the play, where Plautus can comment with satiric effect on marriage customs of the day, dowries, and public morals. Here the **overhearing** device comes into operation as Euclio listens to Megadorus's comments and then interprets them to the audience. The subsequent debate between Megadorus and Euclio introduces a form for comedy on which Bernard Shaw was later to rely very heavily in such plays as *Major Barbara* (1900) and *Man and Superman* (1903).

The introduction of the Young Slave marks the introduction of the honest and trusty caricature of a servant into drama. He begins by **establishing a rapport with the audience** by declaring who he is and explaining his role as his master's slave. He **overhears** Euclio, is discovered, and is beaten. Already the play has been broken up and is clearly **episodic in construction**. The art of the dramatist lies essentially in keeping the action flowing from scene to scene. He does it usually by leaving one character from an episode on stage to introduce or take part in the next. Where this does not happen and the stage is momentarily cleared, as after the Staphyla-Euclio-Megadorus scene or the Slave-Euclio scene, the empty stage signifies a brief passing of time. **The Unities of Time and Place** can be strictly adhered to, in this way; the audience is never lost as to when and where the action of the play is occurring.

Eunomia, a major character from earlier in the play, then enters, introducing for the first time another character, Lyconides, the lover of Eunomia's daughter who has already been referred to. The plot is progressing by a series of **interlocking episodes**. Immediately a crisis occurs with the cries of Phaedria in labour coming dramatically into the plot; now the climax is there with the threat of discovery, the complication of the tissue of lies that has been built up, and the destruction of Euclio's happiness when he has to decide between his gold and his money (*cf.* Shylock in *The Merchant of Venice*: 'this is my day of doom, disaster, and damnation'.) The *dénouement* comes about after further complications, misunderstandings, and explanations through the Slave. The minor character provides the solution to the main plot's problems (*cf.* Dogberry in *Much Ado About Nothing*).

This play, therefore, embodies features of comedy that would run on for centuries even into the farces of the mid-twentieth-century. Above all, it shows a flexible and skilled use of a stage that might have appeared somewhat inflexible. Plautus faced the essential problem of stage-audience relationships and solved them by skilful plot construction, maintained pace, easily

---

* H. Bergson's famous and important work on comedy: *Le Rire: Essai sur la signification du comique* (1900).

recognisable characters, and devices which in themselves provided not only intrigue but *dénouement* as well.

Publius Terentius Afer, usually known as **Terence** (*c*. 190 BC–159 BC), was born at Carthage and became the slave of a Roman senator. His master later gave him his freedom in Rome and his first play, *Andria*, found favour with Caecilius, one of the most successful playwrights at Rome. After suffering some attacks from Luscius Lavinius, a less successful playwright than Caecilius, Terence went to Rome where he studied Menander's comedies. He died very young in Greece, never having returned to Italy. The six of his comedies that have survived all seem to have been firmly based on Greek plays from the later period, four of them on plays by Menander: *Andria*, *Hecyra* (or 'The Mother-in-Law'), *Heautontimorumenos* ('The Self-Punisher') and *Eunuchus*, *Phormio*, *Adelphoe* ('The Brothers'). The Prologue to 'The Self-Punisher' makes a point of saying it is 'an entire play from an entire Greek source': *ex integra Graeca integram comoediam.*

The **soliloquy** played a large part in Terence's plays; the action of 'The Mother-in-Law' is largely played out with the use of this device; in a sense, the soliloquy became one of the lasting developments of the Greek Chorus in later drama. The **Prologue**, too, was becoming more flexible; not only did it serve to give the setting, explain to the audience what they needed to know to follow the plot, and to introduce the major characters and early major dramatic complications in the plot, but it also allowed writers to comment on the current scene. Terence, for example, in one of his plays carries on his literary war with a critic in one of his prologues.

Contrast is often a major feature of Terence's plays. In 'The Brothers', each of them begins with his own rigid code of morality; one lives in the country and brings his son up strictly, whereas the other lives in the town and encourages his adopted nephew to indulge in an easy morality. The strictly brought up son commits excesses for which the nephew is blamed, but on discovery of the real truth the brothers adapt their positions and draw nearer each other.

Terence has been criticised because he seems at times more interested in presenting moral problems than in writing plays. His characters are often earnest, it has to be admitted, and Terence's own complaint that Roman audiences preferred dances and rope-walkers to his comedies is as much a condemnation of Roman popular taste as it is of his plays. Nevertheless, none other than Ben Jonson praises Terence for his contribution of **dividing comedy into acts and scenes** and observing **the Unity of Time** so that 'the whole argument falls within the compass of a day's business'. Julius Caesar found Terence's plays lacking in comedy but the playwright became well-known in the tenth century and during the Renaissance. Nicholas Udall's play *Ralph Roister Doister* (*c*. 1553) with its absent merchant, swaggering simpleton, a mischievous stirrer-of-troubles, and the caricature of a widow owes something to the characterisation and dilemma of characters in the plays of Plautus and Terence. A clear view of the way Terence was seen at the start of the eighteenth century is available from a study of Richard Steele's play *The Conscious Lovers*

(1722) based on Terence's *Andria*. It allowed Steele the chance to air his own social views on duelling, and the way men and women should behave towards each other. An orphan, obedience to parental wishes, an avaricious pedant, the rediscovery of a long-lost daughter, dowries and a neat, tidy *dénouement* are marked features of a play long since out of fashion.

3.8 Roman Tragedy

The work of one Roman writer of tragedies, **Lucius Annaeus Seneca** (died 65 AD) had such a wide and profound effect on the development of British drama in the Elizabethan and Jacobean periods, that his work needs to be considered in some detail here. He was born in Spain of rich Roman parents and was brought to Rome as a child. He studied hard and became a respected advocate, although Caligula became jealous of his abilities when he pleaded a case with the Senate before the emperor. He had an affair with Julia, Claudius's niece, and was banished to Corsica, but Agrippina, Claudius's new wife, succeeded in having Sencca recalled to Rome in 49 AD. He became tutor of Domitius, afterwards better known as the Emperor Nero. Seneca grew very wealthy indeed and supported Nero against Agrippina. But Rome was a city of intrigue and after the conspiracy of Piso in 65 AD Nero became convinced that Seneca was involved in the plot and sent a tribune to the philosopher and playwright commanding his suicide. He met death in the Stoic tradition; he embraced his wife, Pompeia Paulina, and she interposed herself as the blow fell and died with her husband.

Seneca was a philosopher as well as a playwright. His most famous work was *De Beneficus*, a long debate on moral philosophy in seven books, but it is the ten tragedies he wrote which make him important in the development of drama in Western Europe: *Troas*, *Thyestes*, *Hercules Furens*, translated by Jasper Heywood, *Oedipus*, translated by Alexander Neville, *Agamemnon*, *Medea*, *Hercules on Oeta*, and *Hippolytus*, translated by John Studley, *Octavia*, translated by Thomas Nuce, and *Thebais*, translated by Thomas Newton, all appeared in England between 1559 and 1581. All these translators were scholars rather than playwrights but their translations made Seneca's works available in English to a generation of dramatists the like of which Britain had never known before and would never know again: Kyd, Marlowe, Greene, Lodge, Lyly, Peele, Nashe, Shakespeare, Webster, Middleton, Rowley, Tourneur, and so on.

The first printed editions of Seneca's tragedies were produced by Andreas Gallicus at Ferrara in 1474. The *Troiades* was produced at Trinity College, Cambridge, in 1551 and other productions of Seneca's plays followed. The form of verse used in the English Senecan translations was adopted for one of the very earliest English tragedies, Thomas Preston's *Cambises* (1570) (see page 124), but this verse form was not suitable for stage representation; it was the language of the scholar and the study.

Seneca is sometimes thought to have been responsible for ghosts on the Elizabethan stage. Ghosts appear in *Thyestes* (Tantalus), *Agamemnon* (Thyestes), *Octavia* (Agrippina); In *Troas* Achilles and Hector play a major part off-stage and in *Oedipus* Laius, the ghost, plays some part in the action but never appears before the audience. In *Hamlet* and in Kyd's *Spanish Tragedy*, ghosts appear at the start of the plays, in the first seeking revenge and in the second as a witness brought on by the allegorical character Revenge to observe, as the play goes on (and he sits watching the action alongisde the audience), how he was conspired against.

Seneca's plays were more likely to have been composed for public declamation than for stage production. As a result, **set, declaimed speeches** assume major importance; rhetoric abounded in his plays. The **characters are clearly delineated but lack a subtlety** in their representation. Conflict in Seneca is often that of a **conflict of passion, temper, or appetite against duties imposed from an outside power** (*cf.* Hamlet's predicament). The opening speeches by the Ghost and Fury in *Thyestes* richly illustrate these characteristics of Senecan tragedy; (see E. F. Watling, *Seneca, Four Tragedies and Octavia*, 1966, pages 45–49). The Chorus in Seneca was often reduced to an impressive series of lines outside the main action of the play, full of moral philosophy and comment:

> It is not worldly wealth that makes a king,
> Nor the rich diadem encompassing
> His royal head, nor the proud gaudiness
> Of gilded halls and Tyrian purple dress.
> A king is he who has no ill to fear,
> Whose hand is innocent, whose conscience clear;
> Who scorns licentious greed . . . etc.
>
> (*Thyestes*)

Seneca has often been blamed for the bloodthirsty horrors found in plays such as *Titus Andronicus*, *The Jew of Malta*, or *The White Devil*. T. S. Eliot suggested that Seneca would have shuddered himself at such horrors; the revival of Seneca in France produced a quiet, controlled, decorous drama, although in Italy Seneca's name was associated with the bloodthirstiness of drama but was not really the cause of it.

Death allowed men and women the greatest stance. People listen to the dying; the last words of a person are always considered significant. **The dignity of the human being facing disaster** was a central feature of Senecan tragedy. The stoicism of Seneca's plays was borne out in the way he faced his own death. The dignity of Medea when she says *Medea superest* is echoed in Webster's heroine when she says 'I am Duchess of Malfi still'. Lear's defiant cry, 'Ay, every inch a king!' echoes down through the ages as we look upon the spectacle of the 'poor, infirm, weak, and despis'd old man' he became. Man's dignity remains and cannot be taken from him unless he voluntarily gives it up. This is the Senecan stance:

> But we must not complain, nor fear;
> Too fond of life is he who would not die
> When all the world dies with him.
>
> (Chorus in *Thyestes*)

In one of his letters Seneca quoted from Virgil's *Aeneid* (viii, 352):

> In every good man there dwells what god
> We know not, but a very god.

Questions

1   Describe how you would present and use the Chorus in a production today of a classical play *or* of a modern play in which there is a chorus or chorus-type character.

2   How useful do you find Aristotle's theory of tragedy in considering a play you know well for production?

3   What do you understand by the term *deus ex machina* when it is applied to modern plays? Give examples to support your description.

4   What have either (*i*) directors or (*ii*) actors today to learn for their own work from the way Greek plays were staged?

5   What elements in *The Bacchae* (or another Greek tragedy you have chosen) would you emphasise today if you were directing the play?

6   Take a Greek or Roman play you know well. What difficulties would you find in presenting it in a theatre with a proscenium arch?

7   From your study of a Roman play, show what it owes to the Greek theatre.

8   If you were taking the leading role in a revival of a Roman play (*e.g.* Euclio in *The Pot of Gold*) what elements in the character would you try to bring out?

9   'There is no drama without conflict'. Show where the 'conflict' lies in a tragedy by *one* of the following: Aeschylus, Sophocles, Euripides, Seneca.

10   *Give an account of the stage devices and properties available in the Greek Theatre. How would you have used them in staging a play you know well?

The questions marked* could form the basis of project work.

4
Medieval Drama

4.1

You should first read and understand the account of the development of the stage in Britain throughout the medieval period given in Sections **2.4** and **2.5** on pages 20–24. These sections dealt in some detail with the way medieval drama was staged in churches, on 'pageants' and in the halls of great houses.

There are essentially two difficulties for the modern student of medieval drama: to break through the problem of understanding the language of the period in which the plays were written down; and to recreate and appreciate the elaborate, complex, and changing context (historical, religious, social, political) in which the drama was created.

4.2 The Language of the Plays

Following the Norman invasion the native language of the English (Anglo-Saxon or Old English) came under immense pressure to change. An examination of the Lord's Prayer in English (St. Matthew, vi, 9–13) at four periods in the development of the language will quickly show how great the changes have been over a thousand-year period:

(a) Fæder ure þu þe eart on heofonum; Si þin nama gehalgod to be cume þin rice gewurþe þin willa on earðan swa swa on heofonum. urne gedæghwamlican hlaf syle us to dæg and forgyf us ure gyltas swa swa we forgyfa ð urum gyltendum and ne gelæd þu us on costnunge ac alys us of yfele soþlice.

(from a manuscript in Corpus Christi College, Cambridge, written about 1000)

(You will notice that Anglo-Saxon uses some letters no longer found in English today: þ = th; ð = th (voiced); æ = a vowel pronounced like the 'a' in the modern English words either *hat* or *bare*.)

(b) Oure Fadir that art in hevenes halowid be thi name/thi kyngdom come to/be thi wille don in erþe as in hevene/geve to us this day oure breed ovir othir *substaunce*/and forgeve to us oure dettis, as we forgeven to our *dettouris*/and lede us not in to *temptacioun*; but delyver us fro yvel. Amen.

(*Wycliffite Bible*, 1382)

(This is Middle English; some of the words – those in italics – clearly show from their spellings that they bore a strong French pronunciation.)

(c)   Our Father which art in heaven, Hallowed be thy name. Thy kingdom come. Thy will be done in earth, as it is in heaven. Give us this day our daily bread. And forgive us our debts, as we forgive our debtors. And lead us not into temptation, but deliver us from evil. Amen.

(*The Authorised Version*, The King James Bible, 1611.)

(This is the English of the period in the decade in which Shakespeare died. It is easily intelligible now to modern readers.)

(d)   Our father in heaven
May your holy name be honoured;
May your kingdom come;
May your will be done on earth as it is in heaven.
Give us today the food we need.
Forgive us the wrongs we have done, as we
forgive the wrongs that others have done to us.
Do not bring us to hard testing
but keep us safe from The Evil One.

(The Good News Bible, Today's English Version, British Usage Edition, 1976)

The second of these extracts, (*b*), was written at the very period of maximum change when English was passing through its major transition period from Anglo-Saxon (Old English) to Modern English (beginning with the Renaissance period). The language of this transition period of **Middle English** is marked by the following features:

(*i*)   The consolidation in English of some Celtic words (*e.g.* place names including the words *tor*, *coombe*, *brock*, *Exe*, etc.) or Norse words (*e.g. sky*, *skin*, *scrape*, *their*, etc.), which the Anglo-Saxons adopted from the earlier inhabitants of the British Isles (the Celts) or from invaders before William the Conqueror (the Vikings).

(*ii*)   The consolidation of several hundred words from Latin drawn into the language of English across many centuries to include contacts with the Romans whilst the Anglo-Saxons were still inhabitants of the Continent of Europe, contacts with Roman civilisation when the Anglo-Saxons arrived in England, contacts with Roman missionaries (*e.g.* St. Augustine in 597 AD), contacts with those leading reform in the Church (*e.g.* the leaders of the so-called Benedictine Reform of the tenth century).

(*iii*)   The introduction of huge numbers of Norman French words into the language during the thirteenth and fourteenth centuries once the native people and the descendants of the Norman invaders inter-married, established stronger social contact, and began to see themselves as one nation, challenged as they were, once again, by the claims of France on English lands during the Hundred Years War (1338–1453).

(*iv*)   The loss of some native English runic letters (see page 71) and changes in the grammatical structure of English.

The English language during this **transitional, Middle-English period** is the language of native medieval drama. Those producing the plays today, in order to make them intelligible to a modern audience, have to face the question of whether to use a 'translation' (with all the loss of atmosphere, contact, and the risk of distorting the meaning involved), or to keep the original language but try to give it some kind of modern, up-dated pronunciation. Either choice would seem to be a compromise to those who would prefer to recreate the drama *as it originally was*.

4.3   The Religious Origins of Drama

The medieval cleric was trained to see and interpret events and stories on four levels. These levels were embodied in the homiletic (or sermon) material of the period: the literal level (*sensus literalis*), the moral level (*sensus moralis*), the allegorical level (*sensus allegoricus*), and the spiritual or mystical level (*sensus anagogicus*). If the story of the Good Samaritan, for example, were examined for interpretations it could be seen as a narrative of a passer-by who helps another man in distress (*literal*); it raised the issues of what were the responsibilities and duties of all those who saw him and did nothing about it (*moral*); the figures in the story were capable of being seen as the Christian/the brother on the road of life helping someone else (*allegorical*: this level must not be taken too far – *e.g.* the doting and self-indulgent father of the story of The Prodigal Son ought not to be interpreted as God); it depicted God's readiness to help those in need whatever the circumstances (the *spiritual, mystical* or *anagogical*). The Morality Plays of the later medieval period (e.g. *The Castle of Perseverance, Everyman, Mankind*) need to be appreciated on these four levels so inherent in medieval religious thinking.

Secondly, the use of the **liturgy** in Church services was highly dramatic. It was *vivid, moving,* and *significant*. It made use of *dialogue* (between priest and God and between priest and choir/congregation). It involved *actions, gestures,* and *movement*. It had to be interpreted on *many levels* and used *impersonation, role-play* and *symbolism*. Moreover, it was closely related to festivities and the church calendar. It is not without some significance that the names given to early plays included the following: *officium, ordo, processio, representio, historia, similitudo, miraculum, misterium* – all liturgical words.

The ritual of the church involving the Mass and the canonical offices used readings of narrative accounts of the lives of Christ and his followers, antiphons (questions-and-answers, chanting and counter-chanting), songs, prayers, addresses. Gradually readings and special forms of service became closely tied to specific annual celebrations – the Nativity, St. Stephen's feast, Holy Innocents, Circumcision, Epiphany – and so on throughout the year.

Thirdly, in the eighth and ninth centuries musical amplifications of passages from the liturgy grew up in an attempt to beautify them. These musical amplifications led on to **tropes**, phrases interpolated into different parts of the mass, often with embellishment (Greek **Τροπος** = a turn). These tropes remained in use until Pius V (Pope from 1566–72) banned both them and the books (*Troperia*) into which they had been collected.

In a ninth-century manuscript from St. Gall comes the most famous and perhaps one of the first examples of a trope which served as an introduction to the introit of the Mass. It contains, in Latin, a dramatic exchange between two groups arranged antiphonally in the form of question and answer:

> Quem quaeritis in sepulchro, O Christicolae?
> Iesum Nazarenum crucifixium, o caelicolae.
> Non est hic, surrexit sicut praedixerat.
> Ite, nuntiate quia surrexit de sepulchro.

> (Whom are you looking for in the tomb, you Christian women?
> Jesus of Nazareth, the one crucified, heavenly ones.
> He is not here; he has risen as it had been foretold.
> Go and tell, since he has risen from the tomb.)

In later centuries this simple Easter trope became more and more elaborate. It was used at the start of the twelfth century in the Benedictine abbey at Monte Cassino. The chanted *Quem Quaeritis* to the accompaniment of mimed action by monks was set out in detail in the tenth century *Concordia Regularis*, a book drawn up by Æthelwold, Bishop of Winchester, as part of the Benedictine Reform in England; it shows very clearly how the tropes were becoming closely linked to ritualised gestures.

As an introit trope the *Quem Quaeritis* became linked to ceremonies at the sepulchre itself at Easter. The trope was already drama in Church liturgy. The play was chanted and not spoken by those in orders or choir-boys. Other plays based on the *Quem Quaeritis* model grew up alongside the Easter trope to apply to other occasions – Christmas, for example:

> Quem quaeritis in praesepe, pastores, dicite?
> (Whom are you looking for in the crib, Shepherds, tell us?)

Other 'playlets' grew up, too. A drama about *Rachel* lamenting the death of her children (the Slaughter of the Innocents) and about the three kings (*Tres Reges* – sometimes called *Magi Herodes* or the *Stella*) also emerged. Throughout Europe the Biblical incidents and narratives were becoming elaborated into drama. (A full account of the development of these liturgical plays is found in E.K. Chambers, *The Medieval Stage*, II, 1903, 1–67.)

4.4 The Secularisation of Religious Plays

Whilst the religious plays remained in the Church, their content and interpretation of Biblical events and their comments could be regulated. The Church was accommodating and in the *Concordia Regularis* there are very clear instructions on how the *Quem Quaeritis* was to be played, down to the last detail of costume, action, property, and gesture. The 'stage directions' are full:

> While the third lesson is being read, four of the brethren shall vest, one of whom,
> wearing an alb as though for some different purpose, shall enter and go stealthily

to the place of the 'sepulchre' and sit there quietly, holding a palm in his hands. Then, while the third respond is being sung, the other three brethren, vested in copes and holding thuribles (censers) in their hands, shall enter in their turn and go to the place of the 'sepulchre', step by step, as though searching for something. Now these things are done in imitation of the angel seated on the tomb and of the women coming with perfumes to anoint the body of Jesus. When, therefore, he that is seated shall see these three draw nigh, wandering about as it were and seeking something, he shall begin to sing softly and sweetly, *Quem Quaeritis*. As soon as this has been sung right through, the three shall answer together, *Ihesum Nazarenum*. Then he that is seated shall say *Non est hic. Surrexit sicut praedixerat. Ite, nuntiate quia surrexit a mortuis.* At this command the three shall turn to the choir saying *Alleluia, Resurrexit Dominus.* When this has been sung he that is seated, as though calling them back, shall say the antiphon *Venite et videte locum* (Come and behold the place), and then, rising and lifting up the veil, he shall show them the place void of the Cross and with only the linen in which the Cross had been wrapped. Seeing this, the three shall lay down their thuribles in that same 'sepulchre' and, taking the linen, shall hold it up before the clergy; and, as though showing that the Lord was risen and was no longer wrapped in it, they shall sing this antiphon: *Surrexit Dominus de Sepulchro* (The Lord has risen from the tomb). They shall then lay the linen on the altar.

When the antiphon is finished, the prior, rejoicing in the triumph of our King in that he had conquered death and was risen, shall give out the hymn *Te Deum Laudamus*, and thereupon all the bells shall peal.

(Quoted and translated by Karl Young, *The Drama of the Medieval Church*, 2 vols (Oxford 1933), I, 249.)

Here the action is given a local setting; the properties carried by the 'actors' are specified; their movements are clearly laid-down to represent journeys. There is also an awareness of audience. Here are the ingredients of the later 'stage play', although the setting remains symbolic with no attempt at realism.

The development of drama *within* the Church posed some dangers but it was **not** expelled from the Church as it has sometimes been argued. The dramatic representations of Biblical events could be widened to include the Creation, the Annunciation, the Passion, the Ascension, the Last Judgement. The words, too, of any single play could be added to and expanded. The vernacular was used increasingly in drama, particularly as laymen replaced clergy as the main participating actors. The nuns of a French monastery turned incidents in *Quem Quaeritis* into the vernacular in the fourteenth century – the practice had become common throughout Europe by then.

Some churchmen were beginning to have doubts about what was happening. They did not object to the secularisation of the plays so much as to abuses that accompanied them. Indeed, there is evidence that the Church approved of and helped dramatic performances outside the building. Matthew Paris in his account of the lives of the Abbots of St. Albans narrates how Geoffrey, a Norman, borrowed some vestments (*capae chorales*) from the Abbey for a performance at Dunstable. The vestments were burnt and Geoffrey, distraught, became a monk at St. Albans and later the Abbot there in 1119.

Between 1236 and 1244, the Bishop of Lincoln, Robert Grosseteste condemned the entertainments in his diocese, including miracle plays, drinking bouts, athletic contests, and the Feast of Fools. The Registers of Hereford Cathedral for 1348 prohibited plays in church. At the end of the thirteenth century William of Waddington, an Anglo-Norman, objected to the sins of the 'miracles'. The notion that Pope Innocent III in 1207 banished plays from church has sometimes been used as an example of church disapproval of plays, but, in fact, Innocent III banned the *ludi theatrales* associated with the ribald Feast of Fools and yet it might be argued he allowed those plays at Christmas and Easter which stimulated devotion.

4.5   Play 'Cycles'

Miracle plays in England were formed into the great professional cycles immediately after the establishment of the Corpus Christi festival in 1311 (see page 21). The Chester cycle is thought to have been founded in 1328 according to a municipal document, but the first record of the actual performance of such plays dates from 1462. Those at Beverley are mentioned in 1377, those at York in 1378 and those at Coventry in 1392.

Usually, the long cycles were given annually under the governance of the corporation of a large city. The action of the drama, man's progress from the Fall of Lucifer and the Creation to the Last Judgement, was divided into separate scenes or 'pageants' each under the control of a craft guild. The governors of a town would decide well ahead of the proposed date of performance whether the cycle of plays should go ahead; plague, war, or local conditions sometimes prevented the productions. Officers of the town read the proclamation or 'banns' of the play and an official version of the text was kept by the corporation, who adjudicated in any dispute between the guilds themselves. They also kept order during the performances and punished those who infringed the rules or the law. They also demanded that the plays should make use of properly qualified actors, who were not to give more than two performances a day. The corporation provided entertainment if important people came to watch the pageants, but the expense fell almost totally on the craft guilds, who had a sacred duty to provide the plays. There are several accounts dating from the fifteenth century to show just how expensive the maintaining of the productions was – to repair, ornament, clean, strew rushes in the street, rent a pageant home, pay actors, minstrels, and a prompter, to revise and copy texts, to provide costumes, and to make available refreshments. Occasionally the craft guilds in one town received financial help from members of the guild in neighbouring towns. All the citizens were expected to contribute to the guilds' productions by offering to help with the work but there is only a single oblique reference to spectators having to pay to watch the drama.

Elsewhere, outside the main 'play-cycle towns' single plays were sometimes put on by local clergy or officials of the parish church; such performances are known to have taken place at Kingston, Oxford, Reading, Salisbury, Bath, Tewkesbury, Leicester, Bungay, and Yarmouth. Such plays were occasional, rather than annual, productions to raise money. *Vexillatores* would go round neighbouring villages to publicise 'banns' of the play and to call up support.

The Chester Cycle probably contained twenty-five plays beginning with *The Falling of Lucifer* to *Domes Daye*. One source gives the list as twenty-six plays and adds a play after that called *Whitsonday ye makeinge of the Creede* on the subject of the Assumption of the Virgin Mary. This play was performed in 1477 and at least three more times separately in 1488, 1497, and 1515, but – as in York – was finally dropped because of Protestant influence. The extant manuscripts of the Chester Cycle give the list as twenty-four plays, since they merge *The scourginge of Christe* with *The Crusifienge of Christ*. Tradition assigns these plays to the time when John Arneway was mayor of Chester (1268–77), which would make these the oldest of our miracle plays. E.K. Chambers (*The Medieval Stage*, Oxford 1933, II, 352), after careful analysis of the evidence, prefers the mayoralty of Richard Erneis or Herneys (1327–9) to have been the more likely date of origin for the cycle to have been actually established. Probably 1575 was the last year in which the plays were performed as a complete cycle. The plays and the Corpus Christi procession originally took place on Corpus Christi day itself but later the 'banns' were proclaimed on St. George's Day and the plays were put on throughout the first three week-days of Whitsuntide: nine on Monday, nine on Tuesday, and seven on Wednesday.

The York Cycle is contained in a manuscript (Ashburnham MS 137) which dates from about 1430–40. It contains forty-eight plays ranging from *The Creation and the Fall of Lucifer* performed by the Barkers (or Tanners) to *The Judgement Day* performed by the Mercers. The fragment of a play on *The Coronation of our Lady* was added later. The first mention of the plays at York is in 1378; in 1397 Richard II was present to watch them. Performances of the plays in the cycle became irregular about the middle of the sixteenth century but in 1535 the Creed play and in 1558 the Paternoster play were performed instead of the cycle. Earlier, in the first or second week of Lent the town clerk at York set in motion plans for the cycle of plays. On the eve of Corpus Christi a proclamation forbade 'disturbaunce of the kynges pees, and ye play, or hynderyng of ye processioun of Corpore Christi'. The pageants were to be played at the places assigned; the men of the craft guilds were to appear 'careynge tapers of ye pagentz' and to provide 'good players and openly spekyng'. The pageants were to be ready to start at 4.30 am, and one should follow the other in unbroken succession. The plays and the Corpus Christi procession were staged on the same day at first but a special Corpus Christi Guild, set up in 1408, to manage the affairs of Corpus Christi, later separated the two 'entertainments' and the plays were moved to the day before Corpus Christi itself. In 1476 the council further stipulated how the plays were to be put on. Actors were not to play in more than two separate pageants and the stations, at first limited to twelve, were later extended from twelve to sixteen for the performances. Again, the crafts were responsible for building, repairing, decorating and pulling the pageant; they also had to provide costumes for the actors. The duty of providing a pageant was a heavy one.

The Wakefield Cycle (sometimes called 'The Towneley Cycle') of plays is found in a late fifteenth century manuscript which was once in the possession of the Towneley family of Towneley House near Burnley, in Lancashire. There are thirty-two plays in all, beginning with *The Creation* and ending with an incomplete play on the hanging of Judas Iscariot (*Suspencio Iudae*). Unfortunately some leaves of the manuscripts are missing; there is a large gap after the first play (for *The Fall?*) and another after the incomplete play on the Ascension of Christ (*Ascencio Domini*) where possibly a play on Pentecost once stood. The pieces in this 'cycle', if that is an appropriate term for the Towneley plays, have been 'composed' to form a cycle.

The manuscript of these plays is a 'register', that is, an official text copied from the originals kept by the craft guilds themselves; it is clearly a copy and contains errors likely to have been made by a copyist. The plays are associated with Wakefield in Yorkshire and A. C. Cawley (in *The Wakefield Pageants in the Towneley Cycle*, Manchester 1958), has shown that there are a number of local geographical allusions in some of the plays to confirm this.

The Wakefield plays provide some unanswered problems to questions about the way they were staged. It is not known whether they were produced on various stages around an area such as that used for *The Castle of Perseverance* later (see pages 22–24), or whether they were part of a procession of pageants such as was used at Chester, York, and Coventry. Some of the plays (*e.g. Mactacio Abel*, the Killing of Abel, and the play about Noah, *Processus Noe cum Filiis*), require huge sets if they are to work, and some stage directions, which require the movement of actors from one 'mansion' to another, would have made 'pageant' production impossible. Moreover, in the play about the offering of the Magi (*Oblacio Magorum*), the three kings have to enter from separate directions and on horseback.

Nevertheless, it is now accepted that five plays and probably a sixth in the Towneley manuscript known as 'The Wakefield Group' were the work of one man, given the title of **The Wakefield Master**.

The Wakefield Master

The five plays from Wakefield thought to be by the same author are: *Processus Noe cum Filiis* ('The Pageant of Noah and his Sons'), *Pagina Pastorum* ('The Shepherds' Play'), *Secunda Pastorum* ('The Second Shepherds' Play'), *Magnus Herodes* ('Herod the Great'), *Coliphizacio* ('About the High Priest Caiaphas'). A sixth play, *Mactacio Abel* ('The Murder of Abel') was also probably written by the same man.

The evidence to support the common authorship is considerable. Five of the plays use a common nine-line stanza form not found anywhere else outside or in the Towneley Cycle, which normally used a thirteen-line stanza. This nine-line stanza was particularly flexible in expressing change of moods and rapid dialogue. The language of all six plays contains a racy, colloquial idiom and there are some surprisingly close verbal parallels to be found from play to play. There is, too, some very clear and explicit emphasis on gesture and movement in the plays; in *Processus Noe*, for example, there are to be found carpentry, spinning, brawling, using a plumb-line, steering the ark with a tiller, and stripping off a gown in order to get down to the carpentry work. All six plays contain a satiric attack on contemporary abuses and seem to lay heavy stress on sharp characterisation. Very importantly, they also contain much material which is not of Biblical origin; *The Second Shepherds' Play* goes further and adapts the crib scene of the traditional nativity play to extract humour – it is not a parody of the Biblical material itself but it might well be one on the way 'crib scenes' were usually approached in drama. The plays also include such elements as the religious lyric, the sermon in the native tongue, proverbs, and references to traditional folk tales, such as the Madman of Gotham and the story of Moll and her pitcher of milk. Folk plays themselves, such as the Mummers' plays about the battle between St. George and Slasher and other combatants, dealt centrally with the fight of good versus evil and the ultimate triumph of the good; here, too, the basic conflict between the forces fighting for the possession of man is treated humorously. Oddly, in plays so heavy in detail, costume is rarely specified in these six works by The Wakefield Master. (The best edition of these plays is that of A. C. Cawley, *The Wakefield Pageants in The Towneley Cycle*, Manchester, 1958, who analyses many of these characteristics in detail.)

Although the final great cycle of mystery plays is known as **The Coventry Cycle**, it is now doubted whether they are at all connected with the town of Coventry. Early librarians responsible for looking after the fine collection of early English and medieval manuscripts in the possession of Sir Robert Cotton (1571–1631) ascribed the plays to Coventry and suggested in their description of them that they were acted by mendicant friars and not by craft-guilds. The 'pageants' are not divided off in the manuscripts. There are seven opening plays on the Fall of Lucifer, the Creation, Cain and Abel, Noah's Flood, Abraham and Isaac, Moses and the Prophets. A prologue spoken by a character called Contemplation separates these from others on Joachim and Anna, Mary in the Temple, the Betrothal of Mary, and the Annunciation. A scene between Contemplacio, the Virtues, the Father, Veritas, Misericordia, Iusticia, Pax, and the Son intervenes and is followed by two more plays on the Doubt of Joseph and the Visit to Elizabeth. There is a conclusion to the group of plays so far, an 'Ave regina coelarum'. Sixteen more plays appear from the Trial of Mary to the Mount of Olives and then Contemplacio reappears as 'an exposytour in doctorys wede'. There is a group of plays on Herod, the Trial before Caiaphas, the Death of Judas and Christ's trials, Pilate's Wife's Dream, the Condemnation, the Crucifixion, the Burial of Christ, and the Harrowing of Hell. This group is followed by a *Quem Quaeritis*, Hortulanus, Peregrini (*i.e.* a play on the disciples' experiences on the road to Emmaus), Thomas's Doubts, the Ascension, Pentecost, the Assumption of the Virgin Mary, and Doomsday. The groupings of the plays and their division is still open to academic debate but there seem to be forty-two plays in all, the last incomplete.

4.6 Single 'Mystery' Plays

Norwich. There is an eighteenth century copy of an earlier 'Grocers Pageant' which seems to be two plays. *The story of ye Creacon of Eve, w^t ye expellyng of Adam & Eve out of Paradyce*, and a second version 'newely renvid & accordynge unto ye Skrypture, begon thys yre A^o 1567. A^{o}7 Eliz'. Both versions of the story begin with the creation of Eve; the first ends with the expulsion from the Garden of Eden and the second adds a further character (an angel); the pair are threatened by *Dolor* and *Myserye* and are confronted by the Holy Ghost. The pageant plays at Norwich were probably Whitsun plays rather than Corpus Christi plays. In one year it was, apparently, even played in October (1537) in 'ye Processyon for ye Byrthe of Prynce Edward'. From Norwich there is also an inventory of the 'particulars appartaynyng to ye Company of ye Grocers a.d. 1565' which includes a description of the 'pageant' used: a square top to be set over the pageant, a gilt griffon to set on the top, some flags of iron, some stained garments for Eve, Adam, and the Serpent, an angel's coat and over-stockings, some painted curtains for the pageant. 'A face and heare for ye Father', wigs for Adam and Eve, weights; the pageant itself is described as 'a House of Waynskott paynted and buylded on a Carte w^t fowre whelys'.

Newcastle. In 1736 an editor, H. Bourne, published *Noah's Ark: or The Shipwrights' Ancient Play or Dirge'*. The manuscript has since been lost. The play deals with the way the ark was made but never reaches the Flood itself. It had as its main characters God, an Angel, the Devil, Noah, and Noah's Wife. We know that there were craft-plays for Corpus Christi in existence in Newcastle, performances of which were last given in 1561 and 1562. E. K. Chambers thinks there might have been 'as many as twenty-three' such plays at Newcastle (*The Medieval Stage*, II, 424). An amusing feature of the play is Noah's reluctance at 600 to take up a new craft!

The Digby Plays are so-called since they are found in the Bodleian Digby Manuscript 133. There are four dramatic pieces: *The Conversion of St. Paul* where St. Paul is shown as a boastful, pompous, and very verbose knight; *St. Mary Magdalene*, based on the legendary life of St. Mary Magdalene in *The Golden Legend* and introducing very many characters and some allegorical representations of the World, the Flesh and the Seven Deadly Sins; this play also has an 'Imperator' who commands the audience to be silent, a Hell underneath the stage, a sepulchre, a tavern, an arbour, a castle, thrones, a palace, a heathen temple and even a ship! *The Massacre of the Innocents* has a comic knight, Watkin, who is the fore-runner of other versions of this stock figure in Elizabethan times and there are dances of minstrels and virgins. The drama has come a long way from simple Biblical narrative by the start of the sixteenth century. There is also a fragment of a Morality Play, *Mind, Will and Understanding* (sometimes called *Wisdom*).

Other mystery plays appear in manuscripts, now in Dublin, from the fifteenth century (*Abraham and Isaac*, and the Croxton play on *The Sacrament*) and in the Bodleian Library at Oxford (Cornish plays on the Origin of the World, the Passion of Our Lord, and the Resurrection of our Lord). In a commonplace book, *The Book of Brome*, from 1470–80, now in the possession of the owners of Brome Manor, Norfolk, there is a play on the subject of Abraham and Isaac. There are numerous references to mystery plays from a host of places in the British Isles including Abingdon, Appledore, Bath, Bethersden,

Billericay, Bungay, Bury St. Edmunds, Camborne, Cambridge, Canterbury, Easterford, Fyfield, Great Chart, Halstead, Hythe, Kendal, King's Lynn, Kingston-upon-Thames, Little Baddow, and so on (see E. K. Chambers, *The Medieval Stage*, II. 329–30 for a very full list).

4.7 'Miracle', 'Mystery' and 'Morality'

Religious drama in the Middle Ages in England included plays based on Scripture, plays based on the *Apocrypha* and the lives of saints, plays about miraculous happenings, and plays which deliberately set out to make a moral point. The first two kinds of plays are now usually referred to as *mysteries*, since they were played mainly by guilds, or other craft guilds and the word 'mystery' means a 'trade' or 'craft' (Latin *mysterium*). The third kind based on miraculous happenings (*e.g. The Croxton play of the Sacrament*) are now often called **miracles**, although, at one time, this term was used to cover all four types of medieval religious drama. The fourth type of play dealing with moral conflicts, allegorical in design, are now usually called **Moralities**. The terms are still debated and interchanged by scholars, however.

4.8 The Second Shepherds' Play

Sometimes the Biblical and non-Biblical elements are mingled, moreover, and the strict division of plays into 'types' breaks down. One of the most successful plays of the period **The Second Shepherds' Play**, written by the Wakefield Master, illustrates this.

The Shepherds who were watching over their flocks at the time of Christ's birth are found in the Bible narrative: *St. Luke*, ii, 8–20:

> And there were in the same country shepherds abiding in the field, keeping watch over their flock by night . . . the shepherds said one to another, Let us go even unto Bethlehem, and see this thing which is come to pass . . . and they came with haste, and found Mary, and Joseph, and the babe lying in a manger . . . and the shepherds returned, glorifying and praising God . . .

The story of a visit to the new-born Christ in *St. Matthew*, ii, 9–12, tells of wise men who followed a star to Bethlehem from the east where they offered gifts of gold, frankincense and myrrh to the infant Christ. These wise men (the Magi) became kings from the east in Christian tradition and were given the names of Gaspar, Melchior, and Balthazar. In *The Second Shepherds' Play* the two stories are run together: The Biblical angel that appeared to the shepherds enters the play as God's messenger but it is a star which they follow and it is they who think of giving gifts to the child Jesus, not the gifts of the Magi (or the Three Kings of Orient) but a bob of cherries symbolising midwinter fertility (it is a miracle that cherries were available at Christmas, although they would have been plentiful at Corpus Christi!), a bird symbolising the Trinity (*cf.* the dove at Christ's baptism), and a ball symbolising a globe or the world.

The liturgical office, *Officium Pastorum*, grew out of the Latin Christmas trope, *Quem Quaeritis in praesepe, pastores, dicite?* (see page 74).

Based on Biblical narrative and 'office', the Wakefield Master has the basis for his plot. However, he decides to write a parody in order to produce comedy. First, he needs to establish his major characters – and they are quickly but subtly drawn. The First Shepherd is frozen by the English winter (although the play is being put on in midsummer!), he is downtrodden and over-taxed by the nobility, and has to suffer feudal oppression without complaint. This is telling and courageous social satire! The newest upstart with a 'pointsleeve or a brooch' behaves arrogantly and the poor are 'held under'. The Second Shepherd is also oppressed – but by his wife. The hen-pecked husband was well-established as a stock figure in medieval mystery plays; Noah fares little better. He warns young men off marriage, but his wife is somewhat ugly:

> . . . I have one to my fere (companion)
> As sharp as thistle, as rough as a briar.
> She is browed like a bristle with a sour-loten
> (sour-looking) cheer.

The Third Shepherd is a young man who is also oppressed – by the master-men; he is badly paid and often paid too late. He does not intend to overwork:

> . . . for the fare that ye make,
> I shall do thereafter – work as I take.
> I shall do a little, sir, and among ever take
> (and between times I'll amuse myself all the time).

The first scene consists, then, of three separate speeches. The shepherds end it by singing together – the Second Shepherd, despised by his wife, taking 'the treble so high'. Already, social comment, stock characters, identification with the problems of the audience, and diverting song to entertain have become part of the play. It is all non-Biblical so far.

Mak, the arch-villain, enters; in Victorian times the stock character would have wrapped his cloak around him (Mak does have a cloak) and twirled his moustache. The dialogue moves on faster and speeds up the action of the quickly united three against the isolated one. The villain's character is quickly established with the audience: 'Is he come? Then ilkone take heed to his thing'. Mak adopts a pose and links with the earlier exchanges by adopting the pose of a yeoman from the south. In good northern fashion he is soon demolished:

> Now take out that Southern tooth,
> And set in a turd!

Mak's conversation echoes the opening speeches of the three Shepherds: he plays the part of a man of high position demanding reverence; he complains about his wife; he cannot make ends meet.

The thief's speech is an incantation; he weaves a charm in best Anglo-Saxon manner by mixing English and bits of Latin that he clearly does not understand, both heathen and Christian.

The second scene in Mak's cottage begins the parody of the manger scene. Gill is the opposite of Mary and the impatient Mak the opposite of Joseph. It is the wife who devises the scene to hide the stolen sheep. Implicit in the parody is the fact that Christ was seen as the lamb of God.

The third scene opens with more debased Latin – the language sounds like a magical, liturgical incantation. As Mak cursed by the Devil, so the Shepherds curse by Christ. Dreams, the crowing of the cock, the cross, all feature in the dialogue as Mak declares his innocence. The parody is inverting moral qualities, where the good are deceived and the thief is proved innocent.

Again, the scene shifts back to the cottage. This switching of scene is clumsy in some ways but it does allow the passing of time to be indicated. Gill 'swaddles' the lamb in the cradle, still echoing the Biblical text. 'And she . . . wrapped him in swaddling clothes, and laid him in a manger'. (*St. Luke*, ii, 7). The decision of the Shepherds to visit Mak is taken at the Crooked Thorn and the next scene swings back to Mak's cottage. Only on leaving do the Shepherds realise that they have not offered the child a present; kissing the child, they find the lamb and Gill's explanation about elves and magic no longer deceives them. Mak is then tossed in a blanket.

The last two scenes make a transition between the Mak plot and that of the Gospel but the shepherds are still individuals as they praise the quality of the angel's singing of the Gloria; they set off for the second time in search of a child. When they find the child they greet him in formal, stylised verse, although the language is still that of the realistic shepherds seen earlier in the play. The search ends in success and with the hope of salvation.

This plot also shows a skilful use of scene-changes. The characters, the verse, the action itself, as well as the language are arranged antiphonally. Mak, the devil, is discovered and punished so that the innocent can pursue the path of salvation. Social comments abound and the normal Biblical transposition of the child into a lamb is inverted and the lamb becomes a child. Humour, pace, contrast, deception, search and discovery are major features of the comedy. Exaggeration, allusion, magic, stock characters and farcical incident are at its heart.

4.9

The York pageant play **The Creation and the Fall of Lucifer** seems clumsy beside the *Secunda Pastorum*. It is, of course, the opening of a cycle of plays. The stances of the major characters are stereotyped. God, Alpha, the first, opens the play just as God, Omega, the last, ends it. The pattern of *Genesis*, i, 1 ('In the beginning God created the heaven and the earth') is followed with echoes of the Athanasian Creed running through it. The first section ends with the liturgical *Te Deum*. The casting out of Lucifer from heaven, prefaced by a singing of 'Holy, holy, holy, Lord God of Hosts' from *Isaiah* vi, 3, is linked with God on his throne surrounded by elders in *Revelation* iv, 8, the sole book (xx, 10) in the Bible which deals with the casting out of the devil into a lake of fire and brimstone. The heavy alliterative rhythms which gave dignity to God merely give banality and a comic quality to the words of the devil: 'Oh, what I am featous and figured full fit!' The final ignominy for the devil in hell is that he is deserted and rejected by his followers; in Anglo-Saxon tradition, as the Roman historian Tacitus pointed out, the desertion of a leader by his men (*comitatus*) was the greatest shame and disaster that could happen. The final scene resumes the Biblical narrative of the Creation, but God does seem rather smug about his victory over Lucifer.

This York play resembles other plays in the York Cycle where the action demonstrates the battle between good and evil; here Pride, the first and most deadly sin, comes to its inevitable fall. The characters are symbols of man's own real conflict between good and evil; it is the good which is able to create: the evil merely destroys.

Seen as the Prologue to a play-cycle, the mystery of **The Creation and the Fall of Lucifer** can be accepted as a statement of what is to follow; there is little attempt to dramatise the action subtly, although Lucifer does fall through the trap-door into Hell at one point and there is some singing to act as a diversion from the heavy main plot. The devil has not, apparently, yet learnt how to be funny, a quality which would save him for many audiences. The Creed-like utterances of God, however, would find an echo in a York audience, since it was in that town that the great dramatic rivals to the pageant plays were the guild plays on *The Paternoster* and *The Creed*.

4.10

The second play in the York Cycle dealt with the Creation until the fifth day. The third play, **The Creation of Adam and Eve** could have allowed the drama to spring into life with the introduction of human beings. Instead, the scene is the World; there is little dramatic intercourse between the three major characters, (God, Adam and Eve) who are arranged in a triangle; God speaks and Adam and Eve respond predictably. The dialogue, such as it is, is in the form of hymns; the verse is dull and unvaried, often with end-stopped lines. This is a play of stances and attitudes. There is no triumph since, given that God is omnipotent, his creation of man and woman seems comparatively unremarkable. Here there is no dramatic emerging of the character; neither Adam nor Eve respond to each other's attractiveness but continue to praise God in a very dull fashion. The real drama of Adam and Eve lies, perhaps, not in their creation but in their disobedience and fight against the Creator and their subsequent fight with each other. Here lies the substance of drama – conflict.

4.11 The Morality Play

It is with the development of the Morality play in England that the link with the traditions of the Church reasserts itself. It has been pointed out that the trained medieval mind was quick to interpret life and its dramatic representation on different levels: the literal, the moral, the allegorical, the anagogical (see page 73).

The medieval sermon stated rather than argued propositions. Its strength lay in its structure and use of examples and exemplary material but its ultimate authority lay in its dependence upon, first, Scripture and, secondly, the lives of the Saints. The homiletic tradition runs back strongly into Anglo-Saxon times when the works of the Fathers were studied and their sermons, particularly those of Peter the Deacon, were known and translated. Ælfric and Wulfstan were masters of the art of preaching at the turn of the tenth and eleventh century and by the fourteenth century the friars had taken the pulpit into every village and settlement.

The art of allegory was linked with preaching. In literature there was a well-established line of poetry that became popular, following the thirteenth-century *Roman de la Rose* by Guillaume de Lorris and Jean de Meung. The allegorical love poem mingled with the Dream Vision during the time of Chaucer. Asleep, the poet is taken on a conducted tour of landscapes and into adventures full of allegorical significance. The best known works of Chaucer in this tradition are *The Legend of Good Women*, *The House of Fame*, *The Book of the Duchess*, and *The Parlement of Fowls*.

It is essential for the student of fifteenth and early sixteenth-century drama to bear these two traditions of **preaching** and **allegory** constantly in mind if the Morality play is to be appreciated. Those critics who have tried to trace the source of medieval allegory in drama have begun at Prudentius's work **Psychomachia**. Prudentius was a Christian Roman poet, born in 343 AD. His *Psychomachia* gives a description of a battle where Virtues fight Vices and win. The representation of man's struggle in terms of a battle or fight runs through medieval drama (*e.g. The Castle of Perseverance*) to Bunyan's *Pilgrim's Progress* (1678). As in Bunyan, the earlier dramatists sometimes linked this struggle with the journey of Mankind from birth to the grave. *Everyman* is a Morality play of the sixteenth century which represents the struggle as a journey, for example. Preaching or didacticism seems fundamentally the main purpose of such plays; allegory is merely the manner used to convey the message. The characters of the plays are abstract qualities – virtues or vices – which operate around man, Mankind, Humanum Genus, or Everyman. The conflict of man is an internal one for his own salvation but the conflict is externalised and represented in actions and settings that are allegorical. Often the vices appear more attractive than the virtues and are recognised quickly by their swaggering, boasting, and skill in embroiling. (The emergence of the Vice as a major character on the stage is considered in more detail later, see pages 93–94). They adopt stock attitudes and usually establish their role with the audience very early on in the play, sometimes by means of soliloquys. The conflict in man arises from his vulnerability caused by greed or pride; he has free-will and is determined to exercise it. (It will be remembered from the long discussion about free-will and predestination in Chaucer's *The Nun's Priest's Tale* that this topic was a popular one in the Middle Ages.) Death and Folly often play major roles in Morality plays and such characters quickly encourage satirical approaches in drama, since they put man and his life into perspective very quickly indeed.

At the heart of the Morality play is man's dilemma; he is forced to make choices – part of him insisting that he should seek salvation and another part succumbing constantly to temptation. Theologically, only the acceptance of God's grace, offered freely by God and available for man to accept according to St. Augustine, can redeem him from the consequences of making wrong choices.

Those who followed what has been called 'the Darwinian approach' in dramatic criticism (*e.g.* F. J. Furnivall) used to argue a linear progression in the development of English drama from tropes to mysteries to moralities to interludes. Such a progression is untenable since Moralities grew up alongside mysteries. It is a fact, however, that long moral plays with large casts were followed by shorter moral plays with large casts but fewer actors who 'doubled up' their parts, and such plays became known as moral interludes. There are eight plays in English that are usually given the title of 'Moralities':

The Pride of Life remains only in an incomplete form but it contains a whole sermon delivered by a Bishop. Fortunately there is a synopsis of the action of the play given in its prologue (lines 1–112).

The Castle of Perseverance was probably written between 1400 and 1425 and contains a plan of how it was to be staged (see pages 22–24). It sets out the attack on mankind by the World, the Flesh, and the Devil through the Seven Deadly Sins; man is helped into the Castle by Confession, where he is comforted by the Seven Virtues. Backbiter, called upon by the Bad Angel to help, stirs up trouble with the Seven Deadly Sins but the adversaries of man lay siege to the Castle. It lasts a long time, a very long time. The Virtues defeat the Vices by attacking them with roses (the symbol of love?) but Avarice finally lures out man who is struck down by Death. The Soul is carried off to Belyal's scaffold but the Four Daughters of God debate man's case in a formal disputation and judgement is given in favour of man who is rescued from Belyal and taken to find God's salvation on God's scaffold. The play is ritualistic and intellectual in its debate but it is dramatic in its conflict – not only physical but moral and mental.

Wisdom (sometimes known as **Mind, Will and Understanding**) dates from the last part of the fifteenth century. Anima (the Soul) is presented as a young, pure, innocent girl who has never sinned. Lucifer seduces Mind, Will, and Understanding who are really the three parts of Anima. Wisdom finally brings about a conversion. The play is important since it introduced a number of non-speaking actors who could mime or act as in a masque. It also includes minstrels and songs and dances and there is even a suggestion in the play that Lucifer should snatch a boy from the audience and make off with him.

Mankind dates from the same period. It is a humorous play with a distinct moral purpose. The plot concerns the attempt by Mercy on the one hand and Mischief, helped by Nought, New Gyse, Nowadays and a Vice-like character cum devil, Titivillus, to win man's soul. The play tries to differentiate characters by adapting verse forms but there are some good moments of knock-about comedy. Some critics have seen in Titivillus the precursor of the Elizabethan embroiler.

Part of the allegorical movement in the Middle Ages found expression in The Dance of Death, the *danse macabre*. This showed Death, often in the form of a skeleton, dancing through life with representatives of Mankind, ranging from the King and Popes down to the ordinary peasant. The dance was depicted in a number of frescoes and engravings that are still extant. Holbein's work (1497–1543) is the best known on the theme but there is an early painting accompanied by verse dialogue between the living and the dead in the cemetary of the Innocents in Paris, dating from 1424. *The Pride of Life* (see page 86) showed Death dancing with the King who is reluctant to repent. But the best of the Morality plays, *Everyman*, uses the theme of the danse macabre to make its point.

In **Everyman**, probably written in English at the end of the fifteenth century, Death appears as a dignified character rather than a rattling collection of old bones. He carries a dart and declares he is afraid of nobody. Everyman has time to arrange his affairs and dies, smitten by the dart, fortified by the rites of the Holy Church. The plot is set out in the form of a journey, a pilgrimage but the play is called a 'treatise' in an opening statement 'in the manner of a moral play'. A Messenger explains the plot to the audience before the action begins:

The *Summoning of Everyman* called it is,
That of our lives and ending shows
How transitory we be all day. . .
The story saith: Man, in the beginning
Look well, and take good heed to the ending,
Be ye never so gay!
Ye think sin in the beginning full sweet,
Which in the end causeth the soul to weep,
When the body lieth in clay.
Here shall you see how Fellowship and Jollity,
Both Strength, Pleasure, and Beauty,
Will fade from thee as flower in May;
For ye shall hear how our Heaven King
Calleth Everyman to a general reckoning:
Give audience, and hear what he do say.

It is clear that the emphasis is on the moral message; it is also clear that it is a play intended to be heard (a treatise) rather than seen (a spectacle). The characters are numerous but the actors might well be fewer: Messenger, God, Death, Everyman, Fellowship, Good Deeds, Goods, Knowledge, Confession, Beauty, Strength, Discretion, Five Wits, Angel, and a Doctor. God sends Death for Everyman; all desert him in his need – except Good Deeds. The moral is clear.

In **Mundus et Infans** (The World and the Child) there is an interesting concept of character. The central figure changes from Infans through Dalliance, Wanton, Love-Lust, Liking, Manhood, Shame, Age and Repentance as the 'plot' unfolds. Other characters include Conscience, Folly, and Perseverance. This concept of the rolling, developing character has at its heart the 'five/six/seven ages of man' view of life; the stage of life which has seven ages set out in Shakespeare's *As You Like It* (II, iii, 138 *ff*). The idea of life being a stage goes back to the Greeks and Romans; Lucian and Petronius both worked out the idea elaborately. The Greek Solon is thought to have divided man's life into seven periods of ten years each. Hippocrates used the seven-fold division but arranged the years within them differently. The twelfth-century Hebrew scholar, Abraham ben Meir (the 'Rabbi ben Ezra' of Browning's poem of that name) divided man's life into ten stages.

The play is important in the history of drama, too, because it insisted on very few characters, in contrast with *Mankind*. The metre is varied to suit character and there is a marked selection of the dramatic material used – the parade of the Seven Deadly Sins is omitted, for example. There are some pictures of contemporary London as Folly exploits its temptations, and a satiric element creeps into the realistic presentation of low life. There is an attempt to relate the action on the stage to the audience but a very bad metrical version of the ten commandments shows just how far the didacticism had still to go before it could be made dramatic. Old Age has to recapitulate the plot, too, in a very dull fashion; it might have seemed that this kind of reminiscing is what Age does, but it makes for very dull drama. The play, at its end, also feels it has to set out the twelve elements of faith needed to reach heaven; the preaching continues to the final scene.

John Skelton's **Magnyfycence**, 'a goodly interlude and a mery', is a long play, written for court, possibly in the 1520s. Its satirical and allegorical approach is in the tradition of Langland's *Piers Plowman*, a long poem written between 1360 and 1399 which condemned abuses in the Church and upheld Poverty and Love as supreme virtues. Skelton was a satirical poet whose attacks on Wolsey made him seek sanctuary at Westminster where he remained until he died in 1529. Earlier in his life Skelton had been the tutor of the young Prince Henry and had instructed him in the kingly virtues – especially that of authority. He wrote a *Speculum Principis* ('Mirror for a Ruler') for the prince and he saw the Morality play as a way of teaching and of being satirical at the same time.

Magnyfycence represents the kingly virtue of magnanimity, the greatness of the ruler as he exercises authority and judgement. The ruler is exposed to vices as he progresses through the world. Felycyte, in an opening speech, introduces many of the main themes: man's reason; the use of wealth; prudence; the conflict between will and reason. Liberty rejects all restraint; Measure (Moderation) tries to reason for control. Magnyfycence insists that Measure must control Liberty and Felycyte.

The characterisation of the 'villains' is handled in an interesting manner in this play; they 'shift their shapes'. Counterfet Countenaunce is joined by Crafty Conveyance and Clokyd Colusyon; their alliance is made firm by Fansy. But then, in order to deceive, Crafty Conveyance becomes Sure Surveyaunce, Counterfet Countenaunce becomes Good Demeynaunce, and Clokyd Colusyon becomes Sober Sadnesse. Things are never what they seem in Henry VIII's court! The circumstances for satire are thus set up. Other aliases are established as the plot unfolds and the audience needs some help in following the shape-shifting. All is part of a concerted attempt to destroy Magnyfycence. Courtly Abuse, Lechery, Anger, Will, Lust-and-Liking, Appetite, and Folly all proceed to the attack. God himself sends Adversity but also Divine Justice (the earlier figure of Death in the Moralities). Magnyfycence is beaten and robbed, Poverty takes over and gradually Wanhope (despair of God's ultimate mercy), Despair, and Mischief suggest suicide. Good Hope brings God's grace and Magnyfycence repents and confesses his sin. Redress gives him a new garment to wear and Sad Cyrcumspeccyon arrives to deliver the play's morals.

The whole play was to be enacted by five players only; there is an elaborate system of ensuring that only certain characters are on the stage at any given time in order to ensure this is possible. The good and bad characters, as a result, never meet; whilst this makes for clarity, perhaps, it reduces conflict. There are fifty-one stage directions, twenty-three of which are in Latin. For really important episodes an elevated style of verse is used (rhyme royal – a seven-line decasyllabic stanza rhymed *A B A BB CC*, used extensively in Chaucer's work). The dialogue is often racy and the language of some of the exchanges down-to-earth.

This Morality play marks a major step forward in the use of stage devices, satire, characterisation, and language in the development of drama.

The eighth of the so-called Morality plays is Sir David Lindsay's **Satire of the Three Estates**, performed in 1540 before James V of Scotland at Linlithgow Palace. This, then, is a clear indication of an early drama production in a great hall, whose ruin today still shows a huge fireplace in the south end with a great window in the east wall, where the dais and high table for the royal party would have been set up. There is a kitchen at the north end of the hall and a minstrel's gallery was set up there. The west wall contained the main windows for the hall and had a balcony running its full length – a suitable gallery for drama productions. Two other productions of Lindsay's play are recorded during his lifetime, one at Cupar in Fife in 1552 and the other in Edinburgh in 1554, the latter in the open air in a playfield set up at the Greenside. It seems that the performance of this play developed from a court performance to a very large public spectacle in the fourteen years between 1540 and 1554. The two extant manuscripts of the play seem to be those of the Cupar and Edinburgh productions rather than that of Linlithgow Palace, which must have been much more intimate and involved, containing, according to one eye-witness's account, only thirteen players. There are fifty-three named parts in the play and thirteen is the maximum number of actors required on stage at any one time. There must have been some doubling-up of parts by actors but some of the roles (*e.g.* Flatterie, Dissait, Falset, and the Fools) are sufficiently well developed to require professional actors.

The title of the play makes its intention clear, a satire on the three estates of the realm, the Lords Spiritual, the Lords Temporal, and the Commons. The first part shows how Rex Humanitas, served by Solace, Wantonness and Placebo, is seduced by Sensuality. The court vices of Flatterie, Falset, and Dissait, taking aliases such as Devotioun, Sapience, and Discretioun, offer to help the King. Gude Counsall is expelled and Veritie and Chastitie are put in the stocks. King Correctioun arrives, almost like the Seventh Cavalry in Westerns, to resolve the problems.

Then an *Interlude*, coarse in tone, separates the first part of the play from the second. The second part now comes to grips with the three estates. Some argue that the allegory weakens here since the programme of reforms proposed is more real than symbolic. John the Commonweil comes to Parliament to put on trial the Temporalitie and the Spiritualitie. The Spiritualitie refuse to abandon their lechery and greed. Flatterie, always taking the role of deception, accuses Dissait and Falset after changing sides and has them hanged. John finally enters Parliament itself.

Only through Parliament would the abuses in Scotland be put right; this is the mood of Reformation and the King is dropped from the second part of the play, significantly.

The structure of the plot is episodic. There are two sermons, a trial, and Parliament to be portrayed in session; the banns of the play at Cupar suggests that it would last four hours.

4.12   Tudor Interludes

Before the opening of the first London playhouse in 1576, the term **Interludes** was often applied to the shorter moral dramatic pieces included in the repertory of Tudor acting groups, but the term had applied from the end of the thirteenth century to dramatic actions such as that of the farcical *Interludum de Clerico et Puella*, (the Interlude of the Cleric and the Girl), only two scenes of which have survived. The term *interludum* 'appears to be equally applicable to every kind of drama known to the Middle Ages' (E. K. Chambers, *op. cit.*, II, 182). There is no evidence that farces were played out as Interludes (*i.e. inter*(between) + *ludes* (plays)), although Lindsay's *Satire of the Three Estates*, as was shown earlier, does have a farcical 'Interlude' to separate Part One from Part Two. Chambers preferred to understand the *inter*-prefix to refer not to a 'ludus' played out between other plays but between other players: 'The term would then apply primarily to any kind of dramatic performance whatsoever' (*op. cit*, II, 183).

The term 'Interlude', nevertheless, Chambers continues, 'was the normal name, varied chiefly by 'play' and 'disguising' for plays given in the banqueting-halls of the great'. Interlude-players also found themselves giving public performances before the municipal authorities of towns and villages in the guildhall or on a stage on the green – or even in the church, perhaps, although the abuse of 'common plays, games or Interludes' in churches or chapels was condemned in Bourner's *Injunctions* of April, 1542. The play *Pyramus and Thisby* put on by Bottom and the rude mechanicals in the court of Athens before Theseus and Hippolyta in *A Midsummer Night's Dream* is an example of a farcical interlude. Moreover, that scene gives the reader today some idea of what kinds of properties and acting-styles were in use by bands of Interlude players late in the sixteenth century in England. Sir Thomas More, as a young man in the house of Cardinal Morton, would 'sodenly sometymes stepp in among the players, and never studinge for the matter, make a parte of his owne ther presently amonge them' (see page 24).

Interludes were known at the Inns of Court, in schools, and at the

Universities. It was between 1490 and 1550 that a group of intellectual young men associated with Sir Thomas More produced some plays which are sometimes referred to as Tudor Interludes, but the term 'Interlude', it must be remembered, is by no means restricted to their plays, as has been shown (see page 90).

Henry Medwall was Chaplain to Cardinal Morton, Archbishop of Canterbury from 1486–1500, and wrote **Fulgens and Lucres** towards the end of the fifteenth century. It is one of the first secular dramas in England and takes a classical theme as its topic; it is essentially a discussion on the nature of nobility. The play is divided into two parts, the second of which opens with a summary of the first. There is a distinct attempt to order the events in a clear sequence and a comic sub-plot which reflects the action in the main plot. An interesting episode occurs when Sone tells of a beating and exaggerates the details for humorous effect; one is reminded of Falstaff's account of his beating in *Henry IV, Part One*. The play is still openly didactic, but the audience is invited to share in the action of the play.

Another of Medwall's plays found less favour with his audience. His moral play *The Fynding of Troth* played at Christmas, 1513, seemed so long to Henry VIII that he left the performance and 'departyd to hys chambre'.

John Rastell wrote **The Nature of the Four Elements** (*c.* 1517); **Calisto and Melibaea**:

> a new comodye in englysh in maner of an enterlude ryght elygant & full of craft of rethoryk wherein is shewd & dyscrybyd as well the bewte & good propertes of women as theyr vycys & euyll cōdiciōs with a morall cōclusion & exhortacyon to vertew;

and **Gentleness and Nobility**. It is for the first of these plays that John Rastell is best remembered:

> a new interlude and a mery of the nature of the .iiii. elements declarynge many proper poynts of phylosophy naturall and of dyvers strange landys and of dyvers strannge effect and causis, which interlude, if the whole matter be played, will contain the space of an hour and a half; but if you list you may leave out much of the said matter, as . . . and then it will not be past three quarters of an hour of length.

Rastell was a conscious artist and one who thought drama had a role to play in making social comment. There is a topicality in his work and an expansion of elements he thought were humorous.

John Heywood (1497?–1580?) was the husband of Sir Thomas More's niece, Elizabeth Rastell, daughter of John Rastell. He was a singer and a player on the virginals at the court of Henry VIII. His Interludes included **The Four P's** (about 1545), **Play of the Wether** (1533) in which Jupiter listens to conflicting arguments about which weather to supply, **A Play of Love** (1534), and he was also possibly the author of **The Pardoner and the Friar** and **Johan the Husband, Tyb the Wyf, and Syr Jhan the Preest**. In the first of these Interludes a Palmer, a Pardoner, a Pothecary and a Pedlar, as judge, debate who could tell the biggest lie. The Palmer wins in the end by declaring that he had never seen a woman out of patience. It is based on the notion of medieval debate, but the dialogue is witty and full of vitality. Again, the satire is conscious and direct. **The Play of the Wether** is more light-hearted. There are no allegorical figures in it, except perhaps for Merry Report who is in the tradition of the Vice; there is no real plot – actors come and go with little interaction between them, somewhat in the manner of most of Chaucer's pilgrims. The humour in the play springs from the absurdity of the requests for one form of weather rather than another from Jupiter; one little boy, however, wants snow in order to make snowballs.

John Redford took as his theme in **Wit and Science** (about 1548) the importance of being devoted to study. There are still some abstract characters in the play (*e.g.* Learning and Intelligence); Tediousness appears as a character in the tradition of the Vice. The dialogue is realistic at times but characters such as Idleness, Ignorance, Fame, Riches, Worship, Honest Recreation, and Comfort make the moral emphasis very clear.

4.13 The Folk Play

Until now, this Chapter has been concerned with the development of drama during the medieval period which had its origins in religion and in religious practices. Folk remedies, charms, and rituals were well known amongst the Anglo-Saxons. Elements of witchcraft, magic and incantations survived the even more powerful forces which the Christians claimed to control.

Drama has always been associated with festivals since the time of the Greeks. Contests form part of the ritual, as in the Ludlow tug-of-war on Shrove Tuesday; the Easter Monday hare-pie scramble at Hallaton in Leicestershire, and the Haxey hood struggle on Epiphany (in Haxey, Lincolnshire), for men to fight for a roll of sacking or leather to take back to their own public houses are survivals of earlier festival activities. Punishments, forfeits, the chanting of place-names in children's games are also thought by some to be the relics of earlier dramatic rituals. The Hock-tide *ludus* on the second Monday and Tuesday after Easter Sunday, still practised in many places, combines both contest and ritual; on Hock-Monday the women 'hock' the men, catching them, binding them, and exacting a forfeit; the next day the men do the same to the women. It is argued that 'hocking' goes back to the time of the Viking invasions when the women were carried off by the Danes.

Country dances and festivals, particularly in May at the start of the natural annual rebirth of the countryside, abound. Song, dance, contest, and myth combine to form an entertainment. The burial of winter and of Death, and the resurrection of Life often mark the folk drama that arose from such ritual activities in the countryside. Morris dances, sword dances and Maypole dances may well be associated with this use of myth, not only in England but throughout Europe. The dances were often accompanied by characters dressed in grotesque costumes, one of whom was called Maid Marian. Sometimes there was a dragon and a hobby-horse ridden by St. George. A feature of many of the folk-dances was a character who rushes between them and is killed; a doctor is on hand who proceeds to bring the dead person back to life. **The Mummers' Play of St. George** combines many of the folk elements; it is found throughout England. There are local variations but E. K. Chambers (*The Medieval Stage*, I, 211) has summarised the parts of the play as follows: *a Presentation* where an actor speaks a prologue and introduces the characters; *a Fight* with a doctor to revive the dead; *the Quête*, where other characters enter and a collection is taken up. The central hero of the fight is St. (sometimes Sir, Prince, King) George; a second character is a Turkish knight, sometimes with a blackened face; a third is Slasher (Captain Slasher or Bold (Bean) Slasher). This character is a swaggering braggart. There is a fight, one of the champions is killed, but he is revived by a doctor. The town of Lydd had its St. George play in 1456 and in 1511 a play of St. George was acted at Bassingbourne in Cambridgeshire.

Clearly, during a period when learning was in the hands of the Church and those associated with it, texts of religious plays were written down. Folk plays were left to survive by oral tradition and local custom.

4.14 The Vice

Finally, with the end of this period arose the figure of **the Vice**. L. W. Cushman ('*The Devil and the Vice in the English Dramatic Literature before Shakespeare*', *Studien zur Englischen Philologie*, vi, 1900) argued that the Vice came into English drama through the moralities as 'an allegorical representation of human weakness and vices, in short the summation of the Deadly Sins'. He, Cushman argued, later became synonymous with the buffoon. E. K. Chambers rejected the explanation since it disregarded plays in which the Vice occurred and read him into plays where he did not.

The 'Vice' is not given that name in plays where he does appear. He appears primarily as a figure whose main purpose is to make fun. M. C. Bradbrook (*The Rise of the Common Player*, 1962) pointed out that the traditional role of the Vice was that of providing a witty, mocking challenge to authority. He partly instigates action in the play and partly explains it by providing a commentary. Because he stands mainly outside the action, however, he can stand midway between the players and the audience and so involves the spectators in the spectacle. He often declares what he will do and points out the tricks he will use to the audience and deliberately undertakes a false role, for example, that of the Mime, in order to make his points obvious. His language is usually vivid and waggish and his attitude shows irreverence and a lack of respect for those in authority. (One is reminded of The Fool in *King Lear* who says things to the King which no one else dare say; he is called the 'all-licensed fool' but at one point, when he goes too far, Lear warns him: 'Take heed, sirrah: the whip'.) The Vice, similarly, is a privileged figure who can attack the over-virtuous or the representative of officialdom. His role is an amoral one – he is not trying to adopt or put forward a moral position but merely trying to make the audience laugh. This is not to say, however, that satire is not part of his weaponry.

There have been some ingenious explanations of the term 'Vice'. Some argue it is from the French *vis d'âne* (donkey's mask) or *vis* (a mask); others that it comes from the Latin *vice*, because he seems the Devil's representative; others that it derives from *device*, 'a puppet moved by machinery' (see E. K. Chambers, *op. cit.*, II, 204).

One thing is certain: he appears as a stock character many times in plays of all kinds from the beginning of the sixteenth century to the interludes, in many guises. In John Heywood's play *A Play of Love* (1534) he features as Neither-Loving-Nor-Loved; in his play *Play of the Wether* (1533) he is Merry Report; in John Pickering's *Interlude of Vice or Honestes* (1567) the Vice enters the play as Courage and reassures, falsely, the hero that the gods have sent him to bring vengeance. He is rarely equated with the Fool as a character, however, although in *Misogonos* (about 1560), a play by Henry Medwall, one of the characters is called 'foole' and 'nodye' but not Vice although some contemporary writers speak of the Vice's 'long coat and lathen sword, common trappings of the domestic fool' (see E. K. Chambers, II, 204–5).

As Politicke Persuasion in *Patient and Meek Grissell* (1559) the Vice falls from the gods but manages to unite Olympus, Heaven, and London. His aim is to disrupt true love or the government – in fact, he is a Lord of Misrule, a figure associated, some argue with English folk festivals and May Games, and others with Tudor revels at court, where the Lord of Misrule was known as the Abbot (or the Abbot of Unreason in Scotland), and whose job was to supervise the revels and sports at Christmas. The task of the Vice in *Common Conditions* (1576) is avowedly to bring about as much confusion as he can, and so he plays a prominent part in the complexities of the plot. As Subtill Shift in *Clyomon and Clamydes* (1570), the Vice is:

> Like a demigod, here I sit in the sky
> And wretched fools' secrets heedfully o'er-eye

He mocks the lovers, kills a flying dragon, sets the prisoners of an oppressive ruler free, and steals his gold.

One of the features of the Vice is often his readiness to spill out a long list of words and place names; he originated in this respect as a devil, Titivil or Titivillus, whose job it was to collect up all the words in the divine service that were dropped, mumbled, or omitted. It is thought that Titivil was the creation of monks; the earliest mention of him comes in a Latin sermon said to be by Petrus de Palude, a Burgundian at Paris, who later became patriarch of Jerusalem and died in 1342. Titivillus is the name given to the main embroiler in the Morality play, *Mankind* (see page 86). Haphazard in *Apius and Virginia* (1565) by 'R. B.' also displays this same characteristic of word-tumbling on his entry.

A very early tragedy in English, Thomas Preston's *Cambises* (1569) (see page 94), has a Vice-character in Ambidexter who laughs throughout the play alongside the three comic soldiers, Huf, Ruf, and Snuf (whose names also appear in documents associated with the famous Marprelate controversy at the end of the century). In Shakespeare's *The Winter's Tale* Autolychus (IV, ii) describes himself as 'a snapper-up of unconsidered trifles' in the best Titivillus tradition and yet laments that he was not 'out of service'. Autolychus claims that he has been robbed and he describes himself, as a Vice-character, to the Clown:

> AUT.   I knew him once a servant of the prince. I cannot tell, good sir, for which of his virtues it was, but he was certainly whipped out of the court.
>
> CLOWN   His vices, you would say: there's no virtue whipped out of the court: they cherish it, to make it stay there, and yet it will no more but abide.
>
> AUT.   Vices, I would say, sir.

In Act IV, iii, the words of Autolychus bubble out and he shows 'what a fool Honesty is!'. This is the development of the Vice in British drama. The character of the comic embroiler will be replaced by the more sinister figure of the malcontent, the Machiavellian embroiler of Jacobean drama.

Questions

1 Select a major character playing the central role in a Mystery play you are studying. Show how his or her appearance, speeches, and behaviour would have emerged in a medieval production.
2 What do you think would be the major difficulties for a modern director of a medieval play you have been studying? How could the difficulties be overcome?
3 Show the importance of *one* of the following in a medieval play you have been studying: grouping of characters; ritual; the blend of Biblical and non-Biblical elements.
4 *Take a Biblical incident not shown in a medieval play, so far as you know. Write a scene, as it might have been written in medieval times, for a Mystery play presenting the main features of the incident. (Do not try to write in medieval English.)
5 Given that the audience might well have known the main details of the plot already, show how the medieval playwright, in a play you know well, has tried to engage the audience's attention.
6 How far would you, as the director of a production, help your audience to appreciate the allegorical elements in a Morality play you have studied? (Give as many examples as you can.)
7 Outline the uses to which humour has been put in the drama of the medieval period that you have been studying.
8 Show how the writer has tried to reconcile the demands of teaching and entertaining in a play from this period that you know well.
9 What do you consider were the lasting contributions of the Middle Ages to the development of theatre in Britain?
10 *If you could choose to act any part you wished from medieval plays, which part would you choose? Show how you would interpret it for an audience today *or* how you would have interpreted it for a medieval audience had you been living in this period.

*The questions marked * could form the basis of project work.*

5
Elizabethan and Jacobean Drama

5.1

You should first read and understand the development of the stage in Britain until the closing of the theatres in 1642 given in Section **2.6** and **2.7**. You should also study Chapter Four (pages 71–95) on the medieval period, since many of the features of early drama underlie the development of plays and the theatre during the reigns of Elizabeth (1558–1603) and James I (1603–25).

5.2

The period considered in this Chapter runs from about the time of Elizabeth's accession to the English throne to the Restoration of Charles II to the throne in 1660, one of the most exciting, action-packed periods in English history and in the development of drama.

5.3   The Development of Comedy

The distinction between comedy and tragedy is not an easy one to make and a much harder one to maintain. It is not necessarily the topic or subject that makes one event comic and another tragic. Even the 'slipping-on-a-banana skin' situation may be comic if a pompous, strutting proud man suddenly finds himself in an undignified position, but it is not necessarily comic if someone breaks his or her back and is paralysed for life through slipping over. Even death, itself, may be treated as comedy in order to make a special effect.

Horace Walpole in 1776 said 'This world is a comedy to those that think, a tragedy to those that feel'. Bottom in *A Midsummer Night's Dream* describes the play-within-the-play of Pyramus and Thisby as 'a sweet comedy' to Peter Quince who had earlier described the play as 'the most lamentable comedy, and most cruel death of Pyramus and Thisby'.

The word 'comedy' is linked with the Greek *kóμos* or comic Chorus where the essential feature was the happy outcome of the events shown. Certainly, for the Middle Ages 'comedy' meant just that; Dante's *Divine Comedy* (begun about 1300) is so-called because the plot progresses from hell to purgatory and ends in the happiness of paradise (Inferno-Purgatorio-Paradiso). This seems to be at the centre of the notion of comedy: it is a series of events that ends happily, even if it has to show the trials and tribulations experienced on the way to happiness.

The Elizabethan, Sir Philip Sidney, would not have been happy, however, with such a definition. For him, in *An Apologie for Poetry* (about 1583), a comedy had to be a comedy throughout: 'the whole tract of a comedy should be full of delight'. He distinguished carefully delight from laughter: 'we laugh at deformed creatures, wherein certainly we cannot delight'; 'Delight hath a joy in it, either permanent or present. Laughter hath only a scornful tickling'; 'We delight in good chances, we laugh at mischances . . . But I speak to this purpose, that all the end of the comical part be not upon such scornful matters as stir laughter only, but, mixed with it, that delightful teaching which is the end of poesy'. Comedy, then, for Sidney at least, had a moral purpose. Above all tragedies should not 'thrust in clowns by head and shoulders' but should remain tragedies throughout; similarly comedies should remain 'right comedies'. 'The mongrel tragi-comedy' was to be avoided. Look at Shakespeare's thin disguising of his own amusement at such a rigid view of tragedy and comedy in *Hamlet*, II, ii, 423 *ff*:

> . . . tragedy, comedy, history, pastoral, pastoral-comical, historical-pastoral, tragical-historical, tragical-comical-historical-pastoral, scene individable, or poem unlimited.

Comedy seems happier than tragedy with types; such types within a recognisable setting would provide a 'comedy of situation'; such types in a setting but with one type set off against another would lead to a 'comedy of manners'. Certainly, Sidney was voicing a fifteenth and sixteenth century view of comedy when he spoke of its didactic or moral purpose – to laugh someone out of folly. The representation of folly on the stage, however, was one which the Puritans of the Elizabethan age *e.g.* Stephen Gosson, *The School of Abuse*, 1582, Philip Stubbes, *The Anatomie of Abuses* (1583) strongly disapproved of, and John Northbrook, *Treatise wherein Dicing, Dancing, Vain Plays are reproved*, (1577) thought that going to plays taught one 'how to be false and deceive your husbands . . . how to ravish, how to beguile, how to betray, to flatter, lie, swear, forswear . . . murder . . . poison . . . rebel,' etc.

5.4

Nicholas Udall's *Ralph Roister Doister* (about 1553) has been called 'the earliest known English comedy' and it comes rapidly to grips with the problem of 'mirth mixed with sadness' and the moral objectives of comedy from the outset:

THE PROLOGUE

What creature is in health, eyther yong or olde,
But som mirth with modestie wil be glad to vse –
As we in thys enterlude shall now vnfolde?
Wherin all scurilitie we vtterly refuse;
Auoiding such mirth wherein is abuse;
Knowing nothing more comendable for a mans recreation
Than mirth which is vsed in an honest fashion.
For myrth prolongeth lyfe, and causeth health;
Mirth recreates our spirites, and voydeth pensivenesse;
Mirth increaseth amitie, not hindring our wealth;
Mirth is to be vsed both of more and lesse,
Being mixed with vertue in decent comlynesse –
     . . . auoidying all blame.

The play was probably played by boys from Westminster School at the time when Udall was headmaster there. Its plot tells how Ralph, a swaggering oaf, tried to court Cristian Custance, who is betrothed to Gawin Goodlucke, a merchant who is absent for a time. Matthew Merygreeke, the fun-maker and embroiler and a Vice-character, leads Ralph on; poor Ralph is rejected and beaten by Custance and her maids. Goodlucke, on his return, is deceived by false reports but finally makes up with Custance and the play ends happily.

The Prologue acknowledges the play's indebtedness to the comedies of Plautus and Terence and this classical influence led to the play's division into acts and scenes, the coherence of the plot (in contrast to the kinds of plots seen in some Morality plays), an insistence on the Unities of Time and Place, and the very skilful entrances and exits on which much of the comedy depends.

The names of the characters indicate their 'types': Tristram Trusty, an old friend to Goodlucke and Custance; Tom Trupenie, a boy, servant to Custance; Sym Suresby, loyal servant to Goodlucke; Madge Mumblecrust, an old woman; Tibet Talk-a-Pace and Annot Alyface, maids to Custance. The Morality 'types' are given sharp characteristics for the purposes of comedy. The play is full of vitality and has at its heart the enjoyment of everyday life. In spite of the Prologue, the didacticism is never assertive. Udall has managed to introduce a number of features which will echo through comedy for centuries: the figure of the parasite; the manipulation of a comic episode – the mock funeral; the proud disdainful lover in Custance (*cf.* Olivia in *Twelfth Night*); and the use of comic stage directions – *e.g.* 'Pretends to be looking for a house'; 'she struts like a grand lady'; 'runs into him'; 'he bumps hard into Roister'; 'bumps him again'; 'rubs his head roughly'; 'Roister Doister advances on Custance; she beats him', etc. (This elaboration of stage directions will go to extreme lengths in a later period with Shaw's very detailed directions running to a page or more.) It is worth mentioning, too, the way in which Udall has learnt from earlier drama in England how to use racy dialogue and repartee as well as slapstick. Unfortunately the versatility of the dialogue is too often held back by the repetitive, heavy, short-rhymed doggerel in which the play is written.

5.5

Gammer Gurton's Needle (acted in Christ's College, Cambridge, in 1566) embodies many of the comedy features noticed in *Ralph Roister Doister*. The play is written in rhymed doggerel, is divided into five acts with new scenes opening with new characters, the action takes place in a single day in a single street and so the Unities of Time and Place are observed, and it makes use of 'type' characters: Diccon, the Bedlam; Dame Chatte; Doctor Rat, the curate; Scapethryft, a servant; and, interestingly, Mutes. The characters are comparatively few compared with the long lists found in some of the Morality plays. Hodge is the typical farm labourer, Diccon the half-witted wanderer (to lead on in tradition to Poor Tom and Wandering Willie) and Gammer Gurton is the village gossip (still found in *Coronation Street* and other 'soap operas' today).

This play, too, opens with a Prologue which sets out in twenty lines the whole of the dramatic action. If the audience is told what is going to happen, they share the secret with the playwright, but some of the suspense in drama goes; the interest moves from 'What will happen next?' to 'How will they get out of it?' or 'How can the playwright resolve that situation?' Such a technique uses the situation of the Mystery plays where the plot was known already and throws the audience into watching the action for its technique and intricacies. The conclusion is one of mirth if not surprise!

> Sodenlye the neele Hodge found by the prickynge,
> And drew it out of his bottocke where he felt it stickynge.
> Theyr hartes then at rest with perfect securytie,
> With a pot of good nale they stroake vp theyr plauditie.

There are, moreover, some important developments in comedy to be found in this play. The plot depends on misunderstanding; slapstick – where the Curate is caught without his clerical gown creeping into a woman's house and his repulsion by the maids who beat him; the development of the heavy drinker as a comic character; and the introduction of a 'court-type' scene with accusation and counter-accusation which serve to tie the knots even tighter in the plot before the swift conclusion, when Diccon gives Hodge a smart blow on the buttocks, all of which are elements of comedy that will be found again in English drama.

It is essential in a play of this kind, where characters come and go, clash, retire, and then re-emerge later, for all the characters – even the minor ones – to be clearly differentiated. Here, the playwright attempts to do this through language differences. Sometimes this characterisation by language is over-played, as in the case of the simple Hodge (Act IV, ii) who concludes every line he utters, in his embarrassed response to Doctor Rat's invitation to tell what he knows about the loss of Gammer Gurton's needle, with the hesitant, bumbling, awkward phrase ' – see now? . . . – see now? . . . – see now?'.

The stage directions in the play are full and detailed. The opening stage direction is of special interest to the student interested in the development of drama, since it indicates setting and lighting and shows that the Italian interest in perspective (see page 30) has reached England:

> *A village street in perspective. Gammer Gurton's house on one side, Dame Chat's ale-house on the other. The time, Saturday evening after sun-down.*

This sixteenth century precursor of a 'Coronation Street' set is particularly interesting, since it will allow characters to have swift entrances and exits.

In this play, too, there is a very real attempt to produce a fast-moving dialogue which builds up tension and raises the temperature between the characters. The set speeches of the medieval mystery plays seem some way away. Pace is essential to farce; swift-moving dialogue, slick changes in scene, and a smooth but intricate plot are of the essence of comedy.

5.6 Comedy and Learning

The comedy of *The Second Shepherds' Play* in the medieval Towneley mystery cycle (see pages 81–83) had, at its heart, a parody of a well-known Biblical story, that of the Nativity, but its humour, with the concluding scene of tossing Mak in a blanket, was down-to-earth and popular in appeal. The comedy of both *Ralph Roister Doister* and *Gammer Gurton's Needle* also has a down-to-earth, popular, and slapstick quality but it was more sophisticated, since it was played out in schools or colleges and was heavily dependent, in its construction at least, on classical models. As comedy moved on towards the close of the sixteenth century in England it came increasingly under the influence of Italian critics such as Minturno and Castelvetro (through Sir Philip Sidney) with their emphasis on classical tradition, and the Italian professional comedy of the *commedia dell'arte*, with its emphasis on stereotyped characters, (the lover, the braggart, the cunning politician) who used stock jokes, told by professional actors each playing a single part such as Harlequin, Pantaleone or the Doctor.

The Italian critics of the late sixteenth century relied heavily on Aristotle and Horace. They saw their role as one of defending poetry against church criticisms; they eventually abandoned moral and religious justification for literature and moved towards aesthetic ones. They were joined in their justification and insistence on the development of a literary language in France by Du Bellay (*Défense et illustration de la langue française*, 1549–50) and in England by Thomas Wilson (*Art of Rhetorique*, 1553). The critical works in Italy flooded from the presses, beginning with Vida's *De arte poetica* (1527) and moving on through works by Prissino, Daniello, Robatelli, Maggi, Trincio, Minturno, Scaliger, Castelvetro, Patrezzi and Tasso before the century was out. The Dominican monk Savonarola (1452–98), before he himself was executed as a heretic, had raised yet again all the objections to literature that had been current since Aquinas's accusation (1225–74) that it destroyed calmness of mind, and Boethius's earlier suggestion (late fifth, early sixth centuries) that it weakened the will. The Italians insisted that the poets must teach, delight, and persuade (Daniello and Cinthio) particularly by providing beautiful examples (Vacci). The good would be rewarded and the evil punished. In England the sixteenth-century poet Edmund Spenser tried to put many of these principles into practice in his verse (*The Fairie Queene*). The Italians thought that suitable topics for tragedy were the death of kings and the fall of great empires, but above all that *decorum* (see page 51) should prevail. They considered that order, composition and the integrity of tragedy as tragedy should be of prime importance. Comedy should not merely cause laughter, but should laugh people *out of folly*; there was a moral purpose to comedy. We laugh because we feel superior to those at whom we are laughing.

The significant contribution to Renaissance drama made by the Italian critics, however, came from their discussion of the Unities – Time, Action, and Place. Aristotle had insisted centuries before on the need for **Unity of Action** (see page 49). Cinthio (1504–73), whose stories later provided plots for Shakespeare's *Othello* and *Measure for Measure* and for plays by Beaumont and Fletcher and James Shirley (1596–1666), was the first to insist on the need for **Unity of Time** – 'one day or a little more'. Others went further and insisted on 'twelve hours'. Castelvetro (1505–71) thought that **Unity of Place** was vital – 'the scene of action must be constant, not restricted to one city or house but to one place alone visible to one person'. The impact of these critics on the French dramatists Corneille and Racine was to be profound.

The Italian critics also entered the debate about epic and romance. The romantic epic *Orlando Furioso* by Ariosto was published in its complete form in 1532. It was a story of war, heroes, knights, a beautiful heroine, escape to the woods, madness, the course of true love, a flight to the moon, and death before dishonour. This was followed by other romances which were defended by Cinthio but attacked by Speroni and Minturno who attacked their lack of unity and coherence. Tasso (1544–95) came to the rescue of romance with his *Jerusalem Delivered*, a story of Christian knighthood, a wicked sorceress, love and enchantments. The discussion of romance would continue in France, in theory, in the work of Boileau (1636–1711) and in England, in practice, with the publication of *The Fairie Queene* (1589–96). Into this climate of debate come the English playwrights trained in the classical tradition who would turn to comedy and romance, chief of whom was John Lyly (1554?–1606).

5.7 Romantic Comedy

Before John Lyly, however, romantic comedy established itself in England. It ran through English drama until well into the Caroline period after the Restoration, when it was seen as a major theme of plays enjoyed by the aristocracy. The Italians and the French had long argued that drama should break away from the restrictions of classical subjects and move into the realm of romance. The Greek story of Damon and Pythias was adapted and extended into a play about friendship in Richard Edward's play *Damon and Pithias* (printed in 1571); he called his work a 'tragical comedy'. The romantic theme of friendship is matched by that of chivalry, stories of knights and distressed damsels. Many of these chivalric comedies have been lost but there were many of them whose titles we know: *Cloridon and Rodiamanta, Paris and Vienna, Predor and Lucia, Herpetulus the Blue Knight, The Red Knight*, etc. About 1577 the Queen's Men produced a romantic comedy that has survived: *The History of the Two Valiant Knights, Sir Clyomon Knight of the Golden Shield, Son to the King of Denmark, and Clamydes the White Knight, Son to the King of Suavia*. This was a play of love and rivalry, farce, adventure and derring-do, and included such characters as noble heroes, distressed damsels, and cruel giants. By 1576 the term 'Interlude' had been dropped from descriptions of plays; they were now 'comedies', 'tragedies', or 'histories'.

The romantic convention demanded love and lovers, disappointment and tribulations, the search, the triumph of virtue over wickedness, intrigue, epic-like adventures and magic – all presented in elevated style, with easily recognised stock figures, and an ordered progression towards the realisation of the ideal, accompanied by music and song. It is an old medieval convention which Chaucer and his contemporaries drew on. *The Romance of the Rose, Troilus and Criseyde*, and *The Fairie Queene* illustrate some of its most spectacular manifestations. In England the love tradition moved back to the *Flos Amoris* or *Ars Amatoria* of Andreas Capellanus (Andrew the Chaplain) written about 1200. In this manual of love the rules for literary compositions about love are set out:

love must be kept a secret; it always increases or grows less; the lover is obsessed with the image of his co-lover constantly; easy winning makes love despicable – the difficult is held dear; the one in love is always fearful; love is only deserved by those showing prowess; the lover always seeks the happiness of his lover and eats and sleeps little – and so on. The stock characters are emerging, and are well represented by Troilus in Chaucer's romance *Troilus and Cresseid* and satirised by Chauntecleer in *The Nun's Priest's Tale*.

In drama these features of romance emerge – along with their satirical treatment, accompanied by themes of innocence, rustic simplicity and virtue set against courtly intrigue, the driving mad of lovers by passion (*cf.* the madness of Shakespeare's Malvolio) and purity, all set out with ballads, music, and songs in elegantly constructed plots that work themselves out like a game of chess.

Rosalind, in Act III, ii, of *As You Like It* set out many of the traditional romantic features:

(my uncle) taught me how to know a man in love . . . a lean cheek, a blue eye and sunken, an unquestionable spirit, a beard neglected, hose should be ungartered . . . your shoe untied and everything demonstrating a careless desolation . . .

Love is merely a madness, and, I tell you, deserves as well a dark house and a whip as madmen do . . .

Malvolio is a parody of them. Sir Toby Belch and Sir Andrew Aguecheke are parodies of knighthood as is Ralph, drawn from the spectators, to play 'the puissant Knight of the Burning Pestle' in Beaumont and Fletcher's play of that name (about 1610). The 'knights' released from the Barber's Shop in Waltham in the same play guy the romantic chivalric tradition – with the barber's being a giant's cave and the customers, of French tradition of course, being entrapped knights freed by Ralph; one man says,

I am an errant knight that followed arms
With spear and shield; and in my tender years
I stricken was with Cupid's fiery shaft,
And fell in love with this my lady dear,
And stole her from her friends in Turnbull Street,
And bore her up and down from town to town,
Where we did eat and drink, and music hear;
Till at the length of this unhappy town
We did arrive, and coming to this cave,
This beast us caught, and put us in a tub,
Where we this two months sweat, and should have done
Another month, if you had not reliev'd us.

Many of the features of romantic comedy are well parodied here.

5.8

In **John Lyly's** plays we find the model for romantic comedy established. He brought to the vigour of English comedy seen in *Ralph Roister Doister* and

Gammer Gurton's Needle the kind of elegance, order, and reserve – decorum, in fact – that sprang from the classical tradition. He is best known for his long prose romance *Euphues: The Anatomy of Wit* (1578) and *Euphues and his England* (1580). The plot is slight: Euphues, a young Athenian, becomes friends with Philautus, an Italian, whose sweetheart, Lucilla, he steals – only to be supplanted by one Curio. Philautus and Euphues condemn Lucilla 'as most abhominable'. Later, when Philautus visits England and begins his amorous adventures he ignores Euphues's advice. Euphues adopts the role of giving advice to the ladies of Italy by describing the excellent institutions of England. The language of *Euphues* is what makes the book, in its two parts, memorable; it is lofty, Latinate, and full of antithesis, alliteration, and allusions which sometimes ignore the sense. 'Euphuistic' has become a term applied to bombastic, overwritten, pompous prose today.

Lyly's dramatic style was similarly ornate. He was well acquainted with the revels and masques of the Court. He was particularly associated with the bands of child actors which sprang up in schools, such as Merchant Taylors and Westminster, and in Bristol. Boy actors were grouped into companies such as the Earl of Leicester's Boys, The Earl of Oxford's Boys and Mr. Stanley's Boys, and posed some threat to professional adult groups of actors. Shakespeare refers to the boys in *Hamlet* as 'the aery of children, little eyases, . . .' (see also page 24). Lyly's plays were reserved, decorous, and elaborate. The masques of the court, which deeply affected him, were often slight in plot but full of spectacle and music. Lyly, deputy master of the Children of St. Paul's, wrote plays that mirrored the elegance of court manners in a language that was elegant; they contain no brawls, no raw passion, no ribald jokes; instead they show control in plot-construction, and orderly movement. The roles and the relationships between characters are well-established; the play's concern is with the mind rather than the emotion. Often the dialogue consists of set speeches rather than interaction and exchange of conversation. Love is seen as a disease which attacks and robs men and women of their dignity. Lyly is assured and because he is writing from and for a stable society his satire of literary conventions of love, of women, of social standards needs never be strident in order to make its effect.

Alexander and Campaspe (1584) has a plot derived from Pliny's 'Natural History'. Alexander the Great loves a Theban captive, Campaspe, and asks the painter Apelles to paint her portrait. Campaspe and Apelles fall in love and the painter continually spoils the portrait to prolong the time he can spend with Campaspe. The noble Alexander learns of the trick, gives Campaspe to Apelles and goes back to fight. The style of the prose used by Lyly is elevated – and dull, but the action is interspersed with chatter, riddles, and songs to mitigate the heaviness of the main romantic plot. *Endimion, The Man in the Moone* (1591) is the story of Endimion's abandoning of Tellus (the earth) to seek for Cynthia (the moon). A conspiracy with a witch puts Endimion to sleep for forty years but Cynthia breaks the spell and releases Endimion with a kiss. Some argue that the play is an allegory of the rivalry between Elizabeth (Cynthia) and Mary Queen of Scots (Tellus) for Leicester (Endimion) together with other minor allegories on court intrigues. *Midas* (1592) is a heavy prose, romantic, drama indebted to Ovid, and *The Woman in the Moon* (1597) covers the story of the shepherds of Utopia who ask Nature to provide a woman to comfort them; Nature offers Pandora and gives her the qualities of the seven planets who change her mood one by one with strange effects on the shepherds. In this play Lyly tried to contrast the language of lovers and clowns but the satire of love, in all its ridiculousness, is self-evident in the way Pandora behaves. The play contains the famous debate between Concord and Discord but only a goddess can reconcile the irreconcilable.

Lyly's plays, however, are 'artificial', in the classical sense that they are artefacts, made by a skill that is conscious and they use a premeditated form and have a preconceived purpose operating within narrow social and literary conventions.

Whilst Lyly and the boys' companies were occupied with artificial romantic comedy and used 'simultaneous staging' for the productions (*i.e.* several locations indicated by different placings on the stage), the adult players were probably turning to a more robust treatment of romantic themes.

5.9

Robert Greene (1560?–1592) in two of his plays, *Friar Bacon and Friar Bungay* (*c.* 1588) and *James IV* (*c.* 1590) used a historical setting of some kind, often vague, to produce a romance which involved love, magic, and adventure.

In *Friar Bacon and Friar Bungay*, written in verse and prose, Greene embodies the legends of two rival magicians, Roger Bacon (1214–94) who wrote Latin treatises on the sciences and alchemy and who was regarded as a wizard who had created a brass head capable of speaking, and Thomas Bungay, a Franciscan friar and an astrologer of the same period. In the play Bacon watches the head for three weeks and finally gives over the watch to the servant Miles who hears the head say 'Time is . . .' but neglects to do anything; the head then says, 'Time was . . .' and then 'Time is past . . .' before falling down and smashing. Bacon wakes up but the chance has passed and the bungling servant is cursed by his master. The play is embellished, too, by the story of the loves of Lord Lacy and the Prince of Wales (later Edward I) for Margaret but the Prince surrenders her nobly to Lacy in the end (*cf.* Alexander in Lyly's *Alexander and Campaspe*, page 104), and a scene where Bacon, Bungay, and a German magician display their respective powers to the German emperor and other Kings. The play ends on a jingoistic note – under Edward I England would prosper:

> And peace from heaven shall harbour in these leaves
> That gorgeous beautifies this matchless flower:
> Apollo's heliotropon then shall stoop,
> And Venus' hyacinth shall veil her top;
> Juno shall shut her gilliflowers up,
> And Pallas' bay shall 'bash her brightest green;
> Ceres' carnation, in consort with those,
> Shall stoop and wonder at Diana's rose.

King Henry's response echoes that of the audience:

'This prophecy is mystical!'

In this play, however, the romantic elements of history, magic, the court, and rustic life are brought into a single plot. Shakespeare would learn from Greene (*cf. As You Like It*).

Greene's play *James IV* also combines the history of a Scottish king, Oboram, King of the Fairies, and a romantic love story of Dorothea. *Orlando Furioso* (*c.* 1591) is indebted to Ariosto's poem of 1582; Orlando is the Italian form of the name Roland, and, of course, Roland was a hero of the Charlemagne romances of the Middle Ages, especially the 'Chanson de Roland'. In Greene's play Orlando has become a wandering knight; it opens with a procession of kings who have come to woo Angelica (*cf.* the wooing of Portia in *The Merchant of Venice*) who chooses Orlando. The hero is driven mad by love elegies hung on trees (*cf. As You Like It*) by the wicked Sacrapant. This madness is exploited by Greene for some low comedy but a good fairy appears who utters a Latin incantation over Orlando, who goes on to lead an army – equipped with cooking spits and pans – to victory. The play is a kind of dream which mingles history, magic, the love convention, rustic life, and courtly manners. It has fairies and moves on from one event to the next without any great sense of inevitable sequence. The decorum of Lyly provides a marked contrast to the lively exploration of language and dramatic situation in Greene.

Sacrapant, a Magician, appears in another interesting transformation of romantic comedy in George Peele's *The Old Wives Tale* (printed 1595). This play is intended as a satire on the romantic plays of the late sixteenth century. Madge, the old wife of Clunch, the Smith, is persuaded to tell a story to three wanderers, Antic, Frolic, and Fantastic. She does so and the characters of the narrative come to life in the play-within-the-play. Two brothers look for Delia, their sister, held captive by the wicked Sacrapant. They are captured by the Magician but are rescued by the gallant wooer of Delia, the knight who bears the impressive name of Eumenides, helped by the ghost of Jack. Friars, magic wells, harvesters, rustic scenes, fiddlers, furies, music, an old countryman, and a parish waster make up the setting for the play. The learned decrees of the Renaissance critics have been replaced by lively, diverse, dramatic, romantic entertainments.

5.10

Shakespeare certainly continued in the tradition of the romantic comedy of this period. *Romeo and Juliet* (1593) takes up the theme of romance but becomes a tragedy; *A Midsummer Night's Dream* (*c.* 1594), *The Merchant of Venice* (*c.* 1595), *Much Ado About Nothing* (1599), *As You Like It* (1599), *Twelfth Night* (?1600), and *The Tempest* (1611) resume the development of Elizabethan romantic comedy.

Romeo and Juliet begins with an ominous fight between Sampson of the Capulets and Abraham of the Montagues but Romeo's entry is marked by talk of Cupid, dance, love, questions, masks, dreams, and Mercutio's description of the fairies' midwife Queen Mab, the embroiler and Vice-like character; Romeo is madly in love with 'the fair Rosaline'. At the sight of Juliet he forgets Rosaline. The play moves into the magic of the friar and the earthiness of the nurse, but music and poetry are never far to add to the realm of romantic love. The fate of the star-crossed lovers strikes, however, and the romantic elements assume tragic dimensions. In fact, they complicate rather than resolve the plot; they destroy rather than rescue the heroine in distress.

A Midsummer Night's Dream, however is romantic comedy at its most fantastical. Lovers at court are mirrored by lovers in the land of fairies; Athens is an idealised classical world linked to Elizabethan London only by the stage. The court is balanced in bizarre antithesis by the mad world of the crude mechanicals and all the time the air is full of the strange music of love-talk, bewitchings, complications in love, magical interference, the sweet battle between men and women, music, shape-shifting, masques, a play-within-a-play, potions, song, dance, mysterious woods, incantations, wrong pairings of lovers, and happy resolutions of plot. Here is romantic comedy in its most profuse manifestation. The verse is elevated for the court scenes; the prose is low enough for the mechanicals to try to say what they think they mean. The language of the 'Pyramus and Thisby' play is sufficiently differentiated to mark it off from the other dialogue and yet odd enough for Shakespeare to satirise the literary style of romantic comedy. This play is a consummate piece of artistry where the conventions of romance are used, explored, satirised, and above all enjoyed by artist and player.

The style of romantic comedy is one of exaggeration; it depends for its effect on balance, antithesis, contrast, pace, and sudden movements from one event to another, from one mood to another. It is given to the mechanicals to indicate the method. There are two plays where Shakespeare leaves us some clear indication of Elizabethan dramatic production. One is *Hamlet*, where Shakespeare talks to the players about how they should act parts and present their play to the court, and the other is *A Midsummer Night's Dream*. In fact, from their very first appearance Bottom, Quince, Snug, Flute, Snout and Starveling represent a parody of Elizabethan actors and acting. There is a 'company', a 'script', an 'interlude', a summary of the plot, a *Dramatis Personae*, and a sense of audience:

> let the audience look to their eyes; I will move storms, I will condole in some measure. To the rest: yet my chief humour is for a tyrant. I could play Ercles rarely . . . (I, i.)

The actors divide up the parts, with Bottom claiming the lion's part for himself. Pyramus is assigned to him. In Act III, i, the rehearsal scene becomes interlinked with the fairies' plot, but not before Bottom and his friends have discussed how to mix comedy and tragedy, utter a prologue, write verse, involve the people in the audience, depict moonlight, use and design stage properties, and take up cues. Act IV, ii touches briefly on payments to actors but it is Act V, i where the play of 'Pyramus and Thisby' is put on that shows us more about declamation, interpretation, and the playwright's views about the stupidity of some actors. Above all, the scene is a brilliant parody of the language of earlier romantic comedy:

> O grim-look'd night! O night with hue so black!
> O night, which ever art when day is not!
> O night! O night! alack, alack, alack! . . .
> And then, O wall! O sweet, O lovely wall!
> That stand'st between her father's ground and mine;
> Thou wall, O wall! O sweet, and lovely wall!
> Show me thy chink to blink through with mine eye.

After this, Shakespeare came to *The Merchant of Venice*, where the conventions of romantic comedy are blended in with the main plot of Shylock and the Merchant. The wooing of Portia, the love-lorn Bassanio and the clear-headed heroine, the disguise of Jessica in boys' clothes, magic caskets and incantations, references to masques, music, choice in love, love thwarted, love triumphant, songs, letters (love-letters play important parts in romantic comedy; *cf.* the letter 'found' by Malvolio in *Twelfth Night*), youth, beauty, a clown (Launcelot Gobbo) and old age (Old Gobbo) make up the interwoven tapestry of romance here. Above all, the language is delicately matched to reflect the intrigue of the court scene as well as the idyllic mood of romantic love in the Lorenzo-Jessica scenes, for example. The beauty of the antiphonal 'song' of the lovers lingers long in an audience's memory:

> LORENZO   . . . in such a night
> Troilus methinks mounted the Trojan walls,
> And sigh'd his soul toward the Grecian tents,
> Where Cressid lay that night.
> JESSICA   In such a night
> Did Thisbe fearfully o'ertrip the dew,
> And saw the lion's shadow ere himself,
> And ran dismay'd away.
> LORENZO   In such a night
> Stood Dido with a willow in her hand
> Upon the wild sea-banks and waft her love
> To come again to Carthage.
> JESSICA   In such a night
> Medea gather'd the enchanted herbs
> That did renew old Æson . . .
> I would out-night you, did nobody come.

The court scene in the play is in itself descended from the notion of the medieval debates of the romances, although here it is adapted to the purposes of the main plot.

Much Ado about Nothing has the romantic comedy of the main Hero-Claudio plot echoed by the sub-plot of Beatrice and Benedick. The contrast between youth and age emphasises the qualities of passion and judgement in love but the romantic theme of friendship between Hero and Beatrice and between Claudio and Benedick are emphasised. The device of overhearing and of the embroiler (Don John) are used to advantage and the rustic buffoons of

Dogberry and the Watch have a long tradition in romantic comedy.

As You Like It, however, is the play where Shakespeare takes up the conventions most strongly and uses and adapts them. The banished court with its friendship, disguise, thwarted love, purity, love-letters, magic, rustic settings and its innocence is set against the corruption of court; music, rustic simplicity and love, dance, old age and youth, the wise character, the knock-about humour, the satire on abuses, the language of the proverb and of the lyric all combine to provide a happy issue to all the afflictions. The music, even of simple exchanges in dialogue, stays with an audience:

PHEBE	And I for Ganymede.
ORLANDO	And I for Rosalind.
ROSALIND	And I for no woman.
SILVIUS	And so am I for Phebe.
PHEBE	And I for Ganymede.
ORLANDO	And I for Rosalind.
ROSALIND	And I for no woman.

The masque-like element comes naturally into the play at its ending with the entrance of Hymen to marry the lovers; myth and reality meet in the hymn of rejoicing.

Twelfth Night pursues the element of satire into the convention of romantic comedy. Malvolio, the anti-lover is tricked into becoming the lover of the convention so that the romantic hero can be seen for the ridiculous creature he really is. Moreover, the trick is easily worked on him: the conventions of overhearing, the love-letter, misunderstanding are used against him. Madness is treated in light-hearted fashion, although some think that the treatment of Malvolio goes too far. The haughtiness of Olivia, the frustrations of Orsino, shipwreck, the obvious deception (derived from Roman comedy) that comes about from confusing twins – especially when one is already disguised as a boy, loyal but betrayed friendship, the satire of the knight unable to do deeds of daring, and the Clown who comments sadly on the events – all these combine to form the rich satire on romantic comedy that constitutes this play. The opening speech of the Duke ('If music be the food of love . . .') is in itself exaggerated but the clue to the meaning of the play lies in the words 'so full of shapes is Fancy, That it alone is high fantastical'.

Some of these conventions appear again in *The Tempest*, but here the shipwreck, the banishment of innocence, the disguise, the magical potions and chants, the Clown (Trinculo), usurpation and resolving of brotherly quarrels and the use of fairy-like agents are all supplemented by an elaborate masque and the central character who is a magician. Significantly, the last words of the magician invite the audience in the theatre to release him from his part: 'Let me not . . . dwell In this bare island by your spell'. Reality and romance have become inextricably woven in the magic of the theatre.

5.11 Satirical Comedy
Satire was an essential part of drama in England from its move away from the Church but M. C. Bradbrook (*The Growth and Structure of Elizabethan Comedy*,

1962, and *Shakespeare: The Poet in his World*, 1978) has argued that 'The War of the Theatres' (1599–1601) saw a new phase in the development of the stage which gave a new boost to satirical expression.

A new theatre, the Swan, opened in 1597 with a new play by Thomas Nashe and the young Ben Jonson, *The Isle of Dogs*. This play was thought to contain 'very slanderous and seditious matter' and it was rigorously suppressed by the Privy Council; it has not survived. Jonson was jailed and Nashe fled London. On his release Jonson murdered a former jail acquaintance and was condemned, but, branded with a T (for Tyburn) on his thumb as a final warning, he emerged from prison, now a converted Roman Catholic.

The Privy Council began to regulate the theatres very strictly, allowing one south of the Thames and one north. Francis Langley, who had built the Swan, opened the Boar's Head in Whitechapel with Worcester's Men as his company of actors and the Swan fell into disuse. Other theatres waned until the former Choristers' Theatres at Blackfriars and St. Paul's were revived. The Inns of Court and writers took new critical looks at society, and satirical comment grew in fashion. Jonson's *Every Man in His Humour* was put on in 1598 at the Curtain with Shakespeare in the cast. It was followed by *Every Man out of His Humour*. John Marston of the Middle Temple began to attack Jonson and from 1599–1601 the so-called Theatre War raged between them. At the heart of the conflict were the relative merits of the Poet on the one hand and the Player on the other. The satirical 'war' was played out in the theatre by the child actors, such as the Boys of St. Paul's and the Children of the Queen's Chapel. A. Harbage (*Shakespeare and the Rival Traditions*, New York, 1952) has calculated that three-quarters or so of the plays produced in London between 1599 and 1613 were satires; the rest were tragedies or tragi-comedies. M. C. Bradbrook sees this 'war' as a watershed in the development of comedy in England.

5.12

Ben Jonson's early play *Every Man in His Humour* (1598) set out some of his views about comedy. He intended to show:

> . . . deeds and language, such as men do use,
> And persons, such as Comedy would choose,
> When she would show an image of the times,
> And sport with human follies, not with crimes;
> . . . such errors as you'll all confess,
> By laughing at them, they deserve no less.

Jonson used the division into acts and scenes, becoming popular from the study of Latin drama, and used by John Lyly in *Endimion* and by Marlowe in *Tamburlaine*; he also observed the Unities argued by the Italian Renaissance critics as being classical. The Prologue to the play states his objection to showing the whole life of a man in a single play, or a whole war represented by 'three rusty swords', or a journey abroad in the words of the Chorus, or ridiculous stage effects such as thunder represented by drums rolling, or squibs to frighten the gentlewomen. *Every Man in His Humour* establishes, again in theatre history, the use of 'types' for satirical purposes, the irritable father, the jealous husband, the boastful soldier, the merry magistrate, etc. In the medieval theory of humours man was composed of four humours, hot, cold, wet and dry. When the humours were in balance health came; when they were out of balance sickness struck. If one humour-mix predominated, the character of a person might be melancholic (an established 'type' on the Elizabethan stage: Jacques, Don John, Hamlet) or phlegmatic or sanguine. It will be remembered that Chaucer's Doctor of Physic was particularly skilled in knowing.

    . . . the cause of everich maladye,
    Were it of hoot, or coold, or moyste, or drye,
    and where they engendred, and of what *humour*.

It was only with William Harvey's exposition of his theory of the circulation of the blood to the College of Physicians in 1616 that medicine took a new turn into modern science.

Jonson's satirical comedy would depend, then, on classical models of form, type characters, observing people as they are, and laughing people out of their follies. *Cynthia's Revels* (printed in 1601) satirised some court types, such as the traveller who has drunk at the fountain of self-love (Amorphus) or the foolish young gallant (Asotus); Hedon represents voluptuousness, Anaides impudence, Argurion money, Moria folly, and so on. *Volpone* (acted in 1606) contains the stage miser, the parasite (Mosca), the rapacious opportunist (Corvino), the absurd traveller who wants to sell red herrings in Venice (Sir Politick Would-Be) and the voluble female bore (Lady Politick Would-Be). The names of the cast, as in the old Morality plays, indicate their characters: Volpone (the Fox), Mosca (the Fly), Voltore (the Vulture), Corbaccio (the Crow) and Corvino (the Raven). *Epicoene, or The Silent Women* (1609) has Jonson's satirical purposes at its heart and uses a similar method of characterisation. Dr Johnson thought it the most perfectly constructed of plays. Morose, an old bachelor, hates noise and wants to marry a silent woman. He also disinherits his nephew who he thinks is laughing at him. Cutbeard finds a silent woman, Epicoene (= having the characteristics of both sexes). After the wedding Epicoene, the silent, becomes Epicoene, the garrulous, and in order to rid himself of this noisy wife, Morose offers a large annual allowance to his nephew, who promptly pulls off Epicoene's wig to reveal 'her' as a boy. Other type figures abound: Captain Otter (always corrected by his wife), Sir Amorous La-Foole (a boastful coward) and Sir John Daw (a braggart knight). *The Alchemist* (1610), *Bartholomew Fayre* (1614), and *The Devil is an Asse* (1616) followed. Puritans, pick-pockets, out-of-touch judges, hypocrites, simpletons, bawds, bullies, gamesters, the gullible, 'projectors' all come in for their share of Jonson's satire. The humour depends on the recognition of corruption, deceit, pretence, pompousness, and stupidity; the world seems a dangerous place for the innocent. The sole comfort is that the wicked undo themselves:

                    . . . Mischiefs feed
    Like Beasts, till they be fat, and then they bleed.

                                                                (*Volpone*)

Jonson affirmed his practice in a Prologue to *Epicoene*,

The ends of all, who for the scene do write,
Are, or should be, to profit and delight.
And still't hath been the praise of all best times,
So persons were not touch'd, to tax the crimes
        . . . poet never gain'd
By writing truths, but things, like truths well feign'd.

5.13

John Marston (1575?–1634) quarrelled with Jonson and was attacked by him in *Every Man Out of His Humour, Cynthia's Revels* and *The Poetaster* but later he combined with Jonson and George Chapman to produce *Eastward Ho!* (printed in 1605), played by the Children of the Revels at Blackfriars. Eight lines in the third act offended the court since they were held to be derogatory to the Scots (James I was, of course, James VI of Scotland); the three playwrights were imprisoned for a time. The plot tells of the careers of the hard-working apprentice Golding and the idle apprentice Quicksilver. Their master, Touchstone, has two daughters, modest Mildred who marries Golding and immodest Gertrude who marries the adventurer Sir Petronel Flash. Golding becomes deputy alderman; Quicksilver and Flash fall into bad ways but finally repent. The names of the characters in *Eastward Ho!* indicate their natures: Security, an old usurer; Bramble, a lawyer; Scapethrift and Spendall, gentlemen adventurers; Holdfast, a prison officer; Potkin, a tankard-bearer; Sindefy, a mistress; Mistresses Fond and Gazer, neighbours. The passage in this play which annoyed the court contains a satirical attack on the authorities in England, too; the sea-captain tells all in the tavern:

SEAGULL: You shall live freely there (i.e. in Virginia), without sergeants, or courtiers, or lawyers, or intelligencers; only a few industrious Scots, perhaps, who, indeed, are dispersed over the face of the whole earth. . . . You may be an alderman there and never be scavenger; you may be a nobleman, and never be a slave. You may come to preferment enough, and never be a pandar; to riches and fortune enough, and have never the more villainy nor the less wit.
SPENDALL: God's me! And how far is it thither?

This satirical technique is, of course, that of Sir Thomas More's *Utopia* (1516) where a traveller tells of his adventures abroad in order to comment on the contemporary state of life in England. Swift would use it later to telling effect in *Gulliver's Travels* (1726). The playwrights of *Eastward Ho!* point up their moral at the end:

. . . Now, London, look about,
And in this moral see thy glass run out.

Marston's *Antonio and Mellida* (1602) is in two parts: the first is a satirical romantic comedy. Antonio, son of the Duke of Genoa, loves Mellida, daughter of the Duke of Venice. The two states are at war. Antonio disguises himself as an Amazon and goes to the Venetian court to seek Mellida. The lovers are caught but appear to be forgiven. Part Two immediately becomes a tragedy. Piero kills Andrugio, has Mellida dishonoured, plans to murder Antonio, and wins Andrugio's widow's hand in marriage. Mellida dies of a broken heart. Antonio, driven to revenge by the ghost of his murdered father, disguises himself as a fool and kills Piero. The two parts simply fail to go together in style, character, plot, or mood: one seems a 'Romeo-and-Juliet', thwarted young lovers situation, and the other a typical revenge plot in the style of *The Spanish Tragedy*.

5.14 City and Social Comedy

Part of the reaction against social comedy and part of the move to blend satire and comedy were plays that dealt with the City of London and its social manners and customs. The playwrights whose work may be considered here are Thomas Dekker, Philip Massinger, Thomas Middleton, Thomas Heywood, and Beaumont and Fletcher, although some of Jonson's plays might also have been grouped under this heading.

It was during the Elizabethan and early-Stuart period that England became concerned with increasing economic, industrial, and commercial power. The medieval guilds had lost their religious significance and now increased their economic activities but insisted that they should regulate their own affairs; disputes between masters and apprentices were settled by the guilds. Commercial enterprises began to flourish and trade increased, leading to an established middle-class. Money and gold from the New World began to affect London's trade and its merchants; Drake's return from his third voyage in 1573 showed the wealth that lay abroad for the taking. An increased supply of gold and silver raised prices and the speculator was able to move in to reap profits over the heads of those lower classes who worked for wages. Medieval systems of taxation continued, however, and government finance ran into difficulties. James I made some efforts to deal with coinage but heightened the financial crisis rather than improved it. English trade increased enormously and foreign lands and foreigners received new attention in the literature of the period. Donne's *Songs and Sonnets*, for example, contain many references to journeys and travels, and Shakespeare's plays reflect the new interests in overseas exploration (see E. G. R. Taylor, *Late Tudor and Early Stuart Geography, 1583–1650*). Profits from this new economic activity made a small cross-section of the English population rich, but poverty, disease, and deprivation were rife elsewhere.

Textiles, wool, tin, copper, glass and soap were developed as part of industry, and coal-mining was of immense importance to the country. Monopolies and patents protected the already-rich but a new trading class grew up, open to financiers, merchants, and entrepreneurs. The rich bought land and promptly enclosed it; rents increased and the exploitation of the land for profit began in earnest. Greed, social-climbing, pompously held rights newly acquired, and scheming to get rich constitute the dramatic material used by playwrights, but the act of writing about such topics involves some kind of comment, implicit or explicit, merely in the choice of one set of details rather than another. This comment is the substance of satire.

Luxury, the tricking of heirs and heiresses out of their inheritances, fortune-hunting through marriage, usury, the poor, the imminence of death caused by plague-outbreaks, and the huge economic depression of the 1620s concentrated the minds of the playwrights wonderfully.

The rigid structure of society was insisted upon for stability in the realm. The famous speech of Ulysses in the first Act of *Troilus and Cressida* embodies much of Elizabethan attitudes:

> The heavens themselves, the planets, and this centre
> Observe degree, priority and place,
> Insisture, course, proportion, season form,
> Office and custom, in all line of order. . .
> . . . O when degree is shak'd
> Which is the ladder to all high designs,
> The enterprise is sick. How could communities,
> Degrees in schools, and brotherhoods in cities,
> Peaceful commerce from dividable shores,
> The primogenitive and due of birth,
> Prerogative of age, crowns, sceptres, laurels,
> But by degree, stand in authentic place?
> Take but degree away, untune that string,
> And hark! What discord follows.

'Degree', however, was being challenged. This 'centre' (Earth) was no longer astronomically the centre of the Universe and, as a result, man, who was the centre of the God's creation, became almost overnight – with the rejection of the earth-centred view of the Universe (Ptolemaic) for the sun-centred view (Copernican) – a speck of dust rather than God's magnificent work of art at the heart of things. Harvey's theory about the circulation of the blood propounded in 1616 raised doubts about the uniqueness of man's bodily systems. How did he differ physically from animals? The 'province packed up in two yards of skinne', as Donne called it, needed further exploration:

> Have not all soules thought
> For many ages, that our body's is wrought
> Of Ayre, and Fire, and other Elements?
> And now they think of new ingredients,
> And one soul thinkes one, and another way
> Another thinkes, and 'tis an even lay.
> Knowst then but how the stone doth enter in
> The bladder's cave, and never breake the skinne?
> Know'st then how blood, which to the heart doth flow,
> Doth from one ventricle to th'other goe?. . .
> What hope have wee to know ourselves, when wee
> Know not the least things?

(J. Donne, *The Second Anniversary*)

This was a time of social, economic, political, and intellectual upheaval:

And new Philosophy calls all in doubt,
The element of fire is quite put out;
The Sun is lost, and th'earth, and no mans wit
Can well direct him where to looke for it.

(J. Donne, *The First Anniversary*)

Satire normally requires a stable order, a stable society. In Shakespeare's time the order remained but new developments were coming. By John Donne's time (died 1631) the order was changing. 1642 saw the immense upheaval in the political world in England with the overthrow of the monarch and the start of the Civil War. It is during this period of transition that Thomas Dekker (?1570–1632), Philip Massinger (1583–1640), Thomas Middleton (?1570–1627), Thomas Heywood (died 1580), Francis Beaumont (1584–1616), and John Fletcher (1579–1625) lived and wrote.

5.15

Thomas Dekker was essentially a journalist and a pamphleteer as much as a dramatist. He had an eye for detail, and observed (and categorised) behaviour fills his plays. He has been accused of over-struggling with plot construction and it is true that some of his later plays are overcrowded with complications and intrigues. He was attacked, along with Marston, by Ben Jonson in *The Poetaster* at the start of the Theatre War, and responded in *Satiromastix* in 1602. The play bore the eloquent sub-title of 'The Untrussing of the Humorous Poet', with the play on the word 'humorous', directing it immediately at Ben Jonson. Dekker even dared to use two of the characters from Jonson's satire – Crispinus (Dekker) and Demetrius (Marston) – in his own satirical response. Horace (Ben Jonson) is struggling with a poem on a wedding but he is ridiculed for his dress and vanity and is finally crowned – not with laurels but with nettles. Dekker, unlike many of his contemporary dramatists, was not rich. He had a constant struggle with poverty and went to prison for debt, but his love of London and its people shines through the darkness of his own problems. The satire in his attack on Ben Jonson had been preceded by two comedies *The Shoemaker's Holiday* and *Old Fortunatus* in 1600. In the first play, the jovial, kindly shoemaker, Simon Eyre, becomes the Lord Mayor, but not before love intrigues, disguise and adversity have played their roles in providing comedy. *Old Fortunatus* tells of a beggar who meets Fortune and is offered a choice of wealth, wisdom, strength, health, beauty, long life, or riches. He chooses riches, goes off on a tour of the world, encounters magic in Turkey, where he finds a hat which will allow him to go where he wishes, but Fortune deprives him suddenly of his life.

The loose 'chronicle-type' plot of Dekker's plays, the characterisation by bold, rather than subtle strokes (*e.g.* Simon Eyre's characteristic use of 'Go to' at the end of many of his remarks, and the bumbling, stumbling Hodge), and the sympathetic understanding of London life at all levels mark Dekker's plays, produced with the sharp observation of the journalist. Without necessarily trying to show the world as it was, Dekker reflects London society and its manners.

5.16

Middleton's early comedies, *Blurt, Master Constable* (1602), *Michaelmas Term* (1607), *The Phoenix* (1607), *Your Five Gallants* (1608), *A Mad World, My Masters* (1608), *A Trick to Catch the Old One* (1608), show detachment in the satirical presentation of society, the society found in the tavern and the brothel. The plays are given settings which might be found anywhere, and some of the characters have names according to their 'Morality' type: 'Falselight, Easy, Lucre, Follywit; but Middleton refuses to take sides. He recognises that love and sex are commodities; parasites are part of a society which has chosen one set of values towards the acquisition of wealth rather than another; he saw what was ridiculous rather than what was corrupt. In *A Chaste Maid in Cheapside* (printed 1630), the characters sometimes seem grotesque in the way that clowns are grotesque; the situations are grotesque in the way that music-hall situations are grotesque. Exaggerations, selection, intrigue and contrived complications give both a bizarreness to the action (for example, Moll and Touchwood Junior rising from their coffins), and an impact to the satire in order to expose. Both the dramatist and the audience can detach themselves from the action and yet remain part of it as human beings and members of society. Middleton's plots are intricately constructed and easily manipulated with considerable force and liveliness.

5.17

Philip Massinger was a sound constructor of plots and one of the playwrights who was becoming increasingly interested in psychological confrontation. The use of character to motivate plot is less important than the presentation of the character in a dramatic manner. His stage directions are usually very precise and indicate exactly how an actor was to portray a part. Massinger, after all, had become the main dramatist working for the King's Men after the death of John Fletcher in the plague of 1625.

His best known comedy is *A New Way to Pay Old Debts* (1625). Sir Giles Overreach, a character based on the historical extortioner Sir Giles Maupesson, treats his prodigal nephew Frank Wellborn, whose property he has managed to acquire, in a shameful manner. A widow of some wealth, Lady Allworth, offers to help Frank by suggesting she was ready to marry him and immediately Overreach changes his attitude to his nephew. Tom Allworth, Lady Allworth's stepson, and Margaret, Overreach's daughter, are in love, but her father plans a 'higher' marriage to Lord Lovell. The plot becomes more elaborate until Overreach is driven mad and sent to Bedlam. Wellborn receives a commission, the young lovers marry, and Lord Lovell and Lady Allworth are wed. The plot is intricate with one character interacting with another and one pair of characters interacting with another. Confrontation, deceit, and some other minor 'Morality' characters appear: Greedy (a hungry Justice of the Peace), Marrall (a parasite), Order (a steward), Amble (an usher), Furnace (a cook), Watchall (a porter), Tapwell (an alehouse keeper) and Willdo (a parson). Tapwell's wife is called Froth!

This was, after all, the age when **characters** became a minor literary genre with books such as *Microcosmographie* by John Earle (1628) which included sketches such as 'A modest man', 'A poor man', 'An upstart Knight' and 'A plodding Student'; Bishop Hall's *Characters of Virtues and Vices* (1608) and Sir Thomas Overbury's *Characters*, written by Overbury himself and others, including the playwright John Webster. In *Characters* there appears 'A Character of a Character' and the following three meanings are offered: 'a deep impression'; 'an impress or short emblem, in little comprehending much'; 'a picture (real or personal) quaintly drawn in various colours, all of them heightened by one shadowing'. This view of 'character' is seen in much of the comedy of the period. The study of 'characters' might have arisen following a new interest in the work of Theophrastus of Lesbos (371–287 BC), a pupil of Aristotle, whose work was translated into Latin by Isaac Casaubon in 1592, which was translated into English by John Healey a year later. Certainly there are some 'character-type' descriptions to be found in Jonson's *Every Man in His Humour* and in Webster's *The White Devil* (1608) when Vittoria asks, 'Whore! What's that?', Cardinal Monticelso quickly replies,

Shall I expound whore to you? Sure, I shall;
I'll give their perfect character. . .

and he does so by painting a 'character' in the tradition of Theophrastus.

Now comedies, and tragedies too for that matter, turned increasingly towards this kind of interpretation of character, where the action depended not so much on the revelation of character but on the confrontation of one psychological 'character', clearly delineated, with another psychological 'character', just as clearly delineated.

Massinger, in many ways, looks forward to the kind of play found later in the period, particularly in tragedy, than to the earlier period, but he is a Janus-like figure, facing both backwards and forwards in his conception of plot, satire, and character. L. C. Knights has described him as 'the last of the Elizabethans' (in *Drama and Society in the Age of Jonson* 1968, 298), whilst Una Ellis-Fermor judged that 'the greater part of Massinger's work belonged in date and in spirit to a later age' (than the Jacobean) (in *The Jacobean Drama*, fifth edition, 1965, x).

5.18

Thomas Heywood (died 1650) was at one time a member of The 'Lord Admiral's Company' and at another a member of 'The Queen's Players'. Kathleen McLuskie in 'The Plays and the Playwrights: 1613–42' (in *The 'Revels' History of Drama in England*, IV, 1613–1660) has suggested that in Heywood's plays 'the tension between old and new in Stuart drama is perhaps best illustrated'. She pointed out that the two parts of *Fair Maid of the West* were written twenty years apart: Part One (1597–1610) deals with Bess's virtue and courage and is 'robust, episodic', fast-moving, with dialogue switching quickly from blank verse, colloquial speeches to high-flown verse, and with dumb-shows and chorus to speed the plot; Part Two (1630) deals with sexual passion and revenge and is concerned with absolute standards of love and humour.

The psychological tension (*cf.* Massinger) is there; soliloquies emphasise doubt and complex emotional reactions are explored.

Heywood's earlier plays certainly deal with the startling adventures of familiar 'types' or 'characters'. Often he has not a single hero but several (*e.g. The Four Prentices of London*), and deals with the situation of a 'prodigal' character faced with a choice. His plays sometimes have contrived plots, since they have to deal with surprise, several characters, and difficult choices; his success depended on his ability to weave plots and then to resolve them.

John Webster saw Heywood, along with Dekker and Shakespeare, as being prolific and spoke of their 'right happy and copious industry'. He is best known today, perhaps, for *A Woman killed with Kindness* (1631). In the first of these two plays, Anne, the 'perfect' wife is found by her husband Frankford, a country gentleman, in the arms of Wendoll, an ungrateful profligate. She repents and is forgiven by her husband before dying from remorse! *The English Traveller* (1623) is a romantic comedy dealing with plot and counterplot in love; although the heroine of the play dies at the end, the sub-plot is a 'prodigal' play based on Plautus's *Mostellaria*, where a father returns from a voyage only to discover that his prodigal son has wasted his father's goods but is prevented from knowing the truth for a time because of the machinations of a servant.

A word needs to be said about Heywood's defence of his profession in an elaborate work, *Apology for Actors* (written about 1608 and published in 1612). He reminded preachers such as William Crashaw (Richard Crashaw's father) that Christ and his Apostles had not attacked the *ludi* of the Romans and, by reiterating the arguments of the humanists against the Puritans, pointed out that, whilst deploring abuses of morality on the stage, many of his colleagues in the theatre were men 'of substance, of government, of sober lives and temperate carriages . . .'; he deplored the growing tendency of some to attack, through the theatre, 'the state, the court, the law, and the city'. This contribution defending the actors against the continuing onslaught from the Puritans is interesting in the struggle which would culminate in Prynne's *Histriomastix* (1633) which set out the Puritan arguments at length and led to the closing of the theatres once the Long Parliament took control of the country. (At the Restoration the stage of Heywood's period was seen as a model of decency and order, as E. K. Chambers has pointed out in *The Elizabethan Stage*, I, 263).

5.19 Collaboration

G. E. Bentley (in *The Profession of Dramatist in Shakespeare's Time*, 1590–1642, Princeton, 1971, 199) has calculated that 'as many as half of the plays by professional dramatists in the period 1599–1625 incorporated the writing at some date of more than one man'. The demand for drama productions required the constant supply of new plays, and collaboration between authors was one of the ways of meeting this demand efficiently. Sometimes plots were based on topical scandals or trials (see *The 'Revels' History of Drama in England*, IV, 1981, where it is pointed out that both *The Jeweller of Amsterdam* (1617) by Fletcher, Field and Massinger and *Sir John van Olden Barnaveldt* (1619) by

Fletcher and Massinger were based on the Dutchman's trial and execution).

The best collaboration resulted in a coherent play rather than what Una Ellis-Fermor has termed 'stage joinery'. Normally, playwrights would agree to write specific acts or specific scenes within an overall plan. Sometimes this worked well and sometimes left loose ends in the plot, as in *Love's Pilgrimage* (1616) by Fletcher (with Beaumont, perhaps).

The Witch of Edmonton (1621?) provides an excellent example of successful collaboration, in this case between Dekker, Ford, and Rowley. The printed quarto version of the play published in 1658 describes the play as 'A known True Story. Composed into a Tragi-Comedy by divers well-esteemed Poets, William Rowley, Thomas Dekker, John Ford, &c'. Critics have tried to disentangle the various contributions of the three main writers:

> The business of the Witch, the rustic chorus, and certain other parts mark themselves out as mainly Dekker's. The conception of Sir Arthur Clarington and the subsidiary domestic plot is no doubt mainly Ford's. Rowley's share is more difficult to ascertain. The intimate collaboration of all three can alone be held accountable for some of the scenes and indeed in even the passages most characteristic of any one of the authors, the touch of another often shows itself in a chance word or phrase.
>
> (Ernest Rhys, *Thomas Dekker*, 1949)

Modern scholarship is less hesitant. Kathleen McLuskie (*The 'Revels' History of Drama in England*, IV, 1613–1660, 1981):

> There are three distinct actions involving different sets of characters, but since each is concerned with the effects of evil forces their juxtaposition creates a cross-current of irony which is no less powerful for being fortuitous. The Devil appears in each action in the figure of a black dog, but the device is treated in different ways by each dramatist. . .
> *Rowley's* part in the play deals with Cuddy Banks. . . he asks the witch to make Katherine Couter fall in love with him but he is ducked in the river by a spirit resembling Katherine; Banks tries to cajole the dog (the Devil). *Dekker* treats witchcraft with serious psychological attention; the dog is linked with a miser, 'this black cur' who is a bloodsucker. In *Ford's* plot Frank Thorney carries full moral responsibility for murdering his bigamous wife, Susan, but the Black Dog none the less appears at the crucial moment, seeming to precipitate the almost casual violence of the action itself.

The Witch of Edmonton was based on a pamphlet written by Henry Goodcole in 1621 about Elizabeth Sawyer, late of Islington, executed in 1621 for witchcraft. Its authors leave the audience in no doubt about the subject of the play, even before the plot begins.

> Forced marriage; murder blood requires:
> Reproach, revenge; revenge hell's help desires.

The integration of the plots lies in the theme of witchcraft and its symbolism. The sudden surprise or shock when the Black Dog first speaks to Mother Sawyer comes after a slapstick, knockabout scene with Morris Dancers and the cursing of the miser by the old lady. The Devil claims her for his own by sucking blood, ironically the very feature she had just been complaining about in the miser's behaviour. He engineers the ducking of Cuddy Banks and ties up Frank after the murder of Susan to help him avoid being accused of the deed. The Dog reappears in another Morris Dancers' scene and jumps from farce to tragedy and back to farce again – but the Constable is on the track of the 'murderers'. All the time the interweaving of prose with verse provides both pace and a texture to the play; the prose diverts and amuses but the verse advances the serious action, and yet all the time there is a grotesque brooding sense of evil in the form of the talking Black Dog. A good example of the transition from prose to verse comes at the start of Act IV. Ann's entry into the plot as a madwoman, bizarre as it is, is heightened by a return to prose. Cuddy Bank's description of the Dog in negatives illustrates the way evil operates negatively in Elizabethan and Tudor drama (see, for example, the number of times 'No', 'Nothing', 'Never' occur in *King Lear* or in one of Webster's tragedies). Susan re-enters the play first as a spirit and then as a body. At the end the Witch recognises the Dog as 'a lying spirit', but he betrays her to her enemies. The themes of the Witch's Familiar, the shape-shifting, the evil, the madness, the dissembling come together at the end. Evil is punished and the audience must 'make of all the best'.

Thomas Dekker collaborated extensively with other dramatists. For example, he wrote *Patient Grissell* (1600) with Chettle and Haughton; *Sir Thomas Wyatt* (1602) with Webster and possibly with Chettle, Heywood, and Smith; *The Honest Whore* (1604) with Middleton; *Westward Ho!* (1604) with Webster; *Northward Ho!* (1605) with Webster; *The Roaring Girl* (1610) with Middleton; *The Virgin Martyr* (1602) with Massinger; and *The Sun's Darling* (1624) with Ford.

In comedy and romantic comedy, however, the collaboration of **Francis Beaumont** (1584–1616) and **John Fletcher** (1579–1625) is probably the best known but amongst the hardest to disentangle. Their collaboration began about 1608 and lasted for about four or five years. E. K. Chambers argued that Beaumont was the ruling spirit, and their collaboration covered plays not only for the Queen's Revels but also for the King's. Beaumont and Fletcher seemed to have shared a house together, but in 1613 Beaumont married an heiress and began to withdraw from the stage. Fletcher at that time wrote plays independently and looked for others with whom to collaborate (The Elizabethan Stage, III, 216–17).

Fletcher's work in comedy has the stock figures of the period; the hypocrite, the miser, the Jewish usurer, the boasting soldier and the comic madman, often the victims of love which throws men into melancholy and sadness. The study of melancholy is one, of course, well examined in Shakespeare (Jaques, Hamlet, Don John, and Malvolio) and one which was boosted later in the period by Burton's *Anatomy of Melancholy* in 1621. There are the distraught lovers rendered speechless, in Fletcher's plays, the rivalry of young men in search of the same girl, contests, disguises, the dressing-up of men as girls and girls as men. Beaumont (and Fletcher?) in an address to the readers of *The Knight of the Burning Pestle* wrote: 'the author had no intent to wrong any one in this comedy, but as a merry passage here and there interlaced with delight, which he hopes will please all and be hurtful to none'. This, then, was the aim – not to satirise but to delight, not to instruct but to give pleasure. It runs counter to Plato and to Sidney (*An Apologie for Poetry*) but ensured success on the stage. Nevertheless, at the heart of *The Knight of the Burning Pestle* are still the implicit comments on the new citizen's longing for a romanticism, which would lead to the ridiculous, and the boastfulness of the city's train-bands, a precursor of the Home Guard, also made famous in another form of drama centuries later – *Dad's Army.*

5.20   The Development of Tragedy

The development of tragedy in the English theatre has its roots in the Morality play of medieval times. The link between the early form of tragedy and that of Elizabethan and Jacobean times is to be clearly seen in **Christopher Marlowe's** *Doctor Faustus*, probably first performed in 1588.

The story of a man who sold his soul to the Devil became linked with the name of a Dr Faustus who was a necromancer in the sixteenth century. *Volksbuch*, published first in Frankfurt in 1587, was translated into English and the story it contained of Faust was entitled 'The History of the Damnable Life and Death of Dr John Faustus'. Marlowe follows the translation for his plot but the mere magician becomes in Marlowe's play the embodiment of man's search for omnipotence. The Renaissance man's thirst for knowledge grafted on to medieval Man's search for salvation is corrupted by the deadliest of sins, Pride, and so brings Dr Faustus to his fate. The danger of 'over-reaching' was recognised in Elizabethan times; man still had his assured place in God's Universe; a little lower than that of the angels but at the centre of God's creation (see, however, pages 114–115).

The struggle of Faustus for knowledge in Marlowe's play corresponds to Medieval Man's struggle for Salvation. Pride and the Seven Deadly Sins try to lure him away from repentance or second thoughts; philosophy, the balm of Renaissance humanism, has led Faustus deliberately to reject God's salvation since death would come to all with an inevitability not to be denied. As Everyman and Mankind found themselves faced ultimately with an open, yawning grave, so Faustus finds himself confronted with the Hell, medieval in its flames and torments, that his own arrogance has created; but unlike Everyman and Mankind he calls on God's mercy too late:

See, see, where Christ's blood streams in the firmament!
One drop would save my soul, half a drop: ah, my Christ!

God, however, cannot forgive the sin of Pride, since this is the sin of the Devil himself. Faustus's demands for omniscience set himself up as God and this breaks the First Commandment.

The story has Hell's mouth, the Devil as torturer, a Good Angel, a Bad Angel, Devils, Lucifer, Beelzebub, Scholars, an Old Man (Old Age), and a Clown – all characters familiar to the audiences of Morality plays. The Chorus, imported from the Classical tradition, even utters the Moral, so often in earlier days left to God himself:

Faustus is gone: regard his hellish fall,
Whose fiendful fortune may exhort the wise,
Only to wonder at unlawful things,
Whose deepness doth entice such forward wits
To practise more than heavenly power permits.

The argument, then, rests on God's pre-ordaining of order in the world – degree, in fact. To challenge the *macrocosm* (God's order in the universe) led to disaster; the Elizabethan playwrights would also show in their tragedies and histories that to challenge the microcosm (God's order in the world/state) would also lead to disorder. To challenge one was to challenge both.

Dr Faustus is, of course, much more than a medieval Morality play. Its central character is developed; the action takes place in the mind rather than on the stage; the figures are Renaissance in spirit rather than medieval; the symbolism runs beyond the allegory of the narrative into the very imagery of the play. The plot is well and closely engineered to keep the confrontation of Faustus with himself, his friends, his education, his society, his values, his fears, his hopes, his ambitions, his Devil, and his God, central to the dramatic presentation. The scene is Faustus's study (mind), but the crowns, the physical beauty, the rich apparel, the singing of the Dirge (ironically from the Latin word 'direct', *dirige*), the cup, the book, the bell, the candle, the horns, are the appurtenances of imagination, religion, sexual desire, and intellect.

Just as Tamburlaine tries (and fails) to find his personal salvation through political and military power, and Barabas (in *The Jew of Malta*) tries to find it through riches (and fails), so Faustus tries to find it through knowledge (and fails). Where lies man's hope, then? One answer comes at the very end of Webster's *The Duchess of Malfi* (printed in 1623):

Integrity of life is fame's best friend,
Which nobly, beyond death, shall crown the end.

This was the Jacobean 'moral' – but it is a long way from God's mercy as the sole (Augustinian) way to salvation found at the end of *Mankind*:

Mankend ys wrechyd; he hath sufficyent prowe;
Therefore God kepe you all *per suam misericordiam*.*

Webster's 'moral', however, is not so far from that of *Everyman*:

And he that hath his accounte hole and sounde,
Hye in heven he shall be crounde.

Poor Faustus! 'But Faustus' offence can ne'er be pardoned: the serpent that tempted Eve may be saved, but not Faustus'. The despair, the blackness, the waste, the futility of man in his tragic world were assured.

* Through his mercy

5.21

But where did tragedy begin in British drama? Most find a convenient start in Thomas Norton's (1535?–1601?) and Thomas Sackville's (1536–1608) *Tragidie of Gorboduc or of Ferrex and Porrex* (acted before the Queen's majesty in 1561). The 'argument' of the tragedy is given in a preface:

Gorboduc, king of Brittaine, divided his realme in his lifetime to his sonnes, Ferrex and Porrex; the sons fell to discention; the younger killed the elder; the mother, that more dearly loved the elder, for revenge killed the younger; the people, moved with the crueltie of the fact, rose in rebellion and slew both father and mother; the nobilitie assembled and most terribly destroyed the rebels; and afterwardes, for want of issue of the prince, whereby the succession of the crowne became vncertain, they fell to ciuill warre, in which both they and many of their issues were slaine, and the land for a long time almost desolate and miserably wasted.

Here, then, in one play are found the ingredients of many later English 'tragedies': the premature division of a kingdom; brotherly envy and rivalry; fratricide; revenge; insurrection; rebellion; the nobles in the battle for succession; the problems of the rightful succession to the throne; civil war; and tragic waste.

The setting of a play in early Britain, the foolish division of the kingdom, rivalry between children, parental fury, insurrection, the quarrelling over succession and civil war are, of course, themes in Shakespeare's *King Lear*; Kenneth Muir (*The Source of Shakespeare's Plays*, 1977) has acknowledged that some critics have seen Shakespeare's debt to *Gorboduc*.

Nearer its own time, *Gorboduc*, was both praised and condemned by Sir Philip Sidney in *An Apologie for Poetry* (published 1595); the critic condemned English tragedies and comedies for

observing rules neither of honest civility nor of skilful poetry, excepting *Gorboduc*, . . . which notwithstanding, as it is full of stately speeches and well-sounding phrases . . . full of notable morality, which it doth most delightfully teach . . . yet in truth it is very defectious in the circumstances, which grieveth me, because it might not remain a model of all tragedies. For it is faulty both in place and time, the two necessary companions of all corporal actions. For where the stage should always represent but one place, and the uttermost time presupposed in it should be, both by Aristotle's precept and common reason, but one day, there is both many days and many places inartificially imagined. But if it be so in *Gorboduc*, how much more in all the rest?

English tragedy came at once under the influence of Seneca following Jasper Heywood's translation of *Thyestes* in 1560; later in the same decade Seneca's other tragedies were translated and all of the works were published in translation by John Newton in 1581 (see page 68).

Seneca's influence resulted, in the English theatre, in crude sensationalism manifested in melodramatic action; horrors of a crude kind; the use of long, narrative speeches; the introduction into the dialogue of 'sententia' or moral tags; the insistence on scene divisions; the introduction of ghosts and choruses

124 Drama and Theatre Arts

into many plays; the popularity of revenge themes; the use of 'stichomythia' or rapid exchange of dialogue; the concentration for tragedy on high, noble figures; and the facing of death immovably.

In *Gorboduc* the plot is divided into acts and scenes; there are moral tags; revenge is a main theme; and there is a steadfast facing of death. But the play also contributed to the development of English drama by introducing: 'dumb shows' where forthcoming action would be shown or present action would be commented upon; conventional characters, *e.g.* the parasite; a symmetry in the balancing of characters against each other; and, above all, the use of bank verse in drama, self-conscious as it is with its frequently end-stopped lines. (The Earl of Surrey (1517?–47) had already used blank verse in poetry in his translation of *The Aeneid*, Books II and III.) The play's descriptions are better than its dramatic presentation of action and there is more character revelation than character development in the play. With the exception of Porrex, perhaps, the characters remain static. The length of many of the speeches would strain a modern audience and cause problems for a director bent on action.

5.22

Cambises (1569) by Thomas Preston (1537–98) is less restrained. The title page to the printed edition reads:

> A lamentable tragedie* mixed full of plesant mirth, containing The Life of Cambises, King of Percia from the beginning of his kingdome, vnto his death, his one good deede of execution, after that many wicked deedes and tyrannous murders, committed by and through him, and last of all, his odious death by Gods justice appointed.

The Prologue takes the audience through the details of the plot. The interest of the play in the development of the drama lies partly in the fact that it was obviously designed for performance by a travelling troupe of professional actors, six men and two boys. The thirty-eight characters are divided up on the title page of the original edition and beside each grouped division appears the direction 'For one man'. There are eight divisions, six for men and two for boys (Meretrix, Shame, Otian, Mother, Lady, Queene; Young Child, Cupid). The characters are so carefully arranged that only one character from any single group appears on the stage at any one time.

The play is also interesting as it would have aroused Sidney's condemnation; he thought absurd plays which were 'neither right tragedies nor right comedies; mingling kings and clowns, not because the matter so carrieth it, but thrust in clowns by head and shoulders to play a part in majestical matters, with neither decency nor discretion' and so a 'mongrel tragi-comedy' is obtained; '. . . the whole tract of a comedy should be full of delight, as the tragedy should be still maintained in a well-raised admiration'.

Cambises shows the influence of Seneca but it goes far beyond the Roman for its horrors: Cambises's lord is flayed alive: 'Pull his skin over his eares to make his death more vile'; Cambises shoots a child for target practice and then has its

---

* There is a running title, however, 'A Comedie of King Cambises'!

heart cut out in front of the father. Even Ambidexter, the Vice-like character in the play (see pages 93–94), finds some difficulty in commenting on Cambises's acts when he enters immediately after the horrific scenes. Interwoven with this bloodthirsty wallowing in horror (which cannot easily be shown on the stage without risking the audience's laughter!), there is the pathos of the young child's comments before his death and his mother's lament after it. The play is full of long sermons as part of the didacticism of Tudor drama ('poetry should both teach and delight'), and allegorical figures of the Morality type: Councell, Attendance, Diligence, Preparation, Commons Cry, Commons Complaint, Triall, Proof, Execution, Cruelty, Murder, etc. The theme of the play is the abuse of authority, just as the theme of Skelton's *Magnyfycence* was kingly magnanimity (see pages 88–89). The staging is crude, since the play lurches forward through a series of incidents, and the verse is clumsy, in the form of heavy rhyming couplets. (Shakespeare mocked the verse in *1. Henry IV*, II, iv: 'I must speak in passion,' laughed Falstaff, 'and I will do it in King Cambises' vein . . . Here is my speech. Stand aside nobility.') The play of *Cambises* is not divided into acts. W. T. Jewkes (*Act Division in Elizabethan and Jacobean Plays 1583–1616*, 1958) has shown that about ninety per cent of plays put on in the private theatres between 1583 and 1616 were divided into acts, but only eighty per cent of public-theatre plays were so divided. After about 1607 act-division became much more common, and by 1616 it was the rule rather than the exception. He concludes that inter-act music common in private playhouses must have spread to the public playhouses. It is interesting, however, that the Senecan division (and ultimately Aristotelian) is found in the earliest English tragedy *Gorboduc* but not in *Cambises*, produced only a decade or so later. The comedies, *Gammer Gurton's Needle* (acted in 1553) and *Ralph Roister Doister* (before 1541) were, however, divided into acts and scenes.

Finally, it should be mentioned that *Cambises* introduced to the English stage a device that is still used as an essential part of filming Westerns:

CRUELTY   Even now I strike, his body to wound.
          (*Strike him in divers places.*)
          Beholde, now his blood springs out on the ground!
          (*A little bladder of vineger prickt.*)

Perhaps, today, the vinegar would be replaced with ketchup!

5.23

R. B's **Apius and Virginia** (*c.* 1565) is very primitive in its form but, as a very early tragedy, it is particularly interesting for three reasons. First, it has the character of Haphazard who is a 'Titivillus' character (see pages 94–95), whose words gush out in wild profusion:

Yea, but what am I? A scholar, or a schoolmaster, or else some youth?
A lawyer, a student, or else a country clown?
A broom-man, a basket-maker, or a baker of pies,
A flesh- or a fish-monger, or a sower of lies?

A louse or a louser, a leek or a lark?
A dreamer, a drommel, a fire or a spark? . . . etc.

One is reminded of the machine-gun rattle of some parts of the libretto in a Gilbert and Sullivan operetta. Secondly, the plot of *Apius and Virginia* deals with the abuse of a ruler's power. Virginia, a beautiful young girl, is desired by the judge Apius, who manipulates the law so that she must be his. Virginia pleads with her father for death rather than dishonour at the hands of a man she does not love. Some have seen similarities between this plot and Shakespeare's *Measure for Measure* but it is now held by scholars that Shakespeare probably derived his plot material from Cinthio's *Hecatommithi* (1565), in which he also found the story for *Othello*. Thirdly, the allegorical treatment of Morality themes creaks ominously in this play when Apius is besieged by temptation and cries out, 'How am I divided!' At this point Conscience and Judgement crawl out from his robes. The incident contains dramatic surprise, but the humour of the audience at such a delicate point must have been hard to control.

5.24 The Concept of the Tragic Hero

Aristotle had argued that 'tragedy is the imitation of an action that is serious, has magnitude, and is complete in itself; in language with pleasurable accessories (music and metre), each kind brought in separately in the various parts of the work; in a dramatic, not in a narrative form, with incidents arousing pity and fear, with which to accompany its *catharsis* (purging) of such emotions' (*The Poetics*, Chapter Six). He pointed out that every tragedy had six parts: plot, character, diction, thought, spectacle, and melody. It is an imitation not of persons but of action and life, of happiness and misery. Character in a play, he said, was that which revealed the moral purpose of the persons doing the action – their will. This is most easily revealed by placing a character in a position where the choice of alternative actions is not easy; *e.g.* Antigone has to choose between obeying the state which forbade her burying her brother or her own sense of duty towards her family which required her to bury him.

For Aristotle, tragedy must avoid three kinds of plot: (*i*) a good man must not pass from happiness to misery; (*ii*) a bad man must not pass from misery to happiness; (*iii*) an extremely bad man must not be seen falling from happiness to misery since these will not move us to pity or fear. Pity comes from observing undeserved misfortune and fear, only if the disaster happens to someone very like ourselves. The tragic hero, then, ought to be

a man not pre-eminently virtuous or just, whose misfortune, however is brought upon him not by vice and depravity but by some error of judgement, he being one of those who enjoy great reputation and prosperity: e.g. Oedipus, Thyestes.

The hero must have some defect (**hamartia**: a fatal flaw), moral or intellectual, which gives rise to a disastrous action; he makes 'a tragic mistake'; King Lear is a good example of this kind of hero.

To the medieval scholar, the concept of tragedy was different from that of the Greeks. Tragedy meant a narrative rather than a play. *The Monk's Tale* (Chaucer) narrated a series of 'tragedies', the stories of the fall of famous men, Lucifer, Adam, Hercules, Samson, Nebuchadnezzar, King Peter of Spain, etc. At the end of this series of calamities, Chaucer defines tragedy: it can do nothing else except lament that Fortune will strike down the unwary, particularly if they are proud:

Tragediës noon oother maner thyng
Ne kan in syngynge crie ne bewaille
But that Fortune alwey wole assaille
With unwar strook the regnes that been proude;
For when men trusteth hire, thanne wol she faille,
And cover hir brighte face with a cloude.

Therefore, for Chaucer, the story of *Troilus and Cresseid* was a tragedy; he calls it 'my little tragedy' (*litel myn tragedye*) and in it Fortune plays the major role as Troilus is brought to disaster. Of the Biblical characters, **Job**, approximates closest to the concept of the medieval tragic hero. He was a man 'perfect and upright, one that feared God and eschewed evil'. His servants are killed, his sheep are consumed in fire, his camels are stolen, his sons and daughters are destroyed, he is afflicted with boils 'from the sole of his foot unto his crown' but *he still held his integrity*. Job was not to blame for his afflictions but it was his manner of bearing them that was important.

Throughout medieval drama, however, mankind becomes the central tragic hero who has to face affliction and finally death. But here he is shown as being responsible for his actions; he remains not the passive sufferer but fights back against those afflicting him. He defends himself and is defended, but his adversaries, and the last enemy, Death itself, finally push him into his grave. But hope remains with the Resurrection and God's mercy. In *Gorboduc*, Porrex is a wicked man who kills his own brother (*cf.* Cain) and so triggers off a whole cycle of revenge killings; he is neither a Greek nor a medieval tragic hero. *Cambises* is an evil man who deserves the dreadful fate he meets but in Aristotelian terms his death would provoke neither pity nor fear. In *Apius and Virginia* the central character is not a 'good' man.

By the Elizabethan age the concept of 'the tragic hero' was being revised. The huge changes that had come about in man's view of himself and his relationship to God, to the world, and to his fellow human beings because of humanism, the growth of philosophy, the influence of the Italian Renaissance, the Reformation, travel and new geographical discoveries, and the development of science – particularly astronomy and medicine, had led him to look again at his predicament as a physical, moral, and spiritual being. The frequent outbreaks of the Plague had made him only too aware of his mortality. The feudal system and the growth of the autocratic ruler had raised new doubts about social justice. The firm insistence that man had a definite choice to make about good and evil, God's grace and the Devil, meant that he had to become the master of his own salvation. One thing was certain: he would suffer and the only explanation he could find for the cause of suffering lay in the exploration of sin as a force and in his own responsibility for it. Therefore 'integrity' become an important concept.

Marlowe's heroes, Tamburlaine, Faustus and Barabas were prepared to surrender their integrity willingly in order to have power. Macbeth, too, surrenders his own peace to follow the path of ambition. But characters such as Hamlet, Othello and Lear have their peace taken from them and their own integrity as human beings is challenged, either by thoughts of duty and revenge, or by overpowering love that turns to jealousy, or simply by the foolish act of giving one's children everything. In making the choice, all the characters show they are flawed, that they do have a crack in their natures (*hamartia*) which makes them make a wrong choice *in a given situation*.

The situation is important and the circumstances in which the choice has to be made are crucial. If Hamlet, who procrastinates too long after the Ghost's true reports and provokes the final tragedy, had been in the place of Othello, who responds too precipitately to Iago's false reports and causes the final catastrophe, neither tragedy would have come about. The interaction between 'character' and 'situation', therefore, is important. There is no character *on its own* which is tragic; there is no situation *on its own* which is tragic. Only when the potentially tragic character finds himself in the potentially tragic situation does the catastrophe occur. What, of course, leads to this concurrence of tragic forces is still to be debated. In medieval and in Elizabethan times the goddess *Fortune* would have been held responsible.

The image of Fortune as a wheel was common by Shakespeare's day:

> Out, out, thou strumpet Fortune. All you gods,
> In general synod take away her power;
> Break all the spokes and fellies from her wheel
> And bowl the round nave down the hill of heaven
> As low as to the fields.

> (*Hamlet*, II, 2,489–93)

Fluellen explained that Fortune is turning and is inconstant:

> Fortune is painted plind, with a muffler afore her eyes, to signify to you that Fortune is plind; and she is painted also with a wheel, to signify to you, which is the moral of it, that she is turning, and inconstant, and mutability, and variation: and her foot, look you, is fixed upon a spherical stone, which rolls, and rolls, and rolls.

> (*Henry the Fifth*, III, 6, 31–8)

This was the kind of picture frequently depicting Fortune found in the emblem books so popular in the seventeenth century (see Francis Quarles *Emblems*, 1635; Rosemary Freeman, *English Emblem Books*, 1948).

Elsewhere Fortune appears as a tide (*Julius Caesar*), a star (*Hamlet*), a whore (Webster), and an archer (*Hamlet*); Fortune could so easily intervene in life that character and situation are helpless. Examples in Shakespearean tragedy where the hero is helpless to resist Fate's intervention are when Desdemona drops a handkerchief given her as a love-token and Emilia, Iago's wife happens to find it and innocently passes it on to her husband (*Othello*); or when Friar John, carrying a message to Romeo which would have averted the tragedy, was sealed up in a house of plague where he had come by chance and so could not deliver the letter. These incidents in tragedy come about not through character but through Fortune; then the plot unfolds and the catastrophe follows inexorably. (*cf.* The letter in Hardy's *Tess of the D'Urbervilles* which is caught under a mat and not discovered until after the final calamity.)

The Fall of Man was primarily responsible for the power of Fortune over man; until that point he had had free choice; after that point he had to bear its blows and survive the best he could. He could not, however, abrogate his final responsibility:

> The fault, dear Brutus, is not in our stars,
> But in ourselves.
>
> > (*Julius Caesar*)

For Shakespeare, the tragic hero was *a man of status*, often a prince, a general, a king, an empress, or of similar high birth; the low-born may die but theirs is not the essence of tragedy. He usually has a tragic flaw (*hamartia*): 'vaulting ambition' (Macbeth); 'thinking too precisely on the event' (Hamlet); jealousy (Othello); love which excludes everything else (Antony and Cleopatra); the failure to see the nature of one's own children (Lear). Only the lovers in *Romeo and Juliet* are defeated through being 'star-cross'd'. *His is a world of conflict*, both internal and external; many of his comments are concerned with the nature of this conflict; he is isolated and becomes increasingly so; at the end of *Macbeth*, the hero has lost everything – wife, possession, and hope itself. Death, after all, is the one human experience that we all must face alone; birth is a shared experience, but death is an individual, lonely one. *The Shakespearean hero knows himself better* by his experiences; he undergoes a voyage to self-knowledge. The most he can hope for is to retain his integrity; after all, this is the one thing that a person can retain, since nobody can rob him of it unless he willingly gives it up. His is not the Wordsworthian experience of

> . . . poor humanity's afflicted will
> Struggling in vain with ruthless destiny

but the triumphant declaration of human integrity and triumph over the worst that the world can do. In *King Lear* the tragic situation moves from one of being

> As flies to wanton boys are we to the gods;
> They kill us for their sport

to one where they can be defied to do their worst:

> . . . let fall
> Your horrible pleasure; here I stand, your share,
> A poor, infirm, weak, and despis'd old man.
> But yet I call you servile ministers.

Even Macbeth, deprived of everything, fights to the end:

> And damn'd be him that first cries, 'Hold, enough'.

The tragic hero (or heroine), as the ruler, distances himself (or herself) from the rest of the actors; it is from this kind of treatment that the feeling of isolation comes. It is not without some dramatic purpose that the hero is frequently surrounded by comparatively minor characters at the moments of their deaths: Hamlet, Antony, Cleopatra, Macbeth, and Lear die amidst such characters and are raised to a higher level as a result. In *Henry V* the king's stature grows as he moves amongst the ordinary soldiers. This is a dramatic device well recognised on the Elizabethan and Jacobean stage. Vittoria Corombona dies, like Cleopatra, with her maid, Zanche, in *The White Devil* by Webster. In *The Duchess of Malfi*, the Duchess is strangled along with her maid, Cariola, and her children.

If the tragic hero is a villain, then he is motivated by one of four passions: *ambition, lust, jealousy*, or *greed*. The Elizabethans and Jacobeans were not particularly concerned with subtle analyses of motives. Shakespeare certainly tries to explain why his major characters behave as they do and when he has to admit that some are activated by 'motiveless malignity', as in the case of Iago, he recognises it by offering explanations of jealousy, or lust, or frustrated ambition. But usually the medieval 'type' figure takes over; he is judged by what he does rather than what he says. Tamburlaine rages on in his actions driven by lust; Barabas plots for greed; Dr Faustus over-reaches through ambition; Richard III plots for greed and ambition; Ferdinand (in *The Duchess of Malfi*) acknowledges that he is motivated by greed; and Angelo (in *Measure for Measure*) acts out of ambition. The villain-hero is often characterised by what the Elizabethans saw as a defect: Barabas is a Jew; Aaron, a Moor; Richard III a cripple; and Edmund a bastard. In *Othello* Shakespeare inverts the role of the Moor and makes him the good hero; in *The Merchant of Venice* Shylock, the Jew, is shown as the persecuted as well as the persecutor. Usually, however, outside Shakespeare, the hero, good or bad is an easily recognisable type-character who does not develop, although he may change. In later plays, in the Jacobean period, the minor characters, too, assume Morality type-casting, just as the braggart soldier (Pistol) or the hostess (Mistress Quickly), or the loyal friend (Horatio) or the bumbling counsellor (Polonius) or the loyal courtier (Kent) or the embroiler (Don John in *Much Ado about Nothing*) had appeared in Shakespeare. Characters elsewhere – in *The Revenger's Tragedy* (1607), for example – carry names that would not have seemed out of place in Morality plays: Lussurio, Spurio (a bastard), Ambitioso, Supervacuo, Vindice. The same form of characterisation was noticed earlier in the satirical comedy of the period, especially in Ben Jonson's plays (see pages 110–111).

The hero is often seen as one extreme side of the spectrum, black or white. If he is too black he could be hissed and jeered; Hieronimo in *The Spanish Tragedy*, or Titus Andronicus, or Bosola in *The Duchess of Malfi*; if he or she (and often such a character is a woman) is seen as too white, he or she is seen as the sufferer in the wicked world: Cordelia, Desdemona, and Ophelia may be seen as such types. Sometimes both black and white appear in one character but then the halves are usually kept distinct, as in the case of Vindice in *The Revenger's*

Tragedy. The game of black/white is worked out in Middleton's play *A Game At Chess* (1624) where the characters are chess pieces and

The White Knight, with wit-wondrous strength
And circumspective prudency,
Gives check-mate by discovery
To the Black Knight . . .
Plain dealing thus, by wisdom's guide,
Defeats the cheats of craft and pride.

5.25

The Machiavellian hero is of a special kind, however. Niccolo di Bernardo dei Machiavelli (1469–1527) was a statesman and politician in Florence. He was suspected of being involved in a conspiracy against the Medici and exiled. He wrote *The Prince* in 1513, which examined the concept of producing a united Italy, an ideal not achieved until the time of Garibaldi (1807–82) with the 'Risorgimento'. It was not translated into English until 1640 but a selection of the book was translated into French in 1576 by Gentillet, who also attacked Machiavelli. This work was translated into English in 1602 and it was from this translation that the dramatists of the period derived their ideas about Machiavelli. One writer, however, Hardin Craig, in his edition of *The Prince* (*Il Principe*, 1944), has argued that a version in English was known in England before 1585, at least in manuscript.

The end of the sixteenth century was one full of political uncertainty; Machiavelli's views about man's basic wickedness, the role of religion to keep citizens subservient, and the cruelty needed to enforce the will of the state were emphasised and the need for a firm ruler who was scrupulously just was missed. All of this was to be applied to the Italian political situation. Transplanted into England it became a creed of violence, ruthlessness, oppression, scheming and plotting, and cruel disregard of the rights of others. Rulers mislead, murder, and seek vengeance in the cruellest ways; everything can be justified if it results in power.

Thomas Kyd's *The Spanish Tragedy* (acted 1592, printed 1594) is usually seen as the first exploration of the Machiavellian Law in English drama. The play is set in the context of the victory of Spain over Portugal in 1580. The plot is one of love, jealousy, hatred and murder. Hieronimo, the Marshal of Spain, seeks vengeance on the murderers of his son by putting on a play, in the course of which the villains are discovered and killed, and Hieronimo first bites out his own tongue to avoid confessing his crimes and then commits suicide. The play has a dumb show, a Ghost and a character called Revenge, both of which act as a Chorus to comment on the action. The foes of the Ghost are pursued into Hell by Revenge so that their punishment can be made eternal.

Christopher Marlowe's characters, however, emphasised the essential futility and emptiness of the pursuit of material gain at all costs and the emptiness of soul that such a pursuit leads to, especially when it is coupled with ruthlessness and violence. The despair and frustration that ends the pursuit is its own punishment as both Faustus and Mortimer find:

Base Fortune, now I see, that in thy wheel
There is a point, to which when men aspire,
They tumble headlong down: that point I touch'd,
And, seeing there was no place to mount up higher,
Why should I grieve at my declining fall?

(Mortimer, Edward II)

After Marlowe, others, but not Shakespeare, explored this power-seeking, materialistic 'politician' character which perverted the true Machiavellian doctrine. D'Amville in *The Atheist's Tragedy* (printed 1611) represents the frustration of the man who has trusted Nature rather than God. After a rebuke from a Doctor about his mistake in placing his trust in the wrong things, D'Amville cries:

Now to myself I am ridiculous.
Nature, thou art a traitor to my soul.
Thou hast abused my trust. I will complain
To a superior court to right my wrongs.
I'll prove thee a forger of false assurances.
In yon Star Chamber thou shalt answer it.
 . . . O the sense of death
Begins to trouble my distracted soul.

The Marlovian hero, seeing Death and trying to repent, is not so far away.

John Webster gives the fullest presentation of the Machiavellian hero since Marlowe. Flamineo (*The White Devil*, printed 1612) and Bosola (*The Duchess of Malfi*, printed 1623) have human chinks in their politician's armour. Flamineo's death speech is memorable for his regret and the lines:

My life was a black charnel. I have caught
An everlasting cold.

Bosola dies 'in a mist':

We are only like dead walls or vaulted graves,
That ruined, yield no echo . . .
        O this gloomy world!
In what a shadow, or deep pit of darkness,
Doth womanish and fearful mankind live.

Antonio at the beginning of *The Duchess of Malfi* set out the ideal for a Prince:

. . . a prince's court
Is like a common fountain, whence should flow
Pure silver drops in general, but if't chance
Some cursed example poison't near the head,
Death and diseases through the whole land spread.
        . . . Here's the Cardinal.

The Cardinal is the epitome of 'the Machiavellian hero'. He speaks of Bosola as the ideal spy and recognises Antonio as being 'too honest'. His speeches are 'studied', he lusts after Julia, he dissembles, he bribes, and 'he's nothing else but murder', as Bosola describes him. Bosola wants to repent ('O Penitence, let me truly taste thy cup') but the Cardinal drives on ruthlessly, though he cannot overcome his despair:

> I am puzzled in a question about hell:
> He says in hell there's one material fire,
> And yet it shall not burn all men alike.
> . . . How tedious is a guilty conscience!
> When I look into the fish-ponds in my garden,
> Methinks I see a thing armed with a rake,
> That seems to strike at me.

A minor character utters the last comment on the Cardinal:

> PESCARA   How fatally, it seems, he did withstand
> His own rescue.

Perhaps Flamineo, the politician, (in *The White Devil*) best sums up the role of Jacobean 'Machiavellian heroes':

> We are engaged to mischief, and must on:
> As rivers to find out the ocean
> Flow with crook bendings beneath forcèd banks;
> Or as we see, to aspire some mountain's top,
> The way ascends not straight, but initiates
> The subtle foldings of a winter snake;
> So who knows policy and her true aspèct,
> Shall find her ways winding and indirect.

5.26   The Treatment of the Revenge Theme

A number of plays during this period showed blood, horror, and very violent scenes on the stage. They are usually divided, sometimes arbitrarily, into 'Revenge Plays' and 'Horror Plays'.

The Revenge Plays include Kyd's *The Spanish Tragedy* (1592), Shakespeare's *Titus Andronicus* (1594) and *Hamlet* (1601), Henry Chettle's *The Tragedy of Hoffman* (1602), George Chapman's *The Revenge of Bussy D'Ambois* (printed 1613), Beaumont and Fletcher's *The Maid's Tragedy* (1619), *Cupid's Revenge* (1612), and *Thierry and Theodoret* (1621), Webster's *Appius and Virginia* (*c.* 1609), and Tourneur's *The Atheist's Tragedy* (1611) and *The Revenger's Tragedy* (1607).

In these plays revenge makes up the main action of the play. Often they contain ghosts which appear to urge on the protagonist to avenge the murder or crime against someone close to him and usually he hesitates for a number of reasons before moving into revenge; sometimes he feigns madness or is threatened by madness. Part of the action is often taken up with the attempts of the criminal to avoid the vengeance with which he is threatened. Above all revenge should not be used merely to provide the dénouement to a plot in Act V; it is the essence of the whole action.

Quite often the plays include the following elements: accomplices to help the revenger; the death of the revenger at the moment of his success; and deaths of the most horrible kind. These plays, too, particularly in the later period, proceed by a series of scenes rather than a continuous, smoothly related plot; one scene may show static characters set off in relation to each other and the next the same characters (or others) turned and shown off to reveal a changed relationship to each other. The action progresses, therefore, rather as if the spectator is walking through a picture gallery of characters; he or she makes the connection between one portrayal of an action and the next. The pictures are linked by the characters but depict a part of the action discrete in itself. This view of the construction of Webster's plays is explored fully in Una Ellis-Fermor's *The Jacobean Drama*, fifth edition, 1965, 38 *ff*. *Hamlet* differs from the rest, perhaps, in that the central character does develop in the course of the action, but the play contains many of the elements found in the traditional revenge play.

A look at the two Shakespearean Revenge Plays will show how Shakespeare used and developed the theme. *Titus Andronicus* (1594) is now thought to have been written after *Richard III* and *Romeo and Juliet*, but it is one of Shakespeare's early plays. Titus Andronicus is the Roman General fighting against the Goths. After defeating his enemies, in vengeance for the death of his sons, he has the eldest son of Tamora, Queen of the Goths, hacked to pieces and burnt:

> Alarbus' limbs are lopp'd
> And entrails feed the sacrificing fire.

Tamora, therefore, has cause for revenge and delivers Lavinia, Titus's daughter, to be raped by her sons; her hands are cut off and her tongue cut out so that she could not report who has deflowered her:

> She hath no tongue to call, nor hands to wash;
> And so let's leave her to her silent walks.

Titus's sons are arrested by the Emperor on suspicion of murdering his brother; Aaron, the Moor, persuades Titus to have his hand cut off to secure their release, but Titus merely receives their heads in return. Titus, not unnaturally, becomes distraught; his brother, Marcus, remonstrates:

> . . . see, thy two sons' heads,
> Thy war-like hand, thy mangled daughter here;
> Thy other banished son, with this dear sight
> Struck pale and bloodless; and thy brother, I,
> Even like a stony image, cold and numb.
> Ah! now no more will I control thy griefs.
> Rent off thy silver hair, thy other hand
> Gnawing with thy teeth . . .
> Now is a time to storm; why art thou still?

Lavinia reveals to her father the names of her ravishers, writing them in the dust with a staff held in her mouth and guided by the stumps of her arms. 'Mortal revenge' is now assured. Tamora gives birth to a black child which she sends by a nurse to its father Aaron to be killed. Aaron kills the nurse instead. A Clown enters the action, to lighten it before the final revenges. Aaron is arrested by Titus's forces and makes a full confession of all the Goths' crimes and his own to Lucius, Titus's son. Titus takes Tamora's rapist sons and cuts their throats in front of Lavinia, who collects their blood in a basin. Titus cooks and feeds their flesh to their mother (*cf.* Atreus's serving of Thyestes's two sons to their father in Greek tragedy) after killing his own daughter to free her of shame; Titus kills Tamora and is in turn killed by Saturninus. Lucius kills Saturninus and then is declared Emperor; Aaron is punished in the penultimate speech of Lucius:

> Set him breast-deep in earth, and famish him;
> There let him stand, and rave, and cry for food:
> If any one relieves or pities him,
> For the offence he dies.

Tamora's body is thrown 'to beasts and birds of prey' and, in the best of tragic traditions, Lucius sets about restoring peace to the state:

> Then, afterwards, to order well the state,
> That like events may ne'er it ruinate.

This horrific drama is difficult to produce today, merely because of its horror. The play contains most of the elements of the Revenge Play, with the notable absence of the ghost. Revenge is the motivation; the characters barely develop but respond to each other and events in predictable fashion. The innocent, (Lavinia, *cf.* Desdemona, Ophelia, Cordelia) are swept away as part of what A. C. Bradley (*Shakespearean Tragedy*, 1911) called 'tragic waste'; at the end of the play order in the state is restored, just as Fortinbras restores it in *Hamlet*, Lodowico (with others) in *Othello*, Caesar in *Antony and Cleopatra*, Edgar, Kent and Albany in *King Lear*, and Malcolm in *Macbeth*.

Hamlet is a more mature revenge play. Some see close resemblances between it and John Marston's play, *Antonio's Revenge* (1602), which formed the second part of the *History of Antonio and Mellida*. Both Shakespeare's and Marston's plays have ghosts that visit sons of fathers murdered by poison and mothers who become lovers of the assassins. The sons have sweethearts whose chastity is doubted, both fall into melancholy and feign madness, both lose the opportunity for early revenge, both see the ghosts of their fathers again in their mothers' bedrooms. Both plays have the voices of ghosts beneath the stage and both include dumb shows. The Arden edition of *Hamlet* (ed. Harold Jenkins, 1982) pursues these and other comparisons further. Jenkins has concluded that Marston knew *Hamlet* and drew extensively on it; this evidence would mean that the Shakespeare play must have antedated Marston's and so the date of *Hamlet*, originally thought to be 1603, can be pushed back to a performance possibly before the end of 1599 and certainly by 1600.

This important, new edition of *Hamlet* (*The Arden Shakespeare*) contains a very full history of the play and its analogues, as well as critical sections on 'the embroilment', 'melancholy', and 'the delay'. It also points out (pages 142–3) that the play contains a second revenge plot, that of Laertes against Hamlet for the death of Ophelia. This complication was, of course, one used in *Titus Andronicus*, where there were at least three revenge plots led by Titus, Tamora, and Aaron.

In *Hamlet* the first scene opens with a report of the Ghost's appearance, seen by four very ordinary, sane young men. The Ghost's appearance is linked with potential disorder in the state, just as ghosts ran through the streets of Rome before Caesar's murder. Its appearance heralds upheaval in the state, the threat to the natural order of things (see page 114). Even before seeing the ghost, Hamlet is filled with resentment towards his mother and hatred of his uncle, but the word 'revenge' is not used even when the Ghost has appeared to Hamlet and narrated the details of the murder. Even then revenge, at first, is only hinted at:

> But howsomever thou pursuest this act,
> Taint not thy mind . . . Remember me.

Hamlet decides 'to put an antic disposition on', and realises that he has to set right the time which is 'out of joint'. The play proceeds a long way with the King's counterplot against Hamlet, the introduction of the Players. The word 'revenge' first occurs in Hamlet's soliloquy at the very end of Act III ('O what a rogue and peasant slave am I!'):

> This is most brave,
> That I, the son of a dear father murder'd,
> Prompted to my **revenge** by heaven and hell,
> Must like a whore unpack my heart with words
> And fall a-cursing like a very drab.'

His excuse is that he needs 'grounds more relative' than those of a ghost. The word occurs again as Hamlet is contemplating killing his uncle at prayer but hesitates:

> Why this is hire and salary, not **revenge**.

The central speech in the play on the theme of revenge occurs in Act IV, iv:

> How all occasions do inform against me,
> And spur my dull **revenge**.

There Hamlet surveys his reasons for revenge and concludes the speech with a decision to act. In contrast with Hamlet's hesitation and delay, Laertes's return is full of action and thoughts of vengeance:

> . . . I'll be **revenged**
> Most thoroughly for my father.

Hamlet's 'antic disposition' is balanced against Ophelia's having been 'driven into desp'rate terms'. The King's counterplot takes in Laertes after the failure of that involving Rosencrantz and Guildenstern. It is left to the King to voice Hamlet's problem, whilst considering his own:

> That we would do,
> We should do when we would . . .
> **Revenge** should have no bounds.

The irony is considerable.

Not until Act V, ii does Hamlet summarise his reasons for revenge:

He that hath kill'd my king and whor'd my mother,
Popp'd in between th'election and my hopes,
Thrown out his angle for my proper life
And with such coz'nage – is't not perfect conscience
To quit him with this arm?

Laertes, dissembling, is reconciled to Hamlet before the fencing bout but admits his desire for revenge:

I am satisfied in nature,
Whose motive in this case should stir me most
To my **revenge**.

The play ends with

. . . carnal, bloody, and unnatural acts
Of accidental judgments, casual slaughters,
Of deaths put on by cunning and forc'd cause,
And, in this upshot, purposes mistook
Fall'n on th'inventors' heads.

Nevertheless, the play is not one of fate and chance but rather one of character. The revenge theme in *Hamlet* is constantly present, implicit in both words and actions.

5.27 The Dramatic Use of Violence and the Macabre

The tragedies of this period are shot through with violence and, at times, also the macabre. This is of two kinds: the physical and the mental. The plays containing such horror are many; for example, Shakespeare's *Titus Andronicus*; Philip Massinger's *The Duke of Milan* (1623), *The Roman Actor* (1629), *The Virgin Martyr* (with Dekker, 1622), *The Unnatural Combat* (1639); Thomas Middleton's *The Changeling* (with Rowley, 1623), *Women Beware Women* (printed 1657); John Ford's *Love's Sacrifice* (1633), *The Broken Heart* (1633), *The Lover's Melancholy* (1629), *'Tis Pity she's a Whore* (1633); James Shirley's *The Maid's Revenge* (1626), *The Traitor* (1631), *Love's Cruelty* (1631), *The Cardinall* (1641); Sir John Suckling's *Brennoralt* (1646); and Sir William D'Avenant's *The Cruel Brother* (1630). Other horrors occur in John Webster's and Cyril Tourneur's plays.

In *The Spanish Tragedy* (Thomas Kyd, *c.* 1585) Horatio is stabbed and hanged; Hieronimo goes mad and bites out his tongue. In *Titus Andronicus* Lavinia is raped and has hands and feet cut off; Titus cuts his own hand off. In *The Changeling* a group of madmen shout inanities; De Flores stabs Alonzo in a frenzy of killing and cuts off a finger; the madmen dress as birds and animals; De Flores gives Alonzo's finger and ring to Beatrice. In *The Revenger's Tragedy* Vindice carries a skull 'dressed up in tires' and poisons the lips of the skull which destroys the Duke as he kisses them. D'Amville in *The Atheist's Tragedy* strikes out his brains on the scaffold (Exeter says, 'In lifting up the axe, I think he's knocked his brains out'!). In *The Duchess of Malfi* Julia is poisoned by kissing a book, the Duchess and Cariola with her children are strangled on stage, and madmen dance about uttering a bizarre chant as they galumph around 'to a dismal kind of music'. In *The White Devil* Flamineo appears 'a politic madman', Camillo has his neck broken while jumping a vaulting horse, Isabella dies kissing a poisoned picture, Brachiano is poisoned with a helmet he cannot remove and later his ghost enters carrying a pot of lily flowers and a skull, and most bizarre of all, Flamineo, whom everyone thinks dead, leaps up again to deal with his tormentors:

> . . . I am not wounded;
> The pistols held no bullets: 'twas a plot
> To prove your kindness to me.

Even *King Lear* has its terrifying moment of Gloucester's blinding on stage:

CORNWALL To this chair bind him . . .
　　　　　Upon these eyes of thine I'll set my foot . . .
REGAN　　One side will mock another; the other too.
CORNWALL　　. . . Out, vile jelly!
　　　　　Where is thy lustre now?

There were terrifyingly realistic murders of Beech 'a Chaundler and his boy' by Merry on August 23, 1594 in Thames Street, shown in *Two Lamentable Tragedies* by Robert Yarrington (1601) along with 'a young childe murthered in a Wood by two Ruffins with the consent of his Vncle'. M. C. Bradbrook (*Themes and Conventions in Elizabethan Tragedy*, second edition, 1980) points out that:

> there was a dumb show of particular horror known as 'the bloody banquet' (*The Battle of Alcazar* *, Act IV, Prologue; *A Warning for Fair Women*†, Act III, Prologue; *The Bloody Banquet*, Act V, Prologue). It was rather like a Thyestean feast: the table was set with black candles, drink set out in skulls and the Furies served it up.

There is no doubt that the horrors were realistically depicted on the stage. M. C. Bradbrook (*op. cit.*) says that bladders of red ink and animals' blood were used to simulate human blood. There were property heads and property hands (needed in *Selimus*, *Titus Andronicus*, and *The Duchess of Malfi*).

The real difficulty with horror on the stage lies in the fact that it is most effective when it comes after some build-up and when it comes rarely. (See how Alfred Hitchcock prepares his audience for the horror of the killing in the shower and the discovery of the old woman's grinning corpse in his film *Psycho*.) If horror is to follow horror in rapid succession it needs to be arranged in a series which escalates rather than diminishes tension. It is dangerously easy for a horror production to make an audience giggle uneasily and then explode in laughter as a form of self-defence.

Much has been written about the daily horrors of Elizabethan England.

---

* By George Peele (*c.* 1589).
† By William Aspley (1599).

There were complaints that low people visited theatres with running sores; there are two records of public executions outside 'The Theatre' in 1588 (see E. K. Chambers, II, 396); plague with its horrific physical symptoms was common; and hanging, drawing, and quartering of traitors still took place in public – in John Marston's *The Fawn* (*c.* 1606) there is a reference (Act IV, i) to 'a woman that . . . gives two crowns for a room to behold a goodly man three parts alive, quartered, his privities hacked off, his belly lanched up'.

Sometimes the horror is at its most effective when it carries a symbolism that can be readily understood. The Elizabethan audience was prepared to accept the allegory in disguise – madness or old age or risen ghosts represented by costume. It was only a further step to recognise the significance of Tamora and her sons in their disguises of Revenge, Rapine, and Murder in *Titus Andronicus*, or the colours of the costumes in *A Game At Chess* or the bell carried by the executioners who come to deal with the Duchess of Malfi and Cariola. The blinding of Gloucester in *King Lear* has been represented by some as the not-seeing of Edmund's true nature (Gloucester was punished physically because he had sinned physically in creating a bastard) just as Lear had not seen the true nature of Goneril and Regan; that part of the play was concerned with physical, mental, and even spiritual blindness.

Nevertheless, the main function of violence and the macabre was to provide the dramatic impact of spectacle and shock; if they could provide allegorical meaning, too, so much the better. The theatres and the actors were well-equipped to make the experience of violence and the macabre as realistic as possible. Ghosts moved below the stage, blood was seen to flow, murders, rapes, and mutilations occurred before the audience. Some things, Shakespeare at least realised, were more effectively done off-stage, *e.g.* the drowning of Clarence in the butt of malmsey (*Richard III*), the flogging of Thydeus (*Antony and Cleopatra*), and the beheading of Macbeth's corpse. The play was too often, perhaps, centred on the stage instead of in the minds and imaginations of the audience.

5.28   The Treatment of Historical Events

Interest in history that mounted during the sixteenth century was essentially political in its origin. In about 1501 Polydore Vergil was commissioned to write a history of England in order to establish once and for all the right of the Tudors to the throne. His work, published in 1534, *Anglica Historia*, did not achieve what it set out to do and throughout the century attempts to set out the record accurately continued. The Wars of the Roses, the struggle between York (the white rose) and Lancaster (the red rose) divided the country from 1455 to 1485, when Richard III was defeated at Bosworth Field and Henry VII ended the war by uniting the two houses with his marriage to Elizabeth of York. The interest in history, political as it was, had the effect of producing a mass of information on which the dramatists of the later part of Elizabeth's reign, including Shakespeare, could draw. In 1563 John Foxe wrote *The Book of Martyrs*, in 1565 John Stow produced *A Summarie of Englyshe Chronicles*, and in 1577 Raphael Holinshed published his important *Chronicles of England*,

Scotlande and Irelande. For the official Tudor view in 1548 Edward Hall's *The Union of the two Noble and Illustre Famelies of Lancastre and Yorke*, which was based on Polydore Vergil's work, was published posthumously.

John Skelton's play *Magnyfycence* (1519) (see pages 88–89) had stressed the duty of kings to be magnanimous and had allowed him to satirise corrupt manners at court, particularly the policies of Cardinal Wolsey. John Bale's **Kynge Johan** (*c*. 1536, but revised during the reign of Edward VI and rewritten in 1561 for Elizabeth) is usually considered the first English history play. This play contains mostly stock Morality figures, apart from King John himself: Sedicyon (also Stevyn Langton) Nobylyte, Clergye, Cyvyle Order, Dissymulacyon, Usurpid Power (also The Pope), Privat Welth (also Cardynall Pandulphus), Treason Commynalte, Veritas, Imperyall Majestye, and The Interpretour. A major source of the material in the play was William Tyndale's *Obedience of a Christian Man*, 1528, which showed the oppression of the Papacy and was a strong Reformation document.

Widow England is tyrannised by the Church and asks Johan for help. Johan is advised, attacked, and supported by the allegorical characters and he supports Scripture against the Pope. In the end the virtuous characters, such as Veritas, win and Dissymulacyon is condemned to be hanged. The duty of the King directly to God was stressed essentially to establish Henry's political independence as an English ruler, freed from Papal and foreign influence.

Gorboduc has already been considered (pages 123–124) as part of the development of tragedy in England. It is also, of course, a history play along Morality lines. **Cambises** shows how God will destroy tyrants who neglect or abuse their peoples (pages 124–125).

E. M. W. Tillyard (*Shakespeare's History Plays*, 1947) argued that Hall propounded views of history which Tillyard called 'The Tudor Myth'. This combined two conceptions of English history to support Henry VII's claim to the throne: that the claim to the throne went back to King Arthur, through Welsh ancestry, who would return one day to usher in a new golden age; that the claim showed God's intervention in history to end the evils which had begun with Henry Bolingbroke's usurping of Richard II's throne and brought about the terrible civil wars between York and Lancaster. Shakespeare's *Richard II*, the *Henry VI* plays, and *Richard III* trace this history of disaster, relieved for a time only by *Henry V* against foreigners and the growing success of Bolingbroke in quelling rebellion at home in *Henry IV*.

Shakespeare presented the horrors of civil war and implicitly pointed out what would happen if the old dissensions broke out again on the death of Elizabeth.

At the heart of 'The Tudor Myth', as Tillyard pointed out, was the concept of order in the universe, an order based on hierarchies, either seen as vertical in their arrangement, running downwards from the God-Sun-King set of 'correspondences', or arranged horizontally but also running downwards through a series of planes, 'the divine and angelic, the universe or macrocosm, the commonwealth or body politic, man or the microcosm, and the lower creation. The order in the state duplicated the order in the universe (*macrocosm*). God 'assigned kings, princes with often governors under them, all in good and necessary order' (*Homily of Obedience* in a 1547 book of Homilies). This is the order referred to in Ulysses's speech in *Troilus and Cressida* (see page 114). The King is like 'the glorious planet Sol' that 'corrects the ill aspects of planets evil' (see E. M. W. Tillyard, *The Elizabethan World Picture*, 1943). To challenge the King's place was therefore, by implication, to challenge God's divine order. This would lead to chaos and conflict as Sir Thomas Elyot in the *Governor* (1531) pointed out:

> Take away order from all things, what should then remain? Certes nothing finally, except some man would imagine eftsoons chaos. Also when there is any lack of order needs must be perpetual conflict . . . Hath not God set degrees and estates in all his glorious works? First in his heavenly ministers, whom he hath constituted in divers degrees called hierarchies . . . Behold also the order that God hath put generally in all his creatures, beginning at the most inferior or base and ascending upwards.

This clear statement by Elyot (quoted by Tillyard) sets out the view that chaos would come from overthrowing God's divine order – either in the Universe (the Devil's intended purpose) or in the state (rebellion's intended purpose). Spenser took a softer view, provided the order changed gradually: 'All that moveth doth in change delight' and a fixed order 'is contrare to mutability'; but mutability may rage now, though Nature would ultimately provide an eternal stability.

In terms of drama, the nature of kingship and the state occupied Tudor, Elizabethan, and Jacobean dramatists – especially the nature and duties of a ruler or prince. Skelton's *Magnyfycence*, *Cambises*, Machiavelli's *The Prince*, and the plays of the Jacobean tragedians all examine the qualities of kings and those in ecclesiastical or civil power. In Shakespeare's plays there is the very clear principle propounded that usurpers or their immediate successors cannot benefit from challenging the established order. Henry Bolingbroke's descendents pay sorely for his usurpation of Richard II's throne; Richard III cannot maintain his unlawful claims; Macbeth cannot survive after murdering Duncan in Macbeth's castle 'in double trust':

> First, as I am his kinsman and his subject,
> Strong both against the deed . . .
> > > Besides this Duncan
> Hath borne his faculties so meek, hath been
> So clear in his great office, that his virtues
> Will plead like angels trumpet-tongued against
> the deep damnation of his taking-off.

(I, vii)

In *Hamlet* Claudius cannot survive after having murdered the King and usurped his throne. The conspirators who murdered Julius Caesar are doomed from the moment of their challenge to the state. In *King Lear* the old King tried to pass on his powers to his children but still wanted to keep some vestige or sign of his authority. Mistaken as he was, Goneril and Regan had no right to wrest

142 Drama and Theatre Arts

even that from him and it was ignominious that a foreign power, France of all countries, should have to intervene to restore order. This was the real political danger to Elizabethan England, of course, that foreign intervention in England's affairs, repulsed very dramatically once with the Armada, might be tempted to exert itself again.

The clearest exposition of 'The Tudor Myth' comes in Shakespeare's presentation of kingship in **Richard II**. Here was a King, weak and delicate but nevertheless the lawful King. He tries to put down the conflict between Bolingbroke and Mowbray by exile. Gaunt expresses the view that England is paradise:

> This royal throne of kings, this scepter'd isle,
> This earth of majesty, this seat of Mars,
> This other Eden, demi-paradise,
> This fortress built by Nature for herself
> Against infection and the hand of war,
> This happy breed of men, this little world,
> This precious stone set in the silver sea . . .
> This blessed plot, this earth, this realm, this England.

(Act II, i)

The land, then, is inseparable from kingship. When Bolingbroke challenges the natural order, then the divine claims of the King must be stated and restated. The Bishop of Carlisle reassures Richard as his kingdom starts to crumble:

> . . . that power that made you king
> Hath power to keep you king in spite of all.

Richard states the belief in the Divine Right of Kings:

> The breath of wordly men cannot depose
> The deputy elected by the Lord.

The unlikely, high-blown, exaggerated, allegorical, language of the gardeners (in Act III, iv) provides a commentary on the King's duty to lop off unruly branches, to exterminate the caterpillars of the commonwealth, to govern the garden of England. Even after he has been deposed, Richard compares Bolingbroke with Judas, although he is forced to renounce his vows:

> For well we know, no hand of blood and bone
> Can gripe the sacred handle of our sceptre,
> Unless he do profane, steal or usurp.

The belief is restated quite categorically that:

> Not all the water in the rough rude sea
> Can wash the balm from an anointed king;
> The breath of worldly men cannot depose
> The deputy elected by the Lord.

Balanced against this view of 'order' in the creation during this period was the emerging Renaissance view of man, governed by reason, as a creature who can change things by struggling towards freedom. The 'mutability' in

Spenser's view of the Universe can lead to liberation. Man was seen as having a part to play in his situation and must accept the consequences of his actions. This is the Marlovian view of the creation. Tamburlaine boasts, and uses the imagery of the other 'fixed' view of the universe:

> I hold the Fates bound fast in iron chains,
> And with my hand turn Fortune's wheel about;
> And sooner shall the sun fall from his sphere
> Than Tamburlaine be slain or overcome.

This is the view of man in command of his own salvation, a presentation not vastly out of keeping with that of the 'colossus' Antony, in Shakespeare's *Antony and Cleopatra*, who lives, reasons, judges, and pays for his actions. 'Nature' would take over from 'order' in the Renaissance universe:

> Nature, that fram'd us of four elements
> Warring within our breasts for regiment,
> Doth teach us to have aspiring minds:
> Our souls, whose faculties can comprehend
> The wondrous architecture of the world,
> And measure every wandering planet's course,
> Still climbing after knowledge infinite,
> And always moving as the restless spheres,
> Will us to wear ourselves, and never rest,
> Until we reach the ripest fruit of all,
> That perfect bliss and sole felicity,
> The sweet fruition of an earthly crown.

Faustus, too, has to accept his own part played in his own damnation: 'God forbade it, indeed; but Faustus hath done it'.

The interpretation and presentation of historical events during this period must been seen in the light, then, of these two views of creation and the universe: 'order' and 'nature and mutability'.

The developing sense of growing nationhood under Elizabeth with England's defeats of foreign enemies and their 'knavish tricks', the wealth coming from the newly-established colonies, and the new discoveries, is expressed in plays such as *Henry V*. There the battles of Harfleur and Agincourt show in detail the parts played by the ordinary soldiers as well as the nobility; their contribution is well-acknowledged by the King as he moves amongst them. The play also shows the coming together of the Scotsman, the Welshman, the Irishman and the Englishman into a common nation. Historical events have to be seen in this light. Moreover, foreigners are to be viewed with suspicion, especially Italians (see the plays of Webster), who might easily be connected with Machiavellian politicians. Spain, too, is often seen as the background of intrigue and murder.

Parallels between plots and historical events have been seen by critics. Kathleen McLuskie (*The 'Revels' History of Drama in English*, IV, 1981) has shown that Massinger's *The Maid of Honour* (1621) deals with the refusal of Roberto, King of Sicily, to help Urbino against the Duchess of Sienna, just as

James I refused to aid Frederick of Bohemia, his son-in-law in the Thirty Years War. Similarly, Massinger's and Fletcher's *Sir John van Olden Barnaveldt* (1619) dealt with rebellion in Holland and refers to 'that bloody Powder-Plot' hatched in England by the Roman Catholics. The censors watched plays carefully. Jonson was imprisoned for what was thought a slight on the King and Scotsmen in *Eastward Ho!* (1605 – a very sensitive year!). References to houses shut by the Plague (*Romeo and Juliet*), the still-vex'd Bermoothes or the islands of Bermuda in Sir Thomas Gate's expedition (*The Tempest*), the uprising of Perkin Warbeck at the court of James IV of Scotland (Ford's *Perkin Warbeck*, 1634), the continuous attack on Spain (Middleton's *A Game At Chess*, 1624), the surge of so-called pamphlet plays in 1647–49 (*e.g. The Levellers Levelled*, 1647; *Crafty Cromwell*, 1648) all show the contemporary interest which existed during this period in politics, religion, exploration, civil order, national heritage, and social attitudes. Sometimes the historical incidents form the central part of a play; sometimes they serve as major dramatic incidents; sometimes they occur as passing comments.

5.29   Some Stage Conventions of the Period
The Dumb Show
The film *Les Enfants du Paradis* opens with a clown, played by Jean-Louis Barrault, performing in front of a large crowd (see page 145). He breaks into an elaborate mime of a pickpocket at work amongst the audience. Only gradually do they realise that he's in fact warning them of a real, present danger. This use of dramatic mime to involve an audience dates back to the late medieval period.

The **dumb show** in the Elizabethan and Jacobean periods almost disappeared after about 1620, according to Dieter Mehl (*The Elizabethan Dumb Show*, 1965). Whilst it was used on the stage it provided a powerful adjunct to a play when it was integrated into the action. Silent action or action accompanied only by music is powerful in a play; it can provide, in a sense, a play-within-a-play. The horrific dumb show known as 'the bloody banquet' has already been mentioned (page 138) but some other examples will show how the convention worked. The dumb show in Shakespeare's *Hamlet*, enacted before 'The Murder of Gonzago' is introduced to the royal audience by the Prologue, which playlet formed a play-within-a-play role. The dumb show is elaborately described in detail:

> Enter a King and a Queen, very lovingly; the Queen embracing him and he her. She kneels, and makes show of protestation unto him. He takes her up, and declines her neck; lays him down upon a bank of flowers; she, seeing him asleep, leaves him. Anon comes in a fellow, takes off his crown, kisses it, and pours poison in the King's ears, and exit. The Queen returns, finds the King dead, and makes passionate action. The Poisoner, with some two or three Mutes, comes in again, seeming to lament with her. The dead body is carried away. The Poisoner wooes the Queen with gifts; she seems loath and unwilling awhile, but in the end accepts his love.

Ophelia innocently asks, 'What means this, my lord? . . . Belike this show

Jean-Louis Barrault in *Les Enfants du Paradis* (1944).

imports the argument of the play'? She has stated one of the main functions of the dumb show: to summarise the action for the audience. This task was increasingly taken over by the Prologue or the Chorus. The dumb show here, of course, also carries an enormous dramatic impact in the main plot, since it effectively summarises the Ghost's account of the murder in the orchard. It recalls the Ghost, the demand for revenge, and comments on Gertrude's perfidy in marrying her husband's murderer, in the eyes of her son. Thirdly, it invites the audience to follow the play stage by stage and to observe the King's reaction to every event.

There are two dumb shows in quick succession in Webster's *The White Devil*. The first portrays an action in mime and speeds up the plot, since the events need not be shown on stage. Julio and Christophero poison the lips of a painting of Brachiano; Julia later kisses it and dies; Giovanni and Lodovico express their grief. The second shows how, after a drinking bout, Camillo and others prepare to enjoy vaulting an exercise-horse but he is murdered by Flamineo and his assistants by having his neck broken. Marcello laments; the Cardinal and the Duke are called and 'wonder at the act'. Again, the dumb show has removed a strange action one step further back from the world of reality itself or the imitated world of reality on stage. In this way even the most bizarre acts can be shown; indeed their bizarreness is enhanced by this 'distancing'. The action can be telescoped.

The Induction

A long introductory speech by a Prologue or the main character was another way of telescoping action. *Doctor Faustus* by Christopher Marlowe has both. The Chorus linked the over-reaching theme of *Tamburlaine* with the rise and fall of Faustus and then summarises the main plot of the play. Faustus's Induction provides a detailed way into his mind, into his thought-processes. The motivation of the action is set out. The Chorus in *Henry V* shows that the audience must jump 'o'er times':

> Turning the accomplishment of many years
> Into an hour-glass.

Here the Induction makes a direct appeal to the reader's imagination. In Thomas Kyd's *The Spanish Tragedy* Andrea's Ghost summarises the action of the play for the audience before the action begins. Time, the Chorus, in *The Winter's Tale* moves the action forward sixteen years between Acts Three and Four.

Earlier drama in England portrayed well-known stories (*e.g.* from the *Bible*). The interest could not have lain in what happened next, since the audience clearly knew; the interest must have rested on *how, by what means*, the story would be presented. Similarly, if a Prologue or Induction gives the action of the plot away in advance, the interest must remain in the manner of its telling and the skill used to resolve it. This approach, of course, is different from that of the twist-in-the-tail modern short story or television 'who-dunnit'.

It is usually worth examining in some detail the opening speeches of the exposition of a play performed in this period. They often encapsulate the major points of character, action, and plot as well as indicating any satirical slant (see Jonson's plays), level of language, or allegorical/symbolic interpretation to be used by the audience.

The Play-within-the-Play

This convention carries with it some of the effects borne by the dumb show. In modern films or in television drama the flash-back is a more sophisticated and developed use of the play-within-the-play technique.

'The Murder of Gonzago' (*Hamlet*) and 'The Play of Hieronimo' (*The Spanish Tragedy*) comment on and duplicate the action of the main plot. 'Pyramus and Thisby' (*A Midsummer Night's Dream*) serves not only to provide humour in the way it is acted by the 'rude mechanicals' but serves also to bridge the gap between waking and sleeping as the plots are resolved, and Puck can wave his wand as the fairies disappear.

The language of plays-within-plays is always elevated and distanced from that of the main plot. Because of this and the need to present it to an audience convincingly, we have the two surviving commentaries by Shakespeare on how to present them. Conveniently they throw considerable light on Elizabethan acting conventions (see Hamlet's instructions to the Players and Bottom's cavorting with his acting 'company', where he even gives some idea of how stage 'props' were used).

The Sub-Plot*

This convention is extensively used to reinforce the impact of the main plot. The 'Gloucester' plot in *King Lear* mirrors that of the main plot: both have old men rejected and driven out by ungrateful children; both old men suffer but are helped in their extreme need by the child they rejected; both explore madness; one, however, shows mainly spiritual suffering whilst the other shows physical anguish of the cruellest kind. In *Much Ado About Nothing* the 'Hero-Claudio' plot is matched by the 'Beatrice-Benedick' plot; both are accompanied by the 'Dogberry' plot from which springs the *dénouement* of the other two.

The convention of the sub-plot allowed it to act as a comment on, or a commentary to accompany, the main plot. The 'Sir Charles Mountford' sub-plot in Heywood's *A Woman killed with Kindness* balances and comments on the 'Frankford' plot in matters of gratitude and virtue; both plots are skilfully resolved but a more recent editor of the play (R. W. Fossen, 1961) sees a lack of dimension in the characters in the sub-plot. This, of course, puts its finger on the dilemma facing a playwright using a sub-plot; he must never allow it to eclipse, even in part, the main action. M. C. Bradbrook has referred to a play in which four plots are introduced to form 'a grouping of heterogeneous stories': *Four Plays in One*. Comedy, Professor Bradbrook points out (*Themes and Conventions of Elizabethan Tragedy*), uses the sub-plot more than tragedy but Middleton uses sub-plots in *The Changeling* and *Women beware Women* almost as if they were emblematic, carrying an allegorical significance in the whole

* See R. Levin, *The Multiple Plot in English Renaissance Drama*, Chicago, 1971.

tapestry of the play. There was even a play entitled *Five Plays in One* put on by the Queen's Men in 1585.

The Soliloquy

The proscenium arch makes the use of the soliloquy difficult; the actor simply cannot get to the audience to address them. He can sit to one side (as in Thornton Wilder's *Our Town*, where the Manager acts as a go-between for actors and audience) but he cannot move amongst the spectators. On an apron stage the actor was already amongst the audience.

Prologues and Epilogues were special kinds of soliloquy where the audience could be directly addressed, and the plays of this period use both extensively. The ability to move out of the main action on stage to express thought, as an externalisation of the internal mental or emotional process, is one that Elizabethan playwrights cherished. The best example of all, of course, is found in Hamlet's soliloquies, but Macbeth, too, thinks through his own nightmares and fears aloud: 'If it were done when' tis done . . . ; To be thus is nothing, But to be safely thus . . . '.

The essential dramatic feature of the soliloquy is that it is one kind of speech which is to be taken as true. The characters do not deceive themselves or their audience in uttering them; soliloquies express the true feelings and the true thoughts of those speaking; villains and heroes alike. The soliloquy is of considerable value, therefore, when true motives need to be expressed (see, for example, Flamineo in *The White Devil*, Charlemont in finding his father's monument in *The Atheist's Tragedy*, Richard of Gloucester's opening speech in *Richard III*, or Prince Hal's decision to renounce his base companions early on in *Henry IV, Part One*, 'I know you all, and will awhile uphold The unyok'd humour of your idleness').

Character is revealed by what a character does, what a character says to others, and what other characters say about him. It is also revealed by what a character says about himself; this is one of the major roles of the soliloquy. Daniel Seltzer (*A New Companion to Shakespeare Studies*, 1971, 50–1) has argued that the soliloquy declined rapidly after 1609 as an acting device.

The Aside

This is the half-way stage between dialogue and the soliloquy. The character is engaged in dialogue or action and yet wishes to express innermost thought, comment on what is happening, or address the audience to bring them into a secret.

Vindice (*The Revenger's Tragedy*) comments on his own deceit: 'Spoke to a dying man, shame has no shame'. A little before, Hippolito has commented aloud on most of what Lussurioso has said:

> . . .O villain!
> To make such an unnatural slave of me – but –

and

> And now I shall have free leave to depart!

(aside)

(aside)

and
> Are not my thoughts true?
>
> *(aside)*

Telling use of **the aside** to reveal character and introduce pathos into the play occurs in the opening scene of *King Lear* where Cordelia recognises the falseness of her sisters' protestations of love and her own helplessness to avert the tragedy beginning:

> CORDELIA *(aside)*   What shall Cordelia do? Love and be silent . . .
> Then, poor Cordelia!
> And yet not so; since I am sure, my love's
> More richer than my tongue.

The aside is used for humour, to express thought, to 'point up' an action, to identify an actor with the audience by voicing their thoughts. It is a convention freely used on an apron stage. With a proscenium arch it becomes too artificial to be readily acceptable and is part of melodrama rather than tragedy or comedy; in such a situation it is probably better that actors should observe the convention of talking to each other rather than to the spectators sitting in the darkness beyond the footlights.

Overhearing

This is a clumsy, stylised device which demands that the audience can accept the antiphonal commentary uttered by those doing the overhearing of an action or soliloquised speech uttered by another character. Nevertheless, it is a device used often during this period in order to advance and even complicate the plot; reveal character; or provide the *dénouement* to an action.

The plot is complicated by overhearing in, for example, *Much Ado about Nothing*, where it is contrived that Benedick should overhear Don Pedro and Claudio describing Beatrice's unuttered, desperate love for Benedick. The scene is also punctuated with *asides* to keep the audience 'in on the trick'. Later Beatrice is inveigled into overhearing Hero and Margaret talking of Benedick's hopeless love for her. In this way the Benedick-Beatrice sub-plot can advance. In *Twelfth Night* Maria, Sir Toby Belch, Sir Andrew Aguecheek and Fabian observe and comment for the audience's sake on the way Malvolio is trapped into believing Olivia loves him as they watch his antics from the safety of a box-tree. During all these incidents where the overhearing device is employed the characters of both the overhearers and the overheard are revealed.

In *Much Ado about Nothing* the device is used again to resolve the difficulties of the main plot. The watch overhear Borachio telling Conrade of his trick to deceive Claudio into thinking that Hero was deceiving him; they misunderstand and misinterpret what they hear, for comedy purposes to amuse the audience, with a display of their ignorance. Later their evidence is crucial in exploring Don John's plot against the young lovers. Earlier in the play, of course, the device had been used yet again – with complications: Claudio had overheard Margaret (Hero's maid) exchanging love-conversation with Borachio but had believed that Margaret was really his sweetheart playing him falsely with a lover.

In all these instances, the audience is taken into the confidence of some character in the play, or the playwright himself; they are flattered into feeling privileged and so are persuaded to accept the convention. To make the convention work, however, requires some careful staging and some very stylised acting.

Sometimes, of course, the attempt to overhear leads to disaster. Polonius in *Hamlet* pays dearly for going behind the arras to 'hear the process' of Hamlet's conversation with his mother. In *The Duchess of Malfi* Cariola is sent to overhear Antonio's pledge of love to the Duchess so that the 'contract in a chamber' is seen as the equivalent of a marriage contract itself. The plot advances. One amusing 'twist' in the use of the device comes in *Henry IV, Part One*, where Falstaff is pushed behind the arras by Prince Hal to avoid the Sheriff who has come to search the Boar's Head for the Godshill robbers. After the Sheriff has gone, Falstaff, far from having listened to the conversation, is discovered 'fast asleep behind the arras and snorting like a horse'.

Disguise

This was perhaps the most common device used on the Elizabethan and Jacobean stage. It enabled boys to dress as girls and then to disguise themselves as boys again – which made their acting task so much easier (see Ganymede in *As You Like It*, really Rosalind; Cesario in *Twelfth Night*, really Viola; The Doctor of Laws in *The Merchant of Venice*, really Portia). It enabled the plot to be resolved, for example when Vincentio, the Duke, returns to Vienna, disguised as a friar to discover Angelo's wickedness (*Measure for Measure*) or Lodovico and Gasparo dressed as Capuchins return to deal with Brachiano (*The White Devil*). It allowed one character to masquerade as another and so confuse the plot further, as Montsurry does, dressed as the old Friar (in Chapman's *Bussy D'Ambois*). It enabled characters once banished from the action of the plot to re-enter the play (see Kent and Edgar in *King Lear*). It enabled characters to find out more about themselves and others' opinions of them as well as providing a moment of drama when the disguise is revealed (see the King in *Henry V*). It allowed characters to become invisible on stage (see Prospero and Ariel in *The Tempest*). It allows a character to assume a different character. (See Vindice in *The Revenger's Tragedy*.) It is an integral part of the plot when it allows one character to be transformed into another (see Subtle and Face in *The Alchemist*).

This was a versatile convention. It meant, of course, that the audience had to be let into the secret or at least left able to recognise a character, even when everyone else on the stage is apparently being deceived. Asides, soliloquies and dialogues with other characters who comment on the disguise were ways of doing this.

5.30 Music, Dance and Spectacle

Bruce Pattison (*Music and Poetry of the English Renaissance*, second edition, 1970) has argued that in the first place the men and boys of the Chapel Royal 'were drawn into dramatic entertainments merely to add music. It was only in the sixteenth century that they extended their functions and began to act'. John Heywood (1497–1578) was regarded as both a musician and a poet as well as a dramatist.

The numerous references to music in the plays of the period give some 'internal evidence' about how it was used. Certainly there were minstrels' galleries in the big houses where Interludes, musical entertainments and spectacles were staged as part of the entertainments. Richard Horley (*The 'Revels' History of Drama in English*, V, 1975) has shown that at The First Globe playhouse (1599) plays contain references to music played *within*, and so he postulates that a music station was set up in the tiring-house at the back of the stage. *Julius Caesar*, *All's Well that Ends Well*, *Othello*, *King Lear* and *Macbeth* all refer to music or other noises 'within'. Secondly, he has pointed out from internal evidence within the plays themselves that the Second Blackfriars Theatre 'when they specify the location of off-stage music, invariably call for music *above!*' One of the boxes in the gallery over the stage might have been used as a music room.

Private theatres often had music played between the acts but public theatres put on a performance without any interruption at all. W. T. Jewkes (*Act Division in Elizabethan and Jacobean Plays 1583–1616*, 1958) has shown that after about 1607 the practice of dividing plays into acts increased, so that by about 1616 such divisions were the practice rather than the exception. Hosley, in his excellent survey of Elizabethan playhouses, has also suggested that the box in the gallery was probably curtained off and could allow the musicians (or indeed other actors for certain scenes) to appear dramatically above the stage.

In the interesting Induction written by John Webster to John Marston's play, *The Malcontent*, there are several references to customs in the production of plays in the theatre. Amongst them, Burbage, a well-known player, says in response to a question from Sly about what additions he had made to a play, 'What are your additions?': 'Sooth, not greatly needful; . . . to entertain a little more time and to abridge the not-received custom of music in our theatre'.

Apart from the inter-act music, what part did it play in the Elizabethan and Jacobean theatres? Songs were frequently used to add a new dimension to the emotion of a play. In *The Knight of the Burning Pestle*, the citizen and his wife ask the Prologue:

CIT.   What stately music have you? You have shawms?
PROL.   Shawms? No.
CIT.   Ralph plays a stately part and must have shawms!

At the end of the first act his wife comments on the music being played.

Hark, hark, husband, hark! Fiddles, fiddles! Now surely they go finely. They say 'tis present death for these fiddlers to tune their rebecks before the great Turk's grace; is't not George? But, look, look, look! Here's a Youth dances! – Now, good youth, do a turn o' the toe.

Dancing as well as music are entr'acte entertainment, apparently! In Act II the Citizen's wife asks the musicians to act as witnesses to support one of her stories. After Merrythought has sung a song and the second act has ended, the Citizen and his wife comment on the dreadful music and call for a well-known popular tune to be played, the *Lachrymae* of Dowland:

WIFE   The fiddlers go again husband.

CIT.   Ay, Nell; but this is scurvy music. I gave the whoreson gallows money, and I think he has not got me the waits of Southwark. If I hear 'em not anon, I'll twinge him by the ears. – You musicians, play *Baloo*!

WIFE   No, good George, let's ha' *Lachrymae*.

CIT.   Why, this is it, cony.

The third act ends with George going off to get refreshments during the interval – the beer – whilst the music and dancing goes on. This time the wife wants the tune *Fading*: '*Fading* is a fine jig – Now turn o' th'toe, and then tumble! Cannot you tumble, youth?' But the poor boy cannot. The fourth act ends with songs and a game of catch, and at the end of the play Merrythought entertains the audience with a song: 'Methinks all we . . . should not depart without a song.' Here, then, is a good commentary on how music and song were used in the playhouse. Fiddlers, songs, music, dancing, entertainment – not necessarily related to the play being performed – came and went.

Although in *Twelfth Night*, Sir Toby and his companions give a drunken rendering of an air from Robert Jones's *Book of Ayres*, song is used delicately elsewhere in the play. The Clown's songs, 'O mistress mine! where are you roaming?' and 'Come away, come away, death' add haunting melodies to the romantic theme of the main plot. At the end of the play, Feste, the Clown, sings the sad song:

When that I was and a little tiny boy,
With hey, ho, the wind and the rain . . .

and it is this song which Shakespeare reintroduces and poignantly adapts in *King Lear* where the Fool sits with the king in the middle of a raging storm:

He that has a little tiny wit,
With hey, ho, the wind and the rain,
Must make content with his fortunes fit,
Though the rain it raineth every day.

The application, sharp as it was, to the tragic events of Lear's life, still from the lips of the young fool, provides a moving, dramatic commentary to the play. Here is song being used most powerfully to suggest an added emotional dimension.

Music was used to reinforce emotional scenes between lovers (parodied with the Bergomask played at the end of Bottom's 'Pyramus and Thisby' in *A Midsummer Night's Dream*) as in the ball scene in *Romeo and Juliet*, or Duke Orsino's identification of music and love in the opening speech to *Twelfth Night*. It was used to mark entrances and exits (trumpets, cornets, and alarums sounded). It was used to accompany processions and religious ceremonies: (*e.g.* the Cardinal's instalment in The Duchess of Malfi played out in a dumb show at the Shrine of Our Lady of Loretto, 'during all which ceremony, this ditty is sung to very solemn music, by divers churchmen . . . '). Music was used too, to add to the bizarreness of mood; in *The Duchess of Malfi* madmen dance about to accompany a song by a madman 'sung to a dismal kind of music'.

In **masques**, of course, music played an integral part of the action. Ben Jonson's *The Gipsies Metamorphosed* (1621), an elaborate and popular masque, consisted of five formal masqued dances separated by songs and dramatic interludes. In the second of these dances there are six 'strains' or movements broken up by fortunes told by gypsies. These entertainments were essentially musical rather than dramatic (see page 29).

Spectacle played a large part in the drama of this period, given that the widespread use of realistic scenery did not develop in the popular theatre until much later. Many plays open with elaborate processions and entrances which allowed the players to group themselves about the stage. *Henry VI, Part One*, the first scene of *King Lear* and *King John* provide examples of such impressive entrances.

The staging of plays frequently included properties to indicate rivers, trees, banks, churchyards, battlefields, markets, bedrooms, counting houses, etc. E. K. Chambers (*The Elizabethan Stage*, III, 77) pointed out that 'many Elizabethan actors were half-acrobats, and could no doubt fly upon a wire'.

Some of the devices used for 'spectacle' included: chairs let down by cords and pulleys (*Alphonsus, King of Arragon* Robert Greene, 1587); elaborate banquets set and prepared (*e.g. The Tempest*); squibs and crackers; the placing of hanging tapestries or an 'arras' (*Hamlet*); the shifting of the action to galleries from the stage (*e.g. Every Man in his Humour, The Jew of Malta, Henry IV, Part Two*); walls set up on the stage (*Henry VI, Part One, Henry V*); battles and scaling of walls; military camps; trees on which to hang love-verses. The Red Bull Theatre became famous for its use of spectacular devices: *e.g.* ascents from and descents to the stage; hunting episodes; models of ships and buildings; noises of thunder; fire and pyrotechnics (see E. K. Chambers, *op. cit.*, III, 109–10). Animals could be ridden on or off the stage; the apparel of actors was often sumptuous; war scenes, often sketchy and symbolical (see the Prologue to *Henry V*) were enjoyed by audiences; bears were brought on stage (*The Winter's Tale* and Jonson's *Mask of Oberon*) and used the spectacle seen in London of animals chasing men. One record of a bear-and-bull-baiting scene at Southwark made by a Pomeranian visitor set out what happened in detail; fireworks were used and apples and pears, let out of a rocket, set the audience scrambling wildly for them. Fairies, (*A Midsummer Night's Dream*), a fencing match (*Hamlet*), a wrestling bout (*As You Like It*), drinking sessions, the parade of historical characters and ghostly figures (*Dr Faustus, Macbeth*), witches mixing their brews (*Macbeth*), court scenes (*The Duchess of Malfi, The Atheist's Tragedy, The Revenger's Tragedy, The Merchant of Venice*), murders, parodies of court scenes (*Henry IV, Part One*), brawls (*Romeo and Juliet*) and weddings are merely some of the spectacular events presented in both realistic and symbolic fashion on the stage during this period.

Puritan condemnation of the theatre and of plays reverberated on and on. Some of the condemnation was directed at the extravagance and immorality of what was shown to an audience. Philip Stubbes in *The Anatomie of Abuses* as early as 1583 pointed to what offended the Puritans on the stage: lies, deceit, hypocrisy, laughing, jesting, grinning, swearing, blaspheming, 'devirginating', stealing, committing treason, consuming treasures, singing, talking of bawdy love, scoffing, playing the glutton or drunkard – 'all these good examples may you see painted before your eyes in interludes and plays'. Perhaps such spectacles were the attractions which, as John Stockwood lamented, 'will . . . with a blast of the trumpet sooner call (to a filthy play) a thousand, than an hour's tolling of a bell bring to the sermon a hundred' (J. Dover Wilson's *Life in Shakespeare's England*, second edition, 1949).

5.31 The Elizabethan Actor and Actors' Companies

Attempts at control

The City of London tried hard to eliminate plays from their domaine in 1574–6, 1580–4, and 1597–1600. On each occasion they failed. They objected, first, on economic grounds, since the livery companies wished to treat actors as serving-men who could be supervised, and, secondly, on moral grounds, since they thought acting was not a serious contribution to trade and industry but provoked idleness.

If players were to be controlled, statutes would be necessary. Until 1587 the attacks seemed to have been orchestrated. John Stockwood preached in 1578 at Paules Crosse and condemned 'filthy plays' shown at the Theatre and the Curtain. In the same year Thomas White thought the theatres 'a continual monument of London's prodigality and folly. But I understand they are now forbidden because of the plague'. In 1578, again, George Whetstone was unhappy about 'the abuse of comedies': 'grave old men should instruct; young men should show the imperfections of youth; strumpets should be lascivious; boys unhappy; and clowns should be disorderly' so that instruction is mingled with delight. Stephen Gosson's *The Schoole of Abuse, containing a pleasant invective against Poets, Pipers, Players, Jesters and such like Caterpillars of the Commonwealth* (1579) was a withering attack, with a second edition printed in 1587: 'I take upon mee to drive you from playes . . .' They were indirectly responsible for London's wantonness and attracted lascivious, idle behaviour. In 1580 Anthony Mundy joined the attack with his *A second and third blast of retreat from plays and theatres*. In 1582 Gosson returned to the attack:

> The argument of Tragedies is wrath, crueltie, incest, iniurie, murther eyther violent by sworde, or voluntary by poyson. The persons, Gods, Goddesses, furies, fiendes, Kinges, Quenes, and mightie men. The grande worke of Commedies is loue, cosenedge, flatterie, bawderie, sly conveighance of whoredome. The persons, cookes, queanes, knaves, bauds, parasites, courtezannes, lecherous olde men, amorous yong men.

In 1583 Phillip Stubbes equated theatres with 'unclean assemblies' where were found 'unthriftiness, whoredom, wantonness and drunkenness'. Gervase Babington wrote about 'these prophane and wanton stage plays and interludes' in the same year. William Webbe (1586), William Rankins (1587) and the Marprelate papers of 1588–90 kept up the attack.

Attempts to control the abuses of the stage followed in the wake of such criticisms. Plague and the threats of its outbreak provided the authorities with sufficient excuse. A stage collapsed at the Beargarden in 1583 and there were riots at Whitsuntide in 1584, linked, so it was argued, with performances of plays.

In 1574 the City Fathers allowed the so-called Queen's Men to put on plays twice a week in private houses 'without public assembly'. The Queen's Men would be the only company of actors tolerated. Other companies emerged, however, protected by powerful patrons: Leicester's Men (1576 at the Theatre); the Admiral's Men (1574), Lord Pembroke's Men (1574–6); and Lord Strange's Men (1576–7).

The Theatres
After renewed criticism and the rise of the University Wits (Greene, Lodge, Lyly, Peele, Nashe, and Marlowe), the actors fought back. The *Blackfriars* Theatre had been adapted in 1576 by Richard Tarrant to house the performances of children but on the south of the river the Rose was built about 1592, and the Swan in 1595. In 1596 the City persuaded the Privy Council to ban all plays from its area and 'play houses in Gracious Street, Bishops-gate-street nigh Paules, that on Ludgate Hill, the White-Friars were put down'. These were presumably, E. K. Chambers argues, the Bell, the Cross Keys, the Bull, and the Bel Savage.

In 1596 four theatres remained: the Theatre and the Curtain north of the river and the Swan and the Rose on the South Bank. Cock-pits, bear-baiting, and bull-baiting were common. In 1599 the Theatre was pulled down and the Globe was built from its materials on the South Bank of the river in the parish of St. Saviour's by 1600. There followed the Fortune (built on the model of the Globe) in 1600, sanctioned by the Privy Council, ultimately to replace the Curtain which was to be 'either ruinated or applied to some other good use'. In 1597 the Privy Council had limited London acting companies to the Chamberlain's Men and the Admiral's Men. In 1602 the Queen insisted that they allowed a third, the Earl of Worcester's Men. Other 'privileged' companies of actors must have acted outside London. Of the 'private' theatres, Paul's reopened in 1599 and The Blackfriars in 1600. The Globe (used as the home of the King's Men) and the Fortune (the Prince's Men) continued in use until 1642, when the theatres were closed, although the Globe was destroyed by fire and rebuilt in 1613 and the Fortune in 1621.

The Red Bull seems to have been built about 1606, although little is known of it, apart from the fact that it was renowned for its spectacles, is mentioned in *The Knight of the Burning Pestle* (1607), caused trouble for the Middlesex justices because of its 'notable outrage' and use by pickpockets, and was used by the Queen's Men until 1617 when they were to move to the Cockpit in Drury Lane. It was in use until the time of the Commonwealth but was 're-edified and enlarged' before 1633.

The Companies of Actors

During the early years of Elizabeth's reign boy companies dominated drama performances: *Children of Paul's*; *Children of the Chapel and Queen's Revels*; *Children of Windsor*; *Children of the King's Revels*; *Children of Bristol*; *Westminster School*; *Eton College*; *Merchant Taylors' School*; *Earl of Leicester's Boys*; *Earl of Oxford's Boys*; and *Mr Stanley's Boys*. The building of the first permanent theatres in 1576 marked a change and adult companies were set up; before 1576 only the *Earl of Leicester's Men* and the *Duttons* were known, but after 1576 the *Lord Chamberlain's Men* and the *Lord Admiral's Men* came into existence. In 1578 the Privy Council restricted the companies who could share in the Court's Christmas festivities to six: *Leicester's Men, Warwick's Sussex's, Essex's, The Children of the Chapel*, and *St. Paul's*.

Between 1583 and 1590 the boy companies diminished. The *Queen's Men* became the dominant company, set up in 1583. Between 1592 and 1594 a serious outbreak of plague affected dramatic productions. The *Lord Chamberlain's Men*, with Burbage, Kempe and Shakespeare began to assert itself.

The Actors

Unfortunately, details about many of the actors of this period are not known today, although something of what they achieved has come to light through such studies as those of E. K. Chambers (*The Elizabethan Stage*, Vols. 1–4, 1923) and M. C. Bradbrook (*The Rise of the Common Player: a Study of Actor and Society in Shakespeare's England*, 1962).

A few players are known individually, however. Shakespeare himself acted with the *Lord Chamberlain's Men*. It is tempting to think of him playing minor roles such as Cinna the Poet in *Julius Caesar* who is persecuted by the crowd for his bad verses.

Will Kempe and Robert Armin   Kempe is best known from his own account (*Kemps Nine Daies Wonder*, 1600) of a dance he made from London to Norwich in 1599. Cutpurses, girls, and young men tried to keep up with him but dropped out; he was given an official reception at Norwich. Although this was in no sense a modern 'sponsored' dance, it certainly advertised Kempe's prowess as a dancer of jigs, the entertainment which flourished in the nineties at the ends of plays. The description of the inter-act dances given in *The Knight of the Burning Pestle* is one which tells us something of such jigs. He was called 'Jestmaster and Vice-Gerant General to the Ghost of Dick Tarlton', whom he succeeded as Clown with the *Lord Chamberlain's Men*. He left this company in 1599 for a reason unknown and, in turn, was succeeded by Robert Armin, who wrote plays himself. It was Armin who would have played Feste and Lear's Fool. It is thought that he, too, would have played Thersites in *Troilus and Cressida* and Pompey in *Measure for Measure*.

Richard Burbage (died 1619)   He was the son of James Burbage, the joiner responsible for converting a house into the theatre at Blackfriars. From his father, Richard and his brother inherited a share in the *Theatre*. He was an outstanding actor of the period and 'starred' in plays by Shakespeare, Jonson, and Beaumont and Fletcher, and played Hamlet, Lear, and Othello.

He seems to have begun his major career with the title role of Richard Gloucester in Shakespeare's *Richard III*. His approach was one where the actor 'becomes' the part he is portraying. Richard Flecknoe (in *A Short Discourse of the English Stage*, 1664) described Burbage as:

'a delightful Proteus, so wholly transforming himself into his Part, and putting himself off with his Cloathes, as he never (not so much as in the Tyring-house) assum'd himself again until the Play was done . . . He had all the parts of an excellent Orator animating his words with speaking and Speech with Action . . . never falling in his Part when he had done speaking.

(E. K. Chambers, *op. cit*, IV, 370)

A contemporary elegy also described his ability to enter into his parts:

Oft have I seene him, leap into the Grave
Suiting the person, which he seem'd to have
Of a sadd Lover, with so true an Eye
That theer I would have sworne, he meant to die.

(A Funerall Elegye on ye Death of the famous Actor
Richard Burbedg . . . ; given in Edwin Nungezer,
A Dictionary of Actors, reprinted 1968, 74)

Alexander Leggatt (*The 'Revels' History of Drama in English*, III, 1975) has also pointed out that one of Sir Thomas Overbury's *Characters* is sometimes thought to refer to Burbage's acting.

Edward Alleyn (1566–1626)   He had joined the *Lord Admiral's Men* by the end of the 1580s and played the parts of Tamburlaine, Faustus, and Barabas in Marlowe's plays, Hieronimo in *The Spanish Tragedy*, and Orlando in Greene's *Orlando Furioso*. He married Philip Henslowe's daughter and Henslowe was the owner of the Rose Theatre. Alleyn gradually made his own fortune but on the death of his wife, when he was 57, he married the twenty-year-old daughter of John Donne, Dean of St. Paul's.

G. B. Harrison thought that Alleyn 'strutted and bellowed' his parts but William Armstrong has shown that Alleyn and Burbage were praised for having similar qualities.

John Heminges (died 1630) and **Henry Condell** (died 1627), members of Shakespeare's acting company, were responsible in 1623 for bringing Shakespeare's extant work together into the First Folio. Heminges is thought by some to have been the first actor to play the part of Falstaff.

5.32   The Closure of the Theatres in 1642
The serious outbreak of plague in London in 1625 killed some 35 000 people, including the playwright John Fletcher. The theatres were closed until the very end of the year. King James also died in 1625; King James's acting company became King Charles's, and Queen Anne's company and Lady Elizabeth's company disbanded. King Charles took considerable interest in

dramatic performances at court. The King's Company dominated the theatre until 1636. Massinger became the principal dramatist for this band of actors. In 1636–7 another serious outbreak of plague hit London and the theatres were closed, with a week's respite in February, for nearly seventeen months. The theatres had also been closed in 1630 for a period during an outbreak of plague. These three serious outbreaks of the disease in 1625, 1630, and 1637, with the closing of the theatres which accompanied them, had a debilitating effect on the English theatre after its enormous vitality during the Elizabethan and Jacobean periods.

The political situation in England with the overthrow of the monarchy and the beginning of the Civil War in 1642 resulted in the shutting down of the theatres. The Puritan attack, too, which had maintained its onslaught also contributed to the move. On 2 September 1642 the Lords and Commons ordered that 'publike Stage-Players shall cease and bee forborne'. The order was enforced, although there were clandestine attempts to mount old plays.

With the ceasing of hostilities in 1648, a new order was made arresting any players giving a performance and fining any members of the audience. The drama was firmly suppressed, at least until 1656 when D'Avenant tentatively put on an entertainment at Rutland House. Although he wrote dramatic pieces with music and cultivated the friendship of Oliver Cromwell, D'Avenant trod delicately.

The return of Charles II, following Monk's march on London in 1660, opened up the possibility of a new phase in the development of the English theatre.

Questions

1. 'In tragedy things matter; in comedy they don't.' How useful a distinction do you think this is between the two?
2. What problems would you find in presenting a comedy from this period today if its prime purpose originally was to instruct?
3. Do you see any difficulties in reconciling 'romance' and 'comedy' in any play from this period you know well?
4. What problems would you face in directing a production of a satirical comedy from this period? How would you overcome them?
5. *Either (a) Try to present a scene from a modern play dealing with a social problem in a way that an audience from the Elizabethan period would understand.

   or (b) Rewrite a scene from an Elizabethan comedy or tragedy in such a way that its issues could be immediately understood by an audience today.
6. How far is the concept of 'the tragic hero' useful to your understanding of a tragedy from the period you have been studying?
7. What is the importance to the development of English drama of *one* playwright (other than Shakespeare) whose plays you have been studying?
8. Imagine that you are living during the Elizabethan or the Jacobean period and that you have just returned home from a visit to the playhouse where you have seen the production of a play. Write an account of what interested you for your own personal diary or journal. (Do not try to use an old form of the English language.)
9. Write a dialogue between you and a dramatist from this period as it might have occurred in a TV interview today, for an arts programme, given that the dramatist has been able to travel across the time gap separating you both. (You might like to discuss some of his aims in writing and how he set about realising his work on the stage.)
10. If you, as a drama student, could ask Shakespeare five questions in a face-to-face discussion, what would they be? What do you think some of his answers might be?
11. What changes in conception would you need to make in putting a play from this period written for an apron stage on a modern proscenium-arch stage?
12. If you were casting three major characters for the production of a play from the period you have been studying, what features of each would determine your choice of actor?
13. *Describe the costumes you would use for *three* of the major characters in a

*The questions marked * could form the basis of project work.*

play which has allegorical types in its *Dramatis Personae*. Justify your choices for each one.

14   From your study of plays within this period, what do you think were the major interests *or* concerns of an Elizabethan or a Jacobean audience?

15   What are the main difficulties a modern audience has to overcome in understanding an Elizabethan or Jacobean play you have been studying?

16   What picture of kingship emerges from *two* plays you know well from this period?

17   How far do historical events interfere with, or contribute to, a historical play from this period you have either read or seen in production?

18   How important is an understanding of the philosophical, political and religious backgrounds of the period to an appreciation of the drama of Elizabethan and Jacobean times? (You may restrict your detailed discussion to a consideration of *two* plays, if you wish.)

19   'The desire to produce surprise and suspense often takes the place of moral insight and intellectual honesty'. Do you think this is too harsh a comment on Jacobean drama?

20   Describe the use made by one dramatist of this period of *two* of the following: overhearing; the aside; the soliloquy; music; spectacle; the dumb show.

21   *Investigate as fully as you can the way one actor worked during this period. How did his acting differ from the way an actor today might approach the playing of a particular part in an Elizabethan or Jacobean drama?

22   Choose a play from this period you have been studying which you would like to present in production *either* to delight *or* to instruct an audience. How would your choice of emphasis between 'delight' or 'instruction' affect your production?

23   Given that plot and character are important in a play, what else have you found important in a play from this period which you have been studying?

24   *Design a fixed set for a play from this period for a modern theatre. (You may decide for yourself what kind of stage you are working on.)

25   If you had been a dramatist living in the early seventeenth century, how would you have answered the accusations of the Puritans that the theatre encouraged immorality?

6
Restoration and Eighteenth-Century Drama

6.1 The Restoration

First, read the appropriate sections on the Development of the Stage given in Sections **2.8** and **2.9** in Chapter Two (pages 32–39).

In 1660 the Convention Parliament, consisting of moderate Roundheads of the old Presbyterian party with many Cavaliers, called back Charles II from his exile in Holland. Oliver Cromwell was dead and the authority of the King and the authority of Parliament were seen as inseparable.

With the Restoration two important developments took place in the world of science and the arts. In 1645 the *Philosophical Society* had been founded but its activities were interrupted by the Civil War. At the Restoration it began its meetings again and in 1662 was given its royal charter. It then became the *Royal Society*. Its membership included not only scientists of the calibre of Robert Boyle, the chemist (and formulator of 'Boyle's Law') but men of letters, such as Abraham Cowley, John Dryden, Edmund Waller, John Evelyn, and John Aubrey, the antiquary. Its historian and secretary was Bishop Thomas Sprat (1635–1713) who led a committee which discussed the production of a dictionary of the English language, a grammar and translations of the classics. Although this committee never put any of their ideas into practice, the impetus for studying the English Language, using it 'correctly', and setting up an English Academy (the Italians had had one since 1582, and the French since 1635) was under way.

6.2

Secondly, the development of English drama, which had suffered setbacks from theatre closures because of outbreaks of the plague in 1625, 1630, 1637, and because of the Civil War and Puritan attacks in 1642, could now go ahead. Three important things happened: the actors regrouped themselves into companies; secondly, theatres reopened and were altered in design; and thirdly, women were allowed to act on the English public stage.

6.3 The New Companies

Thomas Killigrew (1612–83) brought together as many of the *King's Men* that he could; Sir William D'Avenant (1606–68), Poet Laureate, who had trodden warily during the Commonwealth period but managed to put on some musical, dramatic, and operatic entertainments (*e.g. The Siege of Rhodes*), collected a new body of young actors about him. The King decided that he wished to keep control of the theatres from the start and so he issued patents to only two companies of actors, one under Killigrew and the other under D'Avenant. Other actors who had wished to set up companies were frustrated. George Jolly, for example, returned from Germany where he had exiled himself with a group of actors, and associated himself in due course with William Beeston who had been, before 1642, the master of the King' Company of child players at Salisbury Court. Beeston reopened the old theatre at Salisbury Court but the monopoly granted to Killigrew and D'Avenant by the King's patents held.

Killigrew's company, *His Majesty's Servants*, played at a number of Theatres Royal and Killigrew himself built a playhouse in Drury Lane in 1663 (see pages 32–33). D'Avenant's company, the *Duke's Men* (named after the King's brother, the Duke of York), played in Lincoln's Inn Fields and in Dorset Gardens. In 1682 the two companies joined together to become one to play at Drury Lane, but by 1695 it had begun to fragment. During this period, in addition to the Drury Lane Theatre, one other theatre in London had opened up, the Haymarket, built under licence granted by William III. Later, in the provinces, during the early eighteenth century new theatres were opened at Bath, Birmingham, Bristol, Liverpool and York.

6.4 The Theatres

During the reign of Charles I, Inigo Jones had collaborated with D'Avenant to produce elaborate masques for the Court (see page 29). The new theatre at Drury Lane, designed by Christopher Wren, had a projecting semi-oval stage, additional side wings, new extra doors up-stage for actors to enter by, proximity between actors and audience, painted sets, machinery (such as 'flyings for the witches'), wings designed in perspective, efficient changes of scenery by means of grooves set in the floor and a stage lit by chandeliers. Boxes were built over the stage but the audience still sat on it (and did so until the time of David Garrick, who pushed the stage back beyond the proscenium arch). (See pages 32–39, for a further description of the development of the theatre and stage during this period.)

6.5 Women actors

In 1660 a woman played Desdemona in a production of *Othello* for the first time. Other actresses immediately played major female roles; among the best-known actresses of the Restoration period were Nell Gwynn, Mrs Barry, Mrs Oldfield, and Mrs Bracegirdle (see above, pages 33–34 for a full account of this development in the English theatre). Women had played on the stage in Europe for some time.

6.6

The audience immediately following the Restoration was becoming more and more exclusive; it was the aristocratic circles who attended the playhouse, although with the extension of the Drury Lane Theatre and the new theatre at Covent Garden (opened 1732) it was recognised that the theatre-going audience was rapidly increasing in numbers. The audience, however, in Restoration times was educated, high-born, and not altogether well-behaved. The plays were sometimes *risqué* enough to raise blushes to ladies' cheeks! Pepys reports that his visit to the King's house to see Beaumont and Fletcher's *The Maid's Tragedy* on February 18, 1667 was spoilt by two chattering women talking throughout the performance to Sir Charles Sedley: 'one of the ladies would and did sit with her mask on all the play'; these masks were worn by fashionable ladies to hide their delicate blushes! One play, *The Parson's Wedding*, acted at the Theatre Royal in 1664 solely by women, was considered indecent by Pepys. Plays were often full of the most vulgar, suggestive Epilogues.

In the 1660s the theatres had difficulty in attracting audiences. If a new play appeared at one theatre, the audience deserted the other. The play-going audience for some years after the Restoration was barely sufficient to support both theatres.

6.7

The companies, the theatres, and the audience gave rise for half a decade to plays that were *artificial*. This term would have been one of praise rather than criticism for the period. Well into the eighteenth century poets aimed at 'art' rather than 'nature'. 'Enthusiasm' (*inspiration* in Latin, 'being breathed into' by the gods) was not encouraged. 'What oft was thought, but ne'er so well expressed' became the aim. Craft, language with the right words in the right place, elegance, and distancing carried much weight as qualities to seek. Objectivity and detachment were increasingly seen as the things to aim at. Decorum was all. (Pope's *Essay on Criticism* (1711), based on Horace's work, sets out an attitude to literature which was based on this concept of *artificiality*, 'made by art'.)

6.8

The influence of France on English drama during the Restoration period asserted itself. Charles II's exile to the Continent had left his court well-acquainted with the work of Pierre Corneille, (1606–84) and Corneille's successor, Jean Racine (1639–99), continued that classical tradition and gradually made his influence felt in England with successful adaptations of his plays, such as Ambrose Philips's *The Distrest Mother* (1712) based on *Andromaque*.

Corneille's works in tragedy were marked by their central tragic heroes or heroines, their lofty moral tone, and their dignified, elevated style. Man is not as 'a fly to wanton boys' killed by the gods for their sport; he was a noble creature, responsible for his own fate. His central characters rise above passion and proudly show the strength that comes through reason. Reason conflicts with passion or with the forces of fate but it can rise above such matters in a moment of self-sacrifice. He concentrated his action to make it intense; therefore the Unities of Time, Place, and Action, carefully observed in *Horace* and *Cinna*, were appropriate. The same conflict that Dryden was to take up in

England later as a theme for drama, that of love and duty, formed the central plot of *Le Cid* (1637), a play warmly welcomed by the audiences but attacked by Richelieu, Chapelain the grammarian and critic, and the French Academy (*Sentiments de l'Académie sur le Cid*, 1638) for faults in style and grammar. A version of *Le Cid* was produced in English by Joseph Rutter as early as 1638. Rodrigue, a Castilian noble, kills his betrothed's father, the Count, for an insult to his own father, Don Diègue. Just as Rodrigue had been torn between love and honour, so his fiancée, Chimène, is now similarly torn between love and honour. She appoints a champion but Rodrigue refuses to defend himself. Chimène pleads with him to fight and win the duel to protect her from her promised marriage to her champion. Rodrigue obliges, but spares his opponent's life. Chimène's fear that Rodrigue has been slain convinces the King that she loves Rodrigue but the ploy does not resolve the issue. Rodrigue goes off to a foreign war hoping that time will provide an answer. The plot moves steadily, relentlessly forward, with high sentiments continuously stated and restated:

> CHIMÈNE Honneur impitoyable à mes plus chers désirs,
> Que tu me vas coûter de pleurs et de soupirs!
> Après mon père mort, je n'ai point à choisir.

Racine's tragedies continue to examine the conflict within the tragic hero (or, more usually, heroine) but here the will wavers; circumstances demand to be considered and taken into account; basic passions come into conflict with each other. *Andromaque* is a tragedy where the heroine, torn between jealousy, love, and anger is driven to make compromises which in the end make it impossible to live with herself. The play ends in death and madness. Racine's plays are concerned with 'the passions of the heart', as the critic Brunetière described them. La Bruyère distinguished his work from that of Corneille by saying, 'Corneille showed men as they ought to be; Racine showed them as they are'. Racine's language was less elevated than Corneille's but he observed the Unities and excluded anything which did not support the main action.

It was Corneille, however, who affected English Restoration tragedy, not Racine. In 1663, D'Avenant, in the first act of *The Play-House to Be Lett* wrote:

> The *French* convey their Arguments too much
> In dialogue: their Speeches are too long.
> Such length of Speeches seems not so unpleasing
> As the Contracted Walks of their Designs.

Translations of French plays popularised the rhyming couplet. Corneille's plays were translated during the 1660s and 1970s: *La Mort de Pompée*, *Horace*, *Héraclius* and, *Nicomède*. Several of his plays were adapted for English performances: *La généreuse ingratitude*, 1657 (Lower: *The Noble Ingratitude*, 1659; and Corye, *The Generous Enemies*, 1671); and *Agrippa, roi d'Albe*, 1660 (Dauncer, *Agrippa, King of Alba*, 1674). Racine's influence came with Crown's *Andromache*, 1674 (*Andromaque*, 1667) and Otway's *Titus and Berenice*, 1676 (*Bérénice*, 1671).

6.9 Tragedy (Rhymed, Heroic)

The use of the rhymed couplet for tragedy owed something to the rhymed translations of French tragedies during the 1660s and 1670s, but its use was not new. Dryden (dedication of *The Rival Ladies*, 1664, to the Earl of Orrery) said that the use of rhymed couplets was 'not so much a new Way amongst us, as an old Way new Reviv'd'. Waller and Denham had used it in non-dramatic literature. However, although tragedies were often written in rhymed couplets, this verse form was not restricted to tragedies, as Allardyce Nicoll (*A History of English Drama*, I, 1660–1900, fourth edition, 1961) has pointed out.

Plays of a *heroic* (or an epic) nature should not deal with ordinary people in ordinary situations; they should deal with *extra*ordinary matters. Dryden praised D'Avenant for 'heightening' his characters in *The Siege of Rhodes* (1656), first presented as an opera, but which he failed to revise satisfactorily as drama. Dryden thought that the play was not full enough, lacked variety of characters, had no extraordinary incidents and the characters were not sufficiently noble. A glance at Dryden's own work will illustrate the matter further. He took the theme of *Antony and Cleopatra* and rewrote it, without, strangely, using the heroic couplet. He concentrated on the last phases of Antony's career, besieged in Alexandria and torn between *honour* (represented by Ventidius, his general, Dolabella, his friend, and Octavia, his wife) on the one hand, and '*Love* (represented by Cleopatra) on the other. He called his play, significantly, *All for Love, or the World well Lost* (1678). Honour almost wins the struggle but Antony's jealousy of Dolabella's imagined love for Cleopatra throws him back to her and he loses the world. Here the plot is concentrated into one short period of time, keeps to one geographical location, and simplifies and concentrates the action on one theme. The characters are noble and elevated – so much so that they are almost removed from the human sympathy of the audience.

Roger Boyle, Earl of Orrery (1621–79), wrote heroic plays and deliberately set out to imitate Corneille. His *History of Henry the Fifth* (1664) deals with the conflict between love and friendship. Pepys saw the play on August 13, 1664, and thought it 'a most noble play . . . full of height and raptures of wit and sense'. He also attended the first performance of Orrery's *The Black Prince* on the afternoon of October 19, 1667, and sat in a box for the first time in his life at Drury Lane at the cost of four shillings, since 'there was no room in the pit' because 'the house (was) infinite full', although he got there early at two o'clock; the King and the Duke of York were both present. In the play the clash between love and duty comes again and again, in the best tradition of Corneille. The drama of Orrery is marred, as Allardyce Nicoll, (*op. cit.*, 109) has pointed out, by sophistry and argument 'inaptly imitated from the French theatre'. The audience did not approve of some of the scenes where speeches ran on for several pages and the thoughts lost themselves in undramatic language, for example:

Since Nature no Religion knows but Love,
He that loves most, does most Religious prove

Nicoll quotes one fantastic example of such tortuous language:

When she her Royal Infant did embrace,
Her Eyes such Floods of Tears show'r'd on her Face,
That then, oh *Mustapha*! I did admire
How so much Water sprang from so much Fire:
And to increase the Miracle, I found
At the same time, my Heart both burnt and drown'd.

It is not hard to see why Orrery's plays have now become the quarry for scholars rather than the treasure-trove of directors.

John Dryden's (1631–1700) heroic tragedies are also strongly influenced by the love versus honour/friendship struggle. He has set out some of his ideas on tragedy in some notes written in the end-papers of his copy of Thomas Rymer's *The Tragedies of the Last Age Considered* (1677; dated 1678). In these notes he examined Aristotle's views on tragedy. He found that the plays of 'the ancients' were 'more correctly plotted' but those of his age were 'more beautifully written'; the characters of the modern plays were numerous and more varied in Shakespeare and Fletcher. The thoughts and the words are more noble and more poetic. He listed the following as parts of a poem, tragic or heroic:

(*i*)   The fable itself.
(*ii*) The order or manner of its contrivance in relation of the parts to the whole.
(*iii*) The manners or decency of the characters in speaking or acting what is proper for them, and proper to be shewn by the poet.
(*iv*) The thoughts which express the manners.
(*v*)   The words which express those thoughts.

(See John Coraghan, *Dryden: A Selection*, 1978, 551.)

Plot, the arrangement of the plot, appropriate 'manners' and thoughts, and appropriate language, therefore, are of the essence of *tragedy*.

The notes in *Heads of an Answer to Rymer* are amplified in *The Grounds of Criticism in Tragedy* which followed Dryden's Preface to his adaptation of Shakespeare's *Troilus and Cressida* (1679). The **plot** ought to be one, with a beginning, a middle, and end; it ought to have great persons, ought to be probable, but not necessarily historically accurate; it ought to instruct by precept, and excite pity and fear. In this work Dryden compares the merits of Shakespeare and those of Fletcher. **Manners** (motives) in a play Dryden defined as 'those inclinations, whether natural or acquired, which move and carry us to actions, good, bad, or indifferent, or which incline the persons to such or such actions'. 'These *manners* arise from many causes . . . They must be apparent . . . suitable or agreeing to the persons', and they must 'resemble' the character being portrayed, *i.e.* they must be in accordance with the generally accepted view of the character in history – Ulysses is angry, Achilles patient, etc. Finally 'manners' must be maintained throughout a play. The **hero** in a tragedy should be more virtuous than vicious. The audience must be carefully prepared for the passion shown in a play; everything in a discourse must contribute to the moving of the passions; trifling thoughts should be banished. Love and virtue should be shown as bringing rewards and hatred and vice as bringing punishments. Virtue may, however, be shown as being 'unfortunate' and vice 'triumphant', though it is detestable (see *Thyestes*, 1681, by John Crowne or *The Duke of Guise*, 1683, by Dryden with Nathaniel Lee). Dryden saw a 'great affinity' between tragedy and epic and Thomas Hobbes (1588–1679) saw tragedy as 'The Heroique Poem Dramatique'.

Allardyce Nicoll (*A History of English Drama*, I, 1660–1900, fourth edition, 1952, 111–12) has argued that Dryden's play *The Indian Queen* (1663/4), written in collaboration with Sir Robert Howard, contains nearly all the main features of Dryden's heroic plays during the Restoration period: a noble hero, desperate love rebuffed, crossed love-plots posing questions of love, honour, virtue and vice, the death of the minor 'wicked' characters, the survival of few but essentially noble characters. The sequel to the play *The Indian Emperor* (1665) has a more involved plot, increased spectacle (with magic caves, temples, and prisons) but retains the essential characteristics of the earlier play. *Tyrannick Love* (published 1669) contains similar themes but was so full of ranting speeches and exaggerated attitudes that it attracted the ridicule of George Villiers (and his collaborators) in *The Rehearsal* (1672), which satirised the heroic tragedy of the period by parodying passages from several plays loosely strung together to form an absurd plot. Dryden's last 'rimed' tragedy was *Aureng-Zebe or The Great Mogul* (1675).

Other writers of such heroic tragedies in this period included Thomas D'Urfey (1653–1723); Samuel Pordage (1633–91?); Nathaniel Lee (1653?–92); John Caryll (*The English Princess*, 1666, seen by Pepys on March 7, 1666); John Banks (*The Rival Kings*, 1667, *The Unhappy Favourite or The Earl of Essex*, 1681); Thomas Shipman (*Henry the Third of France, Stabb'd by a Friar*, 1672); Elkanah Settle (*Cambises, King of Persia*, 1671, *Love and Revenge*, 1674, *The Conquest of China*, 1675); Aphra Behn (*Abdelazer, or The Moor's Revenge*, 1676); and Sir Charles Sedley (*Antony and Cleopatra*, 1676).

The types of 'serious drama' in the Restoration period have been categorised by Robert D. Hume, *The Development of Drama in the Late Seventeenth Century*, 1976, 192–229, as follows:

Ideas of Greatness: The 'Heroic' Play
The Villain on Display: Horror Tragedy
The Fall of the Hero: 'High' Tragedy
The Musical Spectacular: 'English' Opera
Split Plot and Mixed Plot Tragicomedy
Virtue Rewarded: The 'Pattern' Tragicomedy
Virtue Distressed: Pathetic Tragedy
History and Politics: 'Parallel' Plays.

Such a grouping of plays is not intended to suggest discrete categories, but it does illustrate the types of tragedy which emerged during this period. Tragedy as a form which had flourished during the 1670s rapidly withered away. Opera became the dramatic form in which the tragic mood might be better expressed. In 1708 the two theatres were in such a serious situation with their lack of audiences, that a new union between Drury Lane and the Haymarket tried to ensure the continuity of both by allowing Drury Lane to put on plays without music on six nights a week and the Haymarket to put on operas on Wednesdays and Saturdays. Financial arguments shut down Drury Lane on 6 June 1709 but it reopened in 1710 to leave the Haymarket once more to put on operas twice a week.

Tragedy struggled on again but by 1710 it was all but defunct as a form in the English theatre. For two or three more years, tragedy based on classicism tried desperately to retain a foothold on the stage: John Dennis's tragedy *Appius and Virginia* (1709) was savagely satirised by Pope in his *Essay on Criticism* for its bombast and exaggerated characterisation:

> But Appius reddens at each word you speak,
> And stares tremendous, with a threatening eye
> Like some fierce tyrant in old tapistry.

Ambrose Philips's *The Distrest Mother* (1712) attempted to adapt *Andromaque* by Racine. With Addison's *Cato* (1713), a story of rivalry, love, public duty, liberty, and honour, the 'pseudo-classical' tragedy, as Nicoll called it, the Restoration saw its final successful tragedy.

6.10 Opera

Dryden, in the preface to *Albion and Albanius* (1685), defined what he meant by opera:

> An **opera** is a poetical Tale or Fiction, represented by Vocal and Instrumental Musick, adorn'd with Scenes, Machines, and Dancing. The suppos'd Persons of this musical Drama are generally supernatural, as Gods and Godesses, and Heroes.
>
> (Quoted by R. D. Hume, *op. cit.*, 207)

Even before the Restoration, music had been combined with drama to form an entertainment in *The Siege of Rhodes* (1656), *The Cruelty of the Spaniards in Peru* (1658), and *The History of Sir Francis Drake* (1658). In 1674 Thomas Shadwell produced *The Enchanted Island*, which was adapted from Dryden's adaptation with the same name (in collaboration with D'Avenant) of Shakespeare's *The Tempest*. This was a musical entertainment with '24 Violins, with the Harpsicals and Theorbo's* which accompany the Voices'; it was full of spectacular events:

> This Tempest (suppos'd to be rais'd by Magick) has many dreadful Objects in it, as several Spirits in horrid shapes flying down amongst the sailers, then rising and crossing in the Air. And when the Ship is sinking, the whole House is darken'd, and a shower of Fire falls upon 'em. This is accompanied with Lighting, and several Claps of Thunder.
>
> (Stage direction from *The Enchanted Island*,
> quoted by R. D. Hulme, *op. cit.*, 208)

---

* bass-lutes with large double-necks

Operas became more and more elaborate and more costly to mount: *e.g.* a magic wand calls up a cloud, which, in turn, becomes first a windmill from which millers and girls emerge to dance, and then a witch who conjures up devils to dance before she finally disappears (in *Brutus of Alba or Augustan's Triumph* (1696), by John Verbruggen and George Powell with music by Daniel Purcell). Scenery and costume of an elaborate sort now became used on the English stage more and more. *The Fairy Queen* (1692) by Elkanah Settle with music by Henry Purcell had, as Allardyce Nicoll has pointed out, allegorical masques of Night and Sleep, Chinese dances with monkeys, and a 'transformation scene' which was becoming increasingly used (see the cloud scene in *Brutus of Alba*). Settle's *The World in The Moon* (1697, with music by Daniel Purcell and Jeremiah Clarke) had arches of clouds filled with Cupids, a silver moon which waned by degrees, twelve chariots riding the clouds filled with children, and an arch which rolled away leaving 'the full Prospect terminating with a large Lanschape of Woods, Waters, Towns, etc'. The comic scenes in this opera take the form of a rehearsal for the finished work proper.

Dryden, too, turned to opera with *Albion and Albanius* (1685, with music by Louis Grabut) and *King Arthur or The British Worthy* (1685, with music by Henry Purcell). The first of these operas intended to praise Charles and James, but Monmouth's landing in June put paid to its run on the stage.

Initially all the dialogue in operas was spoken and was interspersed with arias. This was the form of opera Purcell made popular, but by the beginning of the eighteenth century, under the influence of Italy, *recitative* and musical conversation were becoming the rule rather than the exception.

6.11 Comedy

Allardyce Nicoll (*op. cit.* 194) has said that there were four kinds of comedy in existence by the time the theatres reopened in 1660: the satirical comedy of humours (Jonson); the comedy of manners (Shirley); the comedy of romance or humour (Shakespeare); and the comedy of Spanish intrigue. By the end of the century these four Elizabethan/Jacobean types of comedy were joined by a later comedy of manners, farce from imitations of French and Italian works, and, by the end of the seventeenth century, sentimental comedy. 'None of these seven separate schools', said Nicoll, 'can be wholly dissociated from another, and most often we see merely general mixtures of two or three of them more or less successfully welded together'.

More recently, Robert D. Hume (*The Development of English Drama in the Late Seventeenth Century*, 1976) has wrestled with the problem of categorising Restoration comedy. He surveys James Sutherland's view (in *English Literature of the Late Seventeenth Century*, 1969, 152–3) that 'the comedy of Dryden, Etherege, Wycherley, and Congreve is now seen as offering a serious and consistent criticism of contemporary life' but this attitude may have overstated the case; Harriet Hawkins (in *Likenesses of Truth in Elizabethan and Restoration Drama*, 1972), Hume points out, has argued that 'Restoration comedies are about people, not ideas or ethical abstractions . . . they present the complexities and ambiguities of human experience rather than a simple white-or-black picture of what man should or should not be'.

Hume then goes on to summarise what he sees as the substance of Restoration comedies (*op. cit.*, 71–72). It provides a very useful account:

> Stock characters and situations. The young lovers who bring off an outwitting plot, the heavy Fathers, the fops, fools, hectors, country innocents, hapless Frenchmen, cuckolds, old husbands with young wives, lecherous old men, religious hypocrites, social pretenders, young wastrels, witty girls, young men of wit and little money, bawds and whores, long-suffering, stupid, or tricky servants, hapless tradesmen – these are the people of the comedies. The same plots are used again and again: the young man wins his girl and usually reforms in the process; fortune is won; adulterous copulation is achieved, without discovery – or the consequences are evaded. The same perils of discovery are run in comedy after comedy. The wanton wives, young libertines, jealous husbands, and witty young ladies produce highly repetitive patterns of events and situations.

In spite of these enormous similarities, the plot of any one comedy does not emerge the same as any other.

The main writers of comedy in this period were:

(a) **Sir George Etherege** (1634?–91, *She would if she could*, 1668, *The Man of Mode*, 1676);

(b) **George Farquhar** (1678–1707, *The Constant Couple or A trip to the Jubilee*, 1700, *The Recruiting Officer*, 1706, *The Beaux' Stratagem*, 1707);

(c) **William Wycherley** (1640–1716, *The Gentleman Dancing Master*, 1671, *The Country Wife*, 1672, *The Plain-Dealer*, 1674);

(d) **Sir John Vanbrugh** (1664–1726, *The Relapse*, 1697, *The Provok'd Wife*, 1697, *The Confederacy*, 1705, *The Provok'd Husband*, (finished by C. Cibber and produced in 1728)); and

(e) **William Congreve** (1670–1729, *The Old Bachelor*, 1693, *The Double Dealer*, 1694, *Love for Love*, 1695, *The Way of The World*, 1700).

6.12

It was during this last part of the seventeenth century that **Molière** (Jean-Baptiste Paquelin) (1622–73) produced his first work. His influence on comedy both in France and abroad was considerable. In 1659 he wrote his first comedy of manners *Précieuses Ridicules*. *L'école des maris* (1661) followed, and in the same year came the first of his ballet-comedies, *Les Fâcheux*; these were to become very popular at the French court. His *L'école des femmes* (1662) was attacked for its ridicule and for having indecent and irreverent passages in it. A similar attack from religious quarters was directed at *Tartuffe* (1664) and the King banned its public performance; it reappeared with some changes as *L'Imposteur* (significantly!) but it was again banned until 1669, when it achieved immense success. However, Molière's most famous plays *Le Misanthrope* (1666), *Le Medecin malgré lui* (1666), *L'Avare* (1668), *Le Bourgeois Gentilhomme* (1670) won instant acclaim. When he died in 1673, the church raised difficulties about his burial and so he was interred during the night without much ceremony (see J. M. Reid, *The Concise Oxford Dictionary of French Literature*, 1976, for a complete list of his work).

Molière was an excellent observer of mankind's follies, which he observes to the point where they begin to draw pathos and sympathy from the audience. Comedy is often most effective when the audience can keep its distance and laugh at others, not themselves, but it is at its best when there is the implicit assumption that all men are ridiculous, but some more than others because of their pompousness, their positions, or their attitudes to their fellows. Molière exposes hypocrisy and hits every form of affectation wherever he finds it; this, after all, was what roused the anger of the churchmen. Farce was never far from his work and farce is at its best when it takes stock types and stock situations, which the audience can readily recognise. Boileau thought he was a buffoon and others have criticised him for his contrived plots and endings. Nevertheless his *exposé* of the types of men and women he observed at court, in the church, and in the countryside rings true, given changes brought about by time and the change of superficial manners, of human kind. The major English comedy writers of the Restoration period certainly felt his influence.

6.13 The Comedy of Humours

The theory of humours was essentially medieval. The body was made up of four such humours: melancholy (cold and dry), phlegm (cold and moist), blood or sanguine (hot and moist), and bile (hot and dry). These humours combined to form one's 'complexion' and this complexion determined both one's appearance and behaviour: Chaucer's Frankeleyn (*The Canterbury Tales*, Prologue, line 332) is described 'Of his complexion he was sangwyn' and the rest of his portrait sets out the kind of man and behaviour typical of one with a sanguine complexion. When the humours were in balance and the astrological signs were propitious, one would be in good health. When they fell out of balance then one became ill and attempts had to be made to restore the balance of the humours by blood-letting, causing vomiting, or administering a laxative – as well as using astrological influences. Chaucer's Doctor of Physik was a good doctor because:

> He knew the cause of everich maladye,
> Were it of hoot, or coold, or moyste, or drye,
> And where they engendred, and of what humour.
> He was a verray, parfit praktisour.

He knew the right drugs to administer, the astrological signs to take into account, and had chemists who would make up his prescriptions.

This fourteenth century view of man's make-up and his behavioural patterns which followed persisted right through the sixteenth and seventeenth centuries until Harvey's theory of the circulation of the blood (1616) found acceptance after it was tested and vindicated in saving the lives of soldiers on the battlefields of the Civil War; a knowledge of the theory allowed blood to be staunched and wounds to be controlled.

However, the theory of humours as an explanation of human behaviour

continued in drama, popularised as it was by Jonson's plays and characterisation (see pages 110–112). Burton's *Anatomy of Melancholy* (1621) dealt with the
definition, causes, symptoms, and aspects of melancholy. The melancholy man
(Hamlet, Don John, Jaques) had been a stock character in Elizabethan plays.
Jonson's comedies had similar stock figures but had extended the 'types';
Molière's characters (the miser, the misanthrope, the bourgeois gentleman,
the doctor, etc.) used 'type' figures based on the humours and on the old
characters of Romance and religious drama.

In Restoration times Jonson's plays found new currency at the Theatre
Royal in Drury Lane and his satire and characterisation of contemporaries as
'types' opened up again a fertile field for the dramatist living in a Caroline,
William and Mary, or Queen Anne era.

Thomas Shadwell (1642?–1692) fell powerfully under both Jonson's and
Molière's influences. He produced *Sullen Lovers* in 1668, based heavily on
Molière's *Les Fâcheux*. He wrote an opera, *The Enchanted Island* (see page 168),
and drew on his observations of contemporary manners and amusements for
Epsom Wells (1673) and *Bury Fair* (1689). He quarrelled badly with Dryden in
1682, because Dryden had dared to attack, quite gently, Shadwell's idol, Ben
Jonson, and they both published satires attacking the other. In 1672 he wrote
The Miser and acknowledged his debt to Molière, once again. But Shadwell's
comedies were most effective on the Restoration stage when they turned from
satirising general follies (as in *The Humorists*) to sharper examples of fops and
knaves, 'the fittest characters for comedy' as he thought. His personal attacks
on Sir Robert Howard and members of his family in *The Sullen Lovers* led Pepys
and the audiences to see much of interest in what was otherwise a poorly
structured play about misanthropes. The next age in literature, dominated by
Pope, was one which would excel in sharp, personal attacks where the satirised
object would be hidden under invented or classical names (see *The Dunciad*).
Shadwell was particularly interested in exploring new 'humours' on the stage;
in a dedicatory epistle to *The Virtuoso* (1676) he rejected characterisation based
merely on the affected use of words or exaggerated fashions in dress, and aimed
his satire at those who were not naturally buffoons but had made themselves
seem so by their affectations. Lump, 'a methodical blockhead' (in *A True
Widow*) is one such character.

Other dramatists of the late seventeenth century who took up Jonson's
approach to the theory of humours and adapted it for their own use included
Abraham Cowley (1618–68), **John Lacy** (died 1681) who wrote farce, and
Sir Robert Howard (the *Crites* of Dryden's *Essay on Dramatick Poesie* (1668);
(see page 184).

6.14

By 1680 the humours play had fulfilled its purpose and a new kind of comedy,
the comedy of manners asserted itself. Robert Hume (*op. cit.*, 129–32) has
summarised in a very useful manner some of the main characteristics of this
kind of comedy. **The plots**, he argues, use one or more of the following
formulas:

(*a*) *marriage* – where 'male and female outwit blocking characters and make marriage possible';

(*b*) *cuckolding or fornication* – where male pursues female or older woman pursues male;

(*c*) *gulling* – where knaves are exposed;

(*d*) *marriage in disrepair* – where lovers part, the situation is left unresolved, or a reconciliation is effected.

The characters Hume divides into two categories, male and female. The male characters include:

(*a*) the male lead, and (*b*) his friend; (*c*) a would-be friend or rival; (*d*) the heavy father; (*e*) the dolt or gull; (*f*) the butt for humour; (*g*) the trickster; (*h*) the foolish servant; (*i*) professional types – lawyers, parsons, doctors, especially; (*j*) the hypocrite; (*k*) the bully, (*l*) the discontented husband. The female characters include: (*a*) the romantic lead, and (*b*) her friend and confidante; (*c*) the scheming maid; (*d*) the heavy mother or strict governess; (*e*) the mistress; (*f*) the cast mistress; (*g*) the whore; (*h*) the amorous, usually elderly woman; (*i*) the ingénue; (*j*) the abused wife.

This list of plots and characters by Hume is extremely useful, since it summarises most of the situations and types in the 'comedies of manners' as they are called. His work should be consulted by students since it gives examples of these plots and characters in detail and discusses some of the problems that arise in such categorisation.

Some of the plots and characters are, of course, those of the kind seen in the romantic comedies of Shakespeare, much earlier, but *marriage* itself now begins to play a larger part in comedy. In the medieval Romance convention marriage was often seen as a possible block to the ideals of the convention itself; there the plots dealt with courtship and the pursuit of love outside marriage. According to the exponent of the convention, Andreas Capellanus, in his *Flos Amoris or Ars Amatoria* (*c*. 1200), the point is explicitly set down: 'Marriage is not a good excuse for rejecting love'. In the 'comedy of manners' this is a rich source for the playwright.

The 'comedy of manners', however, like medieval romances, depended on the recognition of conventions. The 'manners' are those of society, particularly the society of the upper-class and courtly circles. They are often opposed, by definition, to nature, since they depend on sophistication and culture and are nurtured by custom and interaction in set milieux. Anything that contravenes the conventions is immediately recognisable and the target for humour; anything within the conventions that challenges them or pursues them to the point of folly is considered a fair source of fun. The tools of the dramatist are acute observation and exaggeration. The areas in which the dramatist can explore the conventions for fun lie in the contrasts between country and town, common sense and learning, simple honesty and cultivated deceit, sincerity and foppery, bluntness and polish. The 'games' are worked out in terms of wit rather than deeply-felt emotion. Indeed, once emotion or sympathy enter the arena, the comedy is in danger of evaporating very quickly. (The treatment of Malvolio in *Twelfth Night* where he is driven to the point of madness might have seemed funny on the Elizabethan stage, where madness could be used for fun, but to a twentieth century audience, the 'mad' Malvolio is a pathetic figure rather than a funny one.) Wit and detachment are at the heart of the comedy of manners.

Sir George Etherege (1634?–92?), strongly influenced by Molière, is often seen as the first exponent of the new 'comedy of manners', although Allardyce Nicoll argues that the genesis of the genre is to be seen also in Dryden, Shadwell, Sedley (*Lisideius* in Dryden's *Essay on Dramatick Poesie*), and Rawlins (about whose life little is known, but who is the author of *Tom Essence or The Modish Wife* (1676), based on Molière's *Le cocu imaginaire*, and of *Tunbridge-Wells or a Day's Courtship* (1678)). Etherege is best known for just two plays: *She Would if she Could* (1668) and *The Man of Mode* (1676). An earlier play, *The Comical Revenge or Love in a Tub* (1664) had a serious plot written in heroic couplets dealing with a duel, an attempted suicide, consolation from the sister of the girl whose beauty had provoked the problems, and a comic underplot written in prose, in which a French valet is confined to a tub for his impertinence, Sir Frederick Frolick is courted by a rich widow who is cajoled out of her fortune, and a foolish country knight is tricked out of a thousand pounds by a couple of rogues. All ends happily with the villains being forced to marry as a punishment! *The Man of Mode or Sir Fopling Flutter* has no real plot but shows the complicated interactions of characters set in the artificial society of Restoration times. Its prose dialogue runs on easily and the characters show a genteel libertine (Dorimant) leaving broken hearts and ruined reputations in his wake and a society bent on its own pleasures however ridiculous they seem or become.

William Wycherley (1640–1716) wrote his major comedies within five years or so, between 1671 and 1676: *Love in a Wood or St. James's Park* (1671); *The Gentleman Dancing Master* (1672); *The Country-Wife* (1674); *The Plain-Dealer* (1676). Harley Granville-Barker thought Wycherley 'lacks a sense of the theatre'; in a sense he was right since *The Plain-Dealer* takes a long time to get under way and *The Gentleman Dancing Master* takes a long time to end. Some have seen Wycherley as a playwright bent on teaching rather than delighting and Gerald Weales (*The Complete Plays of William Wycherley*, 1967, Introductions) argues that the dramatist's purpose could be summed up in Lisideius's (Sedley's) view of a play in Dryden's *Essay on Dramatick Poesie*: 'A just and lively Image of Humane Nature, representing its Passions and Humours and the Changes of Fortune to which it is subject; for the Delight and Instruction of Mankind'. Wycherley's debt to Molière is best seen in *The Plain-Dealer*. Here, Manley, a sea captain who wants to escape the world and its ways, trusts only Vernish, his 'bosome and onely friend', and Olivia, his mistress to whom he has entrusted all his money. When Manley returns to find Olivia married to another, she refuses to give him back his money. Fidelia, a young girl, loves Manley and follows him about disguised as a boy. Manley sends Fidelia to Olivia as a go-between but she falls in love with him. (*cf.* Olivia and Cesario in *Twelfth Night*) Olivia's husband rushes into a secret meeting between his wife, Fidelia, and Manley only to be revealed as none other than the 'noble' friend Vernish. Fidelia is hurt in the fight and discovered to be a woman; Manley rejects Olivia and falls in love with Fidelia.

The *misanthrope* character is from Molière; the go-between/girl disguised as a boy in her master's service is from Shakespeare; the sub-plot of the widow Blackacre and her son Jerry, both of whom enjoy going to law, provides the lighter comedy along with Major Oldfox, 'another impertinent fop given to scribbling', My Lord Plausible, 'a ceremonious supple, commending coxcomb', and Novell, 'a pert railing coxcomb and an admirer of novelties'. Manley and Molière's Alceste have in common their detestation of the treachery of human nature and the current fashions in literature, manners and clothes; theirs is a pessimistic view of the world and they both speak constantly in the first person. Manley comes through to a reappraisal of his view of his fellow human beings:

I will believe, there are now in the World
Good-natur'd Friends, who are not Prostitutes,
And handsom Women worthy to be Friends;

but he warns:

Yet, for my sake, let no-one e're confide
In Tears, or Oaths, in Love or Friend untry'd.

After litigation (*cf. The Plain-Dealer*) Alceste is still disillusioned with his fellows in *Le Misanthrope* and goes off to seek honour and liberty:

Je vais sortir d'un gouffre où triomphent les vices
Et chercher sur la terre un endroit écarté
Où d'être homme d'honneur on ait la liberté.

The Misanthrope is a **comedy of character** which springs from the lack of a true philosophy of life in the major characters, and their over-sensitivity to things around them. Alceste cannot cope adequately with anything which conflicts with his views about his ideals; he expects too much from mankind, more than he manages to get from himself. He finds a gap between what he says and what he can do. Philinte, his friend, is calm, thoughtful and faithful, but, above all, tolerant of the faults of others, without trusting them. He is always right, and this in itself leads to comedy. Celimène, a coquette, is loved by Alceste, she has a delight in teasing her friends but is well able to recognise her own faults. At the end the ridicule she has directed at others is turned on her. Her rival for Alceste, Arsinéo, is the aging coquette of comedy who is prepared to use anything, including religion, to get her own way, but she is ridiculous as a woman who refuses to grow old. As a **situation comedy** the play is comic because as the situations change and the relationships alter, the basic characters remain static. In comedy there is usually no great development of character; it depends rather on the progressive revelation of character. As

a comedy of manners *The Misanthrope* explores the relationship of the characters and their affectations to the situations in which they find themselves – the court, the town, the social characters who parade themselves about. As a drama it is sometimes held up by the posturing stances of the characters who pronounce rather like the unchanging but impressive pieces on a chess-board, 'who move and declare their very natures as they do move within their own limits and borders'. As they move, they affect others but they always remain vulnerable in spite of their own self-assumed importance.

The situation and characters in *The Plain-Dealer* are not that much different. The characters posture, almost as caricatures at times, but they are usually one-dimensional. The situations in which they find themselves come about because society with its double-dealing is what it is. The comedy, however, springs from the ridiculous, the gap between what people think they are and what events show them to be. It is in this gap that any moral teaching lies for those that wish to find it.

William Congreve (1670–1729) was born near Leeds but brought up and educated in Ireland. At both Kilkenny School and Trinity College, Dublin, he was a fellow student of Swift. In 1693 he sprang into the dramatic limelight with *The Old Bachelor*. Heartwell, who hates women, is lured into 'a marriage' with Silvia, a rejected mistress of Vainlove. Disguise, pairings and cross-pairings in love, the debunking of the pompous old, the triumphing of the deserving over the cowardly and bullying Captain Bluffe, the discovery that Heartwell's marriage was really a pretence – all these ensured the success that comes from the satirical observation of men and women in society, with their preconceived and prejudiced static attitudes about themselves and others. Congreve's reputation, however, in the field of the comedy of manners lies in *The Double Dealer* (1694), *Love for Love* (1695) *The Way of the World* (1700). Of these only *Love for Love* was an immediate success in the theatre. Allardyce Nicoll (*op. cit.* 243) attributes the failure of *The Way of the World* with its contemporary audiences to the fact that 'it was . . . too rarefied, too refined for the spirit of its time. There is no sentiment in it, no realism, no coarseness', but he concludes, 'the theme is artificial and the conclusion is artificial, if we test it by the standards of everyday life: yet both have a brilliancy and a truth which make *The Way of the World* the master-creation of the school of manners'. It was not a comedy, however, which impressed Charles Lamb in quite the same way:

> I think I must have sat at it (*The Way of the World*) as grave as a judge; for I remember the hysteric affectations of good Lady Wishfort affected me like some solemn tragic passion.
>
> (*The Essays of Elia*)

The works of **Sir John Vanbrugh** (1664–1726) are considered by Nicoll as 'glorified farces' with 'no finesse'. Hazlitt thought he had 'more nature than art: what he does best, he does because he cannot help it'. It was Vanbrugh, however, who constructed the 'Queen's' or the Haymarket Theatre, designed as an opera house, and the new home of the Lincoln's Inn Fields company. The acoustics were so bad for plays that the company moved back to Lincoln's Inn

Fields for a time to allow alterations to be made. However, the new theatre was finally used more for opera than plays.

The Relapse (1696) was a sequel to the 'sentimental' play of Cibber *Love's Last Shift* (January 1696). The tricks of one brother on another in the game of love, a homosexual pimp (Coupler), an enormously caricatured fop (Lord Foppington) and a character called Sir Tunbelly Clumsey give some indication of the nature of the play. It was well received by its first audience and was later adapted by Sheridan as *A Trip to Scarborough* (1777). Vanbrugh wrote one other original play, *The Provok'd Wife* in 1697. Here it is clear that the **comedy of sentiment** has supplanted the 'comedy of manners'. Emotion and feeling have now come strongly into comedy so that its detachment in observation is waning. Constant loves the wife of a sot, named significantly Sir John Brute, but she is trapped by marriage and cannot break free. Bellinda, Lady Brute's niece, however, rejects marriage for wealth and marries the man she loves, Heartfree. Marriage is seen as a convention which both ties and liberates. But the stock characters abound again: Lady Fancyfull who desires Heartfree; the magistrate; Sir John disguised as a parson. The moralising in comedy is becoming more strident in the plays of the turn of the century.

George Farquhar (1678–1707) reveals the new realistic attitudes of comedy in his plays. Nicoll sees his early plays as 'immoral' but Robert Hume describes *The Twin-Rivals* (1702) (*op. cit.*, 465) as 'an angrily moral play'. In this play Farquhar attacks the rakes of the town and the intricacies of the legal system.

The struggle in Farquhar to come to terms with the new moral realism (given a new impetus by the publication of Jeremy Collier's *Short View of the Immorality and Profaneness of the English Stage*, 1698, in which he attacked Congreve and Vanbrugh, and which led to the prosecution of Congreve and Thomas D'Urfey and the fining of the actors Betterton and Mrs Bracegirdle), was borne out in his two final plays *The Recruiting Officer* (1706) and the engagingly fresh breath of country air in *The Beaux' Stratagem*. In these two plays are 'stock' types but the dramatist looks with sympathy on the weaknesses of men and women. All is exaggerated, but inherent in the plays is an understanding of human nature rooted in realistic approaches. Farquhar has shown drama moving on from 'the comedy of manners'.

The Recruiting Officer was revised in the light of an order issued to the Company of Comedians at Drury Lane by the Lord Chamberlain in 1704. Plays had to take care 'to leve out such Expressions as are contrary to Religion & Good Manners'. The actors were not 'to Act, upon the Stage any Play New or Old, containing Profane or Indecent Expressions which may give Offence'. The Master of the Revels, Charles Killigrew, was accused by Colley Cibber of 'striking out whole Scenes of a vicious, or immoral Character, tho' it were visibly shewn to be reform'd'. The play was based on Farquhar's own experience of being a recruiting officer, after he was commissioned as a Lieutenant of Grenadiers in 1704. In 1705–6 he was at Shrewsbury actively recruiting. Young men were often tricked into joining up and often could avoid the recruitment by bribery. Queen Anne's officers needed to enlist men for her armies to fight in the War of the Spanish Succession. Debtors and criminals could be released from prison if they joined the forces but JP's could recruit fit men who were unemployed or without visible means of support.

However, Farquhar wrote to amuse, not to put down the very practices on which his own commission had depended. The play has characters which are recognisable as people as well as types, and so the move towards the 'sentimental' drama of the eighteenth century can be perceived. It has an intricate plot network consisting of three interwoven actions: the enlisting plot, the plot revolving round Silvia, and that turning on Melinda. The success of the play relies partly on the way these plots come together and break free from each other and partly on the pace with which they are tackled. In comedy it is essential to maintain pace. Long, static scenes or exchanges of dialogue do not necessarily make good theatre, although Shaw later exploited the use of verbal exchanges, and confrontations before audiences which enjoyed debate and court scenes, by their very nature, depend on the conflict of accuser/accused for their success.

The Recruiting Officer has humour, magic, deceit, intrigue, frustrated love, disguise, comments on social injustice, and buffoons to amuse its audiences. The play was a success from its first production on April 8, 1706. It was part of the opening season of plays of the National Theatre in the Old Vic in 1963.

The Beaux' Stratagem (1707) was the last play in the amazingly condensed dramatic career of Farquhar. The Prologue, spoken by Mr Wilks, comments on Wycherley's *The Plain-Dealer:*

> When strife disturbs, or sloth corrupts an age,
> Keen satire is the business of the stage.
> When the Plain Dealer writ, he lashed those crimes
> Which then infected most the modish times.

The satire of the comedy of manners gives way in *The Beaux' Stratagem* to a more relaxed but moral approach:

> Follies tonight we show ne'er lashed before,
> Yet such as Nature shows you every hour;
> Nor can the pictures give a just offence,
> For fools are made for jests to men of sense.

The Epilogue includes the lines:

> Forbear, you fair, on his last scene to frown,
> But his true exit with a plaudit crown;
> Then shall the dying poet cease to fear
> The dreadful knell, while your applause he hears.

Two months later Farquhar was dead – probably from tuberculosis.

6.15

The changes which took place in the theatre at the end of the seventeenth century were not as sudden as critics used to suggest. The move towards 'sentimental' comedy, as it is often called, was already under way. Jeremy

Collier's attack in 1698, *A Short View of the Immorality and Prophaneness of the English Stage*, written as it was by a strict non-conformist of uncompromising morals, did not instigate a new attack on the stage but put into words the thoughts of the years leading up to it. On January 24th, 1696, the Lord Chamberlain ordered the licensing of all plays:

> I doe therefore Order and Command that for ye future noe playes shall be Acted but such as shall first be sent (and that in due time) to Charles Killegrew Esqr Master of ye Revells by him to be perused and diligently Corrected and Licensed . . . and I doe further Order & Command the said Master to be very Carfull in Correcting all Obsenityes & other Scandalous matters & such as any wayes Offend against ye Lawes of God and Good manners of the knowne Statutes of this Kingdome.

Samuel Johnson summed up the eighteenth century's view of Restoration comedy with its 'immorality' in a Prologue spoken at Drury Lane in 1747:

> Themselves they studied, as they felt they writ;
> Intrigue was plot, obscenity was wit.
> Vice always found a sympathetic friend;
> They pleas'd their age, and did not aim to mend.

This echoes Collier's condemnation in 1698 of plays such as Vanbrugh's *The Relapse:*

> I observe the moral is vicious: it points the wrong way, and puts the prize into the wrong hand . . . This play perverts the end of comedy: Which . . . ought to regard reformation, and public information. But the Relapser had a more fashionable fancy in his head.

6.16

The first half of the eighteenth century saw three main changes in the English theatre. The so-called 'Patent' theatres (Drury Lane and the Haymarket, formerly the Queen's) were expanded to accommodate an audience drawn from a wider spectrum of society; the theatre-going public grew to include the new middle classes of merchants and their families; a number of minor theatres sprang up throughout the country, many of them called 'The Theatre Royal' (see pages 35, 162, 181).

Although the **theatres** expanded in the second half of the century, in the early part they still kept the boxes, the galleries, the apron stage, the doors for entrances and exits in the proscenium, and the curtain of the Restoration period. Scenery was run on to the stage to change the scene from indoors to outdoors, from country to town but, although the curtain was a feature of the stage, Allardyce Nicoll (*A History of English Drama*, II, third edition, 1952) has pointed out that 'the playwrights did not realise to what uses they might put (it)'. Foreign artists from Italy and the Continent used to paint scenery, and 'machines' were used to provide spectacular effects – clouds, waves, lightning, etc. Costume was the fashionable dress of the period for comedy but tragedy used some clothes to suggest the historical period or place (*e.g.* Roman, Middle-Eastern) the play required.

The increasingly middle-class **audience** came to the theatre to be diverted and to meet other people, and several writers of the period comment on the public taste that demanded farce and ballad-operas. Drunkenness and fights were known, as Nicoll (*op. cit.*) has pointed out, and riots caused by the audience going back stage, a duel on the stage, and assaults on the actors were all recorded. The first nights were looked upon by young 'bloods' as occasions for causing trouble. Even after the new Licensing Act of 1737, the interruptions continued. Nicoll has shown this in the Preface to *The Nest of Plays* (1738) (three short plays collected together) by Sir Hildebrand Jacob, 'the first Play licensed by the Lord Chamberlain since the last Act concerning the Stage';

> *The first Representation of the* . . . Performance *was interrupted, e'er it well began, in the Presence of a numerous and polite* Audience, *by some People, who, it seems, were determined, as they themselves declared, to silence without any Distinction, the* first Fruits *of that* Act *of* Parliament *which was thought necessary for the Regulation of the* Stage.

Some dramatists, *e.g.* Steele, tried to pack the theatres with their friends to make sure any outbursts could be repressed, apparently. Just as disorder on the terraces at football matches today is often blamed on the unruly behaviour of the players on the field, so in the first half of the eighteenth century it seems that the actors often set a poor example to their audiences. Cibber, the player of comedy, 'beat one play down' and 'laid aside' another. Sewell in a preface spoke about Cibber's rudeness to new authors and the author of *A Proposal For the better Regulation of the Stage* (1732) spoke about 'the Tyranny of the Players', Cibber's rudeness and the way playwrights were ill-treated (see Nicol, *op. cit.*, 42–3).

An interesting account of **the actors** during this same period is found in Colley Cibber's *Apology for the life of Mr Colley Cibber, Comedian*, published in 1740. Cibber (1671–1757) was a playwright and an actor and his *Apology*, as it is known, gives detailed accounts of his colleagues such as Betherton, Mrs Bracegirdle, Nokes, and others. His portraits throw considerable light on the acting-styles of the period. Nokes, for example, was always clapped on his first entry into a play and the sight of him always made the audience burst into laughter, but the more they laughed the more solemn he looked: 'and sure, the ridiculous solemnity of his features were enough to have set a whole bench of bishops into a titter . . . the louder the laugh the graver was his look'. The apron stage allowed every detail of his facial expression to be noted by the audience – his rolling eye, his 'vacant amazement', his 'piteous pusillanimity, and a consternation so ruefully ridiculous and inconsolable, that when he had shook you to a fatigue of laughter, it became a moot point whether you ought not to have pitied him'.

Women actors, such as Mrs Oldfield and Mrs Bracegirdle were formidable actresses, but the convention of presenting women dressed as men, common during the Restoration times, continued. These actresses, dressed as dashing young men often spoke the Epilogues to plays. The parts of young boys and even eunuchs seem to have been written, too, especially for the women actors who specialised in these 'dressed-up' roles.

The Licensing Act of 1737, attempted to exercise strict controls over the theatre. James Sutherland (*English Satire*, 1958, 133) attributes the cause of the passing of the act to Henry Fielding's outspoken satire of Walpole and the Whig government in *Pasquin: a Dramatick Satire on the Times* (1735–6), and *The Historical Register* (1736). Walpole, of course, had already come in for some satire in Gay's *The Beggar's Opera* (1728). However, the satirists were not quelled and in 1739 Dr Johson produced his ironical *A Compleat Vindication of the Licensers of the Stage from the Malicious and Scandalous Aspersions of Mr Brooke, author Gustavus Vasa. With a Proposal for making the Office of Licenser more extensive and effectual*. It is certain that following the Act, plays were suppressed in increasing number.

The 'minor' theatres during the first half of the eighteenth century increased. In addition to the two 'patent theatres' other theatres, before and after the Licensing Act, were putting on dramatic entertainments: Punch's Theatre*, which was used by Martin Powell in 1710–12; Punch's Theatre on Tower Hill, used by Harris in 1721; Punch's Theatre (at the Old Tennis Court in St. James's near the Haymarket, used by Clarke (1737–38) and Yeates (1739–40); New Wells in Clerkenwell; Hickford's Room in Haymarket, where musical entertainment was offered in 1739; Crown and Anchor, Strand, where oratorios were given, 1739–40; Sadlers Wells, 1740 onwards; New Theatre in James's Street, Haymarket, used for plays from 1741; New Theatre in Beaux Street, used for plays in 1742; Old Theatre, Southwark, used for plays, 1744–45; and the Puppet Theatre in Panton Street under Madame de la Nash, 1745–46. Other theatres operated fairly regularly in Richmond, Greenwich, Twickenham, Tunbridge Wells and Bath. (This list is derived from Allardyce Nicoll, *A History of English Drama*, II, third edition, 1952, 272–3.)

6.17

By the second half of the eighteenth century English drama was in serious decline. The drama that has survived the intervening critics to the present day is largely represented by the work of Oliver Goldsmith (1730–34), and Richard Brinsley Sheridan (1751–1816). Nevertheless, farces, pantomimes, and poetical plays, as well as operas, also provided entertainment.

Theatres were still noisy and often critics banked their sticks and audiences operated their cat-calls. A cat-call was a shrill instrument whirled in the hand which made a shricking noise and expressed disapproval.

Whu – go the cat-calls – dub-dub-dub – each dreadful critick's stick.
(Quoted by Allardyce Nicoll.)
(Arthur Murphy's *The School for Guardians*,
Prologue, 1767)

---

* See W. Hazlitt, *Lectures on the English Comic Writers*, 1818, for a description of the 'Punch and Puppet-show', which was still running strong.

Even if the writing was dull, this *was* the age of **David Garrick** (1717–79), . one of the great English actor-managers. He made his acting debut at Ipswich in 1741, and played Gloucester in Richard III in the same year. In 1747 he came to Drury Lane to work with Lacy, where they put on a number of Shakespeare's plays. He sold his share in the theatre to Sheridan and two others for the enormous sum of £35 000 in 1776. He was the author of some farces (*The Lying Valet*, 1741; *Miss in her Teens*, 1772, *Bon Ton or High Life above Stairs*). His importance, however, lies in the changes he made to the Drury Lane Theatre with the withdrawal of the actors behind the proscenium arch (see pages 35–36 for a full account of his work) and for his acting skills. He made Partridge's knees knock together in the Hamlet-Ghost encounter (in Fielding's *Tom Jones*): 'Hamlet is acted by the best player who ever was on the stage'. (See also Thomas Davies, *Memoirs of the Life of David Garrick*, 1780, quoted extensively by Stephen Joseph, *The Story of the Playhouse in England*, 1963, an excellent survey of the craft of the theatre.)

Drury Lane was extended in 1762 and 1780 and entirely rebuilt in 1792; its capacity increased during this time from 220 to 3611 persons. Covent Garden, opened by Rich in 1732, was altered in 1782 and rebuilt in 1792 to take much bigger audiences. (It was burnt down in 1808, rebuilt, burnt down in 1856, and rebuilt again by Barry in 1858.) In the eighteenth century the lighting and acoustics were bad and the changes in the theatre led to: a loss of intimacy; a

David Garrick and Susannah Maria Gibber in Otway's *Venice Preserved*.

need to make the scenery more elaborate, and to increase spectacle with novelties, especially strange creatures in pantomimes; the use of the drop-scene; and the introduction of costumes intended to be historically accurate for the time setting and the geographical location of the play. Although the drama was uninspired towards the end of the century, the theatre had made huge strides in the development of its art.

The introduction of de Loutherbourg, the scene-designer, by David Garrick to Drury Lane, in 1771, led to an increase in spectacular stage scenery, especially in pantomimes and spectacles (see pages 35–36). The scenery was usually well-lit and so actors pulled back from the front of the stage to behind the lights amongst the scenery where they could be seen by the audience. This meant that now their words, because of the distance between actors and audience in the newly-reconstructed theatres, had to be shouted and their moods would be better indicated if they were supported by music.

Garrick died in 1779. A year later, Sheridan, the greatest dramatist of his period, wrote some lines to be spoken as a monody at the Theatre Royal in Drury Lane, which set out his enormous skills as an actor-manager:

> The grace of action – the adopted mien,
> Faithful as nature to the varied scene;
> Th'expressive glance – whose subtle comment draws
> Entranced attention, and a mute applause;
> Gesture that marks, with force and feeling fraught,
> A sense in silence, and a will in thought;
> Harmonious speech, whose pure and liquid tone
> Gives verse a music, scarce confess'd its own.

The art of Garrick was clearly attuned to the bigger theatres he had helped to design. All the skills are to do with movement, gestures, expression, silences, and a musical rendering of the verse he spoke.

6.18 Tragedy in the Eighteenth Century
Influenced strongly by Corneille and Racine, the Rules for tragedy became well-established in the eighteenth century:

> Those rules, of old discover'd, not devised,
> Are Nature still, but Nature methodised;
> Nature, like liberty, is but restrained
> By the same laws which first herself ordain'd.
> (Alexander Pope, *An Essay on Criticism*, 1709)

The rules are to be found, argued Pope, in the classics, especially in the writings of Homer, Aristotle, Virgil, and Horace; A work of art is a unity: 'Survey the whole'.

Sidney, in *An Apologie for Poetry* (*c*. 1580), lamented that English tragedy, was 'faulty both in place and time, the two necessary companions of all corporal actions'; 'the stage should always represent but one place and the uttermost time presupposed in it should be, both by Aristotle's precept and common reason, but one day . . . two young princes fall in love; after many traverses she is got with child, delivered of a fair boy; he is lost, groweth a man, falleth in love, and is ready to get another child, and all this in two hours' space'. Sidney argued, too, that the mixing of tragedy and comedy breaks the Unity of Action, thrusting 'in the clown by head and shoulders to play a part in majestical matters, with neither decency nor decorum'. According to these strictures Shakespeare is a poor dramatist, and *Macbeth, King Lear*, and *Hamlet* poor tragedies. Ben Jonson, however, tried to observe the Unities (see page 110).

Dryden, in his version of the Antony and Cleopatra story, *All for Love* (1678) observed all three neo-classical Unities. He discussed them in his critical work *An Essay on Dramatick Poesie* (published 1668). There Eugenius (the Earl of Dorset) speaks at length about classical writers and points out, '**the Unity of Place**, however it might be practised by them, was never any of their rules: we neither find it in Aristotle, Horace, or any who have written of it, till in our age the French poets first made it a precept of the stage. **The Unity of Time**, even Terence himself . . . has neglected. It is true they have kept the continuity, or, as you called it, *liaison des scènes*, somewhat better . . .' Lisideius (Sir Charles Sedley) argues that the French dramatists kept to the Unities:

> In **the Unity of Time** you find them so scrupulous, that it yet remains a dispute among their poets, whether the artificial day of twelve hours, more or less, be not meant by Aristotle, rather than the natural one of twenty-four hours; and consequently whether all plays ought not to be reduced into that compass . . . In **the Unity of Place** they are full as scrupulous; for many of their critics limit it to that very spot of ground where the play is supposed to begin . . . **The Unity of Action** in all plays is yet more conspicuous; for they do not burden themselves with under-plots, as the English do.

Here, then, is a clear explanation of the Rules of plays, and tragedy in particular. Much of the rest of Dryden's *Essay* is taken up with the influence of the French dramatists, the concept of the hero, their beauty and skill in rhyming, their gravity, and their plots. Neander (Dryden himself) defends English drama against Sedley's charges on the grounds that 'there is a more masculine fancy and greater spirit in the writing, than there is in any of the French'.

Dr Johnson, in his *Preface to Shakespeare* (1765), discussed, too, the merits of the 'ancients' and the 'moderns'. Shakespeare held up 'to his readers a faithful mirror of manners and of life . . . his drama is the mirror of life'. He accepts that 'Shakespeare's plays are not in the vigorous and critical sense either tragedies or comedies'. Nevertheless, 'the plots are often so loosely formed, that a very slight consideration may improve them, and so carelessly pursued, that he seems not always fully to comprehend his own design'. He then turns to 'his neglect of the Unities – his violation of those laws which have been instituted and established by the joint authority of poets and of critics . . . His histories, being neither tragedies nor comedies, are not subject to any of their laws. In his other works he has well enough preserved **the Unity of Action** . . . his plan has commonly what Aristotle requires, a beginning, a middle, and an end . . . **To the Unities of Time and Place** he has shown no regard'. These Unities have been held in esteem, Johnson argues, from the time of Corneille, and the Unities of Time and Place arise from the supposed necessity of 'making the drama credible'. 'Whether Shakespeare knew the Unities, and rejected them by design, or deviated from them by happy ignorance, it is, I think, impossible to decide and useless to inquire'. The Unity of Action is the important one, to Johnson, and Shakespeare observed that; 'the Unities of Time and Place are not essential to a just drama, though they may sometimes conduce to pleasure'. Johnson then spoils his concession to Shakespeare by a massive piece of bombast and ignorance: 'The English nation, in the time of Shakespeare, was yet struggling to emerge from barbarity'! It is hard for a twentieth-century writer not to be amused, when he or she considers the contemporary customs and social injustices to which the eighteenth-century writer, Swift, drew attention or the abuses of a barbarous sort which still exist in the twentieth century itself.

Eighteenth-century English drama felt encumbered by the 'Rules'. Allardyce Nicoll believed that, 'Augustinianism held control of the stage and helped towards the suppressing of true dramatic emotion'. Romanticism in English tradition would soon break the classical bonds, he thought. In 1789 the French Revolution would shake to its foundations the classical order in France, the France of Versailles, the court, reason and taste (*le goût*).

Pseudo-classical tragedy in England was not popular, partly because of its classical traditions and partly because it was tragedy. John Dennis's *Appius and Virginia* (1709) or *Iphigenia* (1700) and Dr Johnson's *Irene* (1749), generously put on by his old pupil, David Garrick, but little more than a series of moral dialogues between Mahomet, emperor of the Turks, his attendants, and some Greek captives, hardly seized the audiences' attention by their drama. Ambrose Philips's *The Distrest Mother* (1712), based on Racine's *Andromaque* had better success. Addison's *Cato* (1713) managed to hit on a contemporary interest of the audiences and so managed some success. It dealt with Cato's obstinate and defiant stand for liberty to the point of death at a time when Queen Anne was nearing death and the whole point of succession to the English throne would come up yet again, with all its uncertainties and threats from abroad. His play included a love-plot, too, but Addison's contemporaries continued to emphasise the love element which they thought had made both Racine and Addison successful. In the middle of the eighteenth century James Thomson (the author of *Seasons*) wrote *Sophonisba* (1730), *Agamemnon* (1738), *Edward and Eleonora* (1739) and *Tancred and Sigismunda* (1745) in an attempt to deal with patriotic themes in a classical manner. These pseudo-classical plays achieved less success than the pseudo-romantic tragedies later in the century in the form of **melodrama**.

6.19

Melodrama is a term often used to apply to a form of dramatic presentation in the nineteenth century which runs alongside the development of gas lighting and the new effects consequently made possible. (Drury Lane opened on

September 6, 1817, for the new season, lit entirely by gas, and by 1840 gas was used in most theatres.) It is usually associated with plays such as *Maria Marten or The Murder in the Red Barn* (the 1830s) or the best-known of all melodramas, *Sweeney Todd, The Barber of Fleet Street* (1865). The genre is sometimes thought to end with T. W. Robertson's *Caste* (1867). However, others see the continuation of melodrama after that and well into the twentieth century with plays such as *The Prisoner of Zenda, The Scarlet Pimpernel, The Only Way, Ben Hur* (Stephen Joseph, *The Story of the Playhouse in England*, 1963, 117.) If the ending of melodrama is difficult to establish, so is its beginning. A convenient point of departure might be the work of George Lillo (1693–1739) and particularly his highly successful prose, domestic tragedy *The London Merchant or The History of George Barnwell* (1731), based on an old ballad of 'George Barnwell', which dealt with the seduction of an apprentice by a ruthless courtesan, Millwood, who persuades him to rob his employer and murder his uncle, for which crime both he and Millwood are sentenced to death. This so-called 'domestic tragedy' left audiences weeping and was praised by Diderot and Gotthold Lessing as well as being translated into German, French, and Dutch. Allardyce Nicoll (*British Drama*, fifth edition, 1962, 196) even claims that the play 'marked the downfall of the classical tragedy, and to a large degree established the basis for the modern theatre'.

The word **melodrama** is derived, through French, from two Greek words μελος a song + δράμα action. It means, according to *Chambers Twentieth Century Dictionary*: 'a play with musical accompaniment to the action and spoken dialogue with or without songs: a kind of romantic and sensational drama, crude, sentimental, and conventional'. In France *mélodrames* were played in the *théâtres du boulevard* in Paris from about 1798 onwards in great numbers. René-Charles Pixérécourt (1773–1844) wrote more than 100 melodramas between 1798 and 1835, often adapted from novels of the so-called 'Gothic' type, such as Mrs Radcliffe's *Mysteries of Udolpho* (published 1794). In France, however, well before 1798, Molière had devised comédie-ballet, a dramatic form of ballet played out between the acts of his comedies, in much the same way that music was used between comedies in *The Knight of the Burning Pestle* in England (see pages 151–152); in Molière the inter-act ballets were often satirical or farcical and had some connection with the play's main theme.

In England during the eighteenth century a form of domestic drama grew up alongside the development of the romantic Gothic novel, whose main exponents were: Matthew Gregory Lewis, (1775–1818) who wrote *The Monk* (1796); Mrs Ann Radcliffe (1764–1823), *Romance of The Forest* (1791), *The Mysteries of Udolpho* (1794), and *The Italian* (1797); and Hugh Walpole, *The Castle of Otranto* (1764). Later, in the nineteenth century, the best known of all Gothic novels was produced, *Frankenstein or The Modern Prometheus* (1818) by Mary Shelley, the daughter of William Godwin and second wife of Percy B. Shelley. The reading and popularity of Gothic novels is, of course, satirised in Jane Austen's *Northanger Abbey* (begun in 1798 and published in 1803).

The 'domestic drama' which develops into melodrama in England was not accompanied by music. Such plays demanded gloom and mystery, a hero or heroine whose innocence and vulnerability would excite pity, a series of lofty utterances called 'sentiments', spectacular effects, and a 'villain' who could preferably be reformed in the final act. *Arden of Faversham* (1592) (adapted by Lillo himself and put on at Drury Lane in 1759) might be seen as the first of such domestic dramas but it ends unhappily: Mistress Arden and her lover Mosbie try to murder Arden and finally succeed after hiring two murderous villains, Back Wil and Shakbag. Mosbie and Mrs Arden are caught and executed. The play was based on an actual murder in February 1550 and reported in Holinshed's Chronicles.

George Lillo's *The London Merchant* (1731) has some astonishing black soliloquys and exaggerated dramatic moments:

> BARNWELL   A dismal gloom obscures the face of day. Either the sun has slipped behind a cloud, or journeys down the west of heaven with more than common speed, to avoid the sight of what I am doomed to act. Since I set forth on this accursed design, where'er I tread, methinks the solid earth trembles beneath my feet . . . For him that was my father's only brother – and, since his death, has been to me a father; who took me up an infant and an orphan, reared me with tenderest care, and still indulged me with most paternal fondness? Yet here I stand avowed his destined murderer – I stiffen with horror at my own impiety. 'Tis yet unperformed – what if I quit my bloody purpose and fly the space? (*Going, then stops.*) But, whither, oh whither shall I fly?

It would be hard to act this today without 'hamming' or 'sending it up'.

Lillo had those who tried to follow his success. John Hewitt wrote *Fatal Falsehood or Distress'd Innocence* in 1734 and Edward Moore, *The Gamester* in 1753.

'Monk' Lewis produced *The Castle Spectre* in 1797, and this melodrama *was* accompanied by music. The play is romantic and similarly unsubtle, as Lillo's. Other writers of the eighteenth century who wrote 'melodramas' were Miles Andrews (with Frederick Reynolds), *The Mysteries of the Castle* (1795); Thomas Morton, *Columbus* (1792); Samuel Birch, *The Adopted Child* (1795) and *The Smugglers* (1796); James Cross, *The Purse* (1794); George Colman, *The Iron Chest* (1796) and *Blue Beard or Female Curiosity* (1798). *Blue Beard* has some spectacular effects: a skeleton which comes to life and plunges a dart into a character who is then dragged down into the earth and consumed with fire; pictures, sculpted over a door, which move; rooms splashed with blood; tombs; writing in blood, etc. Actors might have difficulty with such melodramas. The playwrights were clearly writing for effects and deliberately overdoing it. The audiences apparently loved them.

6.20

Shakespearean tragedies as well as melodrama were more popular than the pseudo-classical tragedies after the middle of the eighteenth century. They were often adapted. Allardyce Nicoll (*op. cit.*) has given an impressive list of Shakespearean revivals during the eighteenth century: *Richard II* (at Bath, 1754); *Hamlet* (by Garrick in 1772 and Kemble about 1792); *King Lear* (by

Garrick in 1756, Colman in 1768, and Kemble in 1788); *Timon of Athens* (by Dance at Richmond in 1768, and Hull at Covent Garden in 1786); *Antony and Cleopatra* (altered by Copell and Garrick, 1759, and by Brooke in 1778); and *Coriolanus* (by Kemble in 1789), and *Cymbeline* (by Marsh in 1756, Hawkins in 1759, Garrick in 1761, Brooke in 1778, and Eccles in 1792).

6.21

Foreign tragedies were translated and put on the London stage in great numbers during the eighteenth century. They were mainly adaptations from French and German plays, particularly those of Corneille, Racine, Voltaire, Fénelon, and D'Arnaud or of Lessing, Klopstock, Schiller, Goethe, and most strongly of all the German dramatists, Kotzebue.

6.22 Opera in the Eighteenth Century

On April 9, 1705, Vanbrugh and Congreve opened a new theatre in the Haymarket. It rapidly became a strong competitor for audiences from the Drury Lane Theatre and in December 1707 its performances were limited to operas. Later this theatre became particularly associated with Handel's music and the Royal Academy of Music. On December 7, 1732 the Covent Garden Theatre was opened and plays and operas were put on until 1749; it was reconstructed in 1792.

Henry Purcell (1658–95) during the Restoration period had made his dramatic operas popular. About 1690 he had provided the music to the words of Nahum Tate for *Dido and Æneas*. Songs and music had long been part of the English dramatic tradition, but it was French and Italian opera which made inroads on to the English stage in the eighteenth century. John Dennis, critic and playwright, tried to warn of the dangers to English drama and music in the Purcell tradition in *An Essay on the Operas After the Italian Manner, which are about to be Establish'd on the English Stage: With some Reflections on the Damage which they may bring to the Public* (1706).

English attempts to counter the Italian threat (Addison's *Rosamund* (1706) and English translations of Italian operas by Motteux) failed, and once Handel had put his weight behind Italian opera (beginning with the production of *Rinaldo* in February 1710) the foreign success was assured. Attempts were made to continue the Purcell tradition of dramatic opera in English by Oldmixon, Daniel Purcell, and Settle, but without much success. Acting on the principle 'If you can't beat 'em, join 'em', some writers produced operas 'after the Italian manner'. Henry Carey, John Gay and Thomas D'Urfey are some of the writers who tried to stem the Italians' success.

John Gay, for a time, found the only effective answer by turning to the ballad-opera. Jonathan Swift suggested to Gay that a Newgate pastoral 'might make an odd pretty sort of thing' and in turn Gay produced *The Beggar's Opera* in 1728. It was such a success that both the author and the producer, Rich, made considerable financial gains from it – 'It made Gay rich, and Rich gay'. Peachum receives stolen goods and then makes more money by informing. Polly, his daughter falls in love with Captain MacHeath, a highwayman.

Peachum is furious when they marry and informs against MacHeath, who is sent to Newgate where he meets Lucy, the daughter of Warder Lockit. Lucy and Polly become jealous rivals for MacHeath and Lucy arranges MacHeath's escape. (This opera formed, of course, the source of Brecht's *Dreigroschenoper*, with music by Kurt Weill, 'The Threepenny Opera' in 1928.)

The success of Gay's opera, however, led to a decline in Handel's influence and marked the beginning of the decline in England during the eighteenth century of Italian opera. Ballad-operas became fashionable for a decade or so and then turned to comic opera as in France. Popular tunes, songs from well-known operas, as well as some original music made up these semi-serious operas with sentimental plots. **Dr Thomas Arne** (1710–78) turned his hand to these new operas. *Thomas and Sally* (1760) had a libretto by Isaac Bickerstaffe (died 1812?), a very successful writer of such plots. He helped Arne, too, with *Love in a Village* (1762) which drew on music of sixteen musicians, arranged by Arne, who also wrote the music for the only successful eighteenth-century serious English opera, *Artaxerxes* (1762). R. B. Sheridan's comedy *The Duenna* (1775) had music arranged and partly composed by his father-in-law, Thomas Linley. Other English writers of comic opera were Charles Dibdin (1745–1814), William Shield (1748–1829) and Stephen Storace (1763–96). The comic opera as a dramatic production ran on into the nineteenth century. (For further history of opera see D. J. Grout, *A Short History of Opera*, second edition, 1965.)

6.23 Comedy in the Eighteenth Century
The comedy of the century after 1707 is dominated by two major names: Oliver Goldsmith (1730–74) and Richard Brinsley Sheridan (1751–1816).

William Hazlitt (1778–1830) in his lecture *On Wit and Humour* in 1818 (one of his lectures on the English Comic Writers), surveyed comedy and particularly referred to the comedy of his own generation. It provides, therefore, some insights into views on comedy towards the end of the eighteenth century. We cry as a relief from pressure, tragic or comic, from a sudden and violent emotion. An excess of joy as well as sadness will make us cry.

> The essence of the laughable is the incongruous . . . the disconnecting one idea from another, or the jostling of one feeling against another. The first and most obvious cause of laughter is to be found in the simple succession of events, as in the sudden shifting of a disguise, or some unlooked-for accident, without any absurdity of character or situation. The accidental contradiction between our expectations and the event can hardly be said, however, to amount to the ludicrous; it is merely laughable. The *ludicrous* is where there is the same contradiction between the object and our expectations, heightened by some deformity or inconvenience, that is, by its being contrary to what is customary or desirable. The *ridiculous*, which is the highest degree of the laughable, is that which is contrary not only to custom but to sense and reason, or is a voluntary departure from what we have a right to expect from those who are conscious of absurdity and propriety in words, looks, and actions.

Misunderstandings are another great source of comic humour as well as *ambiguity* and *contrast*. *Excessive* impudence or excessive modesty (as in *She Stoops to Conquer*) is amusing. *Lying* is a species of wit and humour. *Trying to keep within a role or character*, playing a part, an enthusiasm about trifles, and the pursuit of pleasure all provide humour. The examples of modern types of comic humour that Hazlitt gives are from Molière and Rabelais.

The **comedy of manners** exemplified in the work of Etherege, Wycherley, Congreve, Vanbrugh, and Farquhar has already been discussed (see pages 172–178). Other writers in the same genre were William Burnaby, David Cranford, and Mrs Centlivre whose work appeared in the first two decades of the century. Henry Fielding (1707–54) the novelist, also turned his hand to comedy and was influenced by Congreve and the 'manners' school. Gradually, however, his work turned towards burlesque (see pages 193–194). Some critics, including Allardyce Nicoll, delineate another genre of comedy during the eighteenth century, the **comedy of intrigue**, but by 1715 the genre within which Mrs Centlivre, William Taverner and Richard Wilkinson and others worked was in serious decline.

Oliver Goldsmith is best remembered as the author of the novel *The Vicar of Wakefield* (1766) and the poem *The Deserted Village* (1770). In an essay entitled, *The Present State of Polite Learning* (1759) he attacked the sentimental in drama. His first comedy, *The Goodnatured Man* (1768) was rejected by Garrick for Drury Lane and was put on instead at Covent Garden. His principal aim, as he acknowledged in his preface, was 'to delineate character'; he hoped that 'too much refinement will not banish humour and character . . . as it has already done from the French theatre. Indeed, the French comedy is now become so very elevated and sentimental, that it has not only banished humour and Molière from the stage, but it has banished all spectators, too'. The play was moderately well-received, had a Prologue written by none other than Dr Johnson, and made some money for Goldsmith. The Preface to the play, however, set out the playwright's attitude to comedy; he felt plays were too 'genteel', too 'elevated' – in fact, too remote, without 'humour and character'. Ideally, Goldsmith would have preferred a return to Elizabethan comedy.

His second comedy, *She Stoops to Conquer or The Mistakes of a Night* (1773) was also put on at Covent Garden after Garrick and Colman had both initially rejected it. Dr Johnson was present on the first night and handsomely applauded it. The play was originally entitled *The Belle's Stratagem* or *The Old House or New Inn*, but these had been thought unsuitable. The basic plot of mistaking a private house for an inn is thought to have been amongst Goldsmith's own personal boyhood experiences. In the Prologue, spoken by David Garrick, Goldsmith laments the impending death of the comic muse, a muse likely to be succeeded by a 'spurious breed who deals in sentimentals'. The play was Goldsmith's last attempt, the Prologue implies, to avoid the sentimental and give an old comedy, in the Elizabethan tradition rather than that of Congreve.

The play is in prose. (It is worth considering the relation between prose and drama in the novels of both Goldsmith and Fielding, perhaps.) The stiff, contrived dialogue of Goldsmith's earlier dramatic work has gone. The monument in Latin to him in Westminster Abbey refers to him as a 'poet, naturalist, and historian' but goes on to list his qualities:

> who left no species of writing untouched or unadorned by his pen; a powerful master of the passions, whether to move laughter or to draw forth tears; of a genius sublime, vivid, versatile; in expression noble, pure, and graceful.

Where does the skill 'to move laughter' come in *She Stoops to Conquer*? Hazlitt's description of comedy is useful to provide an answer (see page 189). The laughter comes from the incongruous – character to character, character to setting, and class to class; it comes from 'disconnecting one idea from another, jostling one feeling against another'; it comes from the 'ludicrous' and the 'ridiculous'. Misunderstanding lies first in mistaking Hardcastle's house for 'The Three Pigeons', then in Marlow's treating Hardcastle as the landlord, and then in the misjudging of Miss Hardcastle's true position. Ambiguity (double meanings, twin levels of meaning) and contrast heighten the comedy. Excessive impudence by Marlowe and excessive modesty by Miss Hardcastle compound the joke. The challenge to the accepted roles of nearly all the characters is inherent in the original mistake, where positions in society are turned upside down. The pursuit of pleasure, taken to excess, distorts and makes the situation grotesque. Comedy demands the sure, deft handling of plot, a sound control of pace in the action, and in interplay of character in the given contexts of society, morality, sex-role, and manners. If the pieces are moved round, as in a game of chess, the opportunities for intrigue and contradicting an audience's expectations are many.

Richard Brinsley Sheridan, however, working at the end of the eighteenth century, presents a different kind of comedy. He, like Goldsmith, rejected the sentimental comedies of the time but he derives more from the Jonson/humours/Congreve school than Shakespeare. Some of his work might also be categorised as burlesque and as farce.

He acquired Garrick's share in the Drury Lane Theatre in 1776, although his comedy *The Rivals*, written when he was only twenty-four, was put on in that theatre in 1775. In the same year his farce, *St. Patrick's Day or The Scheming Lieutenant* and his comic opera, *The Duenna*, were also performed. In 1777 he produced at Drury Lane the comedy *A Trip to Scarborough* and *The School for Scandal*. His burlesque *The Critic or A Tragedy Rehearsed* followed in 1779. In that year he also produced a melodrama *Pizarro*.

The Rivals met with riots at the first of its performances because of its satirical attacks on the Irish, although Sheridan himself was born in Dublin in 1751 and his grandfather, Dr Sheridan, had been the tutor of the most famous of Irish satirists, Jonathan Swift. Sir Lucius O'Trigger was at the centre of the Irish attack and some of the audience disapproved of Mr Lee's acting in the part. On the second night Mr Clinch took the part of Sir Lucius and was better received. Sheridan approved of Clinch's acting and prepared *St. Patrick's Day* later for him to act in. The names of the characters are in the humours tradition: Absolute, Faul Land, O'Trigger, Malaprop, Languish, Rivalry.

Plans that go awry from ignorance, challenges, mistaken correspondence, and a happy *dénouement* make up the main plot which avoids sentiment, observes, describes, and, by remaining detached, satirises false stances, social attitudes, and what Allardyce Nicoll has called 'sentimental self-torture'. Nicoll sees in the last scene of the play a sinking back into sentimentalism which is not redeemed by being burlesque. He also thinks that, both read and seen, the play is 'a thing of shreds and patches'.

The *School for Scandal*, however, has received more critical acclaim over the years. It is essentially a satire against hypocrisy, a discouragement for anyone to 'play the fool at large on life's great stage'. Sheridan, the 'young Don Quixote' seeks to scotch 'this hydra, Scandal, in his den'. Structurally the plot is complex and only the contrived *deus ex machina*, the screen scene, can resolve it. The success of the play depends on contrast and balance, black and white, bad and good, deceit and honesty, age and youth. Nevertheless, just as Joseph is a hypocrite, so Charles Surface is reckless and a spendthrift. Sir Peter Teazle, the stock figure of the old man with a young wife, is attacked by the humours characters of Backbite, Sneerwell, and Candour. The honesty test, or test of virtues, arranged by Oliver Surface on his return from India allows him to play the stock figure of a money-lender; Charles the good and Joseph the bad are weighed in the balance. All is revealed by deft exits and entrances, conversations overheard, and the clearing up of misunderstanding by removing the incongruity. The plot, however, is well supported by the thrusting wit of much of the dialogue. Satire, as Pope, Swift, and later Oscar Wilde knew, depends on the economical use of well-directed words. The epigrammatic nature of some of Sheridan's phrases must have influenced Wilde:

> When an old bachelor marries a young wife, what is he to expect? 'Tis now six months since Lady Teazle made me the happiest of men – and I have been the most miserable of men ever since! When an old bachelor marries a young wife, he deserves – no – the crime carries its own punishment along with it.

There are a number of occasions when the words 'moral' and 'sentiment' fall beside each other in the play. Sheridan is mocking the plays that deal with either or both. His aim is to delight.

The Critic and *St. Patrick's Day* are discussed in the sections below, *burlesque* and *farce* respectively.

6.24

Burlesque is the art of producing a piece of drama or literature to mock the original on which it is based by some kind of distortion. If mock-heroic takes the trivial and blows it up to enormous proportions in order to satirise it (*e.g.* Pope's *The Rape of the Lock*), burlesque takes the pompously important and reduces it to the comparatively trivial in order to condemn. Parody is its technique; deflation its aim. The word is derived ultimately from an Italian word *burlesco*, meaning 'a little bit of wool, a trifle'. The Restoration period and the eighteenth century used burlesque to comment on manners, sentiment, and literary fashions. In a sense the satirical technique of blowing up the trivial to huge proportions (mock-heroic) and reducing the self-considered giant to a pygmy (burlesque) is at the heart of showing Gulliver in Lilliput and in Brobdingnag respectively.

The prototype of the English burlesque play was *The Rehearsal* (printed in 1672) by George Villiers, the Second Duke of Buckingham, Martin Clifford, the Master of Charterhouse, and Samuel ('Hudibras') Butler. The play satirised the heroic tragedies of the Restoration period by taking passages from them, parodying them, and stringing them together to make a ridiculous plot. D'Avenant and Dryden particularly come in for attack. The 'high' tragedy is reduced to parody. John Gay's *The Beggar's Opera* (1723) was 'a Newgate pastoral' imitating the fashionable operas of the day but playing out the action with convicts, turnkeys, and the low-born instead of princes, rulers and the aristocracy. Henry Carey (died 1743) wrote the burlesque, *Chrononhotonthologos or The Most Tragical Tragedy that ever was Tragediz'd by any Company of Tragedians* (1734). Chrononhotonthologos is the king of Queerummania; two of the characters are called Aldiborontiphoscophornio and Rigdum-Funnidos, one pompous and the other full of good cheer. Henry Fielding produced as burlesques *The Tragedy of Tragedies or The Life and Death of Tom Thumb the Great* (1739). The preface to this play strips the words of ideas:

> no Word (should) by any means enter into a Preface till stripped of all its Ideas; a . . . method of stripping Words of Ideas is by putting half a dozen incoherent ones together.

Critics have condemned the play, said Fielding, because all the characters are killed off at the end; this is better, the author, argued, than killing them off at the beginning as most tragedies do. Secondly, killing a ghost strains probability; but what about the plays entitled, 'Kill my Soul', 'Stab my very Soul', 'Bleeding Soul', or 'Dying Soul'. Some critics did not like the subject, but, said Fielding, *he* did and so there! The characters in the play include: King Arthur, Tom Thumb, Lord Grizzle, Mr Noodle, Mr Doodle, Queen Dollaholla, Princess Huncamunca and Mustacha. All the characters in the play, including the Ghost of Tom Thumb, who has already been eaten by a cow on the way to his wedding, are killed off at the end:

GHOST	Tom Thumb I am – but am not ere alive.
	My body's in the Cow, my Ghost is here.
GRIZZLE	Thanks, O ye Stars, my Vengeance is restor'd,
	Nor shalt thou fly me – for I'll kill thy Ghost.
	(*Kills the Ghost*)
HUNCAMUNCA	O barbarous Deed! – I will revenge him so.
	(*Kills Grizzle.*)
DOODLE	Ha! Grizzle kill'd – then Murtheress beware.
	(*Kills Huncamunca.*)
QUEEN	O wretch! – have at thee.
	(*Kills Doodle.*)
NOODLE	And have at thee too.
	(*Kills the Queen.*)

CLEORA	Thou'st kill'd the Queen.
	(*Kills Noodle.*)
MUSTACHA	And thou hast kill'd my Lover.
	(*Kills Cleora.*)
KING	Ha! Murtheress vile, take that.
	(*Kills Mustacha.*)
	And take thou this.
	(*Kills himself, and falls.*)

Fielding wrote one further burlesque, *The Covent Garden Tragedy* (1732). It survived just one performance. Instead of dealing with the high morality of the court, it dealt with the low morality of the brothel.

Into this tradition of burlesque* , Sheridan introduced his play **The Critic or A Tragedy Rehearsed** (1779). He set out to satirise, as George Villiers had done in *The Rehearsal*, the sentimental drama of the period and also the literary criticism. Fielding had already started this tradition in his brilliant three-fold dismissal of the critics in his Preface to *Tom Thumb* (see page 193). Dangle and Sneer are the spiteful critics; Sir Fretful Plagiary is a would-be poet (a picture of Richard Cumberland, 1732–1811, author of two sentimental comedies, *The West Indian* and *The Brothers*, two novels, and translator of Aristophanes's *Clouds*); Puff is an advertiser of literary goods and the author of an amazingly bad historical play. As Puff's play is being rehearsed the author and two critics discuss it in the meaningless, pompous language of contemporary literary criticism. At a stroke, Sheridan laughs at the dramatic tradition and laughs at the critics who wrote about it. Ironically, perhaps, in the very act of doing so, Sheridan is himself both playwright and critic!

The critics' comments on the rehearsal of '*The Spanish Armada*' allow Sheridan to satirise managers; those who own theatres (remember, he had a large interest in the Drury Lane Theatre himself); pantomime; theatrical advertising; casting; dramatic theory ('the state is the *Mirror of Nature*'); pretentious playwrights; audiences and their responses; plot; distinctions between tragedy and comedy; morality and sentiment; Vanbrugh, Congreve, and other playwrights; the 'patent' theatres; the superficiality of criticism; 'fantastic encumbrances of fine language'; coarseness of style; dialogue; foreign (especially French and Italian) influences (one scene is in 'Franglais' and 'Italinglese' – but Dangle finds the foreigners talk too fast for him to understand!); music in plays; theatrical advertisements; agents; critics' style ('the puff direct, the puff preliminary, the puff collateral, the puff collusive, and the puff oblique, or puff by implication' – all in different forms, Letter to the Editor, Occasional Anecdote, Impartial Critique, Observation from Correspondent, or Advertisement from the Party' – although Puff doesn't realise that his serious account is, ironically, a hilarious send-up of his own art!); secondary critical judgements; passions in plays; prompting; characterisation by trivial details – *e.g.* Sir Walter Raleigh turns his toes out; exaggerated

---

* A good collection of burlesque plays is available in Simon Trussler, *Burlesque Plays of the Eighteenth Century*, Oxford, 1969.

movements about the stage (see the 'kneeling' episode in Act II); noises off; stichomythia (rapid exchange of dialogue); editing and censorship; the mechanical effects; scene changes; clumsy and contrived physical actions on stage; under-rehearsal; . . . etc. Puff's final remark is priceless:

> Well, pretty well – but not quite perfect. – So, ladies and gentlemen, if you please, we'll rehearse this piece again tomorrow.

The Critic gives an excellent insight into dramatic and theatrical conventions and literary criticism in the late eighteenth century. It is a source of much information about play production, just as the rehearsal scenes in *Hamlet* and *A Midsummer Night's Dream* provide details of Elizabethan play production.

6.25   Farce

The word *farce* comes, through French, from Latin *farcire:* to stuff. It originally was used to refer to the extra material included in the liturgy either as explanation or amplification. In drama it applied to the extra material 'stuffed' into a play by actors to expand it to delight or instruct. Now it is used in criticism to mean 'a dramatic work (usually short) which has for its sole object to excite laughter' (*OED*). It is, therefore, a fairly recent word carrying this rather specific sense. It became popular during the Restoration period where *farce* was seen as foreign, in the tradition of the *commedia dell'arte*, the Italian improvised drama of the sixteenth century, performed by professional actors, and derived initially from the so-called *Atellane or Oscan Fables* performed as comic popular farces in the town of Atella amongst the Osci people in Campania in Italy.

In Restoration times *farce* was a new word and a new vogue. Nahum Tate in the Preface to *A Duke and No Duke* (1693) declares:

> I have not yet seen any definition of Farce, and dare not be the first that ventures to define it. I know not by what Fate it happens (in common Notion) to be the most contemptible sort of Drama.
> > (Quoted by J. M. Davis, 'Farce', 1978, in the series *The Critical Idiom*, ed. J. D. Jump.)

In the early eighteenth century a farcical piece of drama was used as an after-play entertainment along with other spectacular shows. It developed in the nineteenth century as a dramatic form in its own right, particularly as translations of the French master of farce, Georges Feydeau (1862 – 1921), were translated.

In his list of plays produced during the second half of the eighteenth century, Allardyce Nicoll (*A History of English Drama*, III, second edition, 1952) lists some seventy playwrights who wrote plays which may be described as farce. The word 'farce' fell out of favour, but the playwrights continued to write plays of the sort describable as farces. Nicoll argues (*op. cit.* 178-9) that they are a 'roughened form of comedy' and may be of the humours, the intrigue, the manners, and even the sentimental sort. He accepts Tate's dictum, however, and does not try to define it further. The most that can be said, perhaps, is that the word changes its meaning according to the age, the writer, of the play to which it is being applied. The so-called 'Whitehall farces' with Brian Rix during the 1950s and 1960s are quite different from what J. M. Davis (*op. cit.,* 28) thinks is the earliest independent farce in English drama, John Heywood's Interlude of *Johan the husbande, Johan Tyb the wyf, & syr Jhan the preest.* The main common quality of the comedy in all farces, however, seems to be its physical robustness.

In the late eighteenth century, Sheridan's *St. Patrick's Day or The Scheming Lieutenant* (1775) is described as 'a farce'. It is possible, perhaps, to describe some of the characteristics which make this play 'a farce' in a contemporary eighteenth-century sense, without necessarily implying that these characteristics make up a definition of 'farce' which can then be applied to all dramatic pieces of the time carrying that descriptive title. The play is short – two acts, in fact. The characters are one-dimensional and easily recognised by their names and positions: Doctor Rosy, Justice Credulous, Sergeant Trounce, Corporal Flint; simple gullible countrymen. The objects of satire are well-defined and easily recognised: women's fashions; Irish soldiers; cures and spa-water; the tricks of the recruiting bands; the insensitivity of the military; the ignorance of doctors. The literary objects of satire are just as clear; heroines who swoon; themes of poison and revenge; artificial dialogue where messengers cannot deliver their message without constant interruption; quotations dragged in from other writers; the use of foreign phrases; the introduction of heavy moralising; disguise which is supposed to deceive everyone on stage but which would fool nobody else; the revelation of character by caricatured speech; plots which hinge on the arrival of the militia in the town.

Some of the action is robust and physical but the pace of the play is not really fast enough, the intricacies of the plot not complicated enough, the solutions and *dénouement* not outrageous enough for the farce to make immediate impact as farce on an audience. If this play is compared with Fielding's *Tom Thumb,* for example, it emerges as one less obvious in its dramatic effects and more subtle in its dialogue.

Farce, in the history of English drama, is usually linked in its origins with the name of Edward Ravenscroft. He derived some of his inspiration from the visits of Italian and French teams of actors to London during the 1660s, 1670s and 1690s. From about 1683 some of these troupes were associated with the Italian *commedia dell'arte.* These are records of a real Italian Harlequin and Scaramouch on the London stage. Ravenscroft adapted very freely some of Molièrés plays in the early 1670s and continued with his satirical farces into the next decade. Nahum Tate, the Poet Laureate used earlier plays from which to write farces in the 1680s and actors such as Thomas Betterton and John Lacy gave farce new impetus. The first two decades of the eighteenth century were enthusiastic about farce with dramatists such as Owen Macswiny, Mrs Centlivre, and Christopher Bullock joining in. By the 1740s Isaac Bickerstaffe and David Garrick himself (*Lette,* 1740, and *Miss in her Teens,* 1746) had made their contributions to the genre. Arthur Murphy during the 1750s and 1760s produced farces with characters in the shape of the humours characters from an earlier period. Sheridan, as has been shown (see page 196), produced his farce in 1775 and towards the end of the century this kind of comedy was moving into farces about the theatre itself (those of James Powell) and 'farces of intrigue', as Nicoll has classified them (those of William Whitehead and Edward Morris). Farce during the period had moved from versions imitative of Molière and using the *commedia dell'arte* tradition, through attacks on the political system of the country, to satire on manners and the theatrical traditions themselves.

6.26 Pantomime

In England pantomimes were the creation of the eighteenth century and they seemed to have been immediately popular. Nicoll has traced four elements in pantomime during the period: classical myth, the *commedia dell'arte*, farce, and satire. Mime and actions were usually combined with speech or music made by other actors simultaneously. Harlequin and Columbine were the central figures but later in the century historical spectacles were introduced with Joan of Arc, Aladdin, and even Robinson Crusoe playing their parts.

These were entertainments rather than plays and can be seen as one of the ways, along with opera and farce, that the theatre was seeking to diversify its appeal after the demise of tragedy and the weakening of comedy throughout the century, after their brilliant flowering during the Elizabethan and Jacobean ages.

Questions

1 How far has Farquhar come to grips with the new 'moral realism' of his age in *The Recruiting Officer*?

2 How would you present *The Recruiting Officer* to a modern audience to bring out its main comedy elements? (Say what aspects of the play you would stress, the problems you would have, and some of the ways you would overcome them.)

3 What makes Sheridan's *St. Patrick's Day* a 'farce'?

4 Explain how you would instruct some actors playing the major roles in *St. Patrick's Day* to approach their parts.

5 What are the problems in *She Stoops to Conquer* for a director who wants to give pace to his or her production? How could they be overcome?

6 How would you defend *She Stoops to Conquer* from the accusation that its plot is contrived?

7 What is meant by describing Molière's *The Misanthrope* as 'a comedy of character'? What implications would it have for a production if your interpretation of the description were applied to the play?

8 Take a scene from *The Misanthrope* and design a set for it *and* a plan for moving the actors about it as the scene progresses.

9 *What have you learnt about *either* literary criticism *or* dramatic conventions in the eighteenth century from your study of *The Critic*?

10 What makes *The Critic* a 'burlesque'?

11 *Describe some of the major changes to stage performances that came about in the decade following the Restoration of Charles II.

12 *Describe the changes in audience that came about during this period.

13 *What were the main effects on staging brought about by the enlarging of theatres during the eighteenth century?

14 Describe three examples of 'spectacle' provided in the theatres of this period.

15 *What do you understand by *either* the term 'the comedy of manners' *or* the term 'the comedy of humours'? (Give examples to support the points you make.)

16 What do you understand by the term 'sentimental' when it is applied to eighteenth century comedy?

17 *Give an account of the major changes in the design of scenery during the Restoration and the eighteenth century.

18 *Explain, with the help of diagrams and examples, how scenery was used in the production of plays during the eighteenth century.

19 What contribution to the notion of *tragedy* did John Dryden make?

*The questions marked * could form the basis of project work.*

20 What are the main features of *melodrama* in the eighteenth century? How would you recreate faithfully a play from the period for a modern audience as *melodrama*?

21 How important is it to present today a Restoration or an eighteenth-century comedy *or* tragedy in the costume of its period? Justify your views by explaining what the production would lose or gain if twentieth century dress were used?

22 * Describe the debt owed to Europe by the dramatists of the period? How far did the debt help or hinder the development of British drama?

23 Take a character from a drama you have studied in this period whom you would most like to play. Say how you would hope to present it to an audience. What problems would it give you?

24 How do you account for the growing interest in *opera* during this period?

25 What effect did the Licensing Act of 1737 have on the development of the theatre in the eighteenth century?

7
Nineteenth-Century Drama and Drama to 1939

7.1

First, read the appropriate sections on the Development of the Stage given in Sections **2.10** and **2.11** in Chapter Two (pages 39–46).

At the start of the nineteenth century the enlarging of the patent theatres and the diversification of drama into farce, melodrama, and pantomime meant that audiences were widened, spectacle became even more important, moral sensibilities were brought increasingly to bear on dramatic entertainments, and writers re-examined their roles in producing work for the theatre. Changes in characterisation by type and in costume led to changes in acting-styles. The growth of the novel as a powerful narrative form and the development of magazines and newspapers and a wider reading public altered fashions in entertainment. Social and political changes throughout the period would also leave their marks on drama. A watershed in the development of the theatre was the passing of the **Theatre Regulations Act in 1843**.

7.2 Theatre Legislation

The Master of the King's Revels had exercised considerable control over dramatic productions, after he had been appointed by Henry VII in Tudor times. Earlier the church had attempted to exert its own influence in regulating drama (see pages 75–76) and during serious outbreaks of plague the theatres had been closed in Elizabeth's reign. The first Act to control the stage was passed in **1605** '*to restrain the abuses of players . . . for preventing and avoiding of the great abuse of the Holy-name of God in Stage Plays, Enterludes, May-Games, Shews, and such like*'. In **1642** the theatres were closed by a Commonwealth ordinance, the *First Ordinance Against Stage Plays and Interludes* and later ordinances in 1647 and 1648 maintained the prohibition. The Restoration of Charles II to the throne brought patents to Thomas Killigrew and D'Avenant to establish theatre companies. On **July 9, 1660**, Killigrew received a royal warrant which allowed him to set up a playhouse and effectively establish a theatre monopoly for himself and D'Avenant, who already held a patent for a theatre issued by Charles I in 1639; Killigrew set up jointly a single company of twenty players at the Cockpit. Both Killigrew and D'Avenant set about establishing new theatres, too, and after a time in a temporary Theatre Royal at Gibbon's Tennis Court in Vere Street, Clare Market, Killigrew succeeded in building and opening (in 1663) a new Theatre Royal in Drury Lane. D'Avenant, similarly, set up his own group of actors quite quickly (the Duke's Men) and began to give performances at Salisbury Court. In June 1661 his new theatre, reconstructed from Lisle's Tennis Court in Lincoln's Inn Fields, was ready. D'Avenant received a new warrant, in exchange for his pre-Commonwealth one, on January 15, 1663. D'Avenant died in 1668 but his company went ahead with plans for a new theatre in Dorset Gardens. In 1682 the King's Men and the Duke's Men formed a united company. With the opening of Covent Garden theatre in 1732, the 'patent companies' had two important theatres and a monopoly.

Minor playhouses had been growing up and performances in them were licensed providing they had only three acts and five songs. Such entertainments were known as *burlettas*, but they soon included adaptations of Shakespeare with some interpolations to make them conform to the law. The **legitimate theatre** put on five-act plays with little singing, dancing, or spectacle, in the 'patent theatres'. (In the nineteenth century, the term 'legitimate theatre' came to apply to serious drama, as distinct from farce, musical comedies and revues.)

In 1737 the **Licensing Act**, which had recognised the performances of these *burlettas*, effectively eroded the monopoly of the 'patent theatres'. In 1808 a serious attempt was made to allow a third 'patent' theatre to be opened for legitimate drama but the Bill was defeated in Parliament. Similar Bills were defeated in 1810 and 1813, and dramatic productions proliferated il-legitimately. Thomas James Thackeray and a group of dramatists met at the Albion Tavern in 1831 and the City of London Tavern in 1832 to get up a new petition. Lord Lytton presented a Bill in 1832 and in the same year a Select Committee approved the proposal. The Bill passed through the Commons but was thrown out by the Lords in 1833.

In 1843 the **Theatre Regulations Act** became law. It repealed all the earlier acts seeking control of the stage. It laid down in detail the structural and other requirements that had to be met before a building could be licensed for performances and set up the Lord Chamberlain's power as the licensing authority over all theatres in London and Windsor, except for Drury Lane and Covent Garden which he already controlled. Outside London and Windsor the authority to license plays was put in the hands of local authorities. This act also gave permission to the Lord Chamberlain to censor plays. Every new play or amendment to an old play had to be sent to his office at least seven days before the performance and if the Lord Chamberlain disallowed the play, or a part of it, then what had been disallowed was not to be presented in performance. A 'stage play' within the Act included 'every tragedy, comedy, farce, opera, burletta, melodrama, pantomime or other entertainment of the stage, or any part thereof'. Licences, once given, could be withdrawn in exceptional circumstances.

What would cause a 'stage play' to be disallowed? Any 'profanity or impropriety of language, indecency of dress, dance, or gesture; offensive personalities or representations of living persons or anything calculated to produce riot or breach of the peace'. There was no appeal against the Lord Chamberlain's decision.

If an unlicensed play was performed a fine of £50 for every offence could be made and a theatre's licence be revoked. In **1853**, **1866**, and **1892** Select Committees of the House of Commons reviewed the arrangements and found them satisfactory. In **1909** a Joint Committee of the House of Lords and the House of Commons came under pressure to modify or abolish the 1843 Licensing Act. However, it survived until September 28, 1968.

The Lord Chamberlain had no power over the publication of plays but merely over their performance. The movements to censor plays moved alongside the creation of such bodies as the *Society for the Suppression of Vice* (1802). The **Obscene Publications Act** of 1857 allowed for the effective enforcement of Common Laws already in existence but it was to be applied only to those works which were written to corrupt the morals of the young or 'shock common feelings of decency in any well-regulated mind'. This Act was repealed and replaced by the *Obscene Publications Act of 1959*, only after a century of interpreting an obscene publication as something intended 'to deprave and corrupt those whose minds are open to such immoral influences and into whose hands a publication of this sort may fall'.

The repeal of the 1737 Act, therefore, opened up the way to a new, competitive theatre, no longer restricted to what could and could not be put on. The meaning of *legitimate theatre* in the nineteenth century shifted from a positive definition of what serious plays should include to the one relying on exclusions to deal with new dramatic developments such as the music-hall. It was not redefined merely to apply to licensed theatres, since all theatres had to be licensed and in that sense be 'legitimate'.

7.3   The Nature of the Audience

Fires burnt down the two 'patent' theatres at the start of the century. Rebuilt in 1792, the *Covent Garden Theatre* was burnt down on September 20, 1808. The actors moved to the *Haymarket*. The new *Covent Garden* was completed on September 18, 1809, to hold 3013 persons, with a fine stage and excellent stage machinery. In 1823 Charles Kemble took control of it and Edmund Kean played there, mainly in Shakespearean roles. Musical shows came in after the repeal of the 1737 Act in 1843, and in 1847 it reopened for opera as the Royal Italian Opera House. The building was burnt down in 1856 and the present Royal Opera House was opened in 1858.

The *Drury Lane* Theatre was burnt down on February 24, 1809. The acting company there moved to the Haymarket and then to the Lyceum. The new *Drury Lane* Theatre was opened on October 10, 1812. It was smaller than the earlier theatre and struggled for audience, but Kean played there, too.

Following the 1843 Theatre Regulations Act, **new theatres**, and some old ones, found themselves licensed. The *Adelphi*, one of the best 'minor' theatres had been built in 1819. In 1858 it was rebuilt and was famous for its special effects and use of animals in productions. The *Alexandra Palace* opened in 1889; the *Alhambra Palace* in Leicester Square opened as a music-hall in 1858 and a theatre in 1871, but was burnt down on December 12, 1882 and rebuilt the following year. The *Comedy Theatre* began performances on October 15, 1881.

The *Court Theatre* opened in 1871 as the *New Chelsea Theatre*, but it was demolished in 1887 and rebuilt the following year; The *Criterion Theatre* opened in 1874 and was reconstructed in 1884 and the *Dalston Theatre* (Hackney) opened in 1898. The *Trafalgar Square Theatre* opened in 1892 but was renamed the *Duke of York's Theatre* in 1895. The *Empire Theatre*, Leicester Square, opened as a music-hall on April 17, 1884. The *Garrick Theatre* opened in 1889, the *Globe* in 1868 (destroyed in 1902) and *Her Majesty's* in 1897. The *Theatre Royal*, Haymarket was altered in 1872 and rebuilt in 1880. The *Lyceum Theatre* in the Strand was erected in 1765 as an art exhibition hall but Charles Dibdin used it for dramatic entertainments abut 1790. In 1794 it was rebuilt and spectacular shows were put on there. In 1809 it was licensed for musical plays but after extensive rebuilding in 1816 it burnt down in 1830. The present building, designed by Beazley, opened on July 14, 1834, for 'the representation of English operas and the encouragement of indigenous musical talent'. The *Lyric Theatre* in Shaftesbury Avenue opened in 1888, and the *Lyric Opera House*, Hammersmith (now rebuilt) in 1890. The *Sadler's Wells Theatre* dates back to 1765 and it enjoyed particularly nautical melodrama. From 1844 onwards, following the *Regulations Act* of the previous year it put on legitimate theatre but the present theatre building is the oldest playhouse building in London. The *Savoy Theatre* in the Strand opened on October 10, 1881 and the *Shaftesbury Theatre* on October, 20, 1888. The *Strand Theatre* was originally called '*Punch's Playhouse*' then the '*Marionette Theatre*' from 1851 to 1852; it was reconstructed and enlarged in 1865. The *Theatre Royal* at Stratford opened in 1894 and the *Vaudeville* in 1870. *Wyndham's Theatre* began in 1899. (This list is selected from Allardyce Nicoll, *A History of English Drama*, IV 222–32 and V, 215–22.) In addition to these major theatres many others opened in London and the suburbs. In addition Nicoll lists another fifty or so music halls and hundreds of theatres all over England, Scotland, Wales, and Ireland. The increase in theatres was enormous after 1843.

The population of the United Kingdom increased from some 12 millions in 1801, when the first census was taken, to 24 millions by 1861 and to 42 767 530 by 1921. By 1843 the railway system had been laid down allowing easy movement about the country. The nineteenth century was the century of the Industrial Revolution, increased popular education (with the 1870 Education Act), the expansion of imperial powers, the development of a new reading public, and an expansion of periodicals (with their theatre reviews), newspapers (with their comment), and novels (with their interest in plot and character).

The increase in theatres, transport, population, and education, together with the removal of monopoly restrictions in 1843, gave powerful new impetus to the production of drama. Some pessimists, however, lived on. In 1878 one complained, 'Though theatres have multiplied of late, it cannot be said that audiences have vastly increased'. Others thought that, inevitably, 'more meant worse', and that the quality of productions would fall; perhaps, however, 'more' would mean 'more competitive' as audiences and productions would struggle to improve themselves, if only to stay in business. George

Bernard Shaw in 1896 thought that 'the respectably literate citizens' could see all that was worth seeing in theatres if they went six times a year.

At the beginning of the century audiences in the two patent theatres were unruly. Even during Restoration times disorder was rife (see page 100) and some young 'gentlemen' came late or left early to avoid paying. A performance of *Richard III* at Covent Garden was interrupted when 'a ruffian' threw a quart bottle on the stage and nearly did the actor Betterton a mischief in 1801. At the *Haymarket* on August 15, 1805, there was a tailor's riot! On February 12, 1827, at the *Adelphi* the battle of *The Pirate's Doom* was matched by a mêlée in the pit. Pepys, earlier, and Hazlitt, in the nineteenth century, speak of the theatres as being riotous, noisy places. Sir Walter Scott in his *Essay on Drama* (1834) complains that the company was scandalous and 'prostitutes and admirers form the principal part of the audience'. The words of Stephen Gosson (1579), William Prynne (1632), and Jeremy Collier (1698) echo down the years! Stalls were not introduced until towards the middle of the century and the 'pit' allowed immediate responses to the production to boil over quite quickly. The introduction of stalls moved the noisier elements away from the stage into the galleries.

The plots and actions that appealed to earlier nineteenth-century audiences were nationalistic, moral, and sentimental; above all, they had to be direct, full of spectacle, and reasonably free from symbolism or allegory.

By the middle of the nineteenth century the riots had disappeared and the audiences in the 'legitimate' theatre were becoming sedate. The rowdy elements, perhaps, had turned to the music-halls. The Church still looked on the theatre as immoral and delivered its usual puritanical salvoes. Even Henry Irving was attacked for his 'delinquencies'. However, the legitimate theatre was becoming proper and even fashionable. Evening performances were pushed back until after dinner and the earlier '**curtain-raisers**' of the pre-1830 period became rarer as matinées were introduced for the 'pre-dinner' audiences. **Matinées** became more and more popular as the leisured audiences were attracted. The censorship of plays remained all the firmer, in spite of attacks on the Lord Chamberlain by **critics** such as William Archer and Shaw. The critics, themselves, with their reviews stimulated discussion. Although Pepys, Hazlitt and Lamb had given their impressions of visits to the theatre, **dramatic criticism** became a new art form in its own right. First-night reviews became of considerable significance for actors and managers alike.

The audiences in the music-halls and elsewhere were different in some ways, although the patriotism and sentimentality still prevailed. The invitation to join in the songs, to respond with comments in chorus, to laugh and weep aloud, produced a lively player-audience interaction. The presentation of spectacle, of short pieces, and of topical items called for immediate, rather than considered, responses. The differences between the two kinds of audience resulted in two kinds of dramatic entertainment: one of *overheard* drama, where the audience sat listening to and watching an action from a darkened auditorium, and one of *direct contact* drama where the lights could be higher and the participation greater. The move, too, from teaching to entertainment, from instruction to delight was almost complete for both of them.

The separation of the two kinds of drama into 'legitimate' and 'non-literary' (or even 'illegitimate drama' as *The Drama's Levée* produced by Planché in 1838 insisted on calling it) and the increase in the theatre-going population meant that longer runs would be possible. Longer runs made additional expense on production, and especially on scenery and effects, more justifiable. Moreover, the growing technical skills that came from better machinery and more versatile lighting, both brought about by electrical power, encouraged audiences to return and become regular play-goers.

7.4 The Theatres: Scenery: Machinery; Spectacle

The manner in which the 'patent' theatres were extended at the beginning of the nineteenth century has already been indicated (page 202) and the alterations that took place to the audience itself have been described (pages 202–204).

Two conventions died in the first half of the century: the use of a Prologue and the so-called 'giving-out' of a play at the end of the performance when the next production was announced, although this was a technique adapted by the cinema later.

Scenery became more and more elaborately painted and there grew up many scene-painters whose skill increased as the decades proceeded. Stanfield and Grieves are amongst the best known but others like Tomkins, Roberts, and Marshall apparently were active. The primitive stage directions of some plays indicate that the older use of scenery running in grooves and flats and wings continued; it was not until T. W. Robertson, Ibsen, and Shaw that stage directions increased in size and detail. Gauze was used for scenery to indicate smoke or clouds which would lift to reveal gods or heroes, although de Loutherbourg (see pages 35–36) had already used it to gain special effects. It was de Loutherbourg, it will be remembered, who opened up a huge scenic entertainment (the **Eidophusicon**) at the Patagonian Theatre in 1781 and used it to give a feeing of great space and panoramic views. This technique of using scenery to suggest huge distances, and vistas full of interesting detail, in perspective, continued into the nineteenth century.

It is from the stage directions that the best indications of what happened to present the play on stage can be found. References to fights, cannon, explosions, prisons and elaborate costumes show how lavish some of the intended spectacles were. Following the Eidophusicon came the **diorama**. In 1823 Daguerre and Bouton opened a diorama in Regents Park where optical illusions could be gained by moving parts of the scenery or by putting scenery on to rollers to roll up one scene as another unfolded. Allardyce Nicoll (*op. cit.*, IV, 36) quotes a scene from Planché's *Paris and London* (1828):

> Deck of the Steamer – Moving Panoramic View from Calais to Dover by various Painted Flats to the Scene.

He also referred to productions where four rooms were represented on the stage at one time, or two floors in a house. The period was moving strongly towards a realistic presentation on the stage, however elaborate this had to be.

The use of **the curtain** became increasingly important to conceal the movement of scenery; here **the traveller**, or a running curtain pulled across the back of a stage, would allow scenery to be changed behind it whilst the action could continue in front of it; this latter development, however, came towards the end of the century. The curtain was used mainly at the ends of acts. An interesting feature of the 1820s and 1830s was the growth of the practice to drop the curtain at a moment when the actors had 'frozen' into an arranged tableau. (Such a 'tableau' of the peasants and poor, arranged according to the painting of 'The Last Supper' and frozen in their postures and gestures, was used much more recently with devastating effect in Buñuel's film *Viridiana*.)

After the 1843 Act the theatres could move off in new directions to entertain the growing population with dramatic spectacles. The Great Exhibition of 1851 gave official approval to the innovatory, the surprising, the experimenting forces in English ingenuity. **Dioramas** grew more popular. Madam Tussaud's museum, which had begun in France with the heads modelled in wax of those who died during the Terror, was transferred to the Lyceum in 1802 and then to Blackheath. Until 1884, the **Exhibition of Waxworks** was at Baker Street, and then it transferred to Marylebone Road (where it was destroyed by fire with many irreplaceable exhibits in 1925, and reopened in 1929). Displays of **fireworks**, the **London Zoo** (the Zoological Society) with its exotic animals on display, and the enormous and swift growth of music-halls were merely some of the attractions that the 'legitimate' theatre was forced to compete with.

The **picture-frame** stage was established during this second half of the nineteenth century. It was intended, with its elaborate two-foot wide border often, to give the impression to the audience that they were watching a moving picture. Now the curtain could be used effectively to hide scene changes, although for a time some managers still tried to change scenery, and even properties, by pulling them on and off stage by means of cords – in full view of the audience. Edmund Kean used folding velvet curtains to hide scene changes.

A new profession grew up in the theatre – that of **stage-manager** whose job it was to supervise and regulate changes of scene and properties.

The work of **Thomas W. Robertson** (1829–71) was vital to the development of stage productions during this period. He began as an actor but left the stage to become a dramatist. His plays *Society* (1865), *Ours* (1866), *Caste* (1867), *Play* (1868), *School* (1869), and *M.P.* (1870), introduced a naturalistic approach to stage presentation. His stage descriptions were more elaborate so that nobody could be in any doubt about what he intended. The opening stage direction of Caste shows the detail, the precision, and the attempt at realism that Robertson aimed at:

SCENE. A plain set chamber, paper soiled. A window, C., with practicable* blind; street

* practicable: able to be operated.

backing and iron railings. Door practicable, R.3E.; when opened showing street door (practicable). Fire-place, L.; two-hinged gas-burners on each side of mantelpiece. Sideboard cupboard in recess, L.3E.; tea-things, teapot, tea-caddy, tea-tray, &c., on it. Long table, L.C., before fire; old piece of carpet and rug down; plain chairs; book-shelf on back L.; a small table under it with ballet-shoe and skirt on it; bunch of benefit bills hanging under bookshelf. Theatrical printed portraits, framed, hanging about; chimney glass clock; box of lucifers and ornaments on mantelshelf; kettle on hob, and fire laid; door-mats on the outside of door. Bureau, R.

Rapping heard at door R., the handle is then shaken as curtain rises. The door is unlocked. Enter GEORGE D'ALROY.

Elsewhere in the play precise details of actors' movements are set down meticulously:

The handle of the door is heard to rattle, then the door is shaken violently. ESTHER crosses to the door; finding it locked turns to POLLY, sitting in window seat, who gives her the key. ESTHER then opens the door. ECCLES reels in, very drunk, and clings to the corner of bureau R., for support. GEORGE stands L.C., pulling his moustache. ESTHER, a little way up R.C., looking with shame first at her father, then at GEORGE. POLLY sitting in window recess C.

ACT DROP

This realism in scenery was matched by a realism in dialogue, too. The type figures which had been the characters of plays until about the 1860s, grotesque and exaggerated, could also become more realistic individuals. In all his plays he set a central problem examined impartially and so anticipated the comedies later of Shaw and Galsworthy; his are dramatic conflicts within society – gone are the black and white 'moral' characters of drama.

The new stage-managers had a major role to play in rehearsals, examining what was desirable and what was possible. A new dimension came into rehearsals; before, the essential elements were **actors** and **action**; now both were joined intimately by **setting**. All three had to interrelate.

W. S. Gilbert (1836–1911) took on responsibility for his own productions of plays and operas, even after he had joined with **Sir Arthur Sullivan** (1842–1900) to work for Richard d'Oyley Carte at the Savoy Theatre to produce the so-called 'Savoy Operas'. He planned the scenery, lighting, chorus-groupings, and 'every gesture of the actors', said Edward Rickett (in *The New York Times*, April 1, 1934, quoted by Allardyce Nicoll). Dion Boucicault (1820?–90) and Sir Arthur Wing Pinero (1855–1934) also exerted firm authority over the rehearsal of their plays.

Scenery became more and more elaborate as the century proceeded. For a time there was a reaction and a call for the return to simpler, conventional settings away from 'real goats', 'real dogs', and 'real litter', as Ellen Terry described the realism of the stage in *The Story of My Life* (1908). **Antoine** at the **Théâtre Libre** in Paris had been a major exponent of the drive towards realism with his sides of real beef hanging in representations of butchers' shops. **Paul Fort** and the **symbolist** movement reacted strongly in an attempt to restore imagination and imagery to scenic design. Fort founded the **Théâtre Mixte** (which was renamed almost immediately the Théâtre d'Art) and he laid down some of the basic ideas that developed into early twentieth-century scenery. The 'perspective' that had been a feature of English stage design, off and on, from the time of *Gammer Gurton's Needle* (see page 100) was banished, and scenery was to be simplified and stylised in order to suggest rather than to depict minutely. Costume and scenery were to be harmonised in the 'spectacle' of the theatre. At a production of *Pelléas et Mélisande* (1892) by Maeterlinck, one of the best known Symbolist dramas of the period, Konstantin Stanislavski (1863–1938) was in the audience and later he acknowledged his debt to Vogler who had helped design the decorations for the play presented at the Théâtre d'Art, which had been renamed yet again as the **Théâtre de l'Oeuvre**. The whole of the symbolist movement, of course, was centred on Mallarmé and reached out to include writers such as Verlaine, Rimbaud, and Laforgue in France, and Maeterlinck and Verhaeren in Belgium. Adaptations of poems were presented at the 'Théâtre de l'Oeuvre' from 1890 onwards and young artists (including Gauguin, Bonnard, and Vuillard) painted the scenery and even illustrated the programmes. The theatre of the movement attracted, too, playwrights of the stature of Ibsen, Bjørnson, Strindberg, and even Oscar Wilde's *Salomé*, a one-act play banned in England in 1893 but produced in Paris in 1896, whilst Wilde was in prison in Reading goal.

When Stanislavski returned to Moscow, however he founded the **Art Theatre of Moscow** and began by declaring his support for the realistic theatre of Antoine (1858–1943) but the symbolist movement in the British theatre would lead on to writers like W. B. Yeats who described his early play *The Shadowy Waters* as an attempt 'to create for a few people who love symbol, a play that will be more a ritual than a play, and leave upon the mind an impression like that of tapestry where the forms only half reveal themselves amid the shadowy folds'. It is interesting that the action and mood of the play are described in scenic terms, underlying the importance of the relationship between 'action' and 'scenery' in the symbolist-type theatre.

It is worth comparing the kind of realism aimed at in the theatre of Charles Kean in the late 1850s, and some of the more spectacular events aimed at in the last decade of the nineteenth century. Kean, himself a keen antiquary, is quoted as saying, 'I may safely assert that in no single instance have I even permitted historical truth to be sacrificed to theatrical effect'. (J. W. Cole, *The Life and Theatrical Times of Charles Kean*, 1859, Vol. 2, 382, quoted by Allardyce Nicoll, *op. cit.*) Kean attempted revivals of Shakespeare's plays in which he aimed at extreme historical accuracy in set and costume.

Samuel Phelps (1804–78) was another actor-manager who tried to portray scenes in his Shakespearean productions in a way that was historically accurate, but as Nicoll has pointed out, in observing Victorian proprieties 'a Roman-clad Antony might stalwartly stand beside a very demure and much petticoated Cleopatra' and Mrs Kean 'as Hermione in *A Winter's Tale . . .* donned underskirt after underskirt in true contemporary style and posed by her pedestal a most un-Grecian statue'. It is clear, therefore, that 'realism' had to take account of spectacle and social customs and adapt historical accuracy to meet them both: *sic tempora sic mores*. By the 1890s

A playbill of the Theatre Royal, Drury Lane, 14 May 1838. (NB The performance of *Blue Beard* to follow *Richard III*.)

changes had taken place and the 'realism' of the 1850s had given way to effects that innovations in the theatre had made possible.

In 1899 a Swiss, **Adolphe Appia** (1862–1928) published a book on staging, *Die Musik und die Inscenierung*. He had been engaged in considering the way Wagner's operas had been staged at Bayreuth and had come to the conclusion that the one-dimensional, flat, scenery took no account of the fact that actors moved and were three-dimensional. In his work, therefore, he proposed uses of stage lighting which would allow the scene to match the actor. His ideas, however, depended on the versatility that electricity could provide for lighting systems.

In 1815 the theatre at *Covent Garden* introduced **gas** to light the Grand Hall and the staircase. The *Olympic Saloon* in Wych Street, or Newcastle Street, in the Strand was opened by Philip Astley on December 1, 1806, and in 1808 was called *Astley's Pavilion*, or simply the *Pavilion*. When Elliston took it over in 1814 he restyled it the *Olympic*; it was rebuilt in 1818 but burnt down in 1849. On October 30, 1815, however, a playbill from the Olympic says that the exterior, part of the interior, and 'the saloon' would be 'lighted by gas'. The Olympic went back to 'wax lights' however in 1822. An item of news in *The Times* of September 6, 1817 describes the gas installation at *Drury Lane* in some detail: there were twelve perpendicular lines of lamps, each containing eighteen, and 'before the proscenium a row of eighty'. The lights were shielded from the auditorium by screens and reflectors and were encased in glasses. The installation of gas at *Covent Garden* around the stage was reported the same week: a great central light hung from the ceiling and there were gas lights fixed to the edges of the wings on each side of the stage. In 1820 the *Haymarket* opened after its rebuilding with oil lamps and candles, and gas was not introduced there for stage lighting until 1843. Outside London, nevertheless, gas was being introduced in theatres at Liverpool (1818), Edinburgh (1818), Manchester (1819), Exeter (1820), Greenock (1829), and Gloucester (1830), usually for the auditorium. During the nineteenth century the concentration of light on the stage produced a glare and dazzled audiences, it seems. However, attempts were made to reduce the glare by sinking the gaslight floats below the stage (Fechter in 1863 was the first to do this) and **the auditorium was darkened** sometimes to help special lighting effects such as the dawn or moonlight.

In order to use gas lights to provide special effects it was necessary to have a central control box to regulate it. Such control had existed from about 1817 but it was left to **Henry Irving** (1838–1905) at the *Lyceum* to begin the exploration of the use of gas for artistic purposes. He began his managing of the *Lyceum* on December 30, 1878, and established the fashion of keeping the auditorium in darkness throughout the whole performance (an approach advocated in 1598 by the Italian Ingegneri). This darkening of the auditorium had been tried out by **Charles Kemble** at *Covent Garden* in 1832 (*The Fiend Father* production) in order to get special effects at different times during the performance. With Irving, however, new effects could be created and he was quick to see the possibilities of electricity, with its greater versatility, and began installing it at

A playbill for Astley's Theatre, 19 September 1831.

the Lyceum in 1891 (although Ellen Terry attributes the installation of electric lighting to Daly after 1902). About 1870 he experimented with using thin pieces of silk stretched on wire guards over the gas lights in order to introduce colour into the scenery, and, by putting his lights on floats and grouping them according to intensity and colour he could achieve different effects. Later on he used glasses stained with lacquers of different colours for his limelights and later his electric bulbs.

Limelight was a development of the nineteenth century. It was sometimes called 'Drummond light' after its inventor in 1816. It was produced by directing a gas jet against a block of quicklime which gave off a brilliant white glare to provide for the stage an intensity of lighting quite different from the mellow, yellow lighting of the normal gas lamps. (The word 'limelight' is now used in modern English in phrases such as 'to be in the limelight'= 'to be in the glare of publicity'.) It was used in the theatre to suggest beams of sunlight or moonlight coming through windows or doors on stage. It was also used as a way of providing a spotlight to follow an actor about the stage until the 'spot' was developed with the use of electric arc-lighting behind glass lenses.

Electricity was used at the Paris Opéra to suggest the rising sun as early as 1846, and in 1860 during a production of a Rossini opera as a spotlight. This had a hood and a lens as well as a light source and was used with a curved mirror to flood parts of the stage. Arc lights and limelights continued to be used in theatres well into the next century.

At the *Savoy* in 1881 a resistance coil was introduced to provide dimming of the light on stage, and in the auditorium of a theatre using only electricity as its light source. Arc-lighting, however, was used in theatres until the invention and dissemination of incandescent bulbs. Early forms of 'electric candles' consisted of arc lights with carbons beside them insulated from each other by kaolin (the so-called 'Jabloch-Koff candle'). But incandescent bulbs were used at the Paris Opéra for its complete illumination in 1886.

Already experiments in stage lighting were taking place, therefore, which led directly to the lighting of the twentieth century. Even float-mounted lights were being replaced by lanterns with bull's-eye glasses in them. The moving spotlights could create shadow, intensity, and colour and, used with scenery, could provide changes in mood and atmosphere to enhance the language and the action. However, the lights were still bedevilled by glare and lack of easy mobility, but the twentieth century would create a whole new dimension to drama with its technological improvements in the control of lighting, with projectors, gels, lenses, lanterns, light battens, spots, and switchboards dependent on new wiring, circuits, transformers, resistances, electric motors, etc.

The end of the nineteenth century also saw the introduction of the revolving stage in a theatre in Munich in 1896 by *Lautenschläger*. The revolving stage could be divided into three segments, each containing a separate scene. As the stage was revolved a new scene was presented to the audience.

7.5 The Actor-Managers

'Star' actors have always played major roles in the development of the British stage. James Burbage (d. 1597), the women stars of the Restoration and early eighteenth century (Nell Gwyn (d. 1687), Anne Bracegirdle (d. 1748)), David Garrick (d. 1779), Sarah Siddons (d. 1831), Edmund Kean (d. 1833) and Charles Kemble (d. 1854) are merely some of the names that spring to mind over the centuries. However, the 'star' system focuses attention on the performance rather than on the part or the play. **William Macready** (1793–1873) who managed the Covent Garden Theatre in 1837–1839 and Drury Lane in 1841–43 was well known in his own time as an actor who insisted on holding the centre of the stage, who reduced other actors to being pawns in the action, as well as one who took liberties with the text in order to achieve results for himself.

The nineteenth century was, however, the great period of the actor-manager. Prime amongst these must be **Sir Henry Irving** (John Henry Brodribb, 1838–1905). As a boy he had a stutter and took elocution lessons to overcome it. He first appeared as an actor in Bulwer Lytton's *Richelieu* at the Lyceum Theatre, Sunderland on September 29, 1856. He played in the provinces, with one unsuccessful return to London, until 1866. He found success in two plays at the St. James' Theatre in 1866 (as Doricourt in *The Belle's Stratagem* and as Rawdon Scudamore in *Hunted Down* by Boucicault). In 1867 he played with Ellen Terry in Garrick's one-act adaptation of Shakespeare's *The Taming of the Shrew*, *Katherine and Petruchio*. He soon went on to further successes at the Gaiety and the Vaudeville theatres. His fame arrived spectacularly on September 11, 1871, when he produced at the Lyceum a play called *The Bells*, an adaptation by Leopold Lewis of Erckmann-Chatrian's play *The Polish Jew* ('Le Juif polonais'). In 1874 he played Hamlet as a man too sensitive to act rather than an irresolute character. He came under critical attack but thrived on the attention. Ellen Terry, his colleague, described him as being a man 'quiet, patient, tolerant, impersonal, gentle, close, crafty, incapable of caring for anything outside his work.' Praise and condemnation indeed!

In 1878 Irving mounted a revival of *Hamlet* to mark his new management of the Lyceum. He recruited artists from other related areas such as music and painting, and even archaeologists in order to give splendour to his productions. Ellen Terry shared in many of the resulting plays, which included the Shakespearean revivals of *Romeo and Juliet* (1882), *Much Ado about Nothing* (1882), *Twelfth Night* (1884), *King Lear* (1892) and *Cymbeline* (1896). He gave up the management of the Lyceum in 1899 but continued to appear on stage as late as 1905. (A survey of Irving's acting method is seen in a collection of descriptions by his contemporaries in *We Saw Him Act: A Symposium on the Art of Sir Henry Irving*, edited by H. A. Saintsbury and Cecil Palmer, 1939.)

Edmund Kean (1789–1833) is best remembered as an actor who used the romantic, passionate style to counteract the eighteenth-century neo-classical style of the late eighteenth century. Even in his own time his manner was recognised by Hazlitt as being one showing 'the hurried, familiar tone of common life' but Macready and Phelps were even more colloquial in their tone than Kean. Another contemporary described Kean as 'deficient in dignity, grace, and tenderness'. He it was who first portrayed Shylock as a black villain lusting for blood and Macbeth in the murder dagger scene as a man transfixed at the sight of his hands dripping with blood. His private life was as intense as his stage performances and he would fail to appear as scheduled and outraged public morality by seducing the wife of an alderman. His son **Charles Kean** (1811–68) was the greater actor-manager of the two. He established his reputation at the Princess's Theatre in 1850–4. He costumed his productions lavishly in the tradition of Charles Kemble at Covent Garden and aimed at historical accuracy as far as possible by researching details down to the last archaeological or even botanical fact.

Whilst Charles Kean was working at the Princess's, **Samuel Phelps** (1804–78) was putting on serious productions, especially of Shakespeare at the Sadler's Wells Theatre. After time spent in journalism he came to the professional stage through amateur dramatics. He appeared at the Haymarket from 1837 and played Shylock, Hamlet, and Othello. Once the theatres had been freed in 1843 he took over Sadler's Wells. He tried to restore the dignity of the theatre in a time when it was turning more and more to the trivial. He left Sadler's Wells in 1862 but he continued acting until the year of his death. His productions were serious and aimed at producing a scene pleasing to the eye without the current appeal to new gimmickry or striving after effect.

William Macready (1793–1873) pursued realism as enthusiastically as J. P. Kemble had done and Charles Kean would do, particularly in matters of historical accuracy, when he worked at Covent Garden in 1837–39 and Drury Lane in 1841–43, but subsequently it was the Bancrofts at the Prince of Wales's who gave even more impetus to realism in the theatre with their insistence on high standards of acting and production in the period 1865–79. The 'Bancrofts' were **Sir Squire Bancroft** (1841–1926) and his wife **Marie Effie Bancroft** (née Wilton) (1839–1921). They were responsible for the fashion set of drawing-room comedies with the scenery and decor of three-wall rooms with a ceiling (the so-called 'Box Set') with real doors and real windows which were 'practicable', ideas adapted from Mme Vestris's concern for realistic scenery at the Lyceum after 1847. Under the Bancrofts the Prince of Wales's Theatre became a huge success after its opening in the transformed Queen's Theatre building, known at the time as the 'Dust-hole'. Squire Bancroft and his wife played the major roles in the domestic comedies they put on; Squire's performance as Captain Hawtree in *Caste* (1867) was especially praised by contemporary critics. Both husband and wife retired as actor-managers on 2 July, 1885, but they continued to give other appearances from time to time. Amongst their innovations was the raising of leading actors' salaries in their employment tenfold from about five to ten pounds to sixty to one hundred pounds per week, and payment for their actresses' clothes; in this way the status of the serious acting profession was considerably raised.

Later in the century, alongside the work of Irving at the Lyceum, were the achievements of John Hare at the Garrick (1889–95), George Alexander at the

St. James's (1891–1918) and Herbert Beerbohm Tree at the Haymarket (1887–1915).

Sir George Alexander (George Alexander Gibb Samson, 1858–1918) managed the St. James's from 1891 until he died. After work in the provinces he joined Irving's company at the Lyceum in 1881 and stayed mainly there until he became an actor-manager in his own right. He was financially successful and deliberately set out to attract English playwrights whose works he could produce. He played and managed with dignity; undoubtedly his contemporaries held him in the highest esteem. His work included productions of plays by Shakespeare, Stephen Phillips, Oscar Wilde, and Pinero.

Sir Herbert Draper Beerbohm Tree (1853–1917) was one of the most famous actor-managers of the nineteenth century. He began work in the office of his father who was a grain merchant but in 1878 turned to the professional stage after having taken part in amateur theatre. In 1887 he became the manager first of the Comedy Theatre and then of the Haymarket Theatre. He built Her Majesty's Theatre and opened it in 1897. Here he carried on the lavish productions of Shakespeare popularised earlier at the Lyceum; he produced eighteen of Shakespeare's plays between 1888 and 1914. Tree was much more romantic than his actor-manager competitors. His was the tradition of Edmund Kean and romanticism, with flamboyance in both interpretation and acting. His performances were patchy – long, flat patches with moments of high passion in which depths of characterisation would suddenly emerge on the stage. His wife, Helen Maud Holt, was a distinguished actress in her own right and she also managed Wyndham's for a time after 1902.

7.6

Associated with the development of 'actor-managers' is the growth in status of **acting as a profession**. The Bancrofts did much to make 'stars' out of players and the tradition of the powerful, stage-dominating actor-manager was one which continued well into the mid-twentieth century in the person of Sir Donald Wolfitt. The Bancrofts did their best to eliminate the wildest, most extreme excesses of actors in the theatre and insisted on a proper profession-alism. Actor-managers were becoming so acceptable in society that some even received knighthoods for their work. The politer audiences attracted to matinees and more comfortable theatres found that even some of the actors and actresses themselves were of 'good breeding'. The organisation of the acting profession became part of this new professionalism in the nineteenth century.

In each of the London theatres a group of players would be engaged for the season. If replacements for actors were required, the managers looked to companies in the provincial theatres and it became the acceptable route through to the London theatre for young, new actors to serve their time in the provinces first. Long runs of plays, brought about by increased population and better transport by both road and rail, ensured stability and better security for the acting profession. The move towards realism in production was matched by a renewed interest in characterisation of the *Dramatis Personae* and increasingly there was the tendency to match parts to actors.

Success in London ensured, too, demands from provincial theatres to see and mount productions put on by touring companies, and so London theatres often had a second or even third company to go off with a production on tour. Companies of actors in the provinces, therefore, became less necessary since managers of theatres outside London wanted to 'book' London productions. Alternatively, London theatre managers could try out a play in the provinces and, if it were successful, then bring it to the capital – a practice which continues today.

Long runs, 'bookings' from London and the need to get experience first, outside the capital, made it hard for those wanting to get a foothold in the profession. The increased status and rewards for those reaching the top made it an attractive career for the ambitious and the determined. Young actors who found a part tried to hold on to it for security and so found the chance of gaining experience by playing a number of roles of varying difficulty. Authors, too, found it hard to break into the theatre, since actor-managers had to mount tried successes in order to attract audiences. Innovation and experimenting, therefore, demanded risks that many were unwilling to take; but writers are always unknown before they become known, and actors begin in obscurity before they can enter the 'limelight'. At first, the independent matinée, where new productions of new plays could be mounted, helped solve some of the problems and provided work for an expanded acting force, but public demand soon began to insist that matinées should be used for earlier performances of established successes. Another attempt to meet some of the problems came with the foundation of '**the stage society**' concept. In 1866 the 'Dramatic Students' was founded, a stage society bent on giving new performances of works not included 'in the ordinary repertoire'. William Poel established an 'Elizabethan Reading Society' in 1887 and put on Elizabethan and Jacobean plays between 1887 and 1898. In 1891 the 'Independent Theatre Society' was founded and became 'The Stage Society' in 1899. Shaw approved strongly of it: 'It is an excellent institution, simply because it is independent . . . independent of commercial success'. It did, however, also allow for independent experimenting in drama in terms of acting, writing, and production.

The demand for young actors for training in the newly acclaimed profession led to a movement to establish **stage schools**. In 1875 at Stratford-on-Avon, there was a proposal to build a Shakespeare theatre and 'a School or University of Dramatic Art . . . with its libraries, class-rooms, homes for instructors, scholarships for students, and special chairs for Professors'. This led to attempts to establish a dramatic academy – in London, of course – for instructing young players. In 1876 the project ran into financial difficulties for want of an endowment and collapsed. In 1879 an 'academy of acting' was proposed and the idea of a Royal Academy of Dramatic Art was raised again. The debate continued in spite of interventions over a period of twenty-five years by Charles Kean, Dickens, W. M. Thackeray and W. E. Henley, Matthew Arnold, and Wilkie Collins amongst others. The discussion moved across into the twentieth century in due course, as did the debate about the establishment of a **National Theatre**, which had begun as early as 1848, with Effingham Wilson (a

London publisher) who had bought Shakespeare's birthplace for the nation and proposed 'A House for Shakespeare', 'the world's greatest moral teacher'. In 1879 a visit by the Comédie Francaise to London (a French National Theatre had been set up in 1680!) gave new impetus to the idea of an English National Theatre. Matthew Arnold lent his considerable support to the movement along with Henry Irving, but the real movement towards the establishment of such a theatre did not begin on a path to eventual success until William Archer and Harley Granville-Barker collaborated in 1904 to produce a detailed scheme. Squire Bancroft, John Hare, James Barrie, Arthur Pinero, Henry Arthur Jones, Meredith, Hardy, Bridges, and Galsworthy joined in giving the movement momentum and George Bernard Shaw gave continuous support throughout his very long life. (See also pages 40, 45–46, for the later development of stage schools and the National Theatre.)

7.7 The Development and Decline of the Music-Halls (1840–1939)

The music-hall, as part of the non-literary theatre movement was peculiarly a development of the nineteenth century. It is true that there were 'music-houses', such as Sadler's Wells, in the eighteenth century where songs, dances, acrobatics, and pantomime were put on as part of the competition to the legitimate theatre. During the eighteenth century, too, and up to about 1840, the flourishing music clubs had been places where refreshment, song, and music went hand in hand. In Covent Garden, Evans's Song-and-Supper Rooms provided entertainment as late as midnight, run by Paddy Green, an *Adelphi* Theatre actor. (*cf.* The Players' Theatre, reopened under the arches at Charing Cross). Burlesque ballads and part-songs formed part of the repertoire.

Public houses soon set aside a large room as the music room and in the 1840s Charles Morton, the publican at the Canterbury Arms, Lambeth, opened a special adjoining hall with a stage, tables and chairs for the entertainment of his customers. Comics, singers and clowns all gave 'turns' at the improvised tavern halls that rapidly became popular. Some of the earliest were Sam Cowell ('The Rat-catcher's Daughter') and George Leybourne ('Champagne Charlie'). Serious sopranos were employed as part of the entertainment and women performers of burlesque songs, such as Jenny Hill, became popular. Alcoholic licences were removed in due course from such tavern rooms, and the music-hall had to break away from public houses.

Twice-nightly 'houses' were brought in to meet the demand for entertainment and the concept of 'Variety' was introduced so that the songs and comics could be joined by dramatic 'snippets' less than thirty minutes in length. Alexander, Beerbohm Tree and Sarah Bernhardt all appeared in such productions at times. George Black introduced 'crazy gangs' who would move into the audience, rampage about the theatre foyer and auditorium, and break up acts in order to amuse the audience. But by the Second World War (1939) the music-hall had been threatened by the success, first, of the silent cinema and, then, of the 'talking-movies' which attracted huge audiences who could buy refreshments, enjoy the social comfort of being amongst a crowd enjoying themselves, and still retain their own private worlds of imagination in which to live and move.

The stars of the music-hall, the 'top-of-the-bill' performers, climbed to their positions the hard way. An 'act' which set out to gain the sympathy and attention of the audience and merit their applause within a very short time was difficult to devise. The two things necessary were an immediate impact on the audience and a distinctive and recognisable 'trade-mark' in the performance. Both could be achieved quickly by means of *distinctive clothes* (coster-clothes, elegant evening dress, ill-fitting trousers likely to fall down – always funny, for some reason); *distinctive appearance* (patches over the eye, kilts, beards, moustaches, extravagant hair-do's, huge bosoms); *distinctive voices* (provincial accents – especially north-country ones, high squeaks from huge men or low, reverberating tones from thin, small men); *distinctive mannerisms* (repeated catch-phrases, stumbling, twitching, sniffing, chumping lips); or *distinctive songs or patter* (trade-mark signing-off songs such as 'Red-Sails-in-the-Sunset' or 'The Boiled-Beef-and Carrots' type routine of a Harry Champion). Tumbling, Juggling, Acrobatics, Trapeze-Artists, Magicians, and even provocative strip-tease acts provided the 'artiste' was never totally unclad and remained still when seemingly naked, were added to the tradition which survived until the Second World War and even just beyond it, when television finally laid it (and the popular cinema at the same time) to rest. Television recognised the appeal of the music-hall in the cleverly reconstructed show of 'The Good Old Days', where the audience donned nineteenth-century dress, the master-of-ceremonies banged his gavel and introduced his acts with an exaggerated patter, and the 'turns' sang, joked, conjured, and danced their way through their routines with a clear awareness of, and a desire to involve, the audience.

The humour, the pathos, the patriotism, the stock characters (hen-pecked husbands, battling wives, downtrodden drunks, the down-and-out, etc.) and the sentimentality were some of the features of the music-hall which gave rise to at least forty-four major music-halls in London alone listed by Allardyce Nicoll (in *A History of English Drama*, V, second edition, 1959, 222).

7.8 The Nature and Development of Popular Melodrama after 1843.

After the Theatre Licensing Act of 1843 **melodrama** took a new turn. The development of melodrama in the eighteenth century, as a dramatic piece accompanied by music, has been traced in **6.19** (see pages 185–187). There the genre was followed from the work of George Lillo (1693–1793) through to *Blue Beard or Female Curiosity* in 1798.

In the early nineteenth century the famous melodrama of *Maria Marten or The Murder in the Red Barn* (in the 1830s) demanded a revised view of the nature of melodrama but some see the earlier definition of 'the play with musical accompaniment to give special effects' as holding sufficiently well to T. W. Robertson's *Caste* in1867.

The 1843 Act removed the *'burletta'* restrictions (see page 201) and so allowed new kinds of non-conventional plays to be introduced which did not require five acts or, necessarily, the accompaniment of music. The 'illegitimate' theatre could be redefined as 'the non-literary theatre' to embrace farce, musical comedy, revues, and a new, popular melodrama.

These melodramas included stock characters such as handsome, gallant heroes, beautiful heroines in distress, sympathetic and contrastingly humorous friends for the heroes and confidantes for the heroines, and villains (often with cloaks, black hats, and twirling moustachios). Action rather than analysis of character dominates the plot and incidents tumble quickly out one after the other. Throughout, the atmosphere is one of unnaturalness; even the killings are so bizarre and the threats so macabre as to defy any links with reality. Dialogue and movements are swift, the excitement is intense, and poetic justice is sure; the mood is 'romantic' or even 'gothic', light and darkness are vital (*NB*   gas was introduced into the theatres in the 1840s; see pages 185–186, 210), and ghosts, magic, and last-minute rescues are common. Action and spectacle can become the substance of the play, as in the huge conflagration scene (Act V, Scene 2) in Boucicault's *The Poor of New York, Liverpool/London* (or wherever it was played) in 1857, where the disguised villain, Bloodguard, sets fire to the house, a hero is trapped, and a gallant rescuer is almost burnt alive in trying to effect a rescue. Deceit, writings in blood, unreasonable hate, envy, innocence threatened and unbridled malevolence were other features of melodrama in the 1840s and 1850s. But aspects of the genre were being emphasised which would lead in their turn to a new kind of melodramatic writing, based less on sensationalism and more on pathos and, in some writers such as **Tom Taylor** (1817–80) and **Charles Reade** (1814–84), sentimentality. Taylor and Reade often drew on historical incidents for their plots and it is worth bearing in mind that the most famous writer of the period, Charles Dickens, used historical incidents and has been also accused of being too sentimental and too full of pathos. The development in the melodrama and in the novel seems to be going side-by-side, at least in these respects. Where Boucicault (1822–90), actor and dramatist, often used historical incident for the sentimental and the comic, Taylor used it for the sentimental and the tragic; neither Boucicault's nor Taylor's dramas, of course, were restricted to historical topics by any means.

T. W. Robertson (1829–71) drew on the melodramatic traditions in his development of a more realistic drama. He wrote very detailed stage directions which laid down precisely what the set was to contain – and the nearer reality the scene could be the better for Robertson. Similarly the characters, language and themes had to be realistic to match. He broke away, however, from type-characters and replaced them with individuals and tried to link a central theme of his plays (*Society, Caste, War, School*) to moralising, where it occurred naturally, however sentimental it may seem today in its treatment. Robertson's *Caste* (1867) is sometimes considered as the end of the 'melodrama' in the nineteenth century, in its strictest form. It shows that this playwright was not a mere social dramatist of the kind that Galsworthy and others at the turn of the century would show themselves to be. In *Caste* Robertson used the spectacular methods of earlier melodrama and applied them to comedy and in this way he showed himself more of a man of the theatre than a social reformer. It was in the theatre that his skill and interest principally lie. He was not an intellectual writer and his comedy succeeds partly in the way he adapts the melodramatic methods to his comic purposes: Eccles, the drunk is not condemned to a dreadful death but to a place where he can drown himself in drink quite happily and cheaply. *Caste* shows the difficulties which arise when two people of different social rank marry, but it shows much more clearly Robertson's skill in the theatre. He avoids caricature in a way that earlier melodramas did not and uses natural, working-class language without any kind of 'heightening' to make it specifically dramatic. There are also passages which set out foreign accents to be used. The plot itself has the melodramatic 'comedy', happy ending when George, thought dead in war by everyone, suddenly returns. After the initial surprise everyone accepts it quite easily and even his wife, Esther, who has been carefully prepared for a surprise by Sam and Polly quickly accepts that the fairy-tale ballet, 'Jeanne la Folle or The Return of the Soldier' really can come true in life. The heavy, emotion-laden moment of rediscovery is reinforced by music, significant in its air and in its crescendos in best melodramatic style:

ESTHER (*slowly looking into Polly's eyes*) You have heard of George – I know you have – I see it in your eyes. You may tell me – I can bear it – I can indeed – indeed I can. Tell me – he is not dead? (*Violently agitated.*)

POLLY No!

ESTHER No?

POLLY No!

ESTHER (*whispers*) Thank Heaven! (*Sam turns on stool, back to audience.*) You've seen him – I see you have! – I know it! – I feel it! I had a bright and happy dream – I saw him as I slept! Oh let me know if he is near! Give me some sign – some sound – (*Polly opens piano*) – some token of his life and presence!
     (*Sam touches Polly on the shoulder, opens piano, takes hat and exits, door R. All to be done very quickly. Polly sits immediately at piano and plays air softly – the same air played by Esther Act II on the treble only.*)

ESTHER (*in an ecstasy*) Oh my husband! come to me! for I know that you are near! let me feel your arms clasp round me! – Do not fear for me! – I can bear the sight of you! – (*door opens showing Sam keeping George back*) It will not kill me! – George – love – husband – come, oh, come to me! (*George breaks away from Sam, and coming down behind Esther places his hands over her eyes; she gives a faint scream, and turning, falls in his arms. Polly plays the bass as well as the treble on the air, forte, then fortissimo. She then plays at random, endeavouring to hide her tears. At last strikes piano wildly, and goes off into a fit of hysterical laughter, to the alarm of Sam, who, rushing down as Polly cries 'Sam! Sam!' falls on his knees in front of her. They embrace. Polly pushing him contemptuously away afterwards. George gets chair R.C., sits, and Esther kneels at his feet – he snatches off Esther's cap, and throws it up stage. Polly goes L. of George, Sam brings music-stool, and she sits.*)

ESTHER   To see you here again – to feel your warm breath upon my cheek – is it real or am I dreaming?

SAM   (*R., rubbing his head*)   No; it's real.

ESTHER   (*embracing George*)   My darling!

SAM   My darling! (*Polly on music-stool, which Sam has placed for her. Sam, kneeling by her, imitates Esther – Polly scornfully pushes him away.*)   But tell us–tell us how you escaped.

GEORGE   It's a long story; but I'll condense it . . .

And George does just that. The script reads rather like that of a silent movie with piano accompaniment. The movements and reactions are exaggerated, the arrangement of the characters in a posed tableau to hear George's account is conscious, and the slapstick jesting of Sam and Polly to relax the tension at the moment of high passion between Esther and George has become a cliché of theatre and film alike. The use of the piano to recall the past plot, reveal gloomy tension, and to express emotions of the other characters and the release of pent-up emotions in the audience itself can almost be a source book of instructions for the use of theme music in later romantic films.

The topics in *Caste* are well-delineated: love and honour; the loyalty of women; the triumph of love over war; patriotism triumphant; the moral of 'Nobody's nobody! Everybody's somebody'. There are pointed-up comments on wealth, the position of actors in society, pantomime, the use of gaslight in the theatres and even a reference to the spectacles to be found at Astley's *Pavilion*. The use of the stage is conscious as people come and go and pose against each other in formal, balanced style (see the balancing of Polly and Hawtree, George and Esther at the beginning and Polly and Sam, George and Esther at the end). The sentimental effect is never missed – the finding by George of the baby he had not known, and the similarity of the dream ballet and real life. The romanticised ending is how life ought to be, however, not, alas, how it is in fact. The audience is indulging its feeling of escapism to the last moment in the melodrama.

Melodrama has now developed into the sentimental and the emotional but it still retains its sense of shock and surprise. W. S. Gilbert in his comic operas would use very similar techniques in the 1870s. The bringing together of romantic theme and realistic dialogue was one that Shaw would use and explore for humour in *Arms and the Man* (1894).

In the 1870s, however, the older form of melodrama, with its stock characters, the handsome hero, the virtuous heroine and the big, bad, bold, villain dragged its way on to self-destruction through caricature, banality, and excess. It must be remembered, however, that this was also the age of Dickens, who had only just died (1870), Kingsley (1819–75), Charles Reade (1814–84), and George Meredith (1828–1909), (who, incidentally, wrote a famous essay on comedy and left the *The Sentimentalists*, a conversational comedy published in the year after his death). In their works the high emotion, shock, contrasts, social moralising, and stock characters of melodrama can be paralleled in prose fiction. But just as prose fiction was developing towards Henry James and Hardy, so the sentimental melodrama was moving towards a truer philosophical and social statement in the plays of **Henry Arthur Jones** (1851–1929), who began firmly in the melodramatic tradition, and the social comedies of John Galsworthy (1867–1933).

Galsworthy's plays *The Silver Box* (1909), *Strife* (1909), *Justice* (1910), *The Skin Game* (1920), and *Loyalties* (1922) are also much in the tradition of Robertson, in spite of their social earnestness and patent homiletic commentary. Class differences result not in marital difficulties but in profound social difficulties, where the law operates differently for the rich and the poor, where families are seen to be expendable for political causes, and the newly successful upstart can come into conflict with the entrenched, apparently unassailable aristocracy.

Melodrama, then, was changing into the heavily-pointed social, satirical, propagandist drama of the turn of the century, where the appeal remained to the heart as well as to the head, where colours were highlighted, and themes were explicit. The conflict was becoming internalised, however, with more individual reactions and fewer stock responses.

By the 1890s British drama had not thrown off the sentimentalism of earlier melodrama but it was becoming surer. This was the decade when the plays of **Henrik Ibsen** (1828–1906) came into the English theatres: *A Doll's House* (revived in 1891), *Rosmersholm* (Vaudeville, 1891), *Ghosts* (Royalty, 1891), *Hedda Gabler* (Vaudeville, 1891) and *The Lady from the Sea* (Terry's, 1891). It was also the decade of **Oscar Wilde** (1854–1900) with *Lady Windermere's Fan* (St. James's, 1892), *A Woman of No Importance* (Haymarket, 1893), *An Ideal Husband* (Haymarket, 1895) and *The Importance of Being Earnest* (St. James's, 1895). **Bernard Shaw**, too, was making his forays into the theatre: *Widowers' Houses* (1892), *Arms and the Man* (1894), *Candida* (1895), *The Devil's Disciple* (1897), *The Man of Destiny* (1898) and *The Gadfly* (1898). **Sir Arthur Wing Pinero** (1855–1934) continued his work, which had been prolific in the eighties: *The Cabinet Minister* (1890); *Lady Bountiful* (1891), *The Times* (1891), *The Amazons* (1893), *The Second Mrs Tanqueray* (1893), *The Notorious Mrs Ebbsmith* (1895), *The Benefit of the Doubt* (1895), *The Princess and the Butterfly* (1898) and *Trelawny of the 'Wells'* (1898). **Henry Arthur Jones** (1851–1929) produced some of his best work during this decade, including: *Michael and his Lost Angel* (1896), *The Liars* (1897) and *The Triumph of the Philistines* (1895).

This was an important decade, therefore, in the development of British drama out of the world of the sentimental melodrama, and into the area to be taken up by 'the problem play'. The action was becoming more internalised in its presentation, and the individual's personal response to, and wrestling with, social, moral, philosophical, and religious problems could be seen as the fit and proper subject of drama. The presentation was, still, often encumbered with sentimentalism and the wearing of one's heart on one's sleeve; the black villains became the forces lining up against the happiness of the individual; the problems facing the hero could not be solved on a social level alone but demanded a personal, internal solution. Throughout there was a pronounced move to polished construction and greater realism in dialogue. The language was not that of ordinary, colloquial speech but it was the language of ordinary, colloquial speech at one remove. Perhaps the contrast between the artificiality of careful, precise plot-construction and the 'realistic' language of the late nineteenth century is best seen in the comedies of Oscar Wilde. In *The Importance of Being Earnest* the language is crystal clear and a guying of the mannerisms of everyday speech according to class:

CECILY	(*thoughtfully and sadly*)	Whatever unfortunate entanglement my dear boy has got into, I will never reproach him with it after we are married.
GWENDOLYN		Do you allude to me, Miss Cardew, as an entanglement? You are presumptuous. On an occasion of this kind it becomes more than a moral duty to speak one's mind. It becomes a pleasure.
CECILY		Do you suggest, Miss Fairfax, that I entrapped Ernest into an engagement? How dare you? This is no time for wearing the shallow mask of manners. When I see a spade I call it a spade.
GWENDOLYN	(*satirically*)	I am glad to say that I have never seen a spade. It is obvious that our social spheres have been widely different.

In this passage the reference to 'the shallow mask of manners' is interesting and important. Allardyce Nicoll has suggested that the 1890s with Oscar Wilde and Sir Arthur Pinero saw a temporary new flourishing of the 'comedy of manners', so popular in the Restoration and eighteenth century (see pages 172–175).

It is, however, towards 'the problem play' that melodrama changed its direction at the turn of the nineteenth century.

7.9 The Problem Play

The term 'problem' in the context of late nineteenth-century and early twentieth-century drama is one that applies to, and delineates, the drama that discusses controversial social questions, such as class differences, wealth in society, attitudes to moral questions, the role of women, family relationships, or the morality or immorality of war and business. Such plays arose from a period when the sentimentality of the old melodrama merged with the reality and social consciousness of a period of change. The work of Ibsen, Shaw, Robertson, and Jones has already been referred to in this context, but now 'the problem play' needs to be examined more closely, particularly in the light of plays by Ibsen and other Scandinavian writers such as Strindberg and Bjørnson.

The plays of **Henrik Ibsen** (1828 – 1906) were produced in London theatres during the 1890s (see page 208). Ibsen's drama began with some romantic plays but even his early work *Love's Comedy* (1863) satirically showed how the dead hand of authority could weigh heavily on love and marriage. For a time Ibsen plunged into the depths of personal despair at his own financial difficulties and the attitude of the Norwegian government towards the war between Denmark and Germany, and he produced *Brand* (1866) and *Peer Gynt* (1867). The first deals with the personal suffering an unbending religious non-conformist attitude can inflict on an individual and his community, where compromises are refused; at his moment of death Brand despairingly realises that God is the God of Love and not a divinity that deals only with extremes. *Peer Gynt* is also a play about despair that comes from 'going round about' instead of following the true path that idealism lays down. Peer Gynt becomes a successful capitalist but runs into inner-searching for truth as he is confronted by Destiny or his other self; he is saved at the end by the patient, unswerving woman in his life. The play is an exploration, in symbolic, even surrealistic terms, of man's search for his own true identity. *Brand* dealt with the bigotry of an idealism which would not compromise; *Peer Gynt* treated the theme of personal irresponsibility and responsibility to himself and to others.

The areas of 'problems' to be considered in drama were beginning to establish themselves for Ibsen. The first of Ibsen's so-called 'problem plays' was *The Pillars of Society* (1877). This dealt with the predicament of a man with considerable power in his community, well-accepted, who is assailed by corruption, weakness and cowardice. The play also introduced a character-type who would be explored later by Ibsen himself, Shaw, Galsworthy and others – the woman who is able and prepared to work out for herself her own attitudes in relation to those around her and the role she is expected to play in society. George Eliot (1819–80) and later D. H. Lawrence (1885–1930) in the field of the novel were interested in just such a character.

A Doll's House (1879) pursued the attitude of society towards women. Men overprotect Nora, both her father and her husband, Torvald Helmer, a successful lawyer and bank manager. Nora commits a minor act of forgery to get money for her sick, work-worn husband to take a holiday, but she is blackmailed and discovered. Her husband, unaware of her motives, condemns her and she realises her marriage was built on ice. Some saw the play as part of the new feminist movement which gave rise to the Suffragettes in England, but Ibsen was much more concerned with 'the trapped woman' who gradually works herself through to self-realisation and self-understanding. The problem is one of all women who have to live in a male-dominated world, which is full of blindness and hypocrisy and cannot find a moment to understand love and truth in its most human sense. Nora is the little girl living in a doll's house until she pushes it over.

Ghosts (1881) continues the exploration of woman's identity and role in an essentially male world. Here, however, Mrs Alving is an intellectually emancipated woman who can think for herself and make decisions for herself. She is torn, like all good Greek tragic heroines, between two possibilities: to tell the truth or to suppress it. Her late husband had been sexually promiscuous and the venereal disease he had inevitably contracted had physically damaged their son, Oswald. Oswald seems to develop into an image of his father and the ghost of the past lives again in the present. The problem for Mrs Alving becomes the more acute when Oswald proposes to marry the maid Regina, who unknown to the girl herself, is the illegitimate daughter of Captain Alving. Not only are we faced, therefore, with a play about syphilis but one about incest – two topics that are boldly considered by Ibsen in an age when social morality was such as to preclude public discussion of either. The 'whited sepulchre' of an orphanage built by Mrs Alving to commemorate her husband's goodness and philanthropy is (symbolically) burnt down and as Oswald burns up from within the audience is left to wonder whether she would keep her promise to her tormented son to administer a way out of life to him or not. To venereal disease and incest is added the third topic never to be debated – euthanasia.

The play created a furore. Marriage, respect for parents, marital love, all seemed to be questioned. Lindberg, the Swedish actor who was refused his request to put on *Ghosts* was told: 'the play is one of the filthiest things ever written in Scandinavia'. In Norway Ibsen was savaged but the dramatist saw Mrs Alving as another statement about women that had to be made after he had written *A Doll's House*. Gradually, however, the play found its way on to stages in Scandinavia, Germany, and France. It then moved to Vienna and Amsterdam. In 1890 it shocked London. However, the essential mistake about the play arose because its symbolism had been largely misunderstood. The play is not really about syphilis but the corruption of soul that is handed down from father to child. It is not really about incest but about the irony of love that cannot be fulfilled because of conventions. It is not about euthanasia but about the inner struggle of what is the greater love – to watch suffering that will lead to more suffering or to release the sufferer in spite of conventional attitudes. The ghosts of the past and the ghosts of the present are everywhere; they will become the ghosts of the future if they are allowed to continue. (In another setting, in another plot, in another country, the ghosts of *A Christmas Carol* by Dickens carry a not unrelated message.) *Ghosts*, too, is important since it opens up for discussion the values of middle-class morality, the influence of the dead past on the living present. The ironic thing about the play, in the light of the criticism it received in its own time, is that it burns with a strongly moral intensity.

An Enemy of the People (1882) shows that however right a scientist may be, unless society will accept the truth it is worth nothing. Dr Stockman (the scientist) is sure that the water supply is polluted (the truth); but society will not accept the fact since it threatens their livelihoods. Society will always compromise the truth for its own end and its passionate advocate will burn himself out or be burnt up, unless he will see his own weakness and compromise. The fanatic, the bigot, the non-self-questioner, the extremist, in Ibsen's plays, carries his own self-destructiveness about with him.

The Wild Duck (1884) similarly explores the extreme position taken up by Gregers Werle, who insists on everyone seeing the truth, so that Hedvig is destroyed. Hjalmer fails to understand the free flight of Hedvig's soul away from harsh reality. Hedvig goes to destroy the wild duck herself but cannot face the destruction of her one route of escape and kills herself. Hjalmar's remorse comes from the depths; the despair is overwhelming: 'Oh, Gina, Gina! How shall we live after this?'

Rosmersholm (1887) pauses to bring together some of Ibsen's earlier themes and characters. Rosmer, who has turned from his vocation in the church, is supported by an emancipated woman, Rebecca, to face the pressures of middle-class, hypocritical attitudes until he learns that Rebecca helped his wife to end her own life. Rosmer is overwhelmed and both he and Rebecca are persecuted by the ghosts of the past. Here the social problems are the context, and not the cause, of the internal moral and human problems of the protagonists. The worm within gnaws away relentlessly to bring despair.

The Lady from the Sea (1888), *Hedda Gabler* (1890), *The Master Builder* (1892), *Little Eyolf* (1894), *Gabriel Borkman* (1896) and *When we Dead Awake* (1900) followed. Ibsen had showed the way to present the dilemma of the individual in becoming reconciled to himself and to society. The theme was not new in drama since the Greeks had taken it up centuries before. The analysis of the dilemma in terms of the cost in love, principles, relationships and life itself was presented in Ibsen in realistic language and within realistic contexts, but with all the dramatic intensity that the sentimental melodrama had exploited.

Following Ibsen, **Bjørnstjerne Bjørnson** (1832–1910), a fellow Norwegian dramatist, took up some of the themes proposed by Ibsen. *Beyond our Power I* (produced in 1889) explored the dangers that an ungoverned idealism ran and the double standards imposed by men on women in *The Gauntlet* (1883) which argued the case that men as well women should be chaste before marriage.

August Strindberg (1849–1912), a Swedish playwright, was a restless figure who married three times, spent much of his thirties travelling about Europe in Austria, France, Germany and Switzerland, and then returned to Sweden to produce some of his best work. His contemporaries called him a misogynist but in fact he hated only those women he called 'Amazons' or 'hermaphrodites' who tried to destroy or subjugate men. He wrote to his brother Axel in February, 1887: 'You know that as a creative writer I mix make-believe and reality together, and the whole of my misogyny is theoretical, for I could not live without the company of a woman'. (Quoted by Mary Sandbach, *August Strindberg: 'Getting Married'*, 1972.)

His dramatic work is sometimes divided into two periods, his 'naturalism' and his 'expressionism' separated by an 'Inferno Period' (1894–96) during which he charted his own psychological and spiritual upheavals and problems in a book called *Inferno* (1897). The term 'expressionism', perhaps needs some explanation; it is used in literature, music, architecture, and art as well as in drama. Expressionism imposes an interpretation on the world which is dependent on one's own internal view of it; it is a subjective interpretation of what one sees; it turns one's own subjective observations in on one's own internal examination of them. Expressionist art brings *out* from the internal workings of the artist's mind what the artist has seen outside him but seen from his own subjective point of view. Impressionism, however, deals with the subjective *internal* responses to an exernal world that can be established objectively; a subjective view of external reality. Expressionism, therefore, turns in on itself and reacts strongly against whatever is outside in terms of 'reality'; the mood is one of anger and pessimism. Ibsen was essentially an *im*pressionist writer, since he wrote about subjective responses to outside forces; Strindberg, in his later plays was essentially *ex*pressionist, since he wrote about subjective responses to outside forces subjectively perceived (see also George E. Wellworth, *World Drama*, ed. J. Gassner and E. Quinn, 1962 on 'Expressionism').

During his early 'naturalistic' period Strindberg produced social drama, *Master Olof* (1881), *Comrades* (1886–1887), *The Father* (1887) and *Miss Julie* (1889). In *The Father* Strindberg showed how, in the battle of the sexes, the woman will triumph because of her strength of will. *Miss Julie* shows the sex-battle this time between Miss Julie (an aristocrat) and Jean (a footman trying to rise in society); Jean is frustrated in his attempts and is crushed by Julie's father, the Count. Julie commits suicide. The class struggle mixed with sexual encounters across class barriers would become an important theme in Lawrence's *Lady Chatterley's Lover* and Tennessee Williams's *A Streetcar Named Desire*, as Richard Vowles has pointed out (in *World Drama*, ed. J. Gassner and E. Quinn, 1969).

After 1899 Strindberg wrote many history plays based on Swedish history, but his major contribution to the development of the problem play lay in his 'expressionist' drama. *A Dream Play* (written in 1901) is episodic, and through the medium of the dream does away with time and place constraints. The world can be interpreted from the dreamer's point of view by the dreamer. Some of the symbolism in the play is closer to medieval times than to the nineteenth century, with an officer imprisoned in a castle waiting for a supernatural liberation, while an Indian deity moves from an earthly marriage to discussions with a poet near Fingal's Cave and a contretemps with university professors. Far from bringing rescue in the best medieval traditions, the deity returns to heaven with the news that misery is at the heart of the human experience. The dream world atmosphere is maintained by the leaps in time and place, by the juxtaposition of east with west, and by the inversion of male and female traditional roles in subjugation and liberation.

The Ghost Sonata (1908) is a play full of grotesque situations and characters; Hummel, in a wheelchair, is a bloodsucker who manipulates the young for his own desires; a student acts as go-between from Hummel to other creatures in society. The Hyacinth Girl is destroyed, Hummel dies, and the student survives to lament the corruption and mortality of life. Again, reality and illusion seem strangely inverted in order to produce the grotesque image Strindberg is apparently seeking. (For a further analysis of Strindberg's plays see R. Vowles (*op. cit.*) and Maurice Valency, *The Flower and the Castle*, 1963.)

7.10

Ibsen's influence on the early Shaw was considerable. Shaw acknowledged his debt to the Norwegian dramatist and saw himself as a 'realist' in drama terms. Nevertheless, his dialogue was not that of natural speech but was one remove from it and his use of epigrams and the quick, witty retort suggest studied conversation, with balances, innuendo, and deliberate 'ambiguities' to give it weight.

The preface to *Plays Unpleasant* (1898) which contained his first play, *Widowers' Houses* (1892), sets out Shaw's initial stance:

The New Theatre would never have come into existence but for the plays of Ibsen
. . . Ibsen, then, was the hero of the new departure. It was in 1889 that the first
really effective blow was struck by the production of *A Doll's House* by Charles
Charrington and Janet Achurch . . .

He describes *Widowers' Houses* as a 'grotesquely realistic exposure of slum
landlordism, municipal jobbery, and the pecuniary and matrimonial ties
between them and the pleasant people with 'independent' incomes who
imagine that such sordid matters do not touch their own lives'. The play was a
startling success because of its social theme and its discussion of 'a problem',
although Shaw saw it more in terms of an 'uproar' than a 'success'. Shaw was
again influenced by Ibsen in his approach to the treatment and role of women
in society:

> In the following year, 1893, when the discussion about Ibsenism, 'The New
> Woman', and the like was at its height, I wrote for the Independent Theatre the
> topical comedy called *The Philanderer*.

He then produced a third play, *Mrs Warren's Profession* 'on a social subject of
tremendous force'; if Ibsen had dealt with syphilis, incest, and euthanasia,
Shaw felt he could deal with prostitution. He ran up against 'the Censorship',
as he called it, at once. The Licensing Act of 1843 reared its head with the full
force of the law. (Shaw has a long tirade in his preface to *Plays Unpleasant* about
the operation of this Act and the Lord Chamberlain.) In his first forays on to
the stage, then, Shaw was indebted to Ibsen for **realism, social theme**, and
the approach to drama through a **problem**. If the social theme could shock, so
much the better and the closer to Ibsen it was. **The persecution of the
lower classes by the upper and the emerging role of women in
society** were suitable 'Ibsen-type' topics.

Shaw, in the same preface, goes on to discuss the relationship between the
text and its performance. Plays need to be able to be read. It was W. B. Yeats
who said, 'We do not think that a play can be worth acting and not worth
reading'. 'The case,' Shaw argued, 'is overwhelming not only for printing and
publishing the dialogue of plays, but for a serious effort to convey their full
content to the reader. This means the institution of a new art'. It was all very
well for Ibsen to have said, 'What I have said, I have said,' – Shaw pointed out,
but 'the point is what he hasn't said, he hasn't said. There are perhaps people
(though I doubt it, not being one of them myself) to whom Ibsen's plays, as
they stand, speak sufficiently for themselves. There are certainly others who
could not understand them on any terms'. Shaw, therefore, proposes the use of
very detailed stage directions:

> there are fifty ways of saying Yes, and five hundred of saying No, but only one way
> of writing them down . . . At all events, I have tried to put down nothing that is
> irrelevant to the actor's performance, and, through it, to the audience's
> comprehension of the play'.

In *Plays Unpleasant* Shaw's intention was explicit:

> 'to force the spectator to face unpleasant facts . . . In *Widower's Houses* I have shewn middle-class respectability and younger-son gentility fattening on the poverty of the slum as flies fatten on filth . . . In *The Philanderer* I have shewn the grotesque sexual compacts made between men and women under marriage laws . . . In *Mrs Warren's Profession* I have gone straight at the fact that, 'the only way for a woman to provide for herself decently is for her to be good to some man that can afford to be good to her'.

Such facts are unpleasant. Social organisation demands that both men and women have to prostitute themselves by selling their affections and their convictions in order to live.

His next group of plays, *Plays Pleasant* (1898) dealt with 'romantic follies and with the struggles of individuals against those follies'. Here, then, is another Ibsen theme: **the entanglement of the individual in a situation from which he or she cannot escape**. In his preface to this collection of plays (*Arms and the Man*, *Candida*, and *You Never Can Tell*) Shaw acknowledges Ibsen's influence once again and argues that, 'The theatre is growing in importance as a social organ'. The theatre was both school and church in a society where public and private life was becoming daily more theatrical; rulers have to act out their parts and the stage was affecting both newspaper behaviour and the behaviour of citizens. Significantly, Shaw goes on to argue, being amongst the first to do so, the case for a National Theatre. He wanted actors to avoid sentimentalism in presenting his plays and to achieve his effects by his artistry rather than the histrionics of an actor:

> When a comedy is performed, it is nothing to me that the spectators laugh; any fool can make an audience laugh. I want to see how many of them, laughing or grave, are in the melting mood. And this cannot be achieved, even by actors who thoroughly understand my purpose, except through an artistic beauty of execution . . . and an intellectual effort.

Allardyce Nicoll has described Shaw as not 'one single author but as three authors working in collaboration': the social propagandist making each play 'a clearly wrought essay on some problem'; a man of ideas who derives delight in contemplating them for their own sake; and thirdly, 'an almost impish creature constantly bubbling over with a sense of fun which he constantly seeks to express in dramatic terms'. (*British Drama*, fifth edition, 1962, 281.) This view of Shaw acknowledges his debt to Ibsen but also shows Shaw's own contribution to the development of British drama.

In Shaw it is not so much the characters which determine the ideas but the ideas which determine the characters. St. Joan doesn't speak as she does because she is a peasant girl from Domremy; she is the character she is because of the ideas she holds. All the better if the ideas of Androcles, or Tanner (*Man and Superman*), coincide with Shaw's own ideas. In a sense, Shaw's plays are not debates but statements, in the same way that Socrates in Plato's *The Republic* doesn't ask questions to elicit answers to advance an argument but merely to give him a chance to expound his own ideas. *Major Barbara* (1905) raises issues about the reconciliation of materialism with religion; *The Doctor's Dilemma* (1906) deals with problems of choice facing the medical profession. *Androcles and the Lion* (1913) demanded a Preface three times as long as the play itself and an Epilogue of another six pages to conclude it; the comments cover a multiplicity of areas, such as the nature of Christ, atonement, the Gospel narratives, the end of the world, the credibility of the Gospels, fashions in belief, modern communism, ownership of property, equal distribution, free will, marriage, the family, inconsistency of the sex instinct . . . an so on. The comments seem to have run riot. *Pygmalion* (1913) has a short preface but a long epilogue. *St. Joan* (1923) has an important preface which discusses sainthood, catholicism, theocracy, history and its distortions, as well as Joan as a woman, a soldier, a suicide, and a politician. In Shaw the problem play moved on to the play of debate, or at least the play of answers, given that the right questions are posed. Just as with Socrates, the answers emerge only if the right questions trigger them off. The wrong questions would lead only to confusion. The success of the Devil in the Don Juan-in-Hell scene in *Man and Superman* depends on Don Juan asking him the right questions and opening up the right topics to discuss. In case the reader (or the spectator?) becomes confused, 'The Revolutionist's Handbook' at the end of the play makes all clear:

> Do not waste your time on Social Questions.
> *or* What is the matter with the Poor is Poverty: what is the matter with the Rich is Uselessness.
> *or* Home is the girl's prison and the woman's workhouse.
> *or* Beware of the man whose god is in the skies.' . . . *and so on.*

7.11

John Galsworthy (1867–1933), primarily a novelist, produced some so-called 'problem plays' on social themes just before and just after the First World War: *The Silver Box* (1909), *Strife* (1909), *Justice* (1910), *The Skin Game* (1920) and *Loyalties* (1922). *The Silver Box* runs two plots that are linked by the unfairness that exists in a social system which imprisons a poor man for stealing a silver box in his drunkenness and turns a blind eye to a rich, young, good-for-nothing who steals a purse from a woman and whose father manages to buy her off 'as a matter of-er-principle', as Borthwick puts it. In the last scene the magistrate and the police refuse to lower the charges against the poor man, Jones, who is sentenced to one month's imprisonment as he calls out:

> Call this justice? What about 'im? 'E got drunk! 'E took the purse – 'e took the purse but (*in a muffled shout*) it's 'is money got 'im off – Justice!

Galsworthy has taken a step towards realism.

His play *Strife* (1909) pursues the theme of justice, but this time it explores not merely the class struggle, but the pig-headedness of Anthony, the Chairman of the Board, who insists on 'No compromise!' without consideration of his colleagues' advice or the condition of his employees, and the pig-headedness of Roberts, the leader of the employees, who refuses to give in in spite of his men's suffering. Enid, the Chairman's daughter tries to intervene to secure an agreement between her old, obstinate father and Roberts, the dour, obstinate labour leader. The strike rapidly becomes a contest between the two opponents. Friendships are lost and families broken as Anthony and Roberts face each other in solitary, hate-filled obstinate opposition. Mrs Roberts dies but the strike drags on: 'There is only one way of treating *men* – with the iron hand'. Anthony's son struggles on in a vain attempt to convince his father:

EDGAR   There is such a thing as Mercy.
ANTHONY   And Justice comes before it.
EDGAR   What seems just to one man, sir, is injustice to another.

Finally, Anthony is outvoted by the Board of Directors; Roberts's extremism is rejected by his men. The play ends with the sad moral:

HARNESS   A woman dead; and the two best men both broken!
           (*Underwood enters suddenly.*)
TENCH   (*Staring at Harness – suddenly excited*)   D'you know sir – those terms, they're the very same we drew up together, you and I, and put to both sides before the fight began? All this – all this – and – and what for?
HARNESS   (*In a slow grim voice*)   That's where the fun comes in!

On this note of extreme irony the play ends.

The play balances character off against character, and moral value against moral value. The overwhelming impressions that the play makes are of anger at the futility and frustration of a social set of values which allows the intransigent to win the day for a time, and of waste, as the good, the sensitive, the caring are swept on in a system they oppose but seem powerless to change. The strife is resolved finally by the democratic solution of a vote, with the majority voice demanding to be listened to.

Where Shaw made people think in his plays, Galsworthy made them think *and* feel. He showed sympathy, admired strength of character, and respected the individual who could retain his or her dignity in spite of the worst that fate or man's pride and greed could inflict. The characters showing these traits and, above all, those showing human frailty, occur again and again in his plays.

Although *Strife* reveals Galsworthy's compassion, he tries to remain detached, to present both sides of the argument. His satire against one side or the other lacks the swift thrust or the savage slash but relies on a cumulative build-up of emotion. The audience sits in judgement hearing the case.

The realism of Galsworthy's play is shown in the settings he uses as well as the language, but the ordinariness of both can make for dull drama. Galsworthy does not have the humour to inject to relieve the inherent dullness; nor does he have the necessary pace to sweep his audience along with the plot. All the time, however, there is the certain feeling that the march to a *dénouement* is inexorable. In some ways, his approach and style are better suited to the novel, where the writer has more space. *The Forsyte Saga* needed considerable space for Galsworthy to work through and gradually disentangle the knots in the Forsyte household. Sometimes Galsworthy falls back on understatements or silence in order to express the deepest feelings of resentment, anger and hurt, and whilst this may be 'realistic' it does not always make for arresting stage drama. The pauses, the gestures, the looks found in the stage directions are those of the early cinema rather than, say, the Jacobean stage.

However, the problem play found a definite statement of method when it was related to realism in Galsworthy's dramatic work. He took up problems as his central themes in his remaining work. *The Pigeon* (1912) dealt with the difficulty of the philanthropist whose hand was bitten by those he tried to help, whilst *The Eldest Son* (1912) uses some of the themes of *The Silver Box*, when two young men, one rich and the other a poor employee, both get innocent girls pregnant – but it is only the poor man who has to see the consequences of his deed through to the end. Again, the play is presented almost as if it were a debate or a court case; sometimes the characters are less important than the arguments.

The Mob (1914) presented a study of a politician who kept to his principles and died for them; for the year in which the Great War broke out it was a curious statement about the dangers of patriotism. *The Skin Game* (1920) takes two families in conflict, the aristocratic Hillcrists and the Hornblowers, who have made a large fortune. The Hornblowers want to exploit a piece of land for commercial purposes but will, in doing so, spoil the view for the Hillcrists. Both families take firm stands on the morality of their cases but both are found vulnerable to moral arguments as the play goes on. The white becomes grey, as does the black. *Loyalties* (1922) has as its subject the quarrel between an officer and a Jew about a sum of money borrowed; the conflict begins with a quarrel between two individuals but soon becomes a moral conflict between the honour of an officer and a gentleman and the honour of a Jew.

In one of his Oxford Lectures in 1909, A. C. Bradley had considered the theory of tragedy propounded by George Hegel (1770–1831). Here Hegel had shown that often tragedy comes about not because of a struggle between *good versus evil*, but of a struggle between *good versus good*. The right of one is pushed into wrong because it denies the right of the other. The end of the tragic conflict results in a denial of both exclusive claims. It is the absoluteness and not the right of a claim that is denied. The battlefield is the character and during the battle the character is affected (*cf.* Orestes and Hamlet). This Hegelian view of dramatic conflict is one that is demonstrable in Galsworthy's work, where there is a human sadness about man's unreasonableness in taking up extreme positions of principle which deny the rights of others to justice.

7.12

Harley Granville-Barker (1877–1946) was better known as an actor, critic, and producer of Shakespeare's plays between 1912 and 1914 than a dramatist. Nevertheless, he did take up the 'problem play' and moved it into the realm of the 'play of ideas'. Shaw, of course, had done this successfully but Granville-Barker's plays were not so successful. His best known works were *The Marrying of Ann Leete* (1901), *The Voysey Inheritance* (1905), *The Waste* (1907), *The Madras House* (1910) and *The Secret Life* (1923). The best of these, *The Voysey Inheritance*, dealt with the moral problem of Edward Voysey who inherits his father's fortune only to realise it had come from deceit and trickery. The doubts and agonising of the young man form the substance of the debate on morality and pragmatism.

7.13

The remainder of the period until 1939 is taken up with drama by writers such as **St. John Ervine**, **John Drinkwater**, **A. A. Milne**, **Frederick Lonsdale** and **Noel Coward** and the work of a host of minor writers whose names are barely remembered outside histories of drama, Edward Percy, Clemence Dane, W. A. Darlington, Herbert Farjeon and Horace Horsnell, Dennis Bradley, John van Druten, J. E. Harold Terry, Richard Pryce, *and so on*. Ivor Novello was writing comic scenes in the main, but the one play that has survived the course of time is **R. C. Sherriff**'s *Journey's End*, produced at the Apollo on December 9, 1928, for the first time. This was a powerful play about the Great War, where the camaraderie and the blood of the trenches were shown in a context of class differences reduced to nothing in the suffering and courage of the trenches. Throughout there is a feeling of waste and horror; at times patriotism and 'the stiff upper-lip' show through almost in a sentimental kind of way. It is not such a powerful statement of anti-war feeling, however, as E. M. Remarque's novel *All Quiet on the Western Front*, which was made into a powerful silent film, or Jaroslav Hašek's book *The Good Soldier Schweik*.

7.14

Three playwrights during the first part of the twentieth century, however, do demand a little further consideration: **J. M. Barrie**, **James Bridie**, and **J. B. Priestley**.

Sir James Matthew Barrie (1860–1937) is best known, perhaps, for *Peter Pan or The Boy Who Wouldn't Grow Up*, produced first at the Duke of York's on December 12, 1904. The play had the skilful knack of appealing to both children and adults (as did Milne's *Toad of Toad Hall* (1929) and Lewis Carroll's story *Alice's Adventures in Wonderland* (1865)). Within two years, between 1902–4, Barrie came from the comparative obscurity of being a novelist and very minor playwright to fame with *Quality Street* (1902 at the Vaudeville), *The Admirable Crichton* (1902 at the Duke of York's) and *Peter Pan*. In these plays Barrie takes up the theme of escape into a world of make-believe, a desert island where a butler takes over and the social order is inverted, or a never-never land where children fly and live happily-ever-after. These are plays of whimsy and they are sentimental. They did not please all: Bernard Shaw said that he had written *Androcles and the Lion* (1912) as an antidote to *Peter Pan*. *Androcles* is too brittly and intellectually clever, once the joke and the terror of the injured lion coming to the hero's rescue and chasing away the wicked empire has been accepted as the jest it was intended. The mixture of fear and laughter is found in both Barrie's and Shaw's plays. For most children, however, *Peter Pan* and Barrie's 'children's' plays were flights from their own homes into the land of the rich, the lavish, the extravagant middle classes of Edwardian England. For them this was the real dream world.

James Bridie (1888–1951) was a Scottish doctor who continued writing until 1951 (*The Baikie Charivari*). He wrote some forty-two plays of very uneven quality but at the heart of most of them was the belief in the value of the individual, who, though beset by fearful difficulties, would come through spiritually enriched. He doubted well-organised enthusiastic politics and religion, but managed to give his audiences spectacle. He played a leading role in maintaining the Scottish theatre and in 1950 founded the College of Drama in the Royal Scottish Academy of Music, Glasgow.

Bridie has suffered through being compared with Shaw in the discussion of 'the play of ideas'. He was essentially liberal in his views of religion, politics, and society and he constantly throws ideas from character to character, so that in changing the point of view, the context, the purpose and the audience he can see how their substances change or are modified. He is concerned, as was Ibsen, with allowing his characters, as individuals, to come into contact with the problems that make them human – the doubts, the fears, the enmities, the facing of death. The bustle and exuberance in a Bridie play sometimes conceal the depth of concern and emotion that underlie them. This, after all, is the paradox of living: life is active, passionate and throbbing by definition, but the environment that man lives in tries to weaken and destroy its very vitality.

His plays, not surprisingly, often carry religious themes: *Tobias and the Angel* (1930), *Jonah and the Whale* (1932), *A Sleeping Clergyman* (1933) and *Susannah and the Elders* (1937). They often carried effects to shock an audience into attention:

> *The belly of the Whale. The stage is utterly dark except for a red spotlight in the insufficient beams of which sits Jonah, crosslegged, like Buddha, and bowing his head before a stream of eloquence that flows from a dozen amplifiers in the auditorium. The audience is to be deafened by the bellowing noise and hypnotised by the small, impassive, red-lit figure on the stage.*
> (*Jonah and the Whale*)

The declaration of faith in the dignity of the individual in Bridie's plays comes nowhere more clearly than in the very closing lines of this same play, although he is usually criticised for producing very poor final acts:

JONAH   What am I to do? What am I to do? My whole life has given way beneath me. I thought I was a great prophet. Everything I did or said was on that understanding. And now I find I am nobody. I am only an ordinary man.

EUODIAS Oh, no, Jonah, no, no, no, no, *NO, NO, NO, NO!*

CURTAIN

THE END OF THE PLAY

Bridie answered his own critics: 'Only God can write last acts, and He seldom does. You should go out of the theatre with your head whirling with speculations. You should be lovingly selecting infinite possibilities for the characters you have seen on the stage. What further interest have they for you if they are neatly wrapped up and bedded and confined?' (*One Way of Living*, 1939, quoted in *The 'Revels' History of Drama in English*, VIII, 1880 – Present Day, ed. H. Hunt *et. al.*, 1978.)Bridie broke from the 'realism' or 'naturalism' of the Galsworthy school of problem plays and moved into the imaginative world to explore the play of ideas.

John Boynton Priestley (1894–1984) straddles the period from before 1939 to the present day. He also straddles the development from the play of ideas centred in realism to an intensification of realism, where things are too real to believe. The audience is faced, therefore, with believing in the unreal-real.

Priestley made his first impact as a novelist, *The Good Companions* (1931). His first significant play, *Dangerous Corner* (1932), introduces Priestley's concern with time in his writing. The play begins realistically with ordinary dialogue, interesting, full characters and yet there is a feeling of threat in the idea of the 'dangerous corner', a spot in time, a spot in life that has to be negotiated; the dramatist begins the play again and shows how 'the dangerous corner' can be easily avoided by different actions and different decisions. The idea raises fascinating, underlying questions: How far do we determine our own destinies? How far can we avoid our own fate? What role does choice play . . . ? *Eden End* (1934) also played with double time perspectives, where the characters look forward to happiness and back to the solid pre-First World War time of happiness in 1912 in order to understand their own anxieties in 1934. The 'time' plays continued: *Time and the Conways* (1937), *I Have Been Here Before* (1937), *Music at Night* (1938), *The Long Mirror* (1940) and *Desert Highway* (1943), dealing with the elimination of chronology and seeing time as a simultaneous slice of events where past, present, and future merge into one pattern, or breaking out of time or seeing past events happening in the present. Time, of course, following relativity bafflingly seems to hold the secret of space, too. Realism seems to be at the heart of the examination of time but the 'time-warp', as it has become known through science fiction, opened up new possibilities for stage presentation and gave a new meaning to the phrase 'the unity of time'! He continued his fascinated interest in time until 1958 (*Anyone for Tennis*), but after 1962 he turned back to other literary forms to express his ideas.

Laburnum Grove (1933) was a crime comedy and in 1945 he wrote another play (this time for the *New Theatre*), *An Inspector Calls*. The play is again dependent on a mysterious time shift. The happiness of an engagement party is shattered by the arrival of a threatening police inspector, one Mr Goole, who does not directly accuse the Birling family and Gerard Croft of anything, but asks enough sharply directed questions to make them accuse themselves. The ensuing self-examination follows 'A chain of events', as the Inspector puts it in Act One. Earlier, during the party itself, the family had looked back beyond the 1914 period in which the action takes place and forward to 1940. Any moment of time, any incident, is seen as one link in a chain that stretches back and forward in time and links events. First the father is made to feel guilty for the girl's horrific suicide, and then Sheila, and then Eric. A photograph of Eva Smith triggers off their memories of the part they played in the chain. Even the hard, aggressive Sybil Birling collapses under the self-accusation when she recognises she had turned the girl away from the Women's Charity Organisation. In case the audience has missed the point Priestley ingenuously spells out 'the moral' in the last words of the Inspector before he leaves as mysteriously as he had arrived:

> But just remember this. One Eva Smith has gone – but there are millions and millions and millions of Eva Smiths and John Smiths left with us, with their lives, their hopes and fears, their sufferings, and chance of happiness, all intertwined with our lives, with what we think and say and do. We don't live alone. We are members of one body. We are responsible for each other. And I tell you the time will soon come when, if men will not learn that lesson, then they will be taught it in fire and blood and anguish. Good night.

Rarely has a moral been so explicit since the time of the old Morality plays. It is a pity that Priestley did not trust his own play to communicate its message without this last homiletic delivery, which seems trite in its apocalyptic explicitness. The Inspector leaves, cannot be traced, and is seen as the catalytic voice of conscience. One thing is sure; the happiness of the family has gone for ever; they now doubt each other and doubt themselves.

The 'realism' of the play has been reinforced throughout by real language, real people, real incidents, real dialogue and real properties on the set. The stage directions point to the use of lighting to reflect mood – pink during the start of the engagement party but 'brighter and harder' when the Inspector arrives for the self-investigation. The play's action is none the less realistic for its shifting from external events to internal doubts, but the Inspector is rather like one of the supernatural beings in a James Bridie play who intervene at a moment in time in human affairs. The play ends with a time-release mechanism where the temporary halt breaks and the clock starts ticking again. In some strange way, the past events in which the family has been caught up have made them look through the present ahead to the future. The promised arrival of the 'real' police inspector should be easier to deal with, at least. They had begun to learn something and then they had stopped; they were 'ready to go on in the same old way'. Therein lay the real threat of 'fire and blood and anguish'.

7.15 Poetic Drama
During the nineteenth century and the first half of the twentieth century there were several periods which saw revivals of poetic drama.

The Romantic and the Gothic revival of the end of the eighteenth century and the start of the nineteenth saw poetic plays by **Robert Southey** (1774–1843), *The Fall of Robespierre* (1794) (written with the help of Coleridge) and *Wat Tyler* ('written in three days at Oxford, in 1794, but published later in 1817 by his political enemies to embarrass him once the left-wing views of republicanism of his youth had been replaced by toryism). **Samuel Taylor**

Coleridge (1772–1834) produced *Remorse* (1813), based loosely on the basic theme of 'good brother versus bad brother' of Schiller's play *Die Räuber*. It was, however, produced at Drury Lane in 1813, in spite of its dramatic flatness and the romantic remoteness of its characters. Earlier he had written *The Triumph of Loyalty*, 'first performed with universal applause at the Theatre Royal, Drury Lane, on Saturday, February the 7th, 1801'. One of his earlier attempts at drama, *Osorio* (on which he later based *Remorse*), had been sent to Sheridan for production in 1797 but had been rejected.

William Wordsworth (1770–1850), was the leader of the Romantic movement in some ways, whose *Lyrical Ballads* (with S. T. Coleridge) was published in 1798 and provided a landmark in English literary history, both because of its poetical content and its discussion about the nature of poetry and poetical inspiration in its 'Preface'. In 1795–96 he wrote a metrical play *The Borderers*, a romantic tale of a contemporary Robin-Hood type figure who is deceived by a villain to bring about the death of an old, blind baron whose daughter he loves. Loyalties, passion, intrigue, darkness, blood, internal doubt – all within the context of idealism, the good of mankind, love, revolution, guilt and sorrow, loneliness and revival form the essence of romanticism at its most intense. Wordsworth, however, was primarily a poet and lacked the stage-craft needed for a theatrical production.

Percy Bysshe Shelley (1792–1822) also tried his hand at poetic drama with *The Cenci* (1819), but it was not produced until 1886, when it was acted by the Shelley Society. It is a piece of poetic writing, heavily derivative from Shakespeare, full of romantic themes and passions. Francesco Cenci is a debauched and vicious count who longs incestuously for his daughter Beatrice, who, unable to escape, plots with her step-mother and brother to kill Francesco and so rid themselves of their common persecutor. They hire assassins to do the bloody deed but the intriguers are caught, tortured, and executed on the Pope's orders. There is enough conflict here to make an effective drama but the poetic imagination, powerful as it is, is not harnessed to drive purposefully on in the theatre. The murder scene contains too many verbal echoes of Macbeth to avoid comparisons between Shelley's and Shakespeare's handling of a murder scene; Shelley's work, however, seems to herald the worst of Victorian melodrama:

LUCRETIA They are about it now.
BEATRICE   Nay, it is done.
LUCRETIA I have not heard him groan.
BEATRICE   He will not groan.
LUCRETIA What sound is that?
BEATRICE   List! 'tis the tread of feet
          About his bed.
LUCRETIA   My God!
          If he be now a cold stiff corpse . . .
BEATRICE   O, fear not
          What may be done, but what is left undone:
          The act seals all.
                   Is it accomplished?

MARSIO		What?
OLIMPIO	Did you not call?	
BEATRICE		When?
OLIMPIO		Now.
BEATRICE		I ask if all is over?

It is hard to suppress the laughter in a theatre that comes from both fear and the incongruous! How *do* serious actors play a scene like that without 'sending it up'?

John Keats (1796–1821), the other poetic giant of the Romantic Revival, was no more successful with his plays, *Otho the Great* and *King Stephen* (both written in 1819), the second being only 'A Fragment'. *Otho the Great* contains some high poetic moments expressed in a low dramatic key that makes them unactable:

LUDOLPH A splendid company! rare beauties here!
I should have Orphean lips, and Plato's fancy,
Amphion's utterance, toned with his lyre,
Or the deep key of Jove's sonorous mouth,
To give fit salutation. Methought I heard,
As I came in, some whispers, – what of that?
'Tis natural men should whisper; at the kiss
Of Psyche given by Love, there was a buzz
Among the gods! – and silence is as natural.

Both these dramatic ventures are sometimes referred to kindly as 'experiments' in drama; they must be seen, alas, as experiments which failed in drama, whatever they achieved in poetry. A distinction needs to be made between dramatic poetry (*e.g.* Keats's *The Eve of St. Agnes*) and poetic drama. The Romantic poets had turned their backs on 'realism' or 'naturalism' and found themselves in 'melodrama'; their intense passions and poetic styles were better suited to verse or to the Gothic novel.

Other poets and writers also tried their hands at drama, with a similar lack of success: **Walter Savage Landor** (1775–1864) wrote *Count Julian* (1812), *Andrea of Hungary and Giovanna of Naples* (1839), *Fra Rupert* (1841) and *The Siege of Ancona* (1846). **William Godwin** (1756–1836) wrote *Antonio or The Soldier's Return* (which was performed unsuccessfully at Drury Lane in 1800) and *Faulkner* (staged at Drury Lane in 1807). Even **Charles Lamb** (1775–1834), the essayist, set dramatic pen to paper with *John Woodvil* (1802), that had been turned down by John Kemble in 1799 in its earlier version entitled *Pride's Cure*; *The Wife's Trial or The Intruding Widow* (1828); and *The Pawn-Broker's Daughter* (1830). The last two plays were published but not performed.

Lord Byron (1788–1824), perhaps because of his personal reputation more than his dramatic skill, was more successful on the stage. He was, of course, also one of the committee of management at Drury Lane. Allardyce Nicoll attributes Byron's failure to three main causes: first, his preoccupation with himself, so that his heroes are subjectively treated versions of himself; secondly, his condescending and essentially unserious attitude to the theatre as an art-form; and thirdly, a 'preoccupation with themes ill-calculated to express the spirit of the age – he looked back to the past and to the continent'. *Sardanapulus* was staged at both Drury Lane (1834, adapted for representation by Charles Kean, and at Covent Garden, April 3, 1837). The structure of the play is good, the historical facts are researched, but his drama often lies more in the narrative stage directions than in the dialogue. The *Two Foscari* (1821) is more poetry than tragedy, but *Marino Faliero, Doge of Venice* was staged at Drury Lane on April 25, 1821, during Byron's own lifetime. The only other play by Byron that was staged was *Werner* (at Bath on February 2, 1830 and at Drury Lane on December 15, 1830, and again at Drury Lane on December 15, 1830) but once more without success. He also wrote two other plays that were published: *The Deformed Transformed* (1824) and *Heaven and Earth: A Mystery* (1822).

One Romantic writer who did have some theatrical success was **Sir Walter Scott** (1771–1832). Between 1814 and up to his death in 1832 he poured forth a succession of novels that were acclaimed. However, his success on the stage came not from writing plays but providing plots in his novels for others to plunder. The nineteenth century was the period, of course, when all could be plundered in spite of the licensing acts of the seventeeth century and the copyright acts of 1709 and 1842, replaced in 1911 by the modern act. (With the advent of photocopiers new regulations have come into force.) Plundering from French drama was common in Dickens's time:

'Do you understand French?'
'Perfectly well.'
'Very good', said the manager, opening the table-drawer, and giving a roll of paper from it to Nicholas.
'There! Just turn that into English and put your name on the title-page.'
(*Nicholas Nickleby*, 1838)

Scott's novels were rendered into stage plays by playwright after playwright. Dickens's work would suffer the same fate later in the 1840s.

Towards the middle of the century **Robert Browning** (1812–89) produced some plays that were staged. *Strafford* (1837) ran for only a few nights at Covent Garden, even with the famous actor Macready playing the title role and its treatment of a tragic historical English theme. *A Blot in the Scutcheon* was staged at Covent Garden in 1843. This was a story set in the eighteenth century of love, dishonour, murder and suicide but Allardyce Nicoll, because of its obscure plot and unclear style, concludes 'Browning was not destined to be a leader of a new poetic drama'.

Alfred Lord Tennyson (1809–1892) produced a number of dramatic pieces which were staged during his lifetime. *Queen Mary* was produced at the Lyceum on April 18, 1876. It presents the main events of Mary Tudor's reign including Wyatt's rebellion, the marriage with Philip, the death of Cranmer, the loss of the remaining French possessions, and Mary's own death. *The Cup* was presented at the Lyceum on January 3, 1881, in which Camma, the wife of the tetrarch of Galatia, poisons a traitor who is collaborating with the Romans, has killed her husband, and seduced her; she then commits suicide. *The*

Foresters, Robin Hood, and Maid Marian had the support of music by Sir Arthur Sullivan and *Becket* (staged at the Lyceum on February 6th, 1893), was produced by Henry Irving himself. The aim of both Browning and Tennyson, like that of Shelley, Coleridge and others before them, was to bring back a poetic drama to the stage to match the glories of the Elizabethans; in the earlier age the poetry gave life to the drama but in the nineteenth century the poetry strangled the drama. In spite of Irving's attempts to revive poetic drama in Victoria's reign, it was into light entertainments and the music of the Gilbert and Sullivan operas that drama was firmly channelled in the 1870s to 1890s. The only poet who achieved any success on the London stage in drama was **Stephen Phillips** with his blank-verse plays *Herod* (1900), *Ulysses* (1902) and *Paolo and Francesca* (1902). Poetic drama was to flourish for a time elsewhere – across the Irish Sea.

7.16 The Irish National Theatre and Poetic Drama

W. B. Yeats (1865–1939) founded an Irish Literary Society in London and another in Dublin and in 1898 he conceived the notion of establishing an Irish National Theatre. He was assisted in the idea by **Lady Gregory** (1852–1932), who later wrote many plays for the theatre once it was established, and **Edward Martyn** (1859–1924), who also founded the Palestrina Choir in Dublin for the reform of liturgical music. These three moved on from the Irish Literary Theatre to join with the National Dramatic Society run by W. G. and Frank Fay in 1902 to form the Irish National Theatre Society. Miss Horniman, also a pioneer supporter of the English drama, and well-known for her work in Manchester with her own group of actors and at the Manchester Repertory Company, leased a Mechanics' Institute in Dublin to the Irish National Theatre Society, modified it, and gave it a small annual grant. The Society renamed the building the *Abbey Theatre*.

The Abbey struggled hard at first; there were squabbles amongst the management, opposition from 'pure Gaelic' dramatists, and little response from the public. Even Miss Horniman withdrew her support in 1909 because the Abbey refused to close on the day of King Edward VII's funeral, but Yeats emerged as the main mover of the new theatre.

Yeats encouraged new work from writers such as Padraic Colum, Lady Gregory, George Fitzmaurice, T. C. Murray, Lennox Robinson, and John Millington Synge (1871–1909). Yeats, Lady Gregory, Synge, and Miss Horniman were Anglo-Irish Protestants and those engaged in the struggle for Irish national independence objected to what they thought was at worst bias and at best indifference in the work at the Abbey Theatre. The 1907 production of Synge's *The Playboy of the Western World* caused a riot on its first night and the police had to be called to break it up. Synge wrote in prose, but his contribution to a theatre which attempted to revive poetic drama cannot be underestimated.

The Playboy of the Western World sets out in its preface Synge's approach to the theatre, which was non-political and therefore detached from the contemporary political troubles but was a revolt against the realism of Ibsenism in the English theatre (see pages 223–226). He was opposed to both the symbolists and the realists, represented by Mallarmé on the one hand and Ibsen on the other:

> Today . . . richness is found only in sonnets or prose poems, or in one or two elaborate books that are far away from the profound and common interests of life. One has on one side Mallarmé . . . and on the other, Ibsen and Zola dealing with reality of life in joyless and pallid words. On the stage one must have reality, and one must have joy; and that is why the modern intellectual drama has failed, and people have grown sick of the false joy of the musical comedy that has been given them in place of the rich joy found only in what is superb and wild in reality.

Yeats wanted to make the theatre a vehicle to awaken the nation's consciousness of its own history and myth and, once awoken, to let it form the impetus at that point to use drama to work towards national rebirth. Synge had no such motives and was not aggressive; he was gentle, shy and unassuming in his person; he knew and understood the attractions and the loneliness, darkness and the threat of his native landscape. He spent his time obscurely in France before Yeats 'discovered' him there but he suffered much illness and depression. He was misunderstood by the nationalists and by the Church, who saw in his references to God only blasphemy and opposition. He stood aloof from Sinn Fein, clerical extremism, and much of the Irish controversy – a solitary man much misunderstood.

The Playboy of the Western World was 'not a play with a *purpose* in the modern sense of the word', as he himself said. It has no realistic, social problem to discuss but the play does contain farce (the resurrection of Christy Mahon's father); it is a 'comedy' which in its very tones cannot end happily with the living-happily-ever-after of Pegeen and her Playboy and Old Mahon and Widow Quin. But at its heart lies, perhaps, the *mock-heroic* where the trivial, everyday incident is elevated to the fights of the gods. T. R. Henn (*Synge, The Complete Plays*, with an introduction and notes by T. R. Henn, 1981) has compared the Playboy with Oedipus ('the man who killed his da''), Christy Mahon with Odysseus (the wanderer cast ashore and seeking help), and Widow Quin with Nausicaa with her chorus of girls. Be that as it may, there are clearer moments of satire throughout the play in the story of the man pursued by the woman.

Synge had already offended the sensibilities of the Irish nationalists with Nora in *In the Shadow of the Glen*, who had thought the portrait an attack on Irish womanhood because of her infidelity to her husband. But this was nothing compared with the riot at the first performance of *The Playboy* on January 26, 1907. Lady Gregory wrote:

> There was a battle of a week. Every night protestors with their trumpets came and raised a din. Every night the police carried some of them off to the police courts. Every afternoon the paper gave reports of the trial before a magistrate who had

242 Drama and Theatre Arts

not heard or read the play and who insisted on being given details of its incidents
by the accused and by the police.

(Quoted by T. R. Henn, op.cit., 59–60)

The first act was applauded, the second left the audience 'a little puzzled, a
little shocked at the wild language'. Near the end of the third act there was
hissing and the play ended in disorder. Irish sensibilities had apparently been
outraged. It was called 'a libel on the Irish race', but Lady Gregory kept the
play running for a week in spite of the riots. It is not hard to see what the
objections were. The people of Mayo take, in their ignorance, Christy Mahon
as a great hero. The wickedness of parricide is inverted to be seen as enormous
courage. Widow Quin and Pegeen fight over the man as if they were
pantomime dames, and the pious Shaun Keogh is shown as timid and only too
ready to hide behind the Church and holy imprecations. After Christy has
undergone all his trials his old father staggers in and the Playboy has to try to
'kill' him a second time in order to live up to the picture others have created for
him. Pegeen and the villagers turn on Christy, who assumes again the role of
the vaunting, pleasure-seeking character of Elizabethan drama. The implicit
gullibility, lack of values, blasphemousness and ignorance of the Irish peasant
in the portraits could easily cause offence – and serious offence – to those
looking to the Abbey for a resurgence of national dignity.

The resurgence of poetic drama in the Irish theatre, however, was left to
others, since Synge's other plays were also in prose: *Riders to the Sea* (1904), *The
Well of the Saints* (1905) and *The Tinker's Wedding* (1907). He attempted one
verse play which was unfinished at his death, *Deirdre of the Sorrows* (published in
1910).

W. B. Yeats's influence on performances at the 'Abbey' was crucial.
Although he was interested in scenery, for him the main impact of drama lay in
the spoken word related to gesture. In a way, he was, therefore, looking back to
Greek theatre. Movements about the stage were to be slow, decorative and
rhythmical 'as if they were paintings on a frieze'. He rejected blank verse and at
the instigation of Ezra Pound, turned to the Japanese **Nō** theatre for
inspiration.

The word *Nō* (*noh*) means 'accomplishment' and is applied to a form of
Japanese theatre which aimed at total 'artificiality', in its basic sense (see page
105). This form of drama began in the fourteenth century and tried to bring
together poetry, music, mime and dance. The plays depicted scenes from
aristocratic life and appealed to the intellectual middle and upper classes.
There are five basic types of *Nō* play, as Henry Wells has pointed out (*World
Drama*, ed. J. Gassner and E. Quinn, 1970): a serious play praising the gods; a
play about a warrior hero; a play where a man dresses as a woman and acts out
a tragic action ('the female-wig' play); a play of violence and emotion, often
with ghosts; and a festival play with much dancing. The plays aimed to instil
into the audience meditation and a state of sublimity or exaltation of spirit.
They were played out on special stages projecting into the audience on three
sides with a bridge leading to a curtained area. Costumes were lavish, masks
were used, verse was kept for elevated emotions and prose was the vehicle of
expression for simpler thoughts.

Yeats used the *Nō* plays for his drama after 1916, especially in his 'Plays for Dancers', *At the Hawk's Well* (1919) and *The Only Jealousy of Emer* (1919), and his later one-act verse plays, *The Dreaming of the Bones* (1919), *Calvary*, (1920), *The Cat and the Moon* (1926), *The Resurrection* (1931), *The King of the Great Clock Tower* (1934), *Purgatory* (1939) and *The Death of Cuchulain* (1939).

Earlier, he had written *Cathleen ni Houlihan* (1902) with which to open the Abbey, *The Countess Cathleen* (1892), *The Land of Heart's Desire* (1894), *The King's Threshold* (1904), *Deirdre* (1907), *The Green Helmet, An Heroic Farce* (1910) and *On Baile's Strand* (1904) amongst others – in verse. He had also written some prose plays, the best-known of which today are *The Pot of Broth* (1904) and *The Unicorn from the Stars* (1908).

Sean O' Casey (1880–1964) used prose for his plays about Irish resurgence. At first the Abbey rejected his work but in 1923 they mounted a successful production of *The Shadow of a Gunman*. This play deals with the period of the Black and Tans, the ruthless auxiliary soldiers sent in to quell sections of the Irish Republican Army. A poet, Donal Davoren, tries to withdraw from the conflict but his neighbours think he is a gunman on the run. The play is concerned with deception, the deception of oneself and the deception of others. Poses as a poet or as a patriot are just as bogus. When Davoren is faced with real choices in the form of a bag of bombs left by a member of the IRA in his room, he starts to see himself as he is, away from the world of make-believe that has already killed the girl who loved him, Minnie Powell.

Linked with the theme of escape from realism into fantasy only to be confronted by oneself is *Juno and the Paycock* (1924). Captain Boyle is a vaunting braggart living in his own fantasy world, insensitive to the pain of others, some of it inflicted by himself. O'Casey, except perhaps in *The Star Turns Red* (1940) which was written as an anti-fascist play, never allows fantasy to overcome reality. *Juno and the Paycock* sets out the disintegration of a family at the time of the great troubles in 1922. The hero 'Captain Jack' (the strutting peacock) is an anti-hero cocooned in his own fantasy world of boasting and drunkenness, but Juno sees through the facade of her husband. It is in Juno that the war of fantasy and reality is fought out with devastating effect.

The Plough and the Stars (1926) provoked the second 'Abbey riots', which made W. B. Yeats shout at the audience, 'You have disgraced yourselves again. Is this to be an ever-recurring celebration of the arrival of Irish genius?' The subsequent treatment of the dramatist drove O'Casey out of Ireland to England. O'Casey's pacifist stand and refusal to glorify patriots, who leave the women to pick up the pieces of shattered lives, provoked the storm, since the play deals with the Easter riots of 1916 leading to the Irish 'War of Independence', which lasted until 1922. He showed the Irish poor dying as well as the British 'poor' soldiers, and the irony of talking about 'the sanctity of bloodshed' whilst squabbles amongst ordinary people are taken into violence. The play has anti-heroes rather than heroes. The so-called 'riot' at the Abbey, however, has been exaggerated in Irish folklore. It was the second act, which takes place in a public house, with talk of dying for Ireland interspersed with snatches from the speech of Pearse over the grave of O'Donovan Rossa, which caused the disturbance in the theatre. But the play was finished and the riot was not repeated, although outside the theatre up and down the country, especially in Dublin, the argument raged.

The Silver Tassie (1928) received W. B. Yeats's rebuke: the scenes are 'almost unrelated', 'There is no dominating character . . . no dominating action, neither psychological unity nor unity of action'; 'among the things that dramatic action must burn up are the author's opinions'. These comments are as much comments about Yeats as about O'Casey. Certainly O'Casey was now using drama to express his own views about the world. *The Silver Tassie* is a powerful anti-war statement, where the strong, fit, heroic Harry Heegan is reduced to a dehumanised wreck crouching amidst ruins on a First-World-War battlefield. The soldiers speak in antiphonal plainsong against the celebration of Mass in a ruined monastery. Harry is then shown as a physical wreck in a wheelchair in a Dublin hospital, deserted by all those who shouted his praise as he marched off, the hero, to war.

O'Casey's later plays also convey much of his idealistic views: *Within the Gates* (1933), a Morality-type play about salvation and damnation; *Cock-a-doodle Dandy* (1949), a play about exile and banishment; and *Red Roses for Me* (1942), based on his own formative experiences during the 1913 Dublin General Strike. His plays raise the whole question of whether playwrights should use drama to convey their own ideas. Certainly earlier drama had grown from the Church's desire to present its ideas as propaganda and earlier playwrights such as Skelton and Marlowe had not shrunk from setting out their own views of man's human predicament. Playwrights after 1956 would think that the expression of their own opinions and views was a fundamental board on their stage.

7.17

The Rebirth of Poetic Drama in England began during the year 1933 but it was not until the 1940s and 1950s that it burst into flame on the English stage with the work of Christopher Fry and the later plays of T. S. Eliot (*The Cocktail Party*, 1949, *The Confidential Clerk*, 1953 and *The Elder Statesman*, 1958, see pages 245–246 and 285).

W. H. Auden's play *The Dance of Death* (1933) treated the theme of the destruction of bourgeois society from inside itself but its satire and clownish humour is, ironically, of appeal to quite a sophisticated audience. The intellectualism of the appeal is, in some ways, ironic for a theme which aimed to point out the medlar-like nature of the society which provided the intellectualism itself in the first place.

His collaborations with **Christopher Isherwood** (*The Dog beneath the Skin*, 1935, *The Ascent of F6*, 1936 and *On the Frontier*, 1938) were similarly esoteric. Sometimes there is some slapstick humour but the drama and its 'message', such as it was, have now worn thin and the plays are rarely staged.

Other poets who turned to drama during the period immediately before the Second World War were **Louis MacNeice** (*Out of the Picture*, 1937, and some radio plays he wrote during the 1940s and 1950s) and **Stephen Spender** (*Trial of a Judge*, 1938).

The most distinguished and the most successful of the poetic dramatists was **Thomas Stearns Eliot** (1888–1965). In 1934 he accepted a commission from the Diocese of London to produce the text for a pageant, showing the difficulty in constructing church buildings from the earliest times to the present day. He completed his commission but when he came to draw up the text of *The Complete Poems and Plays* in 1952 T. S. Eliot omitted all the text of this pageant called *The Rock*, except the Choruses he had written.

He had views about what might be achieved in poetic drama, however. In his critical work, *A Dialogue of Dramatic Poetry*, he said:

> There is no precedent for a nation having two great periods of drama . . . We are not going to be deterred by a fatalistic philosophy of history from wanting a poetic drama.

In 1935 T. S. Eliot wrote *Murder in the Cathedral* as part of a festival at Canterbury Cathedral. It was designed as a verse play for the stage, although it was first produced on a special stage erected in the Chapter House at the Cathedral. In the setting of a religious festival in a religious building, parts of the play about the murder of Thomas à Becket on some steps in the medieval church could be made powerful in dramatic terms. The choruses could almost be choirs used antiphonally in a kind of liturgical commentary on the political actions taking place; the dignity and melody of the verse could echo and re-echo about the roof; the long statements about belief and the clever phrasings of metaphysical thought are, in some ways, nearer the sermons of John Donne (1572–1631), the poet-preacher of St. Paul's. It is, however, a piece of drama which successfully blends together classical conversations, the medieval Morality of man's life through death to salvation and his being tempted cruelly on the way along, historical event, the sermon, ecclesiastical ritual and poetry into a unified whole. This is not the drama for the few but the drama for those who think, and doubt, and believe, and feel, and live and who will one day die.

The Family Reunion (1939) was a play, based on Aeschylus's *Oresteia*, about family life, where Harry is haunted by guilt about his dead wife; in the discussion family skeletons are taken out of the cupboards in which they have been gathering dust, but the drama ends in reconciliation between Mary and Agatha, in keeping with the image of sunlight. It was the Jacobean dramatists and the metaphysical poets of the seventeenth century who had used imagery intensively to give texture and an added dimension to their work. John Webster's plays sometimes have disease and corruption running through them in order to emphasise the moral corruption existing in the state, and images of threat (*e.g.* men armed with rakes rising up from stagnant pools, ready to strike) abound to suggest oncoming madness. T. S. Eliot uses imagery to explore mood, make connections, and suggest rather than make explicit emotions. Throughout *The Family Reunion* the sense of guilt is strong and yet the striving towards reconciliation persists. It is in the area of imagery that the poetic dramatist has additional strength. The connections with, and overtones from Greek tragedy echo and re-echo.

The Cocktail Party was successfully staged at the Edinburgh Festival in 1949 and then in 1950 had successful runs on Broadway and in London. Eliot declared the play to be based on Euripides's *Alcestis*. An unidentified guest breaks into the lives of Edward Chamberlayne, his wife, and their lovers. The unconventional psychoanalyist helps to restore the family equilibrium. In this play T. S. Eliot used a verse form that was close to colloquial registers. *The Confidential Clerk* (1953), based again on a Greek play, this time Euripides's *Ion*, followed, and the poetic drama of T.S. Eliot ended with *The Elder Statesman* in 1958, with echoes of *Oedipus at Colonnus*, perhaps.

In Eliot's verse drama there is often the feeling, as in Greek tragedy, that the characters are being swept along, not always in control, or even aware, of their destinies.

> . . . you are not free.
> Your moment of freedom was yesterday.
> You made a decision. You set in motion
> Forces in your life and in the lives of others
> Which cannot be reversed.

(The Cocktail Party)

7.18 Influences from the Continent

The work of Strindberg, the influence of Ibsen on the early Shaw particularly, and the adaptation of French plays for the English stage have already been discussed.

Two other dramatists might be mentioned, the Italian **Luigi Pirandello** (1867–1936) and the Russian **Anton Chekhov** (1860–1904).

Pirandello was not known outside Italy until the 1920s. His plays are not easy to understand since there is no easy key which will unlock the process. The dramatist was not an uncomplicated character, too; a fascist and strong supporter of Mussolini he came to grips with the fundamental problem of life which concerns the discussion of reality and its connection with appearances. Man cannot understand, let alone explain, what is happening around him and is driven back into himself.

Six Characters in Search of an Author (1921) at least provides a way into the processes of Pirandello, the dramatist. A rehearsal for a play is interrupted by six characters who demand to be put into a play. The interruption of a performance, of course, was not new in the theatre (see page 17), neither was the use of a rehearsal – both Sheridan (*The Critic*) and George Villiers (*The Rehearsal*, 1672) had used it – as the central action for a play (see pages 193–194). The characters, of course, need a plot, but the story of adultery and suicide with hints of incest is not one that they, as artists, can portray realistically. The characters come down from the stage and run through the auditorium where their wild laughter echoes round and round the foyer; the play ends in a situation where the audience can barely distinguish the real from the 'artificial'; the 'characters' seemed to be identified more with themselves than they had realised. The play, therefore, is a play with a form about no form, and a play about characters that are in it but not part of it, and a play with an audience which cannot remain mere spectators. The stage seems to be the author's mind in which the characters move and demand recognition.

The sense of theatre is something that Pirandello tries to explore in this play. As part of the action a stage-hand pulls down the front curtain by mistake and the interval is created when the director and the characters leave the stage to write the plot out. The theatre of human relationships is transposed on to the stage, and, in the transposition, the discussion about relationships in *real* life and their presentation in an *art* form such as drama is opened up.

Enrico IV (1922) and *Right You Are* (1917) are probably his other best-known plays in England. *Enrico IV* begins with a young man's falling from a horse in a calvalcade and then believing that he had become the character whose clothes he was wearing – Henry IV of Germany. For twelve years he suffers the delusion but, coming out of it, he decides to continue the role. A psychiatrist arrives to 'cure' him but makes the situation more confounded. Again, the play explores the illusion/reality relationship in Pirandello. In *Right You Are*, from the start, Pirandello sets out to confuse the audience – they hardly know which character to believe. Here Pirandello breaks the convention that direct addresses to the audience from the stage are to be trusted in order to gain his dramatic effect.

Anton Chekhov was less obviously an experimentalist but his plays carry a powerful dramatic impact in spite of often having no clearly defined plots, little evident variation in dramatic intensity, action off-stage reported as action on stage and the presentation of life as it is, dullness and all. The laments and agonies of the characters are the dramatic cover for the implicit statement in the symbolism of the plays – that life is frustrating and often seemingly full of broken dreams and delusions.

After writing a series of short comedies, Chekhov produced his major works, *Ivanov* (1887), *The Seagull* (1896), *Uncle Vanya* (1899), *The Three Sisters* (1901) and *The Cherry Orchard* (1904).

In *Ivanov* the dull, useless, selfish life of 'John' is contrasted with that of the dedicated, trustworthy Dr Lvov. Gradually Ivanov comes to a realisation of the futility of his life and is faced with what should and could be done about it.

The Seagull was a failure when it was first staged in Moscow, in 1896; it was, in fact, laughed off the stage because its straight production failed to bring out the subtle changes and significances in the dialogue. The play which ironically, begins with, the rejection of a play, written by the young Treplev, his humiliation and loss of his love, is symbolised by the dead seagull that had lived between his family's house and that of Nina, his sweetheart. After several years Treplev finds success (but not understanding), in the world of writing and Masha falls in love with him. Nina reappears in his life but she still loves Treplev's rival and so the writer falls into despair and takes his life. The play is about the loneliness and isolation of each person. For a time hope and social interaction may seem to break down the loneliness but each character speaks in isolation, with points of contact with other characters, often so desperately needed, impossible to make. The frustration results in destruction and burial of the individual's ability to fly away and escape. The death of the seagull reverberates after the first realisation that it can be killed and annihilated. Life is brutal and even brutish and for a time it can be kept at bay by laughter and hope; in the end, however, its ironies and implicit loneliness will not be denied.

At the very start of the play Masha sets the theme:

> I am in mourning for my life. I am unhappy. Medvedenko does not understand: Why?. . . I don't understand . . . You are in good health . . .

This exchange between the schoolmaster and Masha goes to the heart of the human predicament. What constitutes happiness? Health? Money? Security? Contentment? The stifling atmosphere and the coming storm symbolise the impending threat to the happiness of us all. Treplev, at this stage, still hopes, but his mother is bored and jealous. Already the points where lives impinge on each other are being demarcated; the themes are being declared; the symbolism is being established. The *exposition* of a play is important, since it not only introduces plot and characters but indicates levels of interpretation and symbolic meaning. For example, Treplev is the constant reminder to his mother of her past youth and beauty: 'When I am not there she is only thirty-two, but when I am there she is forty-three, and for that she hates me'. Treplev pulls the petals off a flower as he talks about love in the jingle: 'Loves me, Loves me not'. Treplev speaks for Chekhov when he talks about the stage: 'We need new forms of expression. We need new forms, and if we can't have them we had better have nothing'. Here is the *cri de coeur* of the serious, early twentieth-century dramatists, Pirandello and T. S. Eliot amongst them. Before the play-within-the-play, the family groups itself and the cry of Nina, 'I feel drawn to the lake here like a seagull', not only goes to the heart of the symbolism in the play's title, but evokes thoughts of Ophelia, self-destruction and isolation. Treplev makes a connection with the Romeo–Juliet situation of lovers waiting beneath the window at night. With the exchange between the two, the problem of reality versus fantasy or artificiality on the stage is embodied:

> NINA It is difficult to act in your play. There are no living characters in it.
> TREPLEV Living characters! One must depict life not as it is, and not as it ought to be, but as we see it in our dreams.

But what happens when this seagull is killed?

Nina ends the second act with an address to the audience: 'It's a dream!' The divorce from reality leads to isolation, or as Treplev puts it at the very end of the play: 'I am alone in the world, warmed by no affection. I am cold as though I were in a cellar'. Nina's reaction is disjointed, broken and distracted as she identifies herself with a shot seagull, leaving Treplev even more isolated 'still floating in a chaos of dreams and images'. At the very moment that Trigorin and Shamraev look at the stuffed seagull which they could not even remember, Treplev kills himself.

It is hard to see now the play could have been laughed off the stage at its first performance, since the tragedy is not merely the tragedy of the characters and the playwright but also the tragedy of the audience itself. Perhaps they did not recognise *The Seagull* for what it was.

In *Uncle Vanya* Chekhov explores themes of love denied, frustration and bitterness but stops short of the suicide contained in his own short story 'The Wood Demon' which he used for the plot of his play. *The Three Sisters* treats the futility of life (symbolised by the army) and the failure to adjust to the perspectives given by the passing of time, as the image of the migratory birds comes and goes in the play; the life-force is inexorable and moves on to its own destiny, whatever men and women do to divert its path. *The Cherry Orchard* has at its heart the symbol of trees, which had given good fruit in the past, about to be cut down by the new men. The division of the land without the trees on it will provide an answer for some, but Firs, the faithful butler from the past, dies as the play ends with the sound of the future ringing out – 'the strokes of the axe far away in the orchard'.

7.19   The Pantomime in the Nineteenth Century

M. Willson Disher (in *The Oxford Companion to the Theatre*, ed. P. Hartnoll) has offered seven interpretations of the word 'pantomime':

1   A Greek word describing an Imperial Roman actor who wore a mask that could be adapted to represent Mars, Venus, and Vulcan.
2   Eighteenth-century ballets with subjects taken from classical mythology.
3   Christmas entertainments in Great Britain originating from the '*commedia dell'arte*' and Harlequinades.
4   Wordless pierrot plays.
5   Melodrama in dumbshow.
6   Acrobatic and scenic spectacles with clowns.
7   The visual part of acting or dancing, expressive movements, particularly in ballet.

For the nineteenth century in England, however, it was the Christmas pantomime which established itself in its first fifty years. Harlequin was attached to some kind of fairy story: *e.g.* Harlequin and Cinderella. Allardyce Nicoll has shown that Harlequin could be attached to almost any kind of entertainment and he quotes *Harlequin and Poonoowingkeewangflibeedeeflobee-deebuskeebang, King of the Cannibal Islands* as an example. He also lists amongst the many Harlequin pantomimes *Harlequin and Good Queen Bess*, *Harlequin and the World Turned Upside Down*, *Harlequin Jack the Giant Killer* and *Harlequin Nobody or Grey-Eyed Greedy Guts and the Fairies of the Bilberry Hen* (put on at Marylebone in 1843).

Fairy-tales formed the basis of many of these pantomimes and Augustus Harris, manager of Drury Lane and author of *Dick Whittington* (1894), brought in music-hall comedians to play in pantomimes and so gave birth to the modern English entertainment. *The Babes in the Wood* introduces the story of Robin Hood, and Widow Twankey in *Aladdin* (1860s) was derived from the word *twankay*, or green tea, carried by the huge ships coming into the London Docks. These entertainments are still updated with contemporary jokes and references even in the twentieth century. There is close contact between those on the stage and the audience and there is an established routine and patter which must be observed. The ugly, the old and the villains are all rebuffed by the beautiful, the young and the good. The Principal Boy is a beautiful long-legged girl and the Principal Girl is an afflicted down-trodden but pretty girl who receives happiness in the form of riches or a handsome prince in the end.

Questions

1   *What changes to the theatre came about following the passing of the Theatre Regulations Act of 1843?
2   *Describe the changing nature and role of the audience in the theatre of this period. (What effect did they have on plays and performance? How were they affected by alterations in the theatres themselves?)
3   Outline the main differences you have seen between the non-literary and the legitimate theatres during this period.
4   *Describe some of the major changes in attitude to scenery and its use on the stage between 1800 and 1939.
5   *Outline the way that the contribution which music made to drama during this period altered.
6   *What changes to theatre lighting came about after 1800? How did they affect plays and their performance?
7   By comparing the acting styles of two well-known actors or actresses in this period, show how their skills were related to the texts they were interpreting and the theatres in which they were playing.
8   What were some of the advantages and the disadvantages of the actor-manager system?
9   *Describe the development of *either* the music-hall *or* the melodrama after 1843 and try to account for its popularity.
10 Why should *Caste* be termed 'a comic melodrama'?
11 What advice would you give to actors who are about to play the roles of Esther and George in a production which is setting out to recreate the mood of the time when *Caste* was first presented?
12 Show how you would use *either* lighting *or* acting-styles to interpret *Caste* for an audience today.
13 What did 'sentimentalism' have in it to appeal to audiences of this period? (You may illustrate your answer with the help of references to only *one* play you have studied, if you wish.)
14 Where did the **problem** lie in one of the plays by Henrik Ibsen you have been studying?
15 *Discuss the contribution made to the development of the theatre by one of the following: Henrik Ibsen; August Strindberg; Anton Chekhov; Luigi Pirandello.
16 What effect did Ibsen's work have on the early work of Bernard Shaw?
17 What is there in Shaw's early work other than a debate of ideas on stage?
18 How did changing social attitudes affect drama in the first twenty-five years or so of the twentieth century?
19 How did John Galsworthy make it possible to reconcile the presentation

*The questions marked * could form the basis of project work.*

of dramatic entertainment and the preaching of a social message in his plays?

20 What *three* elements in *Strife* would you try to bring out if you were directing a production of it?

21 Describe how you would interpret for an audience the role of either the Inspector or Sheila in Priestley's *An Inspector Calls*.

22 How do you account for (*a*) the limited success and (*b*) the final failure of poetic drama on the twentieth-century stage?

23 What do you find *either* moral *or* poetic in the plays of Synge?

24 What do you understand by the term 'realism' when it is applied to drama during this period? (Use plays you have been studying to illustrate your answer.)

25 What have you found (*a*) dramatically and (*b*) theatrically effective in the work of Sean O'Casey?

26 What problems would you face if you were trying to direct either *Strife* or *The Shadow of a Gunman* or *The Playboy of the Western World* or *The Seagull* for a theatre audience in the 1980s? How would you meet them?

27 Take *one* scene from a play you have been studying from this period and show how you would present it to a modern audience in terms of (*a*) message; (*b*) dramatic effectiveness; (*c*) character; (*d*) costume.

28 Show how you would present the opening scenes of a play from this period to an audience in the 1980s in order to establish (*a*) their dramatic impact and (*b*) their levels of meaning.

29 *Trace the development of pantomime and its relationship with the music-hall during this period. Show how *one* pantomime you know well has more in it than being merely a Christmas entertainment for children.

30 *Outline the presentation and exploration of one of the following themes in the drama of the period, restricting your discussion to the work of *one* author, if you wish: loneliness; social conscience; grotesqueness; follies; self-doubt; authority; guilt; frustration; the relationship between the sexes.

8
Drama after 1939 and Influences on it

8.1

First read the appropriate sections on the Development of the Stage given in Section **2.11** in Chapter Two (pages 42–46).

At previous times in the history of the theatre it has been reasonably easy to discuss movements, to categorise plays, and to see some kind of progression towards or away from a fashion. Since 1939, such classifications have not been easy, largely because the theatre has become a bustling, politically conscious, experimenting, revolutionary, establishment-conscious, cult-aware bullring, where competitors meet, fight for a moment, and then retire. Nevertheless, some dramatists have made major advances in play-writing: Brecht, Pinter, Beckett, Ionesco, Miller – to name but a few. This has been the age, too, of new names to add to the list of great actors: Sir Ralph Richardson, Sir John Gielgud, Sir Laurence Olivier, Dame Edith Evans, Dame Sybil Thorndike and many more. It has also been the time when Censorship was relaxed, the art of the Director grew and the Theatre of the Absurd made its impact on a confused and hesitant audience. Above all, in England, it was the time of the establishment of the National Theatre (see pages 45–46) after decades of frustration.

Any kind of categorisation is likely to be arbitrary during such a time, but a more helpful approach to the richness of the theatre is to look at the contributions of individual writers and directors and of movements where they can be discerned.

8.2   Some Events in the World of the Theatre since 1939

The outbreak of the Second World War in 1939 and the German *Blitzkrieg* on London during 1940 and 1941 led to the evacuation of the population of London and other large cities. The dispersal of huge numbers of people was followed by companies of opera-singers, ballet-dancers, and actors which moved on tour about the country. The *Council for the Encouragement of Music and the Arts* (CEMA) was formed, and until 1942, it was financed by the Pilgrim Trust and the State jointly. After 1942 the State assumed financial responsibility. In 1946 CEMA was incorporated in the newly formed *Arts Council*, but already the theatre was feeling threatened by the popularity of the cinema and of radio. Within a decade television, too, would begin to erode its audiences as well as those of the cinema.

The Arts Council fostered the growth of repertory and helped to subsidise the Old Vic and Sadler's Wells. It tried to give assistance, too, to some private commercial theatres if they could substantiate the claim that their productions were 'partly educational'. The real need, of course, was for a National Theatre but the new National Theatre Company was not to open its first production with Laurence Olivier in *Hamlet* at the Old Vic in Waterloo Road until October 22, 1963. It did not move to its new site on the South Bank until the spring of 1976.

Repertory

During the last decades of the nineteenth century, the theatres sometimes put on morning performances (*matinées*) by groups of actors of older classical plays that otherwise might not have been staged. In 1904 Barry Jackson in Birmingham, along with John Drinkwater, (author *Abraham Lincoln*, 1918) formed a small group of players that would travel about the area giving performances of an old play (*e.g.* The Interlude *Youth* was one of their first.) This group, **The Pilgrim Players** later developed into **The Birmingham Repertory Company**. Other groups had begun to operate elsewhere in the country, but the term 'repertory' came under attack from distinguished critics such as Ivor Brown, Harold Brighouse and Granville-Barker, who described the name as 'silly' or 'inaccurate' or, more simply, 'daft', as Allardyce Nicoll has pointed out. The repertory companies began to erode the differences between concepts of 'the amateurs' and 'the professionals'. Repertory theatre soon began to establish itself country-wide. In the provinces the new companies tried to ensure the regular production of good quality drama for their local populations; the Old Vic in London owes its radical change from a music-hall into a repertory theatre through the active work of Lilian Baylis who alternated Shakespeare and opera there from 1912 onwards. As well as Lilian Baylis, Harley Granville-Barker was inspired by the new repertory movement and fostered its growth at the Court Theatre between 1904 and 1907.

The 1914–18 war slowed up the development of repertory. The repertory theatres set up in Liverpool (1911) and Birmingham (1913) had encouraged others to open, giving performances twice nightly of the same play for a week, before the programme was changed, or the actors moved on. By the 1950s the popularity of these repertory theatres was passing and by the 1960s they had almost died. They were replaced by regional theatres which were better financed, partly by subsidies from local authorities, which provided better recreational facilities, and which put on longer runs of plays. Such theatres, for example, are found in Leicester (the Haymarket), Exeter (the Northcote), Guildford (the Yvonne Arnaud), Scarborough (the Stephen Joseph Theatre-in-the-Round), Colchester (the Mercury), etc.

8.3   The Theatre of the Absurd

The term 'absurd' was applied to a movement in the theatre for the first time in 1961, when Martin Esslin produced his book, *The Theatre of the Absurd*. The names given to 'movements' are sometimes useful to describe attitudes to what the theatre is trying to do, but they rarely provide water-tight categories within which dramatists write exclusively; they are terms used 'after the event', *post-hoc* attempts to describe, rather than classifications of which playwrights were conscious when they were writing their plays: *e.g.* 'The Theatre of Cruelty', 'The Theatre of Anger', 'The Theatre of Contentment', etc.

Arnold P. Hinchliffe in *The Absurd* (1969, 6–7), quotes a list of characteristics of 'The Theatre of the Absurd' drawn up by Irving Wardle in *New English Dramatists 12* (1968):

> Its characteristics are: the substitution of an inner landscape for the outer world; the lack of any clear division between fantasy and fact; a free attitude towards time, which can expand or contract according to subjective requirements; a fluid environment which projects conditions in the form of visual metaphors; and an iron precision of language and construction as the writer's only defence against the chaos of living experience.

Esslin later came to regret his term ' absurd' and acknowledged that a 'movement' did not exist as a rigid category within which writers could be placed. He suggested that Camus, Adamov, Genet and Ionesco were four writers who had become disillusioned but had shown the irrationality that life seemed to present within the old dramatic conventions, but that playwrights like Beckett and Pinter, for example, began to examine the human condition of man 'stripped of the accidental circumstances of social position or historical context, confronted with basic choices, the basic situations of his existence'. (M. Esslin, *The Theatre of the Absurd*, 391). He spoke later of the 'form-smashers', as he called dramatists like Beckett and Pinter, not as destroyers of the traditional basis of the theatre but as wideners of its range and subject matter; explorers, in fact:

> Having renounced the function of telling a story, of exploring character, of discussing ideas, of solving problems, it (The Theatre of the Absurd) has been able to concentrate on the presentation of what is essentially a sense of being, an intuition of the tragicomic absurdity and mystery of human existence. As such the Theatre of the Absurd is an existentialist theatre which puts a direct perception of a mode of being above all abstract considerations; it is also essentially a poetic, a lyrical theatre, for the expression of intuitions of being is the field of lyrical poetry. So, paradoxically, the theatre that attacks language, and above all language that is beautiful and poetical for its own sake, is a deeply poetical theatre, only its poetry is a poetry of situation, movement, and concrete imagery, not one of language. Plays like *Waiting for Godot* or Ionesco's *The Chairs* eminently prove this point.
>
> (M. Esslin, *Brief Chronicles*, 1961)

This statement embodies the suggestion that the beauty and dignity of man lie in his ability to face himself as a human being, hard as it is to reconcile what he perceives as the irreconcilable fears, doubts, and illusions (the absurdity) of his own existence. Esslin's reference to *The Chairs* is very useful in considering the ways in which the 'absurd' emerges on the stage:

> An old man and woman have lived a mediocre life on an island. The old man is convinced that he has something important to say before he dies and, encouraged by his wife, he invites all remaining human beings to come and hear the message. A chair is brought for each guest (all of whom are invisible) and when they are all assembled the old couple leap to their deaths in the sea, leaving the Orator (the only other visible character) to deliver the message. But he is a mute and can only grunt (for what important message can be communicated and who could sum up life in a sentence?) The orator leaves, and for a long time we watch the stage, full of chairs, listening to the waves washing on the walls of the house . . .
> Ionesco intended a purely visual and aural conclusion.
>
> (Summarised by A. P. Hinchliffe, *op. cit.*, 61–62)

The so-called 'well-made play' of the immediate post-war period in England had begun to be questioned with plays such as Priestley's *An Inspector Calls* (1946), where the element of time and its nature are questioned and the play ends not with a resolution of difficulties (the *dénouement*) but with a new set of surprising ones. The inconclusive ending to plays was reinforced in plays like Chekhov's *The Cherry Orchard* (produced in London in 1948), Terence Rattigan's, *The Deep Blue Sea* (1952) and N. C. Hunter's *A Day by the Sea* (1953). Rattigan in *Ross* (1962), a play about T. E. Lawrence's life in the RAF, in which Alec Guinness brilliantly played the title role, and Christopher Fry in *A Sleep of Prisoners* (1951) used flashbacks, a technique from the radio and the cinema, in order to break down time-sequences. John Whiting in *The Devils* (1961) abandoned both the traditional Unities of Time and Place by using an opera stage, using props to indicate place and a change of language to indicate time. (See John Elsom, *Post-War British Theatre*, revised edition, 1979, for a discussion of the way 'the well-made play' had its rules 'bent' but not 'broken' by plays such as these in the post-war period.)

More radical changes were coming over the London Theatre, however, with the production of a play by **Samuel Beckett**, **Waiting for Godot**, in 1955, first at the Arts Theatre Club. The play was written in French in 1947–48 and staged in Paris in 1953. The London production was in a translation made by Beckett himself. The playwright was born in Dublin in 1906 of Anglo-Irish parents, a Protestant, who settled in Paris in 1937 and wrote afterwards almost exclusively in French.

In Paris Beckett came powerfully under the influence of Albert Camus whose essay *The Myth of Sisyphus* (1942) had examined the plight of mankind in trying to see significance in a seemingly purposeless world. Sisyphus was the man in Greek mythology, it will be remembered, who was condemned for his wickedness in this life to role a marble block up a hill in the lower world for ever, only to know that the moment he seemed to reach the top with it, the block would roll back to the bottom for him to start all over again. Some have seen in Beckett's writing a nihilistic reaction to the 1939–45 war with its genocide and nuclear attacks, but his plays and those of fellow 'exiled' dramatists writing in Paris, Ionesco (a Rumanian), Adamov (a Russian), and Arrabel (a Spaniard), reflected the notion of 'absurd' in Camus' essay in terms of man's being trapped in his own human situation and his attempt to examine his relationship with it.

Waiting for Godot liberated the stage, especially in England, for experiment. Ralph Richardson turned down the part of Estragon (although Paul Daneman had accepted that of Vladimir) because Beckett would not explain the meaning and significance of the play. The play at the Arts Theatre Club was uncensored but it was cut by the Lord Chamberlain before it was put on at the Criterion. It was directed by Peter Hall but Beckett, who watched the early production, disapproved of the way the stage was not kept open enough to display the isolation of the two major characters.

The play was attacked by the critics, except for Kenneth Tynan and Harold Hobson. Ivor Brown said he found 'no satisfaction in the moanings of the mentally deficient' and even Brecht thought that the play was attempting to justify doing nothing in society.

By the time of the Royal Court production of 1964 however, with Nicol Williamson as Vladimir and Jack MacGowran as Lucky, the London theatre was putting on a play that was beginning to be understood. Three years earlier Beckett has been invited to help with his staging of it in Paris at the Odéon and

Estragon and Vladimir in the Borough Road College English Department's production of *Waiting for Godot* (1973).

'approved the strong lighting, the thin delicate tree designed by Giacometti, and a stone for Estragon to sit on. It seems that no one had thought to ask the author's opinion before'. (See J. L. Styan, *Modern Drama in Theory and Practice 2*, 1981, for a survey of the play's reception.) Beckett has since taken an active part in productions of *Endgame*, *Krapp's Last Tape* and *Happy Days* and so indicated something of how he saw the plays.

Godot was not God, Beckett once said. There have been some elaborate attempts to explain 'Godot' in terms of Godeau, a famous racing cyclist or a business partner, Godeau, in Balzac's *Le Faiseur* who defects with a huge sum of money only to reappear at the end as a kind of 'deus ex machina' to solve all the problems. If Beckett had intended to say who Godot was he would have done so, but he has consistently refused to comment on his own work; he feels no obligation to explain his expression of life. John Russell Taylor in 'Dramatists and Plays since 1880' (in *The 'Revels' History of Drama in English*, VII, 1978) has pointed out that in *Happy Days* (one play written by Beckett in English and first produced in New York in 1961) Winnie, who has been buried in a mound of earth, first up to her waist and then up to her neck, objects to some passers-by who ask: 'What's the idea? . . . stuck up to her diddies in the bleeding ground? What does it mean? What's it meant to mean?'

Waiting for Godot, however, is in the tradition of farce and of clowns such as Laurel and Hardy or those in the *commedia dell'arte*. J. L. Styan (*op. cit.*, 126–7) argues:

> All the characters of *Godot* and *Endgame*, Vladimir and Estragon, Pozzo and Lucky, Hamm and Clov, Nagg and Nell are essentially pairs of comics or clowns who divert themselves, and so their audiences, with double-acts of cross-talk, tumbling . . . falling asleep, switching hats, and so on.

In the first American production Bert Lahr, a music-hall comedian, played Estragon very successfully.

The quarrels, the contemplation of suicide, the waiting for tomorrow, the bleak stage, the sparse shooting forth of two leaves on an otherwise bare tree, trousers falling down, blindness, violent persecution of the defenceless, doubt, questions asked insistently but without answers, the mixing of the positive with the negative (Yes yes. No no. Yes yes. No no. *Silence*), the gaps, the hesitations, the silences, the childlike language beside the philosophical phrases, the static quality of the stage, the indecision (Well? Shall we go? Yes, let's go. *They do not move*) – all these and many more elements make up the grotesqueness in the relationship between what is and what seems to be in man's attempt to understand, or at least to come to terms with, his own existence. The clowning, the slapstick, the misunderstandings give to the play a quality of humour that is clearly recognisable.

Eugène Ionesco (born 1912) certainly evokes laughter in the theatre. Many of his plays centre on the family. Where Beckett likes the stage to be empty, Ionesco's stages are sometimes full of properties. In *The New Tenant*, for example, the central character barely has room to sit down. Most of the characters are cut off, or encircled by threats of some kind; they seem locked in a kind of hell where pain and laughter seem to come at the same time.

Martin Esslin (*Brief Chronicles*, 1961) has quoted at length Ionesco's own 'somewhat exaggerated' account of how he wrote a play:

> It is obviously difficult to write a play: it requires considerable physical effort; one has to get out of bed which is unpleasant, one has to sit down . . . one has to take up a pen . . . one has to look for paper . . . and one has to sit down at a table. On the other hand it is relatively easy to create a play without writing it down. It is easy to imagine it, to dream it up, lying on a couch halfway between waking and sleeping. One only has to let oneself go, without moving, without trying to exercise control over events. A character emerges . . . and evokes others. The first one begins to speak, the first exchange is established, the basic note has been struck, the rest of the dialogue emerges automatically . . . the imaginary space is peopled by presences; that space has its soil, its sky, its logic, its own laws which derive, quite naturally, from itself. The play is ready; it remains only, as they say, to write it . . .
>
> (Preface to *Les Possédés*, adapted from Dostoevsky for the stage by Akakia Viola and Nicholas Bataille, Paris.)

Tynan criticised Ionesco for having no message; perhaps this was because Tynan favoured plays of social realism of the kind written by Osborne, Wesker, and Delaney. Ionesco clashed sharply with Tynan and insisted that he was a creative artist, but one concerned with living and the exaggeration in the theatre which distorts reality. A useful clarification of Ionesco's view comes in A. P. Hinchliffe's discussion of the dramatist in his book *The Absurd*: 'Ionesco himself has tended to suggest that the opposite of Absurd is Meaningful, and that Absurdity is there to draw attention to a lack of meaning'.

The Bald Prima Donna (*La Cantatrice Chauve*) (1950) is sometimes seen as the first 'Absurd' play. Ionesco described it as an anti-play; its hilarious juxtapositions and jumps from one situation to another made it an immediate success. However, it is a play about not communicating, and exaggerations that spring from a lack of self-understanding about one's own identity – as well as that of others. On one level the play is a parody of the banal conversations and situations of life (and of the theatre). The language is full of meaningless clichés, which, strung together, carry a logic of their own. The stage is cluttered and opens with a 'typical English Mr Smith . . . wearing English slippers, smoking an English pipe, reading an English newspaper, beside an English fire. He is wearing English spectacles, has a small grey English moustache . . . Next to him is 'a typically English Mrs Smith darning English socks. A long English silence. An English clock chimes three English chimes'. Strangers arrive for dinner as the Smiths prepare for bed and the new arrivals, the Martins, discover that they are man and wife, although Mary, the maid, proves they are not and says she is Sherlock Holmes. Embarrassed silence, the arrival of the fire brigade, and a reduction of the conversation to nonsense and a return to the opening dialogue, bring the play full circle to its beginning-end-beginning.

Improvisation (1956) strangely foreshadows Ionesco's own contretemps with Tynan in parodying critics who believe that plays exist only to delight and entertain and those who believe plays must carry a social message. *The Chairs* (see page 256) had already examined the shock and surprise of the clash between the trivial and the encircling sea of death and the way life goes on in its banal manner of delusion and make-believe. The director, Artaud, had maintained that the stage should be crammed but, as Hinchliffe has pointed out, the stage in Ionesco's *The Killer* (1957) is filled with images of death, parodying Zola and his followers who crammed their 'stages with the objects of everyday living'. In this play social problems have all been solved but Death still prowls the streets as man's final and perpetual enemy. Berenger, a clownish figure, attacks the dwarf Death, who draws his knife with a chuckle.

After *The Killer*, Ionesco turned to a kind of play more akin to the old Morality type of allegorical play. In *Rhinoceros*, produced at the Paris Odéon in 1960 by Jean-Louis Barrault and at the Royal Court Theatre, London, three months later by Orson Welles, Berenger, appears again. Jean-Louis Barrault, perhaps the greatest of mime artists and a clown, played the part. Berenger is not influenced by the slogans and fixed social attitudes all around him but, as the play progresses, he becomes more and more isolated until he is surrounded only by the thick-skinned, the brutish rhinoceroses who conform to the herd and bear down on any who will not surrender themselves.

Rhinoceros opens with Berenger entering left and Jean entering right, like a pair of ancient gladiators; the contrast is immediately established. In a welter of clichés Berenger declares that he 'just can't get used to life' but Jean the conformist, admonishes, 'Everybody has to get used to it. Or do you consider yourself some superior being? . . . The superior man is the man who fulfils his duty'. The arrival of the rhinoceroses galloping by at this point is greeted by a chorus of 'Oh's' and 'Ah's'. The audience is left wondering whether the animals are the figment of Berenger's imagination, the drunkard's, madness or reality itself:

JEAN	You're day-dreaming
BERENGER	But I'm wide awake.
JEAN	Awake or asleep, it's the same thing.
BERENGER	But there is some difference.
JEAN	That's not the point.
BERENGER	But you just said being awake and being asleep were the same thing . . .
JEAN	You didn't understand. There's no difference between dreaming awake and dreaming asleep.
BERENGER	I do dream. Life is a dream.*

The conversation switches to logic and by logic the characters arrive at false conclusions. At the end of each episode the fearful thundering of the rhinoceros herd impinges on, and fills, the whole stage; the menace and the threat of the thick-skinned are everywhere. At the end of the first act, firemen, once again in Ionesco, arrive to effect a rescue.

The second act begins with a continuation of the confrontation between Jean and Berenger, with logic, and bigotry intertwined:

* The translation of *Rhinoceros* used here is by Derek Prouse in *Eugène Ionexco, Plays*, 1960.

JEAN	Moral standards! I'm sick of moral standards! We need to go beyond moral standards.
BERENGER	What would you put in their place?
JEAN	(*still pacing*) Nature!
BERENGER	Nature?
JEAN	Nature has its own laws. Morality's against Nature.
BERENGER	Are you suggesting we replace our moral laws with the laws of the jungle?
JEAN	It would suit me, suit me fine . . . We must get back to primeval integrity.

Berenger is accused of talking rubbish, 'just clichés'; Jean gradually, and fearfully, changes into a rhinoceros.

In the third act, with the entry of Dudard, the play becomes an anti-logical discussion about reality and the meaning of words. The Logician becomes a rhinoceros and Dudard continues to struggle on, only to decide he must go along with the herd. Berenger accuses Daisy of not stopping Dudard from going off to join the mass, all of whom look alike; it is impossible to communicate with rhinoceroses:

BERENGER	They can't understand us.
DAISY	They must. There's no other way.
BERENGER	Do you understand them?
DAISY	Not yet. But we must try to understand the way their minds work, and learn their language.
BERENGER	They haven't got a language! Listen . . . do you call that a language?

Daisy begins to doubt herself: 'Perhaps we're the abnormal ones', and she, too, changes, into a rhinoceros, leaving Berenger isolated from society, from logic, from love itself. But he refuses to give in and in a kind of 'I-am-Duchess-of-Malfi-still!' cry asserts, 'I'm the last man left . . . I'm not capitulating'. This affirmation is the most that a man can make in a world, where values are inverted and reality and illusion are not easily divided or separated.

Harold Pinter (1930–   ), actor as well as playwright, has acknowledged his admiration of Beckett, particularly of his novels. His play *The Birthday Party*, written with *The Room* and *The Dumb Waiter* in 1958, was hammered by the critics and was taken off the London stage after six disastrous nights. His early plays centred on bleak surroundings in which characters lived in isolation but also in relation to others, and were threatened by an alien force that insisted on intruding. In *The Birthday Party* two mysterious villains arrive at a remote guest house to kidnap the one solitary resident. In *The Room* a woman is terrified when she learns that a man has been waiting outside the house for days to see her; he is black, like the blind negro living in the basement, and is killed by the woman's husband, but the woman herself suddenly goes blind. In *The Dumb Waiter* two men wait in a basement for orders to kill, their only communication with the outside world being through a serving hatch opening on to a lift (the dumb waiter), which conveys messages from a menacing figure above. In all three plays, the settings are sparse, primitive, filled with a sense of threat and are occupied by isolated, fearful people who find barriers to communication expressed in silences, repetitions, blindness, and sometimes abuse.

The Caretaker (1960) was a success on the stage. As Goldberg and McCann had intruded into the world of Stanley in *The Birthday Party*, so the tramp, taken on as the caretaker, enters the world of Mick and Aston, becomes aggressive and has to be rejected. The violence and threat are implicit in Pinter's drama and operates, as John Elsom (*op. cit.*) has suggested, on the levels of physical violence (usually off-stage), the violence in the outside world with its problems and the violence within an individual that comes from the fear of losing emotional security.

The Homecoming (1965) is seen by some critics as marking a turning point in Pinter's work as a dramatist, 'more complex, richly textured and challenging than its predecessors' (Esslin). Others see it as a play that 'tells its story in an absolutely clear, direct fashion' (John Russell Taylor). Certainly the plot is well mapped out. Max, a retired builder, lives in a London working-class district with two sons, Lenny who is clever and polished in manner and Joey who is simple and dull. The boys' uncle, Sam, lives with them and talks much of his wife and a friend long since dead. The 'homecoming' occurs when a third son, Teddy, and his wife, Ruth, return to the house on their way back to America. The intrusion is accomplished and nobody notices the arrival. Ruth teases and sexually entices Lenny. When Teddy has to leave for America, Ruth stays on and becomes the whore to the whole household. Esslin sees the end of the play as a tableau, wrapped in the atmosphere of a fantasy. Peter Hall, in an interview with Irving Wardle* partly assessed *The Homecoming* in terms of Pinter's overall work:

> I think all of Harold's work relates to a confined space where people confront each other in often very ugly terms. . .what did impress me about the play was its ugly brutality. . . underneath the writing there is a pressure of emotion and an ugliness of motive which I think is a new note in his work.

It is interesting that just as Pinter emphasises silence by the noises off (for example, the flushing of the lavatory in *The Dumb Waiter*) so in *The Homecoming* Pinter emphasises the emotions on the stage by references to two characters off-stage, MacGregor and Max's dead wife – a wife who might, or might not, have been a whore herself. In the same interview mentioned above, Peter Hall spoke about the significance of silence in Pinter's work:

> he defines silence by the noise on either side of it. . . If there is a pause in the proceedings, for a small pause he puts three dots; for a large pause he puts 'Pause'; for a very, very long pause he puts 'Silence'.

Shakespeare, Hall pointed out, used silence in a similar way only once – in *Coriolanus* where the hero answers his mother's plea not to burn Rome by holding 'her by the hand, silent'. Pinter never did anything haphazardly; every detail, every word, every stage direction was seen as part of the planning of the whole.

---

* In *A Casebook on Harold Pinter's 'The Homecoming'*, edited by John and Anthea Lahr, 1974.

Pinter's plays depend partly for their dramatic effectiveness on shock: Bert's kicking in the head of the Negro or Rose's sudden blindness in *The Room*; the dreadful sense of impending threat in the stage directions in *The Dumb Waiter* when 'Ben goes to his bed, but realising what he has said, stops and half turns. They look at each other'; Stanley's attempt to strangle Meg and rape Lulu as he seems to go mad in *The Birthday Party*; the apparent sudden blindness of Edward in *A Slight Ache*; the smashing of the Buddha in *The Caretaker*. The shock is like the violent sense of falling in a nightmare, that awakens the sleeper suddenly, breathless, anxious, and ready to relate the dream to his or her own world.

Implicit violence, pauses and silences, shock, the dream or fantasy held together by images of sex, vans and death in bleak settings threatened from the outside partly make up the world of Pinter's plays. Their meaning remains undefined, since to be able to explain the 'absurd' would render it, by definition, not the absurd but the explicable.

8.4 The 'Angry' Theatre

The force of 'The Theatre of the Absurd' had been spent by 1962, John Russell Taylor and Charles Marowitz have agreed. Similarly, 'The Angry Theatre' burst quickly on the London stage, flourished for a time, and died.

The phrase 'the angry young men' came from an article written by Kenneth Tynan in 1958. He referred to Colin Wilson (*The Outsider*), Kingsley Amis (*Lucky Jim*), John Wain (*Hurry on Down*) Iris Murdoch (*Under the Net*), Stuart Holroyd (*Emergence from Chaos*), Lindsay Anderson (*Thursday's Children*), John Braine (*Room at the Top*) and especially John Osborne, whose play *Look Back in Anger* at the Royal Court Theatre in 1956 had made 'it all come to a head'. Any group of young intellectuals, 'the new intelligentsia, created in the main by free education and state scholarships', was reflected in Jimmy Porter's 'impulsive unargued leftishness, his anarchic sense of humour, and his suspicion that all the brave causes had been either won or discredited'. It was not so much the quality of the play itself that marked a turning point, but what the play represented largely through the central character: a disaffection, a restless insistence that tomorrow must be better than yesterday, a feeling that the politics that led to the Suez Canal clash between France, England and Egypt had to pass away, a new intellectualism that questioned the old establishment to its very roots.

The 'angry young men' of the novel and the theatre were mainly those who had not been to university, however, in spite of Tynan's comments. Osborne, Arnold Wesker, Harold Pinter, Shelagh Delaney and Alun Owen were, as the critic might have put it, 'self-taught', but their work in the theatre burned with a new intensity.

Look Back in Anger, which started it all, did in theatrical terms 'look back', in a way that Pinter, Ionesco, Beckett and Genet did not. **John Osborne** (born 1930), himself, recognises it now as an old-fashioned play in its 'realistic' approach to the theatre. The strength of the theatrical event lay in the vehemence and life of Jimmy Porter's outbursts which really were powerful soliloquys about the frustrating world of the mid-1950s; certainly this is what is most remembered about the Royal Court production of the play – along with the traditional 'open-room set'. Osborne's next play a year later, in 1957, *The Entertainer*, with Sir Laurence Olivier playing the part of the hero Archie Rice, at his own request, did experiment and abandoned realism. It showed the running down of a former music-hall artist who tried to keep going whilst everything around him, and he himself, ran into a despairing decline. The dialogue was interspersed with old music-hall songs and routines which told of former glories; in a sense the 'entertainment' was an allegory of the running down of a former life and of Empire with an awareness of the vacuum which would follow it. *Inadmissible Evidence* (1964) moves forward in a series of monologues with Bill Maitland at the centre of the play and the other characters around him as kinds of projections of his own experience. Characters are switched as they divest themselves of their robes and Maitland is conscious of them as they circle about him and he wears himself down from within. The 'realism' of Osborne's theatre of the 1950s has gone.

In the late 1950s and early 1960s at the Theatre Royal, Stratford in East London, **Joan Littlewood** was directing a number of plays, or 'shows' as she preferred to call them. She called on her actors and actresses to improvise, giving them the essential situation and characters and letting them fill out the dialogue and persons in the play in order to understand them better; they were encouraged to find out for themselves the background, the times, the feelings of the periods and people they were presenting to the audience. Performances, therefore, of plays like Barry Norman's *Fings Ain't Wot They Used T'be* or Shelagh Delaney's *A Taste of Honey* (1958) carried a vitality, at least. The production of Delaney's play was enlivened with games, music-hall jokes, asides, and snatches of music. One of the most vivid 'shows' to come out of Littlewood's Theatre Workshop was *Oh, What a Lovely War* in 1963. This was a powerful anti-war statement which set off the singing of music-hall songs of the Great War period by a troupe of those doing 'turns', the Merry Roosters, and pictures of generals and soldiers projected on a backdrop with the terrifying statistics of the dead and injured, the maimed and the lost in the battles as they raged. The contrast between the haunting gaiety of the songs and the horrific details of the war, set as they were in contrast, provided a powerful evening of theatre. The anger and frustration burst on to the stage with a vitality that audiences were becoming used to.

Arnold Wesker (born 1932) was also 'realistic' in some ways in his approach to the theatre. *Chicken Soup with Barley* (1958) presented a picture of the life of a Jewish family before the war through to the immediate post-war period. It is an account of the loss of conviction, about change in most of the family, as the mother, Mrs Kahn, still struggles to keep alive her political hopes and Mr Kahn runs out of steam, along with his optimism. *Roots* (1959) was the second of the plays in what has come to be known as 'The Wesker Trilogy'. As John Russell-Brown (*A Short Guide to Modern British Drama*, 1982) has pointed out, Wesker saw drama, as he put it himself, as 'a tool, equipment for the enjoyment of living, for its better understanding. . . I want to teach'. The play traces the loss of the enjoyment of living. This is difficult to present on stage unless the loss is replaced by another, more dominant and positive emotion such as resentment or hate. Smouldering frustration which is lapsing into apathetic acceptance is often the way life is, but it makes a hard plot to sustain on stage. In the play Wesker experimented with 'what was not said' on the stage. Silences in Pinter were huge dramatic steps forward, and in Osborne, as Russell-Brown has argued, they were used as 'still centres of dramatic conflict'; in Wesker they form part of the drama of what could not be said and so added to the tension. *I'm Talking about Jerusalem* (1960), by its very title, suggests that the silences must be challenged and broken. It moved Wesker into attempting to show in action rather than words, what could be seen, the essential drama of frustration. The earlier realism of this playwright was giving way to more dramatic experimenting. *The Kitchen* (1959), for example, had been written from his own experience and tried to show life, such as it was, in the kitchen of a large London restaurant, as it happened. *Their Very Own and Golden City* (written in 1964) used time-switches forwards as well as backwards in an attempt to experiment with description on the stage. It is interesting that both Osborne and Wesker began the expression of their frustration using realism that soon matched their medium to their message by trying to break the ties and evolve new and stronger forms of dramatic presentation. It was the technique of radio, film and television with their slipping easily from past to present, fading out scenes and bringing up others, interspersing dialogue with silences or events to watch, all accompanied by the luring, haunting, reinforcing appeal of music which would push drama forward. Increasingly during the 1970s and 1980s young playwrights of quality turned to these new dramatic media: John Mortimer, Alun Owen, Clive Exton, David Mercer and more recently, Frederick Raphael. David Storey had been a film-writer before he turned to the professional theatre with some success.

Brendan Behan (*The Quare Fellow* (1956) and *The Hostage* (1958)) received praise indeed from Kenneth Tynan [*] in his reviews. The first of these two plays was produced by Joan Littlewood and the production was 'a model of restraint, integrity, and disciplined naturalism'; *The Hostage*, according to Tynan was 'a *commedia dell'arte* production' with its 'tragical-comi-cal-historical-pastoral-farcical-satirical-operatical-musical-music-hall combi-nation'. Both plays were of protest; both were angry; but both experimented with theatre and dramatic experience. Behan, however, did not live long enough to 'fill the place vacated by Sean O'Casey', as Tynan had hoped he would.

8.5 The Epic Theatre: Bertolt Brecht and his Influence

There is no doubt that **Brecht** (1898–1956) has been one of the major forces in the development of drama in the twentieth century, both as director and playwright. He was brought up in Augsburg and had his first play (*Die Bibel*, The Bible) published in the school magazine when he was only sixteen. He began to study medicine at Munich and wrote another play in 1918, *Baal*,

[*] See Kenneth Tynan, *Curtains, A Critic's View of Plays, Players, and Theatrical Events 1950–56*, 1961.

which publishers would not print because of its (superficial) outrage to public morality.

Brecht was writing poetry throughout his teens. In 1920 his mother died and he moved to Munich. He had had a love affair with Bie Banholzer who bore him a son but he never married her; instead he married Marianne Zoff, the daughter of a Munich theatrical producer. It was in this town that his first plays were produced, *Trommeln in der Nacht* (*Drums in the Night*), *Im Dickicht der Städte* (*Jungle of Cities* or *In the Swamp*), *Leben Eduard des Zweiten von England* (based on Marlowe's *Edward II*).

In 1924 he moved to Berlin, his marriage broke up, and he had another child by the actress Helene Weigel, whom he married in 1926. Here he wrote *Mann ist Mann* (*A Man's a Man*) in the same year and moved in style from the poetical and expressionist to 'epic theatre', which Eric Bentley summarised (in *World Drama*, ed. J. Gassner and E. Quinn, 1969) as 'narrative, objective, political, didactic'. *Die drei Groschenoper* (*The Threepenny Opera*) opened in August, 1928, and was an immediate success.

By the beginning of the 1930s Brecht had produced *Saint Joan of The Stockyards*, *The Rise and Fall of the City of Mahogany*, *The Measures Taken*, and *The Mother* (an adaptation from a Gorky novel). Brecht's interest in communism and the rise of the Nazi party led to his being accused of high treason, but he fled with his wife in the nick of time. After a short stay in Switzerland he moved in exile to Denmark until the start of the Second World War. During this time he wrote *Mother Courage and her Children*. When the invasion of Denmark by the Germans threatened, Brecht moved on first to Sweden and then to Finland. In May 1941 he went to America overland via Soviet Russia. During his time in America, Brecht wrote *The Caucasian Chalk Circle*, but he was unhappy and was suspected of communist sympathies. Once more he tore up his roots and returned to Europe, to Zurich, until finally the East German Democratic Republic welcomed him to Berlin. There in 1949 *Mother Courage* was produced. But he was once more caught up in political problems until he died in 1956. (For a much fuller account of Brecht's life see Eric Bentley, *op. cit.*, on which this summary is partly based; Bentley also translated much of Brecht's work during the 1960s.)

Brecht's early theatre (1928–34) undoubtedly placed the emphasis on didacticism. A play should teach rather than delight. Ionesco was so opposed to this view of the playwright's art that he called Brecht 'a postman', since he seemed only to want to deliver messages. Later Brecht moved towards a theatre which argued or presented a situation; some have even used the term 'dialectical' to describe the approach. Brecht was concerned with examining the situation in a dramatic action, not what happened in terms of plot but what happened in terms of causes, effects, and the nature of the action. This meant, of course, *first* that he did not want the audience to be so involved in following what Aristotle called 'plot' so that they could not understand an event; to help them, he could, therefore, even tell them in advance what would happen or remind them of what was happening by means of placards or stage directions built into a commentary given by one actor whilst another carries out the instructions in a mechanistic kind of way. *Secondly*, Brecht did not want the audience to identify with any single character, so that they could not examine the whole action from many different points of view. Therefore, actors could not identify with the characters in the way that the Stanislavski or 'method' school of acting demanded. He suggested that it would be necessary to shatter the illusion that came from the proscenium arch/darkened auditorium theatre which effectively cut off audience from action and actors and left them free not to participate. Why not have the house-lights dimmed but not put out so that the audience could see the reactions of others and the actors could see the audience, too? The plot was not vital but the handling of a particular scene was. A director had to be conscious, therefore, of message, medium, and audience; actors had to adopt points of view which challenged audiences to share them or reject them but not to identify exclusively with them. The stage had to take account of this presentation of an action, too; the properties had to be chosen carefully so that they could jolt a response, 'alienate' or 'distance' an audience, into thinking. Whilst it might be important in one scene to have properties as authentic as possible according to time, place and style, 'realism' or 'naturalism' was not necessary. As one critic has put it, if you need to show a moon, why not dangle one down on a piece of string? The audience knows that the scenery is not real; there is no point in trying to make it seem so. Why not use the properties and scenery to jolt the audience into a consideration of the real issues being discussed?

Audience, therefore, is implicit in Brecht's view of the theatre. They are not mere spectators but they need to maintain their objectivity and identities; they cannot and must not be expected to surrender them in total identification with either actor or action. It may be that Brecht's art was to alienate them from their own preoccupations, too, so that they could see reality. The way to do this was not necessarily to present realistic actions in a realistic way.

Brecht's view of the nature of the theatre was embodied, therefore, in a theory which used the theatre's techniques to produce this readiness to analyse on the part of the audience. The way he would do this, would be to 'alienate' them, distance them sufficiently, jolt them into awareness. Such techniques he called *Verfremdungseffekte* ('V-effects' or 'Alienation Effects' – although the trouble with the word 'effect' in English is that it describes a result rather than a cause, whereas the German 'Effekte' embodies the idea of what brings about an effect!). Amongst such 'effects' would be the introduction of the third person, or the past tense, into dialogue, or an aside, or a direct addressing of the audience, to distance or 'alienate' them, by changing direction, altering emphasis, or stopping the plot. Music, songs, the speaking of the stage directions, the use of panels – all helped to mark such breaks in the train of the play, the way it was unfolding. The sets could harmonise with the ideas and moods or contrast with them. The lights had to be harsh and white, unless a conscious need arose of there to be an explicit use of colours.

Brecht did not aim at the kind of shock tactics that Artaud was advocating in order to provoke reactions in the audience. He could indicate responses where he needed to do so by using different levels of language as *Verfremdungseffekte*, different registers – slang, jargon, dialect, formal, informal, etc. The ear would pick up changes quickly.

This view of the theatre, then, drew on elements from the past (the aside, direct contact with the audience, the use of songs and music, concentration on scenes, the careful use of lighting, properties that contributed to the action etc.) but it rearranged them so that they could have a flexible interaction with each other to provide a total theatrical experience where plot, character, message, entertainment, actor, audience, scenic designer, and director join in a shared experience. He deliberately set his face against the kind of theatre which whiled away an hour or two. His theatre was one of enhanced perceptions which changed attitudes or perceptions, not in a moral way necessarily, but perhaps in a political way'; certainly in a 'human' way. [Such a brief summary of Brecht's attitudes, theories, and practice obviously involves some paring down and omissions. Students should consult more detailed expositions such as Martin Esslin's *Brecht: the Man and His Work* (1961) or John Willett's selection of Brecht's theoretical writings *The Theatre of Bertolt Brecht*. See also George Tabori's stage version of Brecht's writings, *Brecht on Brecht* (1963) and Eric Bentley's clear and informative article on Brecht in *The Reader's Encyclopaedia of World Drama*, ed. J. Gassner and E. Quinn, 1969.]

Brecht's influence on British drama has been considerable. 1956, significantly, saw the first major productions of his work on the London stage when the Berliner Ensemble staged *Mother Courage, Trumpets and Drums* (based on Farquhar's *The Recruiting Officer*) and *The Caucasian Chalk Circle*. A year before *The Threepenny Opera* had had a very successful run. Joan Littlewood's production of *Mother Courage* at the Devon Arts Festival in 1955 was savaged by critics like Kenneth Tynan who accused her of 'blunders . . . attributable to sheer perverseness', adding music where Brecht indicated none; it was 'a production in which discourtesy to a masterpiece borders on insult, as if Wagner were to be staged in a school gymnasium'. (*Curtains*, 1961, 101) The production of *The Good Woman of Setzuan* at the Royal Court Theatre, with Peggy Ashcroft in the main role, fared better. But Tynan really did reduce Brecht's art to the absurd in a review of the Berliner Ensemble's production of *The Caucasian Chalk Circle* in 1956:

> I have read a great deal about Brecht's theory of acting, the famous *Verfremdungseffekt*, or 'alienation effect'. What it boils down to in practice is something extremely simple. The small parts are all generalised. They wear masks down to their lips, fashioned like faces in Bosch or Brueghel and so exaggerated that we know at a glance what kind of people they are meant to be – drunken, prying, lecherous, miserly, what have you. We can thus concentrate on the principals, who wear no masks or make-up and play with absolute realism.
>
> (*Curtains*, 390)

This 'boiling down' says much about the critic* and less about Brecht, perhaps. It was the obvious techniques of Brecht, however, rather than his

---

* In 1959 Tynan set down his more considered views on Brecht and productions of Brecht in Germany (See *Curtains*, 459–72).

basic theory which had the initial impact on the London theatre. Wesker experimented in due course with time. Joan Littlewood in *Oh, What a Lovely War* used songs as well as panels to help the narrative along.

Brecht's influence also prolonged 'social drama' for a time but it was greatest in proving, as John Elsom has pointed out (*Post-War British Theatre*, revised edition, 1979), an alternative to the well-made play. The impact of Brecht on London came at a crucial time – in 1956.

John Arden's work shows the influence of Bertolt Brecht at its strongest, perhaps, although Arden does not acknowledge any conscious influence. Martin Esslin, however, is clear about where he sees the influence (*Brief Chronicles*, 95–6):

> The linking of scenes by songs in *Live Like Pigs*, the use of folk song in *Serjeant Musgrave's Dance*, the masks in *Happy Haven* (not long after the Berliner Ensemble had used masks most tellingly in their 1956 appearance in *The Caucasian Chalk Circle*), the whole structure and technique of *The Workhouse Donkey* (with a narrator and copious musical interludes), the parable technique of *Armstrong's Last Goodnight*, all show a deep and genuine affinity with Brechtian concepts.

Jan Needle and Peter Thomson (*Brecht*, 1981) have recently suggested that only one play in the English theatre has 'come close to being *genuinely* in the mode of Brecht' – Edward Bond's *Saved*, a play that was banned by the Lord Chamberlain when it appeared in 1965. William Gaskill, who had taken over from George Devine as Director of the Royal Court Theatre turned the theatre temporarily into a club theatre in order to stage it. The problem lay essentially in a scene where a baby in a pram is stoned to death. The club's regulations were allegedly infringed and in a subsequent court case Laurence Olivier defended the play and England moved that much nearer to the abolition of censorship, which finally came in 1968. The play evoked the bleakness of life in a working-class part of London. It opened with two men fishing, talking about sexual prowess and a loose girl they had shared. They mime tearing a worm in half. The girl arrives with a baby in a pram and leaves it with the men. Four louts enter, pull the baby's hair and, after much obscenity, batter the child and then murder it. The *Sunday Times* critic thought the play sadistic and likely to appeal to only a minority audience. The *Observer* critic saw its bleakness and found the last arid scene a mime of 'life-in-death, the most horrific scene in the play'. The *Daily Telegraph* critic had only one emotion watching the play – 'cold disgust'. The *Daily Mail* critic recognised the silence in the last four minutes of the play but was confused: 'It is a muddled and muddling play. But it is certainly a moral one. It is impossible to be indifferent to the characters' indifference'. Other critics saw only the horror and the *Punch* critic saw the acting as being 'meticulously naturalistic'. (See John Elsom, *Post-War British Theatre Criticism*, 1981, for further detailed criticism, not only of *Saved* but of many other recent plays.)

Brecht's influence in England, however, was on direction rather than on the writing of new plays. Peter Brook and Peter Hall both came under his influence, along with Devine and William Gaskill.

8.6   The Cruel Theatre: Antonin Artaud

'The Theatre of Cruelty' is usually associated with the name of Artaud (1895–1948); the phrase springs from his first manifesto, *Le Théâtre de la cruauté* in October, 1932. In his early career Artaud had been impressed by surrealism and, with Roger Vitrac and Robert Aron, founded the Théâtre *Alfred Jarry*, putting on surrealistic works, including Strindberg's *Dream Play*. Contacts with the Balinese theatre at the Colonial Exhibition in Paris in 1931 led him to write a series of essays, published together in 1938 with the title *Le Théâtre et son double* (*The Theatre and its Double*). An edition of this in an English translation by Victor Corti was published in London by John Calder, 1977, from an *Editions Gallimard* publication issued in 1964.

Soon afterwards he suffered a mental breakdown and spent many years in hospitals before being released in 1946. He died two years later. His work had a powerful influence on dramatic artists such as Jean-Louis Barrault and dramatists such as Genet. Peter Brook and Charles Marowitz were also interested in putting Artaud's ideas into practice. In some of the so-called 'fringe' theatres (for example, the King's Head, Islington, the Open Space Theatre of Marowitz in 1968, and the Traverse Theatre in Edinburgh where the American Jim Harper worked as producer) and in the LAMDA drama school theatre where Marowitz, also an American, ran a theatre workshop for a season under the title of *Theatre of Cruelty 1 and 2*, the ideas of Artaud were influencing production in the 1960s. John Elsom (*Post-War British Theatre*, revised edition, 1979) has shown that during the LAMDA season of *The Theatre of Cruelty*, Brook and Marowitz attempted to 'shock' by using nakedness, mimed defecation, sadistic whipping, invitations to the audience to suggest words on which improvisations could be made, a prostitute lifting her skirt to reveal a mass of scorpions, a reduction of *Hamlet* to a short statement about the Oedipus complex, and even someone biting the arm of God to give 'a spurt of blood' across the stage. Brook's 1970 production of *A Midsummer Night's Dream* in 1970 used, as a set, a gymnasium with trapezes and introduced conjuring tricks to suggest the 'magic' inherent in the play.

However, what did Artaud give as his definition of 'The Theatre of Cruelty' in his writings and indicate as the way it could be manifested in the theatre?

First, the term 'cruelty'. In a letter to a friend written on September 13, 1932, he reluctantly explained:

> This cruelty is not sadistic or bloody, at least not exclusively so. I do not systematically cultivate horror. The word 'cruelty' must be taken in its broadest sense, not in the physical, predatory sense usually ascribed to it . . . one may perfectly well envisage pure cruelty without any carnal laceration. Indeed, philosophically speaking, what is cruelty? From a mental viewpoint, cruelty means strictness, diligence, unrelenting decisiveness, irreversible and absolute determination . . . We are wrong to make cruelty mean merciless bloodshed, pointless pursuits unrelated to physical ills . . . In fact, cruelty is not synonymous with bloodshed, martyred flesh or crucified enemies . . . Above all, cruelty is very lucid . . . there is no cruelty without consciousness, without the application of consciousness, for the latter gives practising any act in life a blood red tinge, its

cruel overtones, since it is understood that being alive always means the death of someone else.*

In another letter, written on November 14, 1932, he expanded his ideas further:

> I use the word cruelty in the sense of hungering after life, cosmic strictness, relentless necessity . . . in the sense of the inescapably necessary pain without which life could not continue. Good has to be desired, it is the result of an act of willpower, while evil is continuous. When the hidden god creates, he obeys a cruel need for creation imposed on him, yet he cannot avoid creating, thus permitting an even more condensed, even more consumed nucleus of evil to enter the eye of the willed vortex of good. Theatre in the sense of constant creation, a wholly magic act, obeys this necessity. A play without this desire, this blind zest for life capable of surpassing everything seen in every gesture or every act, in the transcendant aspect of the plot would be useless and a failure as theatre.

The definition of 'cruelty', so far, has been in partly negative terms. It is not necessarily bloody but it *is* clear and determined for men and women by the fact that they are alive. The forces of cruelty are permanent and even if love and eroticism can set them at bay for a time, their very contact will lead to further impositions of cruelty in an endless cycle of renewal and disintegration – the process is clear and inevitable, a ritual where thoughts and acts can barely be distinguished.

His 'definition' is best seen by studying what kind of theatre Artaud proposed and this is set down in the two documents, the First and Second Manifestos.

Artaud's First Manifesto proposes a way of bringing the theatre into contact with 'reality and danger'. For that the theatre needs its own language and the verbal text is not the best way to achieve the goal: 'instead of harking back to texts regarded as sacred and definitive, we must first break theatre's subjugation to the text and rediscover the idea of a kind of unique language somewhere in between gesture and thought' (see the treatment of *Hamlet* and *A Midsummer Night's Dream* described on page 270).

The 'unique language' can only be defined, Artaud suggests, as 'expressive, dynamic spatial potential' in contrast with 'expressive spoken dialogue potential . . . We must take inflexion into account here, the particular way a word is pronounced, as well as the visual language of things (audible, sound language aside), also movement, attitudes and gestures, provided their meanings are extended . . . Having become conscious of this spatial language, theatre owes it to itself to organise these shouts, sounds, lights, and onomatopoeic language, creating true hieroglyphs out of characters and objects, making sure of their symbolism and interconnections in relation to every organ and on all levels'. (See the improvisation of words given by the audience described above, page 270.)

---

* Translations of Artaud are taken from Antonin Artaud, *The Theatre and its Double,* John Calder (Publishers) Ltd., 1970, from the French, *Antonin Artaud: Oeuvres Complètes,* Editions Gallimard.

Already, then, **text**, **language**, and a concept of **total theatre** are emerging. What is this language? It calls on music, dancing, mime, mimicry, movement, harmonies and rhythms without favouring any single one of them. (Here Artaud makes an implicit comparison with the Balinese dancing he had seen in 1931.) Theatre creates its own free 'language' so that 'our sensibility is put into a deeper, subtler state of perception by assured means, the very object of **magic and ritual**, of which theatre is only a reflection'.

The method of the theatre's illusion is to call on '**truthful distillations of dreams** where the audience's taste for crime, its erotic obsessions, its savageness, its fantasies, its utopian sense of life and objects, even its cannibalism, do not gush out on an illusory, make-believe, but on an inner, level'. Theatre is concerned with the inner world and in order to touch it, theatre must 'transgress the ordinary limits of art and words, actively, that is to say magically to produce a kind of **total creation** in *real* terms, where man must reassume his position between dreams and events'.

How can this 'total creation' come about? Artaud explains in terms of production.

(a)   *The show*:   'Every show will contain physical, objective elements perceptible to all. Shouts, groans, apparitions, surprise, dramatic moments of all kinds, the magic beauty of the costumes modelled on certain ritualistic patterns, brilliant lighting, vocal, incantational beauty, attractive harmonies, rare musical notes, object colours, the physical rhythm of the moves whose build and fall will be wedded to the beat of moves familiar to all, the tangible appearance of new, surprising objects, masks, puppets many feet high, abrupt lighting changes, the physical action of light simulating heat and cold, and so on'.

(b)   *Staging*:   Artaud moves away from concepts of 'author' and 'producer' towards that of 'creator'. The stage will be 'the starting point for theatrical creation'.

(c)   *Stage language*:   'We do not intend to do away with dialogue, but to give words something of the significance they have in dreams'. The 'symbols' or 'hieroglyphs' created on the stage not simply by words, must be 'immediately legible'. There must be connections between the different levels of expression, rhythms, movements, lighting, gestures, words, music, mime, ritual, costume, masks, etc.

(d)   *Musical instruments*:   'These will be used as objects, as part of the set'. In order to create unusual sound properties and vibrations ancient or forgotten or newly-invented instruments should be used to provide 'a new scale in the octave and produce an unbearably piercing sound or noise'.

(e)   *Costume*:   Modern dress should be avoided wherever possible since it suggests a uniformity; age-old costumes may embody ritual and tradition to give the experience new dimensions.

(*f*)   *The stage-auditorium*: 'We intend to do away with stage and auditorium, replacing them by a kind of single, undivided locale without any partitions of any kind and this will become the very scene of the action. Direct contact will be established between the audience and the show, between actors and audience, from the very fact that the audience is seated in the centre of the action, is encircled and furrowed by it. This encirclement comes from the shape of the house itself'.

Present-day theatres should be replaced by 'some kind of barn or hanger rebuilt along lines culminating in the architecture of some churches, holy places, or certain Tibetan temples . . . The auditorium will be enclosed within four walls stripped of any ornament, with the audience seated below, in the middle, on swivelling chairs allowing them to follow the show taking place around them.* In effect, the lack of a stage in the normal sense of the word will permit the action to extend itself to the four corners of the auditorium'. (Compare this suggestion with some of the ritualistic drama in churches in medieval times. See pages 74–75.)

'Special places will be set aside for the actors and action in the four cardinal points of the hall, the show will be enacted in front of washed walls, and galleries will run round the whole building for actors to pursue one another and to give height and depth as well as length and breadth to a show. Lightning, thunder, wind, etc. will be experienced by audience as well as actors and several actions could be taking place simultaneously. But a central area will be kept (but not a stage) to provide a focal point where the action could be concentrated or brought to a climax'.

(*g*)   *Objects-masks-props*: Puppets, huge masks, objects of strange proportions will be used; 'all objects requiring a stereotyped physical representation will be discarded or disguised'.

(*h*)   *Decor*: 'No decor. Hieroglyphic characters, ritual costume, thirty-foot high effigies of King Lear's beard in the story, musical instruments as tall as men, objects of unknown form and purpose are enough'.

(*i*)   *Topicality*: 'News and events, yes! Anxieties, the prerogative of the few, no!'

(*j*)   *Works*: 'We will not act written plays but will attempt to stage productions straight from subjects, facts, or known works. The type and layout of the auditorium itself governs the shows as no theme, however vast, is precluded to us'.

(*k*)   *Show*: 'We must revive the concept of an integral show'.

(*l*)   *The actor*: 'The actor is crucial, since he must be pliant and yet neutral, denied rigorously any individual initiative'.

* See pages 290–291 for a description of the production of *Lark Rise* and *Candleford* in the Cottesloe Theatre.

(*m*)   *Interpretation*:   'The show will be coded from start to finish, like a language. Thus no moves will be wasted, all obeying a rhythm, every character being typified to the limit, each gesture, feature and costume to appear as so many shafts of light'.

In the programme Artaud planned to give expression to his kind of theatre, amongst other things, he intended to stage (*disregarding the text*): a Shakespearean or an Elizabethan play, such as *Arden of Faversham*; the story of Bluebeard, reconstructed from historical records, containing a new concept of cruelty and eroticism; the Biblical story of The Fall of Jerusalem; one of the Marquis of Sade's tales; one or more Romantic melodramas 'where the unbelievable will be an active, tangible, poetic factor'; Büchner's *Woyzek*; Elizabethan theatre, stripped of the words, 'retaining only their period machinery, situations, character, and plot'.

Artaud's Second Manifesto was much shorter and glossed or exemplified ideas contained in the First. It begins with a statement about **audience**: 'Whether they admit it or not, whether a conscious or unconscious act, at heart audiences are searching for a poetic state of mind, a transcendant condition by means of love, crime, drugs, war, or insurrection . . . The Theatre of Cruelty was created in order to restore an impassioned convulsive concept of life to theatre'. It will 'choose **themes and subjects** corresponding to the agitation and unrest of our times' and 'will bring major considerations and fundamental emotions back into style, since modern theatre has overlaid those with the veneer of pseudocivilised man. These themes will be universal, cosmic, performed according to the most ancient texts taken from Mexican, Hindu, Judaic and Iranian cosmogonies, among others'. The Theatre of Cruelty would include 'great social upheavals, clashes between peoples, natural forces, the interventions of chance and the attractions of fate'.

Artaud then went on to gloss what he had said earlier about **form**. Ancient conflicts would be brought up to date, the themes being transferred on to the stage without 'gushing out in words'. Language distorts. A new concept of space was required, 'all possible height and depth sight-lines must be used, and a special notion of time coupled with movement will exist within this concept'.

Silence and rhythm would be used amidst the signs, as part of 'a certain physical pulsation and excitement; . . . words will be construed in an incantatory, truly magical sense, side by side with their logical sense – not only for their meaning, but for their forms, their **sensual radiation** . . . Differing intensities of colour, light, or sound, using vibrations and tremors, musical, rhythmic repetition or the repetition of spoken phrases . . . can only achieve their full effect by using *discords* . . . The set will consist of the characters themselves, grown as tall as gigantic puppets, landscapes of moving lights playing on objects or continually shifting masks . . . There must be no let up, no vacuum in the audience's mind or sensitivity . . . no gap between life and theatre'.

Although Artaud's conception of theatre was put into practice some time ago by Peter Brook and Grotowski, the Polish director, it remains a powerful source of new ideas for improvisation, alternative theatres, experiments and new slants on dramatic meaning. It goes to the heart of the nature of drama as an art form by relating it to life and the dreamlike searches of everyone for an expression, and even an understanding, of the pulsating experiences of living, dying and being reborn, undeformed by society, religion, morality or convention.

Both Brecht and Artaud would leave their audiences with no hiding space. The theatre was not a place to escape but to confront reality. In both there is an aggression, a violence, which the proscenium arch and the darkened auditorium had long protected them from. This violence is more personal than that found in the theatre of the Jacobean tragedy (see pages 137–139); this is the violence, in a sense, of rape. The only escape is back into the paradoxically unreal world of the normal. It does not allow the audience to keep a distance and the theory conflicts sharply with those of other twentieth-century writers on the nature of art and language, such as Edward Bullough ('Psychical Distance as a Factor in Art and An Æsthetic Principle', *British Journal of Psychology*, June, 1912) or Susanne Langer (*Feeling and Form*, 1953): 'All appreciation of art – painting, architecture, music, dance, whatever the piece may be – requires a certain detachment, which has been variously called the 'attitude of contemplation', 'the aesthetic attitude', or 'the objectivity of the beholder' . . . it is part of the artist's business to make his work elicit this attitude'. Bullough's view of drama, and Langer's (made in the context of dramatic criticism) are at the opposite end of the spectrum from Artaud's in the way one regards the theatre.

8.7   The 'Method' Theatre: Konstantin Stanislavski

Vladimir Nemirovich-Danchenko (1858–1943) and **Konstantin Stanislavski** (1863–1938) directed the Moscow Art Theatre at the time when Chekhov was writing and staged many of his plays (see pages 247–249). They reacted sharply to the conventional, declamatory style of acting prevalent on the Russian stage at the time and evolved an approach which involved the actor in personally experiencing or living through the part he was playing. Sometimes, however, they interpreted the intention of plays and playwrights wrongly. Chekhov said he would not let them stage the fourth act of *The Seagull* because it was no longer his in their portrayal of it and he said of *The Cherry Orchard*, 'Stanislavski has ruined the play for me'. There were furious clashes, apparently, between Chekhov and the two Moscow producers. David Magarshack (*Stanislavsky on the Art of the Stage*, second edition, 1960) has shown very clearly how Stanislavski's misinterpretation of the character of Lopakhin by making him a servant in *The Cherry Orchard* led him to distort the scene and the play and to alter stage directions, so that the whole production misrepresented Chekhov's intentions.

Stanislavski's influences would, in due course, stretch wide, but they would have to struggle against other forms of acting already well established. Acting on the English stage in the 1930s, 1940s, 1950s and 1960s had taken on distinctive styles. On the one hand there were the 'type' actors who specialised in presenting *one* kind of character (*e.g.* a cockney sailor, a lord, an eccentric, a dominating woman) almost in the fashion of the seventeenth-century 'character' (see page 117); some of these actors, for example Richard Attenborough, John Mills and Donald Pleasance, later diversified and showed the full range of their abilities. On the other hand, there were those who were in the tradition of Noel Coward, who learned the mechanics of the art of acting – how to cry, how to laugh, how to move about stage, how to enter a set and so on. Coward, himself, acknowledged that he learned practically all he knew about comedy acting from Sir Charles Hawtrey, an actor-manager in Edwardian times:

> He taught me how to laugh. I remember him standing over me at rehearsal, in front of the whole company, and saying, 'Now, boy, you've got to laugh. Now start like this. Ho, ha, ha, ha, ha, ha. But put your breath right.' And he stood over me till I did it. He said, 'Now smile with it a bit,' and I'd go, 'Ha, ha, ha, ha.' That was entirely technical and, of course, it was an enormous help. He could laugh on stage indefinitely.
>
> (Noel Coward, interview in *Great Acting*, 1967, quoted by John Elsom,
> *Post-War British Theatre*, revised edition, 1976)

This 'technical' style of acting was challenged by the newly discovered 'method' style of Stanislavski in the late 1940s. Elsom quotes the story of a 'method' actress who once asked Coward what was her *motive* in crossing the stage. 'Your motive, my dear, is your pay packet at the end of the week', he replied.

However, Stanislavski's 'method' became popular amongst many young actors and actresses, although not many plays on the London stage lent themselves to it. American drama, led by Arthur Miller, Eugene O'Neill, and Tennessee Williams was different, however. Lee Strasberg in New York set up the Actors' Studio in 1947 and based his work on an interpretation of Stanislavski, where his students had to learn about the characters they were playing before going on to learn the techniques they needed to present them.

Stanislavski's views on acting are to be found in *My Life in Art* and *An Actor's Work on Himself* (edited, abridged, and translated as *The Actor Prepares*, in an American edition).

He examines how one is 'to create the enchanting magic carpet of life's truth on the stage'.* Immediately the fundamental problems arise in the form of questions: Is it the purpose of drama to recreate 'life's truth'? Is the process of 'creation' a conscious one? Why is the production compared with 'a magic carpet'? What is the relationship between this active creation and re-creation on the stage and the audience watching it? Some of these questions are answered. Stanislavski recognised the criticism of his approach in the demands it made but he rejected it:

> 'I have often been told that certain people reproach me for asking too much of the

---

* The quotations are taken from David Magarshack's translations in *Stanislavski on the Art of the Stage*, 1960. The introductory essay by Magarshack in this book is a classic in the study of Stanislavski.

actor; they accuse me of demanding that an actor should become almost an anchorite and devote himself entirely to the theatre and his art'.

To renounce all life outside his art, Stanislavski argued, would rob an actor of the basis of his creative work which consisted of 'a series of life-affirming situations'. Nothing is to be sacrificed. In art and through art everything is fascinating, everything interesting. 'In life the artist is always feverishly busy. His heart is wide open to life's troubles, struggles, and conflicts; and no artist can exist if he is expected to renounce life like a monk'. He told his students:

'I want to eradicate all your hackneyed stage conventions and replace them by new principles of creative art which prevent the actor from getting into a groove . . . I hope you will get rid of every kind of overacting as soon as possible and always be natural in your parts'.

Stanislavski recorded that it was his attempt to get inside the part of Dr Stockmann in Ibsen's *An Enemy of the People* which led him to the constantly developing, never stationary, system of acting based on 'creative organic nature'.

'I fell under the spell of Stockmann's personality . . . It was my intuition that suggested to me Stockmann's outward appearance . . . Stockmann's and Stanislavski's body and soul fused organically with one another . . . The whole basis of an actor's life and work consisted of the impossibility of separating his worldly 'I' from his actor's 'I'.

The statement is clear enough. How does an actor accomplish the fusion? How can an actor develop 'the ability of speaking the thoughts of another man on the stage, of putting yourself entirely at the service of someone else's passions, and of reproducing someone else's actions as if they were your own'? He needs a singleness of purpose; education; 'a whole series of tasks and exercises aimed at the attainment of concentration and attention'. He must divest himself of his own private life in order to accomplish the transmutation. By having allowed his thoughts and feelings to develop without impediment, by leaving his mind open to new ideas, by struggling to attain 'greater depth and purity of thought', he can achieve 'the circle of public solitude' in which the creative work of the actor can be performed. To begin with, Stanislavski said, an actor needs: (*a*) **attention**, internal and external; (*b*) **goodwill**; (*c*) **absolute peace-of-mind and repose**; and (*d*) **fearlessness**. An acting studio must be free then of 'quarrelsomeness, touchiness, hysteria, envy, and ill will'.

My system does not consist of written down 'rules' that can be applied indiscriminately; it teaches an art that is every moment different and that can be mastered only through concentration and through watchful discernment of the fundamental and unchangeable nature of things and people.

From the start a student-actor must be taught how to concentrate all his attention on himself, how to relax one set of muscles and switch from one set to another at will. 'Such work cannot be boring', Stanislavski teases!

So far, then, Stanislavski has focused on **concentration, relaxation**, and **control of the muscles** in order to enter 'the creative circle'. The actor must concentrate on the 'given circumstance', the area circumscribed by the plot or the fable by shedding 'all the ties that bind him to his private life' so that he can create a 'now', not a 'then' or a 'tomorrow'.' The experience was present *now*, for the actor. Movement, detailed action, intonation and stress would all then emerge naturally. But before he could enter the circle of 'now', the good actor would have reconstructed the past of the character he was playing, perhaps by **research**:

> 'Let us assume you are Czar Fyodor. You are thinking of your first entrance . . . Are you going to try to remember how a certain actor used to play that part? You must get some history books and enter . . . into the life of that age, all the various facts about that life'. In that way the actor would become 'you—Fyodor'.

This was part of the technique of breaking the part or the play into **pieces** and seeing the **problems**.

The physical side of playing a part was vital for an actor to understand: '**respiration plus rhythm**' formed the foundation of all his creative work, together with concentration and focusing, so that the *how* of the performance was synthesised with the *what*, the manner with the substance or subject being presented. The actor must **believe in the truth** of what he was doing. Students learning to act must 'forget their own personal *I* and put in its place that entirely new man of the part whom the actor ought to be able to understand from now on'.

Actors should not 'play' parts but 'act, that is to say, create' parts. They were not in a game of *let's pretend* but in a presentation of reality. The concentration needed to achieve this must be linked with **alertness** and the preparation of the part over a long, uncluttered time before arriving at the theatre:

> Suppose you are Tatyana . . . If you did not leave your dressing room as Tatyana, and exchange greetings on the way to the stage as Tatyana; if as you put on your make-up you did not experience in your alert attention the dark wintry evenings you used to spend listening to your nurse's fairy-stories; if the rhythm of your heart does not beat in unison with hers . . . the stage will never become your home.

'We have now found,' said Stanislavski, 'the two steps that are common to all who wish to become proficient in the art of the stage, namely, concentration and mental alertness'. Fear would destroy both; courage was essential in all creative work, the entry into the world of *If I*. 'Nobility of mind', 'wider sensibility', and 'gladness' were qualities that make the life of the stage different from everyday life. **Habit** – the habit of being tidy, methodical and ordered was vital for an actor. He must cultivate a **naturalness** of pose and gesture.

The role of the audience in Stanislavski's work was reduced to the way it affected what the actor did and how it changed his view of what was happening on the stage. The ultimate aim of the Stanislavski actor was to enter fully into the *real* life on the stage, not what was represented or symbolically hinted at for an audience. The stage was transformed into reality and it was this that would grip the audience. Not for Stanislavski the shock and involvement of the audience, but rather the living of life on the stage to the full, unaware almost that in the blackness beyond the stage hundreds of eyes were watching and living out their own dramas in their own beings. The magic carpet had conducted the actor on to the real life of the stage. In their imagination, perhaps, the audience could share it – but only if the intensity and rhythm of what was happening in front of them suggested life, integrity, and truth. Playing a part was a lie; the character on the stage must be breathing truth.

8.8 The Art of the Theatre: E. Gordon Craig (1872–1966)

The three great influences on the development of ideas on the art of the theatre this century already considered, *Brecht, Artaud* and *Stanislavski*, were important largely because they freed thought and opened up new fields of exploration for drama. In the most recent biography of Craig, Denis Bablet concludes his book, *The Theatre of Edward Gordon Craig* (translated by Daphne Woodward, 1966), with words in similar vein: 'He has been a liberator and an awakener, a provocation and an inspiration'. He certainly did not begin any new fashions in the writing of plays but he has been the inspiring force behind the advocates of both 'total theatre' where words, visions, sounds, colours, dance, and music combine into a single experience and 'abstract theatre' where, as Bablet put it, nature had been driven from the stage and the actor dehumanised. A survey of his life, based on Bablet's account, will show how Craig developed from an actor into an accomplished influential designer.

Craig's parents were Edward William Godwin, an architect, and the actress Ellen Terry. His mother had married at the age of seventeen to a painter called Watts, but after the failure of the marriage she went to live with Godwin and bore him two children, Craig and his sister Edith. In 1876 Godwin married Beatrice Philip and in 1877 Ellen Terry married an actor, Charles Kelly.

Craig was put on the stage by Ellen Terry when he was sixteen at the Lyceum, directed by Henry Irving. Antoine visited the Lyceum and admired the scenery and the lighting effects particularly. Between 1889 and 1897 Craig learned from Irving and met the leading actors and designers; at the same time he took great interest in sketching at the museums in London and was fascinated by the Renaissance, Dutch, and English painters in the National Gallery. At the age of 21 he met William Nicholson, the engraver, and became interested and competent in the technique. His first production, for which he designed and painted the scenery, and directed, was Alfred de Musset's *On ne badine pas avec l'amour* on December 13 and 14, 1893. The costumes were exact copies of fourteenth-century clothes, which he had researched.

Art and literature and then music played the major parts in Craig's life in the last decade of the nineteenth century. Craig and Martin Shaw, composer and organist, met and began a collaboration which led to a successful presentation of Purcell's *Dido and Æneas* for the Purcell Operatic Society in 1899, when Italian opera was in vogue. Craig said, 'The instrument I worked with was a company – 60 men and women – line and colour – in movement, sound, and scene'. The elements were seen as a totality and the art of Craig as a designer was evolving. W. B. Yeats described Craig's work in a letter (quoted by Bablet):

> Mr Gordon Craig used scenery of this kind at the Purcell Society performance the other day . . . it was the first beautiful scenery our stage has seen. He created an ideal country where everything was possible, even speaking in verse, or speaking to music, or the expression of the whole of life in a dance . . .

Craig's success led to further work and he fell under the influence of Japanese art for a time, but his new kind of scenery demanded new kinds of stage machinery to allow for smoother scene changes. He still collaborated with Martin Shaw and, at the invitation of the poet himself, they prepared a production of Laurence Housman's *Bethlehem* in 1902 at the Imperial Institute at South Kensington. The costumes were colourful and symbolic in their use of colour and lighting was used to signify God's presence; as the cover was pulled back from the crib by Mary, light streamed up from it but no baby was seen.

Craig's work now turned to the professional theatre in London and his work was praised but Ellen Terry's company, with Craig as designer, failed in May, 1903, with *Much Ado About Nothing* at the Imperial Theatre, just as they had failed earlier in the same year with Ibsen's *The Vikings of Helgeland*. He left England and went to Weimar, via Berlin, where he made new friends. In 1904 he went back to Berlin and visited Vienna, too. Craig was exerting a strong influence on German scenic designers and at this time he met and began his affair with Isadora Duncan, the famous dancer, touring through Europe. In 1905 he published his first theoretical writings, *The Art of the Theatre*, a Platonic-type imaginary dialogue between a director and a playgoer. In the same year he produced *The Steps*, a set of designs for the theatre of the future, free of words; the designs (four in number) showed wide flights of steps running up to a platform, each flight symbolising a mood; the central (abstract) character is the flight of steps on which people meet and pass – but the steps are permanent.

In 1906 Craig moved on to Italy, where he established himself and later wrote *The Actor and the Über-marionette*, published in *The Mask*, a magazine on theatre art, and opened his School. He was in great demand now as a designer from Germany, Holland, London, and Moscow.

In 1912 Stanislavski's production of *Hamlet* opened at the Moscow Arts Theatre, designed by Craig although he had been working earlier in 1909 at both St. Petersburg and Moscow with Stanislavski, with whom he had discussed his designs for *Hamlet* over a long period of time. Again, he proposed arrangements of screens and steps with moving projectors to diffuse light, make it shudder, leap out from different directions, or highlight actors and costumes. Craig rejected painted scenes and artificiality of all kinds, but the scenery had, too, to match the theories of acting which the actors found hard to adhere to, because of the verse. The response of the critics to the production was mixed: some found the screens dull but the costumes and lighting were arresting. It was hard to reconcile Stanislavski's ideas, his actors with their limitations, and

Craig's theories. In 1914 Craig's School in Florence was closed with the outbreak of war.

In February 1914, Adolphe Appia, the designer, met Craig, and Craig came under the influence of the older man. Denis Bablet has succinctly summarised the similarities and differences between the two (*The Theatre of Edward Gordon Craig*, 178):

> Both protested against the enslavement of the theatre and wished to restore it to the status of a self-contained art. They disliked realism and all its methods – photographic imitation, *trompe-l'œil*, artificial perspective and sham. They declared that suggestion, evocation, symbolic representation, were far better than a slavish reproduction of reality. When working on a play or libretto, they did not feel bound by the author's stage directions, which they considered to be meant for the reader; they drew their inspiration entirely from the work itself. Neither of them believed in the *Gesamtkunstwerk*, Wagner's idea of a supreme artistic theatre created by the union or fusion of several arts. Both declared there must be harmony between the various means of stage expression – actors, scene, lighting, etc. – and wanted a three-dimensional stage world.

Bablet also pointed out that Appia was grounded in music and Craig in acting. Appia saw music as the determining form of spectacle, then the actor, then space, then lighting and then colour. Craig thought all the elements equally important but needed harmonising. Both stressed movement, Appia of the body and Craig also of other elements set on the stage.

During the 1914–18 war Craig developed his interest in marionettes. After the war he continued his work in Europe and in 1928 he produced his last major work for the stage, Ibsen's *Pretenders* in Copenhagen. After the Second World War he settled in France where he died at the age of 94 on July 29, 1966.

The life of Gordon Craig, so fully documented and set out in Bablet's biography, shows a richness of experience, a width of enjoyment in the arts and contact with some of the most influential people in his contemporary world of acting, poetry, music, engraving, directing and designing. An account of his life reads somewhat like a catalogue of the famous in the arts and theatre between 1890 and 1930.

What emerges of his theory of designing from his own writings? In **The Artists of the Theatre of the Future**, written at Florence in 1907, Craig argued that the scenic designer first took a simple basic design and then explored and developed it, *e.g.* a towering rock capped by a cloud for a production of *Macbeth*. For the colour of the rock and the man's costumes he needed to go back to the text to see if it would help him decide. The design should be uncluttered and not to try to make twenty statements at once. The play demanded the setting-off of supernatural beings from natural ones, some lifted into the air. The rock, therefore, might have paths weaving up it towards a platform. The placing of the characters on these paths would be crucially important to the effect. Costumes needed to be designed with the individual character and the whole set in mind. For example, a barbaric garment for a shy man would differ from a barbaric garment for a bold, tender man or one for an ugly, vindictive man. The 'naturalistic' look should be avoided; only what was necessary should be considered. Craig advocated that all actors after a time should take on the job of stage-manager; in this way they would learn about what was beautiful, what was effective theatrically and that lighting needed to be harmonised with scenery and costume. Sometimes painters, musicians, and even writers have 'used our Theatre as a kind of after-thought. Take care to pay no attention to what they say or what they do'. A man of the theatre needed a ten-year apprenticeship, passing through the years as actor, manager, designer and director.

Craig put much stress on what he called **movement** in the theatre. Music and dance involved and sprang from movement, but essentially it could be envisaged as either a square or a circle on stage. The written play was not essential to the theatre and neither were actors, although both were central to it at that moment.

In **The Actor and the Über-marionette** (1907) Craig took his ideas on acting further. 'Acting is not an art', he argued, for art depended on design and design on calculation; acting depended on man and man was not a substance to be calculated. All the movements, expression, and voice of the actor were at the whim of emotion and therefore as *material* for design he was useless. 'Art can admit no accidents'. Therefore, for actors to be useful, 'they must create for themselves a new form of acting, consisting for the main part of symbolical gesture. Today they *impersonate* and interpret; tomorrow they must *represent* and interpret; and the third day they must *create*'. The artist did not imitate or make a photo-reproduction of a character or event; an actor should not 'get under the skin of the part' but '*out* of the skin of the part altogether'. He should see the emotions within a character, recognise them, rearrange them, and then represent them to an audience, 'feeling as little of them as is necessary'.

Craig saw the theatrical 'artist's' task not as one of 'competing with the strenuous photographer'. He must banish 'the idea of impersonation, the idea of reproducing Nature'; realism on the stage was not art: 'do away with the real tree, do away with the reality of delivery, do away with the reality of action, and you tend towards the doing away with the actor. Do away with the actor, and you do away with the means by which a debased stage realism is produced and flourishes; no longer would there be a living figure to confuse us into connecting actuality and art'.

The actor should be replaced with the **Über-marionette**, therefore, 'who will not compete with life but go beyond it'. Craig described briefly the history of puppets throughout the world and concluded that the return of the *Über-marionette* would draw the theatre back from the chaos into which it had fallen.

In **Some Evil Tendencies of the Modern Theatre** (1908) Craig explained that chaos resulted from a lack of unity. The theatre consisted of several kinds of people: the proprietor, the business manager, the stage-director, business men, the actor, the understudy, other actors, the scene-designer(s), the costume-designer(s), the lighting engineer, the man responsible for the machinery, scene-painters, costume makers, limelight manipulators (*i.e.* spotlight and lighting-effect operators) extras, cleaners and programme-sellers. No one person was proprietor, manager, director, business man, actor, understudy, or designer; there was no unity. Painters were even, then, dragged into help with scenery design; managers advised actors to 'be natural'. All attempts to bring about realism were pointless; they divided and resulted in anarchy. 'Realism is a caricature'. 'What the Art of the Theatre lacks is *form*. It spreads, it wanders, it has no form'.

In **Plays and Playwrights, Pictures and Painters in the Theatre**, (1908), Craig contended that just as the theatre was not a unity, neither was the audience, although actors regarded 'the audience' as a single mass. It was made up of those who had come from a wide variety of motives – curiosity, entertainment, duty, escapism, invitation – but they had all come to *see* something. Painters, playwrights, musicians and even architects thought the theatre was theirs. It was not; it belonged to the men of the theatre themselves. Words and actors were not vital. In a theatre in Germany Craig had seen the words as he entered the stage-door: 'Sprechen strengverboten' ('Speaking strictly forbidden'); for a moment he thought he was in heaven, since they had discovered the Art of the Theatre, but he was disappointed (**The Theatre in Russia, Germany and England: Two Letters to John Semar, I**, 1908).

The Art of the Theatre was the title Craig gave to two dialogues in the Platonic fashion, both between a stage director and a play-goer.

The First Dialogue (1905) began by establishing that the theatre was made up of many parts – acting, the play, scene, dance, action, words, colour, line, rhythm, etc. Drama arose from dancing and was to be seen, it was intended to appeal to the eyes by using the last five of these elements listed. A theatre ideally should not 'perform' plays but have pieces of its own, argued Craig. The *stage-director* was the one responsible for what appeared in the theatre; he was a craftsman but might become an artist. He first read a play to observe its entire colour, tone, movement and rhythm but could ignore the stage directions and scene descriptions since they were for readers and 'he can learn nothing from them'. Shakespeare himself made sparse use of such descriptions, although later editions added a large number. The stage-director must not leave his scene-designing to a scene-painter, as so often happened.

He designed the scenery and the costumes as a whole. He could then fit into this unit actors and the lighting, not to reproduce reality but to suggest it. Everything should harmonise. Rows of footlights should be removed. Then movement about the stage could be planned and not be left to the actors. This would make actors kinds of puppets (see the idea of the *Über-marionette*, page 282). To have an actor-manager was not a sound way of producing a show; the stage-manager must be in sole control.

Plays were not necessary. All that was needed for the theatre was action, scene and voice: *action* = gesture and dancing; *scene* = lighting, costume, and scenery; *voice* = the spoken or sung word, but *not* the read word.

The Second Dialogue (1910) dealt with 'the Affairs of the Theatre' and distinguished the two kinds of theatre possible – the natural and the artificial. The Russian Constan Theatre tried to approximate to actuality as far as possible; there the theatre was full of people purposefully going about their craft and was a school for theatre craftsmen to form 'a standing company'. The

Russian method of training was superior to all others since actors, painters, lighting craftsmen and so on saw each other's crafts and worked together. Everyone involved must have *a passionate love for the theatre*.

'Artists' formed the majority on the board of directors; profits were ploughed back into the theatre and not taken off as dividends. The first dividend had not been paid for ten years but the 'investors' were happy because of their love for the theatre. The New Theatre in New York might be a similar venture, Craig thought. The question of a National Theatre arose but the best that could be hoped for in England for some time would be a Society Theatre, such as the Berlin Schauspielhaus or the Paris Opéra. The Constan model was the one desired.

Craig wanted a college/theatre established – £5000 a year guaranteed for five years will be all we shall require'. It would have two theatres, one open-air and the other roofed-in, for experimental workshops; a printing-press; a well-stocked library; and craftsmen sections. The college would be for thirty men; 'there will be no women'. Craig did not explain why! He thought he would receive support for the idea from people like Sir Herbert Tree, Sir Charles Wyndham, Arthur Bourchier, Weedon Grossmith, Cyril Maude and the Constan Theatre. It might even receive state support. The present theatres with all their experimenting cost £2 500,000; Craig's proposal over five years would cost only £25 000. Such a National Theatre would be ideal, incorporate a simplification of the mechanical appliances of the modern stage, train stage-managers and scene-shifters, train actors to speak and move, and train scene-painters and lighting staff. The College would provide an ideal Theatre for the nation. Craig would leave its direction and management to others, although he would 'never be absent from the College'.

Other works of Craig were essays entitled **On the Ghosts in the Tragedies of Shakespeare** (1910), **Shakespeare's Plays** (1908), **Realism and the Actor** (1908), **Open-Air Theatres** (1909), **Symbolism** (1910) and **The Exquisite and the Precious** – a brief account of some of the materials used in theatrical productions. All the works considered in this discussion of Craig's work were collected together and published by Craig in a single volume under the title of **On the Art of the Theatre**, 1911, published by Heinemann (and since republished in Mercury Books, Heinemann Group, in 1962). As Craig said of the book, 'In brief, this book is the dream, is it not? Why such an ado then, to prevent someone taking the next step to realise something of his dream?' Steps have been taken, but to use Craig's own image, the exploration to the North Pole has not yet ended!

Craig's influence was probably greater on theatres in Germany, Austria, and Russia than in his home country, but his reputation is curiously distorted. J. Michael Walton (*Craig on Theatre*, 1983) has shown that some still say of him, 'Wasn't he the man whose scenery looked fine on paper but fell down as soon as it was put up?' or 'Didn't he want to do away with the actor in favour of the puppet?' or 'Surely he was one of those theorists from the turn of the century who wrote a lot but never *did* anything'. His screens did collapse just before Stanislavski's production of *Hamlet* at the Moscow Art Theatre and he did discuss actors in the context of the *Über-marionette* as is shown above (page 282). Nevertheless, the theatre has been experimenting with Craig's views on visual impact, symbolism, and the role of the theatre beyond the immediate play production ever since his period of initial influence in the first decade of the twentieth century.

8.9 The Post-War Revival of Poetic Drama after 1939

Before 1939, twentieth-century writers like Yeats, Synge, T. S. Eliot, W. H. Auden, and Christopher Isherwood had tried to re-establish poetic drama on the English stage (see pages 244–246). Following the 1939–45 War, **T. S. Eliot** continued with *The Cocktail Party* (1949), based on Euripides's Alcestis, *The Confidential Clerk* (1953), based on Euripides's *Ion*, and *The Elder Statesman* (1958), based on Sophocles's *Oedipus at Colonnus*.

There was a serious move by E. Martin Browne to mount a season of new verse plays at the Mercury Theatre in 1945–46 with productions of works such as **Ronald Duncan**'s *This Way to the Tomb*, **Anne Ridler's** *The Shadow Factory*, and **Peter Yates**'s play about Abraham Lincoln's killer, John Wilkes Booth, *The Assassin*.

Apart from T. S. Eliot, however, the most successful writer of verse plays, post-war, was **Christopher Fry**: *A Phoenix Too Frequent* (1946) a one-act fantasy; *The Lady's Not For Burning* (1948) with John Gielgud playing the lead; *Thor, With Angels* (1948), written for the Canterbury Festival; *Venus Observed* (1950), with Laurence Olivier in the lead; and *A Sleep of Prisoners* (1951). He also translated Jean Anouilh's *L'Invitation au Chateau* and presented it as *Ring Round the Moon* (1950), with Paul Schofield in the lead. His final play, *The Dark is Light Enough* (1954) had Edith Evans playing the role of the countess. The verse drama was powerfully backed by some of the outstanding actors and actresses of the 1950s but after a time it failed commercially, apart from Fry's plays, and has not made a reappearance in any major way.

8.10 Other Playwrights in the 1960s and 1970s

It is not easy to categorise dramatists during this period, mainly because neither the content of their work nor the form of their work denotes a strong 'movement' or susceptibility to a strong influence that classifies them. It is better, therefore to look briefly at some of the more successful in turn.

Edward Albee (born 1928) is an American writer. He began with *Zoo Story*, a one-act play, that was staged first in Germany in 1959 (at the Schiller Theatre in West Berlin), and in 1960 on a bill with Beckett's *Krapp's Last Tape* 'off-broadway'. It is a frightening play with shock, somewhat in the Beckett tradition. Jerry, a dropout, sits beside Peter, a middle-class man, on a park bench. There are barriers to their conversation as Jerry again and again almost tells Peter of a trip to the zoo. Throughout, the conflict between the characters mounts implicitly and explicitly and the shock arrives when Jerry manages to persuade Peter to kill him.

After some more short plays, Albee wrote *Who's Afraid of Virginia Woolf* (1962); it ran for two years and gained some important drama awards. Again, the play dealt with the difficulty in communication between two married couples and also the individual members of each couple. After this play Albee had less success in the commercial theatre, with runs of only a few months for *Tiny Alice* (1964), even with John Gielgud in it, and *A Delicate Balance* (1966). Another play, adapted from a James Purdy novel, *Malcolm* (1966) closed after seven performances.

John Arden (born 1930) is best known for **Serjeant Musgrave's Dance**, produced at the Royal Court Theatre in 1959. It ran for only a week but has established its reputation since. Musgrave and some deserters arrive in a northern mining town where the men are on strike. At first the soldiers are seen as a threat to the strike but, once accepted, reveal that they have the bones of a local boy killed in a far-off country. Musgrave decides that men in authority must be killed as a lesson against war and to revenge five natives who had been executed for killing the boy in the box. Arguments, threats and violence erupt before the forces of law and order arrive to arrest Musgrave and his deserters. Arden presents the case for pacifism but the characters have their own complex stances. He did not think, however, that the theatre should present causes or stereotype character. The detachment from causes and characters leaves the plays sometimes without a unifying, burning direction and some spectators give up the struggle to continue, to their own loss.

Armstrong's Last Goodnight was produced first at Chichester and then at the Old Vic in 1965. It took the story of some frontier barons on the Scottish border in the sixteenth century who attempted to keep down the people; it was thought to relate to the attempt by Lumumba to crush Tshombe in the Congo, just as the 'Musgrave' play was thought to have a link with an incident during the British occupation of Cyprus. Albert Finney played the leading role and *The Times* saw it as a moral-political parable with an ending which was 'a bleak reflection on inevitable and wasteful sacrifice'.

Arden's other plays include *Live Like Pigs* (1958), a conflict between squatters and residents on a housing estate; *The Waters of Babylon* (1957); *Ironhand* (1961); *The Workhouse Donkey* (1964); and *Left-handed Liberty* (1965).

Alan Ayckbourn (born 1939) has been consistently successful with his 'well-made' plays with their clever twists of plot and *dénouements*. He has experimented with plot construction: *The Norman Conquests* (1973) showed the events in three rooms occupied by three different sets of people in the same house over the same weekend; the stories, happening simultaneously, are presented in three consecutively run scenes. *Sisterly Feelings* (1980) has four different versions: two sisters toss up for a handsome intruder and whether to stay in the tent or go off on a cross-country run. The toss of the coin determines which one of the four possible plots are played out on a particular evening. Some critics describe Ayckbourn as merely a writer of light comedies; others see him as a shrewd observer of human behaviour; most admire his 'mathematical' control over plot-structure as the number of possible combinations from a story are worked out. J. W. Lambert (June 9, 1974) in *The Sunday Times* described Ayckbourn as 'the Kingsley Amis of the stage . . . the most remarkable British dramatist to have emerged since Harold Pinter – with whom he has more in common than may seem instantly probable'. Unfortunately, the critic described the comparison neither with Amis nor with Pinter any further in detail.

Ayckbourn, along with James Saunders and David Compton, was set on his road to success with the help of Stephen Joseph, who formed Studio Theatre Ltd and later, at Scarborough, worked in theatre-in-the-round before opening a second company at Stoke-on-Trent in 1962, and it was here that Ayckbourn began his serious career, first as actor and then as playwright. His output of plays has been consistently maintained and his skill displayed. Michael Billington saw him as a writer of 'extremely ingenious farces based on a dazzling theatrical legerdemain' (quoted in John Elsom's, *Post-War British Theatre Criticism*, 1981).

Edward Bond (born 1935): his play, *Saved* (1965), staged at the Royal Court Theatre has already been discussed (see page 269); it produced violent reactions because of its language and a scene where a baby in a pram was savagely assaulted and then stoned to death. The play had been commissioned by the theatre following a Sunday performance there of *The Pope's Wedding* in 1962. *Early Morning* (1968) also provoked problems with the guardians of public morals. Its obvious jokes such as the allegation of Queen Victoria's having had a crush on Florence Nightingale might have caused offence but its dream references to sexual behaviour caused more. The play takes up problems of social barriers. *Narrow Road to the Deep North* (1969) and *Lear* (1971) again raised social and political areas of discussion; his images are violent and some incidents and references shocking in their assault (disembowelling, flagellation, hanging, cannibalism). In *Bingo* Bond deals with the gradual awakening of Shakespeare to the horrors all around him in his own time until he despairs and takes his own life. In a sense the inherent political statement made by Bond is closer to Brecht; man's violence and wickedness are outward manifestations of the violence and wickedness in society itself. Bond's view is a strident, uncompromising one where violence in society of one sort or another has to be exposed for what it is. John Russell-Brown (*A Short Guide to Modern British Drama*, 1982) has seen in Bond's writing 'plays that are hard to stage and challenging to audiences . . . a spearhead for other dramatists – David Hare, Howard Barker, Trevor Griffiths and Howard Brenton'.

Trevor Griffiths (born 1935) is another writer who takes social problems and public attitudes to them as fit subjects for drama in the 1970s. *Occupations* (1971) presents an Italian strike leader, Gramsci, in 1920 who asked a Soviet agent, Kabak, for help in the first step to overthrow capitalism. Soviet interests, however, differed from Gramsci's and he is left disappointed and cheated, with his idealism falling apart. *The Party* (1974) tried to concentrate the discussion of political issues by claustrophobically putting the protagonists into a single room during the Paris left-wing demonstrations of 1968. They all sympathise with the rioting students, but, like Kabak, although left-wing themselves, find reasons not to join in the revolution when it is in the streets outside. At the heart of the refusal lies some kind of corruption of spirit, insensitivity to others' suffering, drink, prejudices, sexual arrogance, and so on. In *The Comedians* (1975) a similar divide occurs – with those laughing at society, those giving in to society and those outside the division who think they could change it if it were not for . . . . . . In some ways, the plays are like those Biblical parables of men who saw the vision to follow Christ, but somehow found reasons not to do so as the opportunities came and went. As with most comics, below the jests there lies smouldering frustration and the deep sadness of disappointment.

Arthur Miller (born 1915) is an American playwright, who found success in the late 1940s with *All My Sons* (1947), influenced by Ibsen with its sense of the past impinging tragically on the present, and *Death of a Salesman* (1949), which won the Pulitzer Prize and explored the canker at the heart of the drive to success; it is particularly interesting for the use of flashbacks, a technique more readily suited to film than stage, perhaps. After a version of Ibsen's *An Enemy of the People* in 1950, he produced *The Crucible* which opened in 1953 at the time of McCarthy's witch-hunt in American politics for reds under the bed. The parallel between Miller's play and the contemporary events made him a target for those seeking out any suspected of so-called un-American activities. He was accused in 1956 before a committee and was found guilty of contempt for refusing to inculpate others.

The Crucible deals with some of the events in the Salem witches' trials in Massachusetts in 1692. Within the Proctor family accusations and counter-accusations of witchcraft are made until Proctor, caught up in an adulterous relationship with a former servant and trapped between the pincers of his cold, puritanical wife, still smouldering under wrongful arrest as a witch, refuses to accuse others of witchcraft (as Miller himself was later to do) and is taken away to be hanged. The play is about a theocracy which 'for good, even high purposes', as the playwright says, tries 'to keep the community together and to prevent any kind of disunity that might open it to destruction by material or ideological enemies'. The witch-hunt becomes a public ritual of cleansing and confession. The play opens with the Reverend Parris weeping and confused; it ends with Parris disorientated by fear; the note 'Echoes down the Corridor' at the end of the play indicates that he walked off into obscurity and oblivion. In trying to defend itself, the community has torn itself apart and sensibilities have been deadened.

Miller also wrote a pair of one-act plays, *A Memory of Two Mondays* and *A View from the Bridge*, staged in 1955. He later expanded and rewrote the second of the two. During the period 1956–61, while he was married to Marilyn Monroe, Miller produced no plays. By 1964 he had written *After the Fall*, seen by some as profoundly autobiographical, and *Incident at Vichy*, a long one-act play. *The Price* followed in 1968, in which one brother, easily tricked out of money but happy, and another, successful and more shrewd, but much less happy, are contrasted. The conflict of sensibilities is never far away in Miller's plays.

Peter Nichols (born 1927) once said: 'I just don't see things tragically; my characters meet adversity cheerfully and humorously, as I try to do . . . I can only write dialogue when I hear people's voices in my mind; my writing is not really creative – it comes from memory and imitation. I've always been a good mimic'. (Quoted in John Russell-Brown, *A Short Guide to Modern British Drama*.) Nichols began his career as a writer of television plays and he had a very impressive run of successes.

His first stage play, *A Day in the Death of Joe Egg* was produced in 1967, and met instant success. It surprises the audience from the start when Bri enters and begins attacking them verbally. On the stage is Josephine (Joe, or Joe Egg as she is known) who is Bri's spastic daughter. Sheila, his wife, also confides in the audience, and so the first part of the play is taken up with dialogue between husband and wife, a silent spastic child on the stage, and the silent audience on the other side of the stage attacked and confided in, in turn, by Bri and Sheila. Tension is there and yet Joe acts as the catalyst for the boiling, turbulent emotions of her parents. The second act deals with a social visit of another couple, Pam and Freddie, who also use the audience to expound their views and attitudes. The tragic tension builds up until, at the end of the play, Bri leaves home for good, the audience is left saturated and worried, and Joe is left playing and alert but unaware of what is happening.

The National Health, originally conceived as a television play, was staged at the National Theatre on October 16, 1969. It operates on one level as slapstick comedy or farce, and on another as a tragic commentary on the social system in which we are all involved. The characters, brought together in a ward, unable to escape, are set off against each other; they make an unhappy lot: obsession, self-pity, depression, frustration, the dying and the dead. Even the young motor-cyclist, discharged at the start, returns at the end smashed up again after another accident. Bed-pans, bottles, slippers, dressing-gowns, nurse-teasing, Sister's terrorising, all the stereotyped music-hall hospital joke situations are set off against the seriousness of the play. As a comment on the social system it is not a profound statement; as a study in tension between the comic and the tragic it is not particularly well maintained; as a play that 'makes 'em laugh and makes 'em cry', it probably succeeds. It is interesting, however, in structure, as *Nurse Norton's Affair* unfolds itself in the TV fantasy going on, heedless of everything else around it on a television screen set up in the corner of the ward, as a kind of antiphonal incantation, where the real world of the hospital and the glamour of the TV series on nurses and hospitals come together like silent armies clashing on the battlefield of life and death.

The interaction between the two plots is carefully worked out to provoke thought and evoke emotion by means of the running commentary of one on the other. Barnet, the orderly, who appears in both the plots, becomes an increasingly sinister figure as the whole play unfolds.

Joe Orton (1933–67) shortly before he was hammered to death, said in an interview: 'People are profoundly bad but irresistibly funny'. The tragic irony inherent in his death is there for all to see.

He began his dramatic career with a radio play, *The Ruffian on the Stair* in 1964. His first stage success was *Entertaining Mr Sloane* (1964), which demonstrated one of the key qualities in Orton's work: the balance and tension between the polished, sophisticated dialogue his characters use and the grotesque, foul events that they talk about. The play is set in squalor, the characters are sexually violent, but Mr Sloane, suave and handsome, enters the spider's web. However, Sloane is a psychopathic murderer, who gradually emerges with frightening inevitability. John Russell Taylor (*The Second Wave*, 1971) has pointed out that the word 'entertaining' changes its meaning in the course of the play from 'providing the entertainment for Mr Sloane to using Mr Sloane as an occasion of entertainment'. *Loot* followed in 1965. It is an amusing parody of the detective story with corpses, coffins, clever inspectors of police, stolen property (loot), near-discovery and chance. In addition, there is added a glass eye to make up the weight. Alongside the grotesque comedy runs the polished language, almost of the comedy of manners, broken occasionally by the sudden descent into the sharply colloquial.

What the Butler Saw was staged posthumously in 1969 as a slickly drawn farce: 'Torture, nymphomania, transvestism, incest, blackmail, bribery parade across the stage while psychoanalytic prattle twists experience into meanings all its own'. (John Lahr, *Prick up your Ears: the Biography of Joe Orton*, 1968 quoted in J. R. Brown, *A Short Guide to British Drama*.) Again the language beside all this remains polite and ordered.

Tom Stoppard (born 1937) achieved instant success with his first stage play; *Rosencrantz and Guildenstern are Dead* at the National Theatre in the Old Vic on April 11, 1967. Some of the qualities of the play in production singled out by the critics were its 'elegant language', 'Beckett-like cross-talk', 'ingenuity', 'delicacy and ingenuity of plot', and its 'many-layered statements'. Not everyone liked it however, and accused Stoppard of 'casting about for what to say next', being 'derivative, familiar, even prosaic,' using language lacking in economy and compression and having central characters 'whimsical to the point of nausea'. One critic thought it 'all very clever' (see J. Elsom, *Post-War British Criticism*, 1981).

The first play Stoppard wrote, however, was one produced on television in 1963 and, under its new title, appeared on the London stage as *Enter a Free Man* in 1968 but this and some of his later work, *Albert's Bridge* (1968), a one-act comedy *The Real Inspector Hound* (1968) and some other pieces for radio and television have been found 'relatively slight' (John Russell Taylor, *The Second Wave*, 1971). *Jumpers* (1972), however, was intended to make an impact in the theatre with its devices, including a dance and scenery which revolves. It also included the TV screen on stage, the device already used by Peter Nichols in *The National Health*, three years before, with similar success.

Keith Dewhurst wrote *Lark Rise* and *Candleford* as two 'promenade' plays for performance in the Cottesloe Theatre (the small theatre of the National Theatre, holding about 400 people), the first on March 28, 1978 and the second on November 14, 1979. Dewhurst described a 'promenade production' as one where 'there is no distinction between stage and auditorium. The seats were removed, the audience could move about, and the actors performed the play amidst them. 'Sometimes the actors could not even see the colleagues to whom they were speaking because there were too many spectators in between'. It also meant, of course, that the 'audience' could not see the whole of the action as it moved about, although all of the plays could be heard. In this way, Dewhurst hoped, the audience would become part of the show.

The show was based on Flora Thompson's picture of village life at the end of the last century in her trilogy *Lark Rise to Candleford*; she worked in the post-office which also served as a blacksmith's. The first two parts of her work present a picture of, rather than a story about, rural Oxfordshire at a time of massive changes taking place in the countryside. Dewhurst's adaptation of the book retains its enormously evocative qualities and sense of community. His two plays or 'shows', as he calls them, present two contrasting days in the life of the people, one in summer and one in winter.

In some ways, the atmosphere and mood of country life by means of cleverly observed incidents is reminiscent of both Dylan Thomas's *Under Milk Wood* and Thornton Wilder's *Our Town*, but there the poet and the stage-manager act as interpreters to audiences who remain 'watchers' rather than 'participants'. There is a carefully paced rhythm to Dewhurst's two plays, with the finely observed contrast between old and young reflected in the language. The songs that are interspersed in the dialogue are celebrations of the countryside. The first play, *Lark Rise*, ends with a 'flash-forward' in time by means of a plaque seen in the local church to the memory of those killed in the Great War; one of the characters, Edmund Timms, recognises his own name inscribed on it, in a poignant reminder that the balmy days of village summers would pass away in the gunsmoke of the Battle of the Somme. The second play, *Candleford*, moves on four years from the earlier one and already the people, the life, and the time have moved on into winter. There is a brooding sadness that seems to be descending as childhood fades and adolescence comes on. The post-office becomes the central focus for the picture given.

These plays are time capsules; the cast refuses to move into the present, in spite of the fact that they are amongst an audience one hundred years and two major wars on. On the contrary, they pull the audience back with them in time to a quieter, slower age. Lighting, song, movement and subtle changes in language, pace and colour are all necessary to make the experience evocative and lyrical.

Lark Rise and *Candleford* are suitable 'shows' to end this survey of the development of Theatre and of Drama contained in Part II. They show how the ideas of 'play', 'text', 'audience' and 'theatre' have evolved without losing sight of the earliest origins of drama. The action is firmly back amongst the people and the wheel has turned full circle.

Questions

1 What advice would you give an actor to help him or her play the leading role according to Stanislavski's method of acting in a play you have been studying?

2 Take the leading character from a play you know well and show how its interpretation on the stage would differ according to whether you played it according to the Stanislavski or the Brecht approach to acting.

3 *Design a set for the dramatic presentation of either a Biblical story or a fable, using a 'Craig' approach.

4 What difference would it make to the production of a play you are studying if the approach to theatre advocated by Artaud were applied to it?

5 Examine carefully the way the dramatist has sequenced his 'plot' in a play you know well. Describe it and show any problems this sequencing might have for a director and how he or she might overcome them.

6 Describe the way humour emerges from Beckett's plays in production. (If you wish, you may restrict your discussion to one play.)

7 By discussing in detail the work of Harold Pinter that you may have studied, show how it has been influenced by Samuel Beckett's theatre.

8 What have you found 'absurd', in an Esslin sense, in any play you have been studying?

9 *What difficulties does an 'absurd' play present to a director presenting such a play for the first time? (You can, if you wish, research and describe the problems some particularly well-known director had when directing a play such as *Waiting for Godot*.)

10 Show how you would bring out a sense of conflict in a play you have been studying by means other than verbal on the stage.

11 By describing a play from the 'angry' theatre show what kind of anger is there and how this could be brought out in a production.

12 What do you understand by the term 'The Theatre of Cruelty' when it is applied to a play you have been studying that is specifically in that tradition.

13 What 'alienation effects', in Brecht's sense, do you see in a play you have been studying. (Make your discussion as sharply defined as you can by using detailed examples.)

14 By discussing the interpretation of a character in a play you know well show how you would try to affect an audience by using *either* a 'Method' *or* a purely technical approach to its interpretation.

15 Show how the presentation of a play would differ if Craig's ideas about Über-marionette' acting were applied to it.

16 *Discuss some of the ways you would present a Shakespearean tragedy to

*The questions marked * could form the basis of project work.*

an audience today using Craig's methods and ideas of scenic design.

17 Where does the dramatic power lie in a play you know well by *one* of the following: Edward Albee: John Arden; Edward Bond; Trevor Griffiths; Arthur Miller; Joe Orton; Tom Stoppard, or John Whiting?

18 Describe the mixture of humour and seriousness in a play by either Alan Ayckbourn or Peter Nichols. What problems does such a mixture present for a director?

19 Show how you would bring out the lyrical qualities in production of a play such as *Lark Rise* or *Candleford*.

20 The evocation of the past is often powerful when presented on the stage. Show how you would direct a play to evoke such a sense of the past.

21 What advice would you give to a cast of amateur players coming to take part in the production of a play from the 'Absurd' school for the first time? (Sharpen your comments by naming the play they will be taking part in.)

22 Show, with the help of detailed examples, some of the various ways you, as a director, would use silence and silences on the stage?

23 How far do *stage directions* help or restrict a team working to put on a play or dramatic show?

24 What do you understand, as a student of Drama and the Theatre Arts, by the term 'a play'. What restrictions does your definition have? (Justify the use of an alternative term, too, if you wish.)

25 In the light of your reading of Chapter One of this book and of your study of a play from this period, show what you understand by its 'text'.

PART THREE

Putting on
an
Act

9
The Production

9.1

First read carefully the ideas about staging a dramatic production put forward by **Antonin Artaud** (pages 270–275), **Bertolt Brecht** (pages 265–269), **Konstantin Stanislavski** (pages 275–279) and **E. Gordon Craig** (pages 279–285). Their work embodies some of the major approaches to direction, stage-management and stage-design, and acting.

The staging of a play or show in the theatre is a complex, technical process, one not easily learnt from a book. The various skills, activities and roles are **interdependent** in producing the magic of a production. No single member of the team can exist without the other. It is possible to describe the main features of most of the tasks but it must be remembered constantly in working on a production that 'no man is an island – and no woman either'.

In this part of this book it is only possible to give an outline of some of the roles played by those involved in a production. There are some very useful, practical, detailed handbooks on all the skills required. Perhaps one of the best comprehensive, practical guides available, certainly for those beginning their work on a production, is Esmé Crompton, *A Handbook of the Theatre*, second edition, 1973, published by Heinemann Educational Books Ltd.

9.2 The Director

Craig wished to see one person in control of the whole process of putting on a play. Ideally he or she was to be director, stage-manager, designer of both scene and costumes, and the interpreter of text, action, music, dance, rhythm, language, etc. However, in the modern theatre the director has some more limited but very important roles to play. There are few rules that are laid down, since his art is one which rests on a personal interpretation of the dramatic material being prepared for staging.

The director was known as 'the producer' in England until 1956, when it was decided to adopt the American usage and keep the title of director for the person interpreting the play and representing it on stage or in the theatre. 'The producer' (known in England as 'the manager') is the person responsible for the administrative and financial matters concerned with a production in American theatres. In France the director is known as the *régisseur*. Until the twentieth century, authors, actors, and actor-managers assumed the direction of productions but now in the commercial theatre professional directors such as Peter Hall and Peter Brook have established the role which is moving towards, but still with some way to go, the super-director/stage-manager as advocated by Gordon Craig at the turn of the century.

The director's first task is to establish the nature of the play, show, entertainment, opera etc., to be realised in production. This means studying the 'text', in terms of plot, character, language, and, above all, context – genres, movements, significance, or message. This will involve research into the period when the work was first devised, author's intentions, former productions, historical conventions and restraints, and so on. In short the director must be steeped in the work as far as is possible. Then he or she will begin to form some appreciation of the source material.

Then the 'vehicle' for presentation will be considered – spectacle (with lighting and sound) and relationships with the audience who will witness/share in the production. At this point constraints will emerge, such as the physical conditions in the building or theatre where the production will be mounted, the actors available, the cost of realising the production, the audience, and so on.

Any work of art involves four essential things:

(1) **a point of view**, or the angle from which the production of the work starts and is mainly sustained;
(2) **content**, or the plot/subject matter;
(3) **context**, the conditioning factors which surround the work as it grows – social, political, literary, financial, artistic, moral, etc.;
(4) **audience** or the people at whom the work is directed.

The Director, therefore, quite literally, *directs* the play towards his or her audience and is involved in a 'directed production' exercise just as a writer is engaged in a 'directed writing' exercise.

He or she is not alone in the venture in quite the same way as the writer or playwright is. The director has a stage-manager, a producer, actors, publicity people, designers, costume-makers, painters, scene-shifter – and a host of others to help him or her, but in the first place a director's task is a lonely one: to establish the fullest understanding and appreciation of the work that is possible. Scholar, critic, financier, musician, artist, personal manager, dress-designer, carpenter and lighting engineer are just some of the important roles the director must play, but above all he or she must be a sensitive, organised human being who understands, at least in part, and cares for fellow human beings.

Once the point of view, content, context and audience have been considered the more practical work can begin to make the 'vision' take shape in the very physical terms that constitute theatre.

First, the work needs to be broken down into its parts; acts and scenes, perhaps, but certainly phases or 'movements'. Its pace, its narrative progression, if it has one, its inter-relationships have to be considered. Stage directions (so firmly rejected by Craig but so important to writers like Ibsen, Shaw, and Brecht, too), exits and entrances, special effects indicated, openings and endings must be reduced to what some writers call 'blocking', where every detail of moves, direction of the speech, relation of actors to the stage and its properties, as well as to each other, are specifically mapped out. The stage, or area of performance, must be used to maximum effect to realise the 'vision'. At this point rehearsals can begin.

Some directors sit down, almost in a classroom situation, with their actors, stage-managers, scene and costume-designers, prompters and lighting engineers to examine **the meaning of the 'text'** of the work they are producing together. The **'blocking' rehearsals** can then be used to realise the 'text' in terms of movement, pace, sound and texture, step by step, scene by scene, act by act. Decisions taken at these rehearsals must be noted down accurately and clearly on a master copy, which will form the basis later of the most important document of all – the prompt copy. This is the working record of what the production is doing, gradually built up to include details of links between scenes, movements about the acting area, special effects, positions, exits, entrances, properties and time-schedules.

Following the 'blocking' of the dramatic show, the down-to-earth, **routine rehearsals** will allow the director to slant the production in the way he or she has seen in his or her 'vision' of the text. Misunderstandings of words or ideas, clarification of movements, pace and gesture, collaboration between actors and actresses on stage can all be dealt with – but the director's task is to direct and not to be deviated from the main purpose of realising the 'text' as it was perceived. As the rehearsals proceed, the technical matters such as lighting, sound, costuming and set-construction can proceed alongside them, but again, they must conform to the original 'vision', contribute to it, and not clash with it. **The first dress rehearsal** usually includes such considerations as the 'costume parade', the taking of photographs, and ways of handling the 'curtain call'. At **the final rehearsal** the director will continue note-making in order to ensure that the details worked out so painstakingly through the weeks of preparation are adhered to. Ad-libbing, paraphrasing, the alteration in the position of the set, or changes in details of properties or costumes can easily destroy the team, affect others' contributions and falsify the director's original intentions.

The director's is a strange, complex task, then. The dream has to be put together in terms of volatile human beings, pieces of wood, pots of paint, sticks of make-up and a host of other 'nuts and bolts'.

9.3 The Stage-Designer

In some ways the truth of Craig's view of how a production of a work of art appears on the stage or in the theatre comes sharply into focus here. The stage-designer needs to be an artist in his or her own right, creatively working to realise an effect. However, the effect aimed at is the director's vision rather than his or her own. Not only does the stage-designer have to study the 'text' just as closely as the director, but he or she also has to study the director's view of it. Obviously, the director's views can be listened to and slavishly obeyed, but that reduces the stage-designer's role to that of puppet at best and mere carpenter, electrician, or painter at worst. Technical knowledge and skills are, nevertheless, required – knowing what can and what cannot be achieved in wood, canvas, paint and light. After all, even Craig's scenery collapsed just before the opening of Stanislavski's production of *Hamlet* in Moscow.

The stage-designer needs, then, to understand the text and the director's interpretation of it. The 'idiom' or the 'texture' of the work needs to be considered very early on and in close, challenging, critical discussion these two key figures in the theatre need to bear in mind how the sets could be modified, painted, easily moved about, stand solidly and, above all, fit and enhance the whole production. Such sets, of course, may be realistic and naturalistic or symbolic; moonlight may, for example, either be simulated accurately or represented by a piece of circular orange card hanging over the acting area, suspended by a piece of string; or it may be left for the words to bring out, as in the Lorenzo–Jessica love scene in *The Merchant of Venice* (see above, page 108).

The stage-designer is also concerned with matters such as **costume**, **lighting and sound**, and **make-up**, although other members of the company will probably assume responsibility for the management of these areas of the production once they have been decided.

9.4 Costume

This is a technically highly-skilled part of a production and decisions about it need to be taken by the director and discussed with the stage-designer at the moment gestation starts, following conception.

The nature of the costuming of a production will be partly determined by the way the director sees the actors' role. If 'dressing-up' is one of the ways an actor *assumes* a character then one view of costume will emerge; if an actor *becomes* the character (*e.g.* in the Stanislavski method) then the dress will express the inner character and costume will be seen from a different angle.

Theatrical costume existed before scenery. Masks to represent character and heads of animals to represent the transformation of character were elements of 'disguise', so beloved to the theatre. Greek tragic actors wore a special coloured and decorated tunic called a *chiton* with special sleeves. In the Old Comedy (see page 19) actors wore padded clothes with a large, red leather phallus and animal heads were used where they were needed (*cf.* Bottom in *A Midsummer Night's Dream*). In the New Comedy popularised by Menander (see pages 63–64) normal, everyday clothes were worn. **Roman** actors used the Greek conventions of dress and took over the use of colour in costumes to symbolise attitudes and emotions. In some mimed productions clothing was very scanty indeed. Masks continued to be used but the costumes became more and more elaborate during the period of the *commedia dell'arte* in Italy. In England, costumes used in the **guild plays** were sometimes sumptuous and were borrowed from the church or the guild members themselves, but no attempt was made to play Romans in Roman dress or Greeks in Greek dress. Figures in the **Morality** plays were dressed in clothes which went some way towards representing the nature of the characters being displayed and props were carried to indicate nature and role. The 'Fool' or 'Vice' characters were often becoming distinctively dressed in productions with coxcombs and bells. The **Elizabethan** actors wore Elizabethan dress but royalty looked like Elizabethan royalty and rogues and ragamuffins looked like Elizabethan rogues and ragamuffins. Inigo Jones in the masques of the period (see pages 29–31), however, aimed at some historical accuracy, particularly where Roman and Greeks were being depicted. The introduction of elaborate scenery in the later part of the century demanded more elaborate costumes to match it. The growth of *rococo* in eighteenth-century France led to elaborate dress for actors performing before the court and a kind of wide ballet skirt became a common stage costume. By the 1780s some greater attempts at historical accuracy in costume came in France but David Garrick abandoned all foreign elaborations in the period 1750–60 and returned to the dress of his own time for productions, although, like the medieval actors, props could be carried to indicate period. Historical accuracy in dress became more popular in England following the Romantic period's renewed excitement over history and, with realism, historical accuracy became an important feature of the theatre. **Expressionism**, however, demanded the use of new forms of costume to suggest, rather than describe mood, and Craig, certainly, saw costume as part of the scenery as a whole design. In this century, costume designers have moved from 'historically accurate' to 'symbolically conceived' to 'modern' dress productions according to the way the director has seen the play or show. 'Historically accurate' when it is applied now, demands very closely re-searched material. The film industry spends much of its time on such work. (For a detailed historical description of the history of dramatic costume see James Laver's article in *The Oxford Companion to the Theatre*, edited by D. Hartnoll, fourth edition, 1983, to which the above summary owes some details.)

In drawing up costumes for a production, therefore, the stage-designer must primarily be influenced by the overall design of the production, its 'idiom' and its mood. Realistic, representational, symbolic, historically accurate costumes will reflect and comment on the nature of the whole production. The actual making of sketches may well fall within the stage-designer's purview, but the measuring of actors, the buying of cloth and trimmings and, once they have been specified, the making-up of the costumes, the fitting-out of actors, adaptations of and modifications of clothes, their issuing and storing and checking-back in, as well as their maintenance and cleaning, will fall to the **wardrobe mistress** and his or her team.

9.5 Make-Up

Bright lighting in the theatres which came about as the result of the use of gas and electricity in the nineteenth century is sometimes given as the reason why make-up was introduced to the British stage. Clearly make-up was used before this time to gain special effects, such as disguise, red noses, sallow complexions or moustaches and beards. Ghosts whitened their faces and blackamoors darkened them. Make-up for more general purposes to enhance appearance, however, was rarely used before the nineteenth century; it seems to have become current on the English stage in the seventeenth century but only amongst actresses, now appearing for the first time following the Restoration of Charles II to the throne in 1660, although there is some real evidence that young men used 'pencils' to transform their faces into those of old men in the first part of the eighteenth century. Garrick used make-up for the purpose of disguise. Although grease, lamp-black, burnt cork, and other pigments such as Indian ink were used for make-up before the middle of the nineteenth century, it was only about then that greasepaints of the kind still used today were sold commercially. Powders go back, it seems to at least the 1740s.

The Road to the Stage (1827) by Leman Thomas Rede is the first book on stage make-up, and it remained the authority almost until the end of the century. He makes it clear that the colours used were put on over a grease base, presumably to make them stick and easier to remove afterwards. *How to Make Up. A Practical Guide to the Art of 'Making-Up for Amateurs, etc.*, written by the pseudonymous 'Haresfoot and Rouge', was published in 1877. This is an invaluable source of knowledge for those wishing to know what materials were available and what techniques were used to make up according to age, nationality, or stereotyped parts, such as clowns and country folk. The instructions are very specific and detailed. Ludwig Leichner (born 1836) was the inventor of commercial greasepaints and after making them at home with his wife he set up the Leichner company in 1873.

Modern greasepaints no longer use lard or suet or tallow as their base but use beeswax or hard liquid paraffin with lanolin. (An excellent article on the history of make-up and the development of the pigments and techniques is to be found in D. Hartnoll's *Oxford Companion to the Theatre*, fourth edition, 1983. It is both comprehensive and enlivening with some interesting and amusing examples.)

Professional actors often make themselves up but in a production the effects produced by make-up, amongst even the most minor of parts, must remain firmly in the hands of the director and his colleague, the designer. The unity of the production as a concept must remain the criterion that is applied, so that no one character is allowed to dominate falsely, or fade away like some 'forpined ghost', or appear inappropriately grotesque.

9.6 Lighting

The history of lighting in theatres and of the stage itself has already been described in the context of the development of drama through the ages (see 'Lighting' in the *Index*).

Again, the lighting of a production is an essential part of design on the stage and is yet another element in constructing the vital 'vision' of the director in collaboration with the stage-designer. Today stage lighting is technically complex and students should turn for detailed explanations of its theory and techniques to modern books which include sections on circuits and computerised control of them such as Francis Reid's *The Stage Lighting Handbook*, second edition, 1982 and Frederick Bentham's *The Art of Stage Lighting*, third edition, 1980.

The director – or the stage-designer for that matter – cannot be expected, or expect, to know the last details of how a modern lighting system operates. But he or she must know first, how lighting will enhance and contribute to the production and its effect, and secondly, whether it is possible technically to be able to achieve what is wanted. The light is an essential part of the scene and must be integrated with it, so that it shines exactly when and how it should, without casting shadows or reflections or being obstructed in any way. Bentham (*op. cit.*, 184) sets out the point clearly and succinctly:

> Whoever is designing the lighting, he or she is responsible to the director alone. While the opinions of the ballet mistress, the scene designer, the members of the cast, the friend of the backer, the theatre owner, and perhaps even the architect, who may not like the way those ugly blue spotlights are disfiguring his new theatre, may have to be endured, they can and must be ignored.

The switchboard **lighting-designer** (and even operator) must keep a plot of the lighting for a production either in a copy of the play or on separate sheets giving the cues and the details of switches that need to be operated. It is important to make sure that the vocabulary used is consistent and accurate: for example, *check*, *dim*, or *fade* may be synonymous or be given special meanings. A multiplicity of words for the same operation is obviously best avoided.

Lighting rehearsals are needed in order to establish exactly how, when, and where the lighting will appear in relation to the scenery and the overall intended visual effect. Some spots may need adjusting, bulbs need replacing (not just the burnt-out ones but the old, weak ones, too) and the 'gels' or colour-filters need inspecting, since they can fade or soften and the glasses darken, become dirty, or lose their quality. Often, the trouble with lighting rehearsals is that, whilst technically informative, they are usually conducted without the cast being present. The scenery and props will be in position but it is essential that some stand-ins for the cast are used for this rehearsal, preferably in costume. Shadows cast by actors and actresses, and clashes of colour between lights, scenery, and costumes should have already been eradicated, but a final full-scale lighting rehearsal leaves one last chance to put any errors right. The director and stage-designer must be present in order to take decisions. At the other lighting rehearsals necessary before this last one the switchboard operator will need to have been present.

It falls to the lighting-designer to be responsible in some productions for the bangs, flashes, smoke and mist required. Flash boxes (made of fire-proof materials with fine wire stretched between terminals to ignite the flash powder) or bombs or maroons (fixed in special tanks) must be operated only when the operator can see the devices. Snow, rain, and reflections off water are other special effects to be sought. Snow can be simulated by soap flakes, and rain falling past a window by real water dripping; but lighting can create just as powerful effects with the help of gauze, sharp-definition lenses, wave-effect attachments (rather like the flame disc) placed before lenses or the 'tubular ripple' (a rotating drum and lamp unit, again rather like the flame drum). For the technical details of how to create such effects, consult Frederick Bentham's book mentioned earlier in this Chapter.

Safety care is paramount in dealing with stage-lighting. Every piece of wiring, every piece of equipment (including chains attached as a precaution to lamps and spots hanging above the heads of actors and audience) must be inspected and fire extinguishers for use on electrical fires must be available. A disaster here may result not only in a dramatic failure but in a fatality.

9.7   Noises Off and Other Effects

Developments in recording techniques have made it possible for many 'prefabricated' effects to be available to the director. In the 1950s and 1960s it was possible to purchase 'records' (as they were then known) of trains chugging uphill or entering a tunnel, ghosts complete with clanking chains, or horses galloping along stony paths. Today, such effects can be prerecorded on tapes, but often the abrupt starts or finishes of the recorded sound, or the quality of amplifiers together with their siting in the auditorium, can give results which diminish rather than enhance the illusion. Therefore, effects are still produced 'live' by other means in the theatre, often in a mechanical way, at the time they are needed. *The Oxford Companion to the Theatre*, ed. D. Hartnoll, fourth edition, 1983, lists some of the following ways of producing effects. A hand-driven drum on which are mounted horizontal, closely-spaced, slats which rub against a canvas sheet draped over them can simulate sounds from a breeze to a raging storm. Peas, lead shot, or small ballbearings shaken in a wooden box can suggest soldiers marching, surf or hail. A long, suspended, iron sheet can be vibrated to simulate thunder. Horses galloping can be suggested by banging coconut shells together or against different surfaces. Pieces of broken glass thrown from one bucket to another can produce a very effective noise of a window breaking. Doors slamming or locks being opened or shut are often produced by a specially made mock-up of a door off-stage.

Other ways of achieving special effects used in the 1930s can be found in A. E. Peterson's 'Stage Effects and Noises Off' in *Theatre and Stage*, 1934 and in Esmé Crompton's *A Handbook of the Theatre*, second edition, 1972.

9.8   The Stage-Manager

The role of the stage-manager in the production of a play or dramatic show is that of *link-man* and *co-ordinator*. He or she is the essential link in the chain between the 'vision' of the director and the stage-designer with what happens and is presented physically on the stage itself. As co-ordinator the stage-manager will bring together the efforts of a large team of people, such as: assistant stage-managers (known in the Theatre as ASM's), prompter, property-manager, call-boy, carpenters, electricians, the wardrobe mistress, dressers, scene-shifters, etc.

His or her work involves ensuring that matters such as the supply of copies of the play, times of rehearsals, the making or borrowing of properties, the buying and supplying of make-up, the hiring of furniture, the establishment of wardrobe and changing areas are attended to. Discipline and quiet conduct behind the scene also fall within the purview of the stage-manager, since his or her task is to ensure the smooth-running of back-stage and off-stage matters. It is not the stage-managers's responsibility to help direct the production or to advise on the design of sets, except where the scenery is clearly impossible to manage or shift. Ensuring that the director's interpretation of the play or stage action is technically possible, and managed, is his or her prime responsibility.

It is normal for the stage-manager to draw up and keep a number of 'plot sheets' which set out details of characters with their wardrobe and make-up requirements, their exits and entrances; *a furniture plot*, which specifies which articles are required exactly when and where on the stage; *a property plot* and a system for arranging the properties needed off-stage so that they are immediately available without fuss and without searching – there is nothing more calculated to destroy the audience's sense of dramatic illusion than a telephone that rings and demands to be answered according to the plot but which is still sitting in the corner of somebody's dressing room or a gun that has to be fired but has been left in the pocket of the wrong character's dressing-gown; and *a sound or effects plot*. Above all, the stage-manager needs to maintain a *prompt copy* of the production which contains all the details of exits, entrances, noises off, scene changes, curtains rising or falling, changes in lighting effects, properties required, and so on. At a glance he or she should be able to establish what is needed.

The careful stage-manager will also maintain and keep up-to-date a bulletin board which tells members of the cast the details of rehearsal timetables, news of the production with its difficulties and successes, publicity, and future plans or revised arrangements. Such a board should be placed where all members of the production team can see it and bring themselves fully into the picture every time they enter the theatre.

It is the stage-manager's task, too, to ensure that the whole stage area and off-stage and back-stage areas are kept safe and in an ordered condition. At the end of every performance he or she should ideally be the last to leave the areas. Again, *safety* is an essential element in mounting a production. The stage is a potentially dangerous place in more ways than one!

9.9   The Prompter

This is a key role throughout every performance. Normally, the prompter is established just off-stage in the wings, usually stage left; on the continent in some theatres, the prompter sits below but centrally down stage, with a box set into the footlights from which to prompt.

The prompter must prompt clearly, when required, but not so decisively as to misinterpret genuine pauses made by an actor or to draw the actor out of his role even temporarily. On the other hand, inaudible prompting helps nobody. Concentration is clearly vital and actors who paraphrase or ad-lib prove a threat not only to other actors who are relying on them for their cues, but to the production as a whole and to the director's 'vision'. Playwrights have taken too much care over their texts to have their meanings jeopardised by actors who cannot learn their lines accurately or who are too careless to bother. The director should, of course, establish this insistence on accuracy during rehearsals, except where improvisation, of course, is at the heart of the production.

It is interesting to note that the person responsible for prompting actors and making sure that they entered the stage at the right time was called the 'book-

holder' in Elizabethan times. Another person, the book-keeper', was responsible for keeping the 'text' of the play secure. Before strict copyright laws,
attempts were made to acquire the texts of 'box-office' successes illegally. To
stop this, or to make it more difficult, a playwright would sell his original
manuscript (his 'foul papers') to the Company for whom he was working and a
'scrivener's copy' would be made from it, endorsed and officially licensed on
the last page; actors were issued only with their own parts and their cues in and
out. These actors' parts were copied out by the book-keeper and issued by him;
actors were required to return all such copies to him when they were not in use
in the theatre. In this way the book-keeper would be held responsible for the
security of the text. Nevertheless, the bribing of actors to lend their parts or to
dictate them, and the practice of taking down details surreptitiously in the
theatre itself led to the publication of many 'pirated' versions ('corrupt' or
'bad' quartos) in Elizabethan times, many of which have survived. Once a
book was published the text became the property of the publisher and the
author had no further rights over it. This concentration of authentic texts in the
hands of a few 'book-keepers' and the heavy security surrounding them may
account for the loss of so many 'original' versions of the texts of Elizabethan
plays. Fortunately, after Shakespeare's death in 1616 two of his acting friends,
John Heminges (died 1630) and Henry Condell (died 1627), collected together
as much of Shakespeare's work as they could and published it in a folio edition
in 1623 (now known as the First Folio). This book together with officially
printed versions (good quarto) and the 'pirated' versions (corrupt quarto) of
the plays remain our sole sources of knowledge of Shakespeare's plays.
Heminges and Condell mention the existence of 'stolen and surreptitious' texts
of their friend's work.

9.10 The Manager (The Theatre Manager)
In England today the 'manager' (called 'the producer' in America) is the
person responsible for the business side of a theatrical show.

The manager is responsible for five main areas of a production. First, it is for
him or her to establish that all rights of copyright and for performance have
been met and royalties paid before rehearsals begin. Secondly, the manager
must ensure that the rent for hiring the building, special equipment such as
lighting rigs, and extra properties has been paid. He or she, too, should ensure
that the budget for the production is carefully and correctly drawn up and
adhered to. Thirdly, the manager should arrange through an agent or another
member of the company for the production to be advertised; with amateur
productions local newspapers will often send a theatre critic to report on what
is happening and on the performance itself. Professional managers will arrange
for press releases on matters of interest about the play, the cast, and the
production itself and for complimentary tickets to be sent to those who can
influence others and publicise the show. Fourthly, it is for the manager to
arrange for the sale of tickets, the drawing-up of seat plans, and the design and
selling of programmes. The selling of programmes can be profitable for a
company or theatre; until recently programmes were sealed at the edge with a

small piece of printed paper to ensure that programme-sellers did not collect unwanted programmes left behind by one audience and sell them again to the next. Finally, the manager is responsible for the 'house', as it is known. This involves meeting all the local regulations governing places to which the public has access, licensing the premises where and as necessary, and ensuring that the local Fire Inspector and Safety Officer have been given the opportunity of visiting the theatre. Amateur productions have sometimes been refused licences, for example, because seats were not spaced or set out correctly or were not fastened securely to avoid further personal accident in a situation of panic, where fire doors or escape routes were blocked or not available, overhead lamps were not equipped with safety chains, or fire-extinguishers, or sand/ water buckets at least, were not provided in changing rooms.

A production requires considerable attention to detail, and it is for the manager to ensure that the administrative plans are adequate and properly carried out.

Questions

1   Describe how you saw your role as a director in a play which you have already staged or how you would see your role in a play you hope to stage in the future.

2   *Outline two different 'visions' of a play you have been studying that a director might have in considering how to present it to a modern audience.

3   What problems would you consider an actor might meet if he or she were also playing the role of 'director' in the production of a play.

4   *Make a model of a set for a scene (or a play) you hope to direct and illustrate the costumes you expect to use for your major characters. Explain how the set and costumes are part of your 'vision' of the production as its director.

5   Write a commentary on the opening scene of a play you are studying which you would present to a cast of actors you are about to direct and take into rehearsal.

6   *Draw up (or model) alternative 'designs' for the set of the final scene of a play you have been studying. Justify what you suggest.

7   Justify your decision to mount the production of a pre-twentieth-century play in modern, contemporary dress. (Make it clear that you recognise some of the difficulties which will follow on from your decision.)

8   *Design (and justify your design) costumes for three of the major characters in a modern production of a play from one of the following periods in the history of drama: Greek; Roman; the Middle Ages; Elizabethan or Jacobean; the Restoration.

9   Describe some of the special effects needed for the production of a play you are studying. Show how they contribute to the interpretation of the whole play and describe how you would achieve them technically.

10 Write a short play-scene of your own where one of the actors continually forgets his or her lines and the prompter comes to his or her aid with increasing irritation. (Show how this affects not only the actor concerned but other members of the cast, too.)

*The questions marked * could form the basis of project work.*

PART FOUR

Criticism

10
Describing a Production

10.1

There is no single way of approaching this kind of critical writing. A glance at the writings of theatre critics' work in newspapers and magazines will reveal some of the more common approaches they use, but the most effective will take account of some of the following, at least:

(a) the nature of the play, its plot and period;

(b) the fundamental angle or angles from which the playwright has tackled the dramatic material;

(c) the 'vision' of the play the director has;

(d) the interpetation of this 'vision' in terms of set, costumes, acting, special effects;

(e) special points of interest in the production: *e.g.* pace, levels of language, climaxes, dénouement, contact with the audience, the cohesion of the production, fundamental moods and overall effects, humour, moral or social significance, the unusual, etc.;

(f) the critic's own stance or point of view;

(g) the audience for which the critical piece is intended.

These points, of course, do not set out the order in which a critic may give his or her impressions of a performance. The list is not an exhaustive one, but it does indicate some of the points critics have to bear in mind in their writing of reports of a production. Some writers, of course, are hard-hitting and need to consider the effect their writing will have on the run a play will have – with all the consequences for the many hundreds of people who normally take part in a production. But critics are responsible people and will maintain their integrity by being honest, and yet sympathetic, in their writing. They remember, too, that they have also a very serious responsibility towards their readers; such readers will not thank the critics for misleading them if they are to spend both time and money in visiting a theatre.

10.2

Examples of critics' writings and reviews of actual productions will show how styles of criticism have changed over the ages, and also what modern journals see as significant elements in theatrical criticism.

(i) **Samuel Pepys   The Tempest**   November 7, 1667

7th. Up, and at the office hard all the morning, and at noon resolved with Sir W. Pen to go see "The Tempest," an old play of Shakespeare's, acted, I hear, the first day; and so my wife and girl and W. Hewer by themselves, and Sir W. Pen and I afterwards by ourselves; and forced to sit in the side balcone over aginst the musique-room at the Duke's house. The house mighty full; the King and Court there, and the most innocent play that ever I saw, and a curious piece of musique in an echo of half sentences, the echo repeating the former half, while the man goes on to the latter, which is mighty pretty. The play no great wit, yet good, above ordinary plays.

(*ii*) **Leigh Hunt** (1784–1859) was dramatic critic first of the *News* and then of the *Examiner* and the *Tatler*. He knew Shelley, Keats, and Byron well. In 1807 he published *Critical Essays On the Performers of the London Theatres* and gave the following advice to theatre critics writing for newspapers:

(*a*) Never take any notice whatever of the author of the play, or of the play itself, unless it be a new one.
(*b*) Indulge an acquaintance with every dramatic writer and with every actor.
(*c*) Say . . . it would have been infinitely more entertaining if a little had been added or a little had been taken away, a probability which few will dispute with you.
(*d*) If you do not exactly understand how to conceal your evil opinion of men's writing or performances . . . always say the direct contrary of what you think.
(*e*) Never exceed six or seven lines, but be sure to notice by name the fashionables in the boxes.

He then went on to give an example of this kind of criticism based on a performance of Sheridan's *The Rivals* at Drury Lane:

DRURY LANE. Last night the *beautiful* comedy of *The Rivals* was performed with great éclat to an *overflowing* house: Bannister was excellent – Mrs H. Johnston looked *beautiful*. Among the company we observed the Duchess of Gordon, the Duke of Queensbury, Lady Hamilton, and many other *amiable* and *beautiful* personages. There was a quarrel in the pit.

As a critical comment on the criticism Leigh Hunt added:

What can be more concise, more explanatory, more critical, than such a criticism? Grammarians undertake to teach a language in five months, musicians, the whole theory of music in five weeks, and dancing-masters all sorts of steps in five hours, but by these rules a man may be a profound critic in five minutes. Let Aristotle and Quintilian hide their huge volumes in dismay, and confess the superiority of a criticism, which, like the magic word *Sesame* in the Arabian Nights, opens to us a thousand treasures in a breath!

(*iii*) **William Hazlitt** (1778–1830) reviewed a melodrama called **The Vampyre** for *The London Magazine* in September, 1820:

The new Dramatic Romance (or whatever it is called) of the *Vampyre** is, upon the whole, the most splendid *spectacle* we have ever seen. It is taken from a French piece, founded on the celebrated story so long bandied about between Lord Byron, Mr Shelley, and Dr Polidori, which last turned out to be the true author. As a mere fiction, and as a fiction attributed to Lord Byron, whose genius is chartered for the land of horrors, the original story passed well enough: but on the

* English Opera House.

stage it is a little shocking to the feelings, and incongruous to the sense, to see a spirit in a human shape – in the shape of a real Earl, and, what is more, of a Scotch Earl – going about seeking whom it may marry and then devour, to lengthen out its own abhorred and anomalous being. Allowing for the preternatural atrocity of the fable, the situations are well imagined and supported: the acting of Mr T. P. Cooke (from the Surry Theatre) was spirited and imposing, and certainly Mrs W. H. Chatterley, as the daughter of his friend the Baron (Mr Bartley) and his destined bride, bid fair to be a very delectable victim. She is however saved in a surprising manner, after a rapid succession of interesting events, to the great joy of the spectator. The scenery of this piece is its greatest charm, and it is inimitable. We have seen sparkling and overpowering effects of this kind before; but to the splendour of a transparency were here added all the harmony and mellowness of the finest painting. We do not speak of the vision at the beginning, or of that at the end of the piece – though these were admirably managed – so much as of the representation of the effects of moonlight on the water and on the person of the dying knight. The hue of the sea-green waves, floating in the pale beam under an arch-way of grey weather-beaten rocks, and with the light of a torch glaring over the milder radiance, was in as fine keeping and strict truth as Claude or Rembrandt, and would satisfy, we think, the most fastidious artist's eye. It lulled the sense of sight as the fancied sound of the dashing waters soothed the imagination. In the scene where the moonlight fell on the dying form of Ruthven (the Vampyre) it was like a fairy glory, forming a palace of emerald light: the body seemed to drink its balmy essence, and to revive in it without a miracle. The line, 'See how the moon sleeps with Endymion', came into the mind from the beauty and gorgeousness of the picture, not withstanding the repugnance of every circumstance and feeling. This melodrama succeeds very well: and it succeeds in spite of Mr Kean's last nights, and without Miss Kelly!

The emphasis was clearly on the spectacle rather than the substance of the plot or their characters and their interpretation. Such comments say more about the reasons why audiences were going to the theatres at the beginning of the nineteenth century rather than indicate any real interest in the 'message' of drama or, indeed, its real medium.

(*iv*) **Charles Lamb** (1775–1834) wrote a criticism of Sheridan's **School for Scandal** for the April, 1822, edition of *The London Magazine*:

> Amid the mortifying circumstances attendant upon growing old, it is something to have seen the *School for Scandal* in its glory. This comedy grew out of Congreve and Wycherley, but gathered some allays of the sentimental comedy which followed theirs. It is impossible that it should be now *acted*, though it continues, at long intervals, to be announced in the bills. Its hero, when Palmer played it at least, was Joseph Surface. When I remember the gay boldness, the graceful solemn plausibility, the measured step, the insinuating voice – to express it in a word – the downright *acted* villainy of the part, so different from the pressure of conscious actual wickedness – the hypocritical assumption of hypocrisy – which made Jack so deservedly a favourite in that character, I must needs conclude the present generation of play-goers more virtuous than myself, or more dense. I freely confess that he divided the palm with me with his better brother; that, in fact, I liked him quite as well. Not but there are passages – like that, for instance, where Joseph is made to refuse a pittance to a poor relation –

incongruities which Sheridan was forced upon by the attempt to join the artificial with the sentimental comedy, either of which must destory the other – but over these obstructions Jack's manner floated him so lightly, that a refusal from him no more shocked you, than the easy compliance of Charles gave you in reality any pleasure; you got over the paltry question as quickly as you could, to get back into the regions of pure comedy, where no cold moral reigns. The highly artificial manner of Palmer in this character counteracted every disagreeable impression which you might have received from the contrast, supposing them real, between the two brothers. You did not believe in Joseph with the same faith with which you believed in Charles. The latter was a pleasant reality, the former a no less pleasant poetical foil to it. The comedy, I have said, is incongruous; a mixture of Congreve with sentimental incompatibilities: the gaiety upon the whole is buoyant; but it required the consummate art of Palmer to reconcile the discordant elements.

No piece was, perhaps, ever so completely cast in all its parts as this *manager's comedy*. Miss Farren had succeeded to Mrs Abington in Lady Teazle; and Smith, the original Charles, had retired, when I first saw it. The rest of the characters, with very slight exceptions, remained. I remember it was then the fashion to cry down John Kemble, who took the part of Charles after Smith; but, I thought, very unjustly. Smith, I fancy, was more airy, and took the eye with a certain gaiety of person. But the weighty sense of Kemble made up for more personal incapacity than he had to answer for. His harshest tones in this part came steeped and dulcified in good humour. He made his defects a grace. His exact declamatory manner, as he managed it, only served to convey the points of his dialogue with more precision. It seemed to head the shafts to carry them deeper. Not one of his sparkling sentences was lost. I remember minutely how he delivered each in succession, and cannot by any effort imagine how any of them could be altered for the better. No man could deliver brilliant dialogue – the dialogue of Congreve or of Wycherley – because none understood it – half so well as John Kemble. His Valentine, in *Love for Love*, was, to my recollection, faultless. He flagged sometimes in the intervals of tragic passion. He would slumber over the level parts of an heroic character. His Macbeth has been known to nod. But he always seemed to me to be particularly alive to pointed and witty dialogue. The relaxing levities of tragedy have not been touched by any since him – the playful court-bred spirit in which he condescended to the players in Hamlet – the sportive relief which he threw into the darker shades of Richard – disappeared with him. He had his sluggish moods, his torpors – but they were the halting-stones and resting-places of his tragedy – politic savings, and fetches of the breath – husbandry of the lungs, where nature pointed him to be an economist – rather, I think than errors of the judgement. They were, at worst, less painful than the eternal tormenting unappeasable vigilance, the 'lidless dragon eyes', of present fashionable tragedy.

Already a number of additional features of dramatic criticism are starting to appear. The critic is beginning to see himself as a professional, able to relate performance to the play's content and to its underlying significances. Comparisons are made which attempt to place the play back into a context, that of sentimental comedy. There is much, too, on the way actors interpreted their parts, but little sense of overall *direction*.

(*v*) **William Archer** (1856–1924) was one of the most eminent of Victorian critics. He also edited all the translations of the latest plays of Ibsen and wrote many books on drama. A year before his death one of his own plays, *The Green Goddess* was successfully staged.

His criticism of Oscar Wilde's **The Importance of Being Earnest** when it was produced in 1895 is now a classic in its own right:

The dramatic critic is not only a philosopher, moralist, aesthetician and stylist, but also a labourer working for his hire. In this last capacity he cares nothing for the classifications of Aristotle, Polonius, or any other theorist, but instinctively makes a fourfold division of the works which come within his ken. These are his categories: (1) Plays which are good to see. (2) Plays which are good to write about. (3) Plays which are both. (4) Plays which are neither. Class 4 is naturally the largest; Class 3 the smallest; and Classes 1 and 2 balance each other pretty evenly. Mr Oscar Wilde's new comedy, *The Importance of being Earnest* belongs indubitably to the first class. It is delightful to see it, it sends wave after wave of laughter curling and foaming round the theatre; but as a text for criticism it is barren and delusive. It is like a mirage-oasis in the desert, grateful and comforting to the weary eye – but when you come close up to it, behold! it is intangible, it eludes your grasp. What can a poor critic do with a play which raises no principle, whether of art or morals, creates its own canons and conventions, and is nothing but an absolutely wilful expression of an irrepressibly witty personality? Mr Pater, I think (or is it some one else?), has an essay on the tendency of all art to verge towards, and merge in, the absolute art – music. He might have found an example in *The Importance of Being Earnest*, which imitates nothing, represents nothing, is nothing, except a sort of rondo capriccioso, in which the artist's fingers run with crisp irresponsibility up and down the keyboard of life. Why attempt to analyse and class such a play? Its theme, in other hands, would have made a capital farce; but 'farce' is far too gross and commonplace a word to apply to such an irridescent filament of fantasy. Incidents of the same nature as Algy Moncrieffe's 'Bunburying' and John Worthing's invention and subsequent suppression of his scapegoat brother Ernest have done duty in many a French vaudeville and English adaptation; but Mr Wilde's humour transmutes them into something entirely new and individual. . . . .

Not that the play is a masterpiece of construction. It seemed to me that the author's invention languished a little after the middle of the second act, and that towards the close of that act there were even one or two brief patches of something almost like tediousness. But I have often noticed that the more successful the play, the more a first-night audience is apt to be troubled by inequalities of workmanship, of which subsequent audiences are barely conscious. The most happily-inspired scenes, coming to us with the gloss of novelty upon them, give us such keen pleasure, that passages which are only reasonably amusing are apt to seem, by contrast, positively dull. Later audiences, missing the shock of surprise which gave to the master-scenes their keenest zest, are also spared our sense of disappointment in the flatter passages, and enjoy the play more evenly all through. I myself, on seeing a play a second time, have often been greatly entertained by scenes which had gone near to boring me on the first night. When I see Mr Wilde's play again, I shall no doubt relish the last half of the second act more than I did on Thursday evening; and even then I differed from some of my colleagues who found the third act tedious. Mr Wilde is least fortunate where he drops into Mr Gilbert's Palace-of-Truth mannerism, as he is apt to do in the characters of Gwendolen and Cecily. Strange what a fascination this trick seems to possess for the comic playwright! Mr Pinero, Mr Shaw, and now Mr Wilde have all dabbled in it, never to their advantage. In the hands of the inventor it produces pretty effects enough:

> But Gilbert's magic may not copied be;
> Within that circle none should walk but he.

The acting is as hard to write about as the play. It is all good; but there is no opportunity for any striking excellence. The performers who are most happily suited are clearly Mr Allan Aynesworth and Miss Rose Leclercq, both of whom are delightful. Mr Alexander gives his ambition a rest, and fills his somewhat empty part with spirit and elegance. Miss Irene Vanbrugh makes a charmingly sophisticated maiden of Mayfair, and Miss Evelyn Millard, if not absolutely in her element as the unsophisticated Cecily, is at least graceful and pleasing. Mrs Canninge and Mr H. H. Vincent complete a very efficient cast.

This piece of dramatic criticism, published in *The World* on February 20, 1895, is well-constructed, sets out the dramatic critic's difficulties, avoids mere plot-narration, links the performance with others for comparison and tries to be as kind as it can to the cast with words of faint praise such as 'elegance', 'charmingly', 'pleasing', 'efficient' and the use of the negative – 'if not absolutely in her element'. With William Archer the dramatic critic established himself as a professional.

(*vi*) **Max Beerbohm** (1872–1956) in his criticism of John Galsworthy's **Justice** in *The Saturday Review* on March 5th, 1910, tried to place it in the context of the discussion about 'artificiality' or 'realism' in the theatre and linked it with the developing art of the cinema. It has much about the play but very little about the actors.

We are getting on. Time was when our drama was so utterly divorced from life that the critics never dreamed of condemning a play for artificiality. It is but a few years since they acquired the habit of judging plays in relation to life. And now (so fast has our drama been moving) they are beginning to decry plays on the ground that they are indistinguishable from life. Well, I am not going to join in the doubts expressed by so many critics whether *Justice*, in the repertory at the Duke of York's, be proper art. 'Cinematographic' they call it. So it is, in a sense. We really do, in seeing it, have the sensation of seeing reproduced exactly things that have happened in actual life. Or rather, we feel that we are seeing these things actually happen. If the cinematograph were chromatic and stereoscopic, and free from vibration, and gramophonic into the bargain, Mr Galsworthy might – no, even then, as I shall presently show, he would not have a dangerous rival. In the first act of *Justice* we do not feel that we are seeing an accurate presentment of the humdrum of a lawyer's office: we are *in* a lawyer's office. The curtain rises on the second act; and presently we have forgotten the foot-lights, and are *in* a court of law. At a crucial moment in the cross-examination of a witness, somebody at the reporter's table drops a heavy book on the floor. An angry murmur of 'Sh!' runs round the court, and we ourselves have joined in it. The jury retires to consider its verdict, and instantly throughout the court there is a buzz of conversation – aye, and throughout the auditorium, too: we are all of us, as it were, honorary 'supers'.

In the third act, we arrive at a prison. Gloomily producing a special pass signed 'John Galsworthy', we are shown over the interior. We interview the governor, the chaplain, the doctor. Through the wire-blind of the governor's office we have, all the while, a blurred glimpse of certain automata, quickly-revolving – the convicts at exercise. Some of these men we see presently at close quarters in their cells. We are haunted by it all afterwards as by an actual experience, not as by a tragic play. And part of this effect is due, of course, to the excellence of the stage-management and of the acting. But of what avail would these things be if the play itself were not true to life? . . .

In some of his works he does certainly lay himself open to a (very superficial) charge of inhumanity. In *Strife* he showed us a conflict, and in *Fraternity* a contrast between the poor and the rich; and the implicit moral of the play was that this conflict would be for ever. If things are irremediable, why, it might be asked, harrow us about them? To which, I take it, Mr Galsworthy's answer would be that to recognize the sadness of things is a duty we owe to honesty, and is good for our souls. In *Justice*, however, there is no fundamental pessimism. Mr Galsworthy sees that our criminal law and our penal system are clumsy, mechanical, mischievous. But he sees them as things not beyond redemption. A little spurring of the scientific intelligence in us and of our common humanity is all that is needed to induce reform . . . When the curtain falls, the auditorium is as silent as the very prison whose silence the convict has just broken by hammering with his fists against his door; and not even when, a moment later, the curtain rises, and we see Mr Dennis Eadie cheerfully bowing his acknowledgment to us, is the horror undone. Cheerfully? No, I am very sure that Mr Eadie is too fine an artist not to shudder at this rising of the curtain – this bland, idiotic attempt, on the part of the management, to undo the horror.

(*vii*)   By the time the critic had reached the post-Second-World-War period criticism had adopted the style of the newspaper in its direct address to the reader and the pointed throwing out of questions, but often the skill of the actors, which occupied much of the critical writing of Lamb and Hazlitt, came in for short treatment. **J. C. Trewin's** and **Lionel Hale's** criticisms of J. B. Priestley's **An Inspector Calls**, when it was produced at the Old Vic in 1946 exemplify this new style of criticism:

The piece shoots its question-marks as the porcupine its quills. Early in the evening we might be sitting at a revival of some doctrinal play of the Manchester school (in the Gaiety's best mood). Presently we ask if the author can be speaking in symbols. Can the Birlings stand for that complacent world of 1912, tottering blindly to its fall? . . . Is, then, this omniscient inspector Priestley's idea of the angel with the flaming sword? Who can tell? He comes in such a questionable shape. He may be an embodiment of Conscience or the representative of a Celestial Watch Committe or another version of the Examiner from *Outward Bound* – or simply (as he claims) an Inspector Goole. Have it your own way, says Mr. Priestley.

The play, not a long one, could have been stripped to half its length: though their offence is rank we feel that the Birlings are hardly worth this elaboration, this prolonged rattling of skeletons (and, indeed, this high place in the Old Vic's repertory). . . .

J. C. Trewin: *Observer*
6 October 1946

Who is the Inspector? Something out of 'The Passing of the Third Floor Back'? Did the dead girl ever exist? The theatre hates indecision. Mr. Priestley, not making up his own mind, does not persuade ours. And Heaven help his chief actor (Mr. Ralph Richardson) for the author won't.

It is an indication of the play's lack of theatrical truth that its author was obliged to put it into an Edwardian scene and costume. Mr. Richardson, looking for something to act in a nebulous part, paraded like some dummy in the Tailoring section of a 'Britain used to make it' Exhibition. A pitiful sight for a fine actor.

And a pitiful play for a dramatist who can write such brilliant introductory scenes for Mr. Basil Dean to direct and for Mr. Alec Guinness and Miss Margaret Leighton to play.

Lionel Hale: *Daily Mail*
2 October 1946

(*viii*)   Kenneth Tynan's criticism of John Osborne's **Look Back in Anger** in 1956 began the trend at the time of linking criticism of the play to events outside the theatre, but explicit comments on the performance of the actors and actresses are still sparse, although, because the characters are treated as real people, a comment on the character becomes a comment on the actor's performance:

"They are scum" was Mr. Maugham's famous verdict on the class of State-aided university students to which Kingsley Amis' Lucky Jim belongs; and since Mr. Maugham seldom says anything controversial or uncertain of wide acceptance, his opinion must clearly be that of many. Those who share it had better stay well away from John Osborne's *Look Back in Anger*, which is all scum and a mile wide.

Its hero, a provincial graduate who runs a sweet-stall, has already been summed up in print as "a young pup," and it is not hard to see why. What with his flair for introspection, his gift for ribald parody, his excoriating candour, his contempt for "phoneyness," his weakness for soliloquy, and his desperate conviction that the time is out of joint, Jimmy Porter is the completest young pup in our literature since Hamlet, Prince of Denmark. His wife, whose Anglo-Indian parents resent him, is persuaded by an actress friend to leave him; Jimmy's prompt response is to go to bed with the actress. Mr. Osborne's picture of a certain kind of modern marriage is hilariously accurate: he shows us two attractive young animals engaged in competitive martyrdom, each with its teeth sunk deep in the other's neck, and each reluctant to break the clinch for fear of bleeding to death.

The fact that he writes with charity has led many critics into the trap of supposing that Mr. Osborne's sympathies are wholly with Jimmy. Nothing could be more false. Jimmy is simply and abundantly alive; that rarest of dramatic phenomena, the act of original creation, has taken place; and those who carp were better silent. Is Jimmy's anger justified? Why doesn't he *do* something? These questions might be relevant if the character had failed to come to life; in the presence of such evident and blazing vitality, I marvel at the pedantry that could ask them. Why don't Chekhov's people *do* something? Is the sun justified in scorching us? There will be time enough to debate Mr. Osborne's moral position when he has written a few more plays. In the present one he certainly goes off the deep end, but I cannot regard this as a vice in a theatre that seldom ventures more than a toe into the water.

Look Back in Anger presents post-war youth as it really is, with special emphasis on the non-U intelligentsia who live in bed-sitters and divide the Sunday papers into two groups, "posh" and "wet." To have done this at all would be a signal achievement; to have done it in a first play is a minor miracle. All the qualities are there, qualities one had despaired of ever seeing on the stage—the drift towards anarchy, the instinctive leftishness, the automatic rejection of "official" attitudes, the surrealist sense of humour (Jimmy describes a pansy friend as "a female Emily Brontë"), the casual promiscuity, the sense of lacking a crusade worth fighting for, and, underlying all these, the determination that no one who dies shall go unmourned.

One cannot imagine Jimmy Porter listening with a straight face to speeches about our inalienable right to flog Cypriot schoolboys. You could never mobilise him and his kind into a lynching mob, since the art he lives for, jazz, was invented by Negroes; and if you gave him a razor, he would do nothing with it but shave. The Porters of our time deplore the tyranny of "good taste" and refuse to accept "emotional" as a term of abuse; they are classless, and they are also leaderless. Mr. Osborne is their first spokesman in the London theatre. He has been lucky in his sponsors (the English Stage Company), his director (Tony Richardson), and his interpreters: Mary Ure, Helena Hughes, and Alan Bates give fresh and unforced performances, and in the taxing central role Kenneth Haigh never puts a foot wrong.

That the play needs changes I do not deny: it is twenty minutes too long, and not even Mr. Haigh's bravura could blind me to the painful whimsey of the final reconciliation scene. I agree that *Look Back in Anger* is likely to remain a minority taste. What matters, however, is the size of the minority. I estimate it at roughly 6,733,000, which is the number of people in this country between the ages of twenty and thirty. And this figure will doubtless be swelled by refugees from other age-groups which are curious to know precisely what the contemporary young pup is thinking and feeling. I doubt if I could love anyone who did not wish to see *Look Back in Anger*. It is the best young play of its decade.

(*ix*) **Irving Wardle's** criticism of Tom Stoppard's **Rozencrantz and Guildenstern are Dead** on April 12, 1967, in *The Times* is more concerned with trying to establish the nature of the play. It manages to convey very convincingly the problems that an audience might have with it. Criticism is increasingly trying to meet the insistent questions of a potential audience: Am I likely to enjoy the play? What is it about? How does it relate to other plays I may know?

As a first stage play, it is an amazing piece of work.

I know of no theatrical precedent for it, but among other things it might be called a piece of literary detection. From the labyrinthine picture of Elsinore, Mr. Stoppard has blown up a single detail and wrenched enough material from it to create a drama.

The shadowy history of Rosencrantz and Guildenstern always sticks in the mind as a classic instance of the fate that befalls little men who are swept into great events. Much is said against them in the course of *Hamlet*, but they hardly deserve it: they are too insignificant to escape anonymous servitude.

For most of Mr. Stoppard's play they are shown in private – abandoned in an ante-chamber of the palace waiting for the next call, spinning coins and playing word games, desperately latching on to the First Player as the only character who will speak to them.

From time to time, the court sweeps on to conduct its incomprehensible business and sweeps out again, leaving the interchangeable nonentities stranded like driftwood on the beach.

What emerges is a compound of Shakespearian criticism, Beckett-like cross-talk, and the mathematical nonsense comedy involving two cyphers. The couple have no memory of the past, no understanding of the present, and no idea where they are going.

All they have is words, and the endless word games they play represent both a way of passing the time and an indefatigable attempt to make sense of their predicament.

Mr. Stoppard manages to relate the material to the Shakespearian action – as where a quick-fire question game (as exciting as a tennis match) is used as a preparation for an interview with the prince, who promptly wins the game and set (' "We were sent for", you said, I didn't know where to put myself '). . . . But the real triumph is in relating the partners' preoccupation with free will to the players, whose profession insists on fixed destiny and who stage a rehearsal of the *Ganzago* prologue forecasting the fatal voyage to England. On the voyage, Mr. Stoppard secures an existential conclusion in which the partners discover their death warrant and choose to deliver it so as to emerge, if only for a second, into lives of their own.

There are times when the author, like his characters, seems to be casting about for what to say next. But for most of the time he walks his chosen tight-rope with absolute security.

In its origins this is a highly literary play with frank debts to Pirandello and Beckett; but in Derek Goldby's production, these sources prove a route towards technical brilliance and powerful feeling.

(x) Milton Schulman's account of the Young Vic's production of Shakespeare's *Romeo and Juliet* in *The Evening Standard* on February 24, 1977, is a very good example of the theatre critic's attempt to relate the production to an audience's possible reactions. It is, nevertheless, a somewhat devastating 'notice'.

ROMEO AND JULIET is a play about the folly of maturity and the victimisation of youth. It is the children of the Montagues and Capulets who are destroyed to satisfy the feuds of their families.

But this production at the Young Vic demonstrates that to illuminate its message and convey its impact, being young isn't enough.

Natasha Pyne, as Juliet, certainly has all the gauche mannerisms of a 13-year-old girl, while Simon Chandler, as Romeo, looks the part of a callow, self-conscious teenage boy.

But what they have for each other never flares into anything more than a casual crush. Star-crossed lovers they certainly are not.

In this modern dress production where jeans motorbike helmets and leather jackets are worn, and flick knives used for the street brawls, there is a valid attempt to link the characters with the experiences of the young audience that frequents this theatre.

Unfortunately, if we pop the plot into the 1970's credibility is strained at the prospect of a 13-year-old Italian girl being hustled into marriage, and the fuss over being banished from Verona to Mantua appears hysterically overdone.

Apparently to avoid testing the patience of the audience too severely, there seems to have been an effort in Denise Coffey's production to take the Bard at his word and try to get the whole thing over in "two hours traffic of our stage."

Even at the speed with which most of these speeches were gabbled they couldn't meet Shakespeare's schedule.

All this, of course, does the poetry no good at all. And without the poetry the balcony scene loses its magic. Mercutio is reduced to a garrulous exhibitionist and the final death scene in the tomb, becomes trite melodrama.

Only in scattered moments did the sweet poignancy of the play break through. The fights staged by Derek Ware had a vicious authenticity which the audience appeared to enjoy.

For those who have never seen the play before, this production is a competent enough introduction.

(*xi*) **Francis King's** review of Bertolt Brecht's **Mother Courage and her Children** on November 11, 1984, in the *Sunday Telegraph*, shows an interesting modern reassessment of Brecht's play and dramatic theory. It deals with both in terms of theatre and never loses sight of the audience. The poor actors and actresses still get a rather swift appraisal of their skills:

In John Napier's set for *Mother Courage and Her Children* (Barbican), Courage's wagon, attached to a spindle connecting it to a weather-vane and a gigantic overhead cogwheel, trundles round and round the same well-worn track. Here, clearly, is a symbol of her life on a treadmill that gets her nowhere.

But here, too, is a symbol of a play that, as the evening progresses, becomes increasingly effortful, cumbersome and repetitious. At the close, one feels that the action has taken place not at the height of the Thirty Years War but for the whole length of the Hundred Years War.

That this should be so is the fault neither of the director, Howard Davies, nor of an unusually strong cast, but of the dramatist, Bertholt Brecht. There are some memorable remarks about war, the exploitation of the weak by the strong, and the general beastliness of human nature. There are also—as when Courage's dumb daughter frenziedly beats a drum from a rooftop to warn a sleeping township of an imminent attack, even though she knows that the action will cost her her life—some truly thrilling scenes. But the constant reprocessing of the same basic material soon becomes numbing.

My high hopes of Judi Dench's Courage were, alas, disappointed. Made to look like a midget male impersonator of Bud Flanagan in an overcoat that reaches to the ground, she is altogether too jolly, sweet and nice for the kind of tough, rasping, rapacious woman who can say that she is not going to have her linen torn up to bind the wounds of peasants.

Trevor Peacock is extraordinarily effective in the Cook's jaunty song-and-dance number near the close of the play, and Zoe Wanamaker is intensely moving, if too attractive, as the unmarriageable daughter.

10.3

From these criticisms it will be seen that fashions in dramatic 'reviews' of productions change according to the times but some things remain constant:

(*i*)   the impact of the play or entertainment on the audience is dominant;

(*ii*) selection of details according to changing fashions, comparative plays and traditions or personal whim gives the tone of the article;

(*iii*) the balance of the items discussed is dependent on the main direction of the critic's approach: satirical, humorous, descriptive, discursive, etc.

Questions

1   Write a review for a local newspaper of an amateur production of a play by a serious author put on in a village or school hall.

2   Write a review for a college magazine of an evening's dramatic entertainment put on by students for their fellow students and friends.

3   Imagine that a production in which you have taken part has been unfairly criticised in the national press, because the critic failed to understand both the play and its director's intentions. Write a full letter to the editor of the newspaper pointing out the errors in the review and the main features of the production. (Don't forget to name the play you choose to write about.)

4   Imagine that you were the director of *one* of the productions referred to in the examples of critics' work given in this chapter and that you had called a meeting of the cast to discuss the review. Write the conversation, in dialogue form, that might have taken place at such a meeting.

5   Imagine that two or three dramatic critics of national newspapers have met in the bar following the production of a play you yourself have just seen in a professional theatre. Write the dialogue that might have taken place between them. (Try to choose a play you know well and have actually seen in production, if possible.)

11
Commentary and Analysis

11.1

Advanced Level GCE examinations, and some others, often require candidates to comment on and analyse extracts from plays. The problem with such
exercises is essentially that, because the passages given are extracts and not
whole plays, it is hard to establish quickly the context of the piece.
Introductory comments or synopses are sometimes given or the passages
chosen are the opening scenes of plays in order to alleviate the difficulties of
establishing a context. Nevertheless, those attempting the exercises need some
practice in finding their way quickly and purposefully into the text.

11.2

(*i*)   First, the nature of the passage as *dramatic text* needs to be considered (see
Chapter One, pages 5–13). It is, of course, lacking 'the performance
dimension' and the only evidence of how the words would be interpreted
and represented on the stage must lie on the printed page of the extract
given. Examine critically, therefore, any clues given in stage directions,
words italicised for emphasis, indications of special effects (*e.g.* noises off,
music), or any indication in the words themselves about set, costumes,
properties, silences, breaks in dialogue, physical actions, etc.

(*ii*) Secondly, it is important to recognise any non-verbal indications of how
the extract might appear when the other dimensions that make up a
dramatic production are added to the text.

(*iii*) Dramatic build-up to climaxes or sudden changes of direction (*peripetes*)
or switches in mood must be recognised within the framework of the
essential conflict which makes the extract drama rather than a form of
narrative prose in dialogue form.

(*iv*) The establishment of characters and the relations and interactions
between them is fundamental to the dramatist's purpose. Questions such
as, '*What* characters are they?', '*How* have the characters been
established?', and '*Why* do the characters behave as they do?', are
fundamental to the understanding of an excerpt from a drama.

(*v*)   The opening scenes of plays, sometimes called the **exposition** have *four*
main tasks which they must accomplish quickly, as well as that of seizing
the audience's attention:

(*a*)   to establish a **context** for the play's action (period, locality, social
or intellectual atmosphere, etc.);

(*b*)   to indicate who the **major protagonists and antagonists** are (such as, characters, opposing ideas, symbolised attitudes, etc.);

(*c*)   to **introduce an action** which will develop and involve complications;

(*d*)   indicate the levels of **language** (the 'registers', as they are sometimes called) on which the play will work to establish its meanings.

The sets and other elements of the production must enhance the meanings which can be established from the 'text' of the play.

(*vi*)   **The technical skill of the playwright** in selecting his or her material and bringing together items that should go together to establish meaning, or contrasting items which oppose each other to jolt audiences into awareness, is another area that is vital to producing a sound commentary or analysis of an extract from a play.

11.3

In the June, 1981 Report of the GCE Examiners of the University of London, the criteria used for assessing the work of candidates and the ways in which candidates' responses were graded in Advanced Level English papers were set out very clearly:

CRITERIA	GOOD	AVERAGE	WEAK
Relevance Coverage of points raised by the question.	Full. Will note subtlety, complexities and possible disagreements: will discuss.	More relaxed application. May follow obvious line: uncritically accepts the terms of the question.	May ignore question. Thin, inadequate, in-complete. The updated, prepared answer
Content Use of text.	Full, relevant and incisive with sufficient and apt example.	Moderately full. Still relevant but perhaps implicitly so. Less controlled and applied.	Irrelevance: narration, summary or account. Incompleteness.
Structure The order and logic of the argument.	Progressive, pertinent. focussed, convincing, well instructed.	Argument should be evident, but probably less controlled and purpose-ful. May plod a bit.	Confused, even non-existent.
Style The quality of the expression.	Clear, incisive, correct, even elegant.	Ordinary, comprehen-sible, perhaps rather colourless.	Slack, incorrect, possibly inappropriate.

The criteria are clear: answers should be **relevant, structured**, and **set out clearly, incisively, and correctly**, and should **make use of the text**.

11.4

In exercises on commentary and analysis what are candidates asked to do? Here is a selection of some typical tasks, ranging from literary/dramatic criticism to dramatic interpretation and presentation:

Identify the principal dramatic effects and say how they are achieved; comment on the style and indicate how appropriate you find the passage as the opening of a play.
Show how the ideas in the passages are developed.

Distinguish the theme(s) of the passage, comment upon the style and indicate how far you find it dramatically effective.

Show how theme and character are revealed . . .

Describe the relationships between the characters.

Describe the events in the scene as they might have been observed from the point of view of one of the characters (*e.g.* a trial scene).

What elements of melodrama/comedy/tragedy do you find here?

Show ways of staging this scene *or* design a set for this opening scene . . .

Where do the audience's sympathies lie in this scene?

What is the point of greatest tension/climax in this scene? How is it reached?

Describe the variation of tone and pace in this scene.

11.5

From these questions, therefore, the following areas or approaches seem to be those focused on:

the establishment, development and revelation of ideas and themes;
the point(s) of view of one or more characters and their inter-relationships;
the language of the text;
dramatic effects and devices;
the establishment of conflict, its climax(es) and resolution (*dénouement*);
progression of dramatic action;
responses of the audience;
elements of a genre used (tragedy, comedy, comedy of manners, farce, etc.);
the staging of a scene;
the dramatic effectiveness of opening scenes.

Published syllabuses for examinations in Drama and Theatre Studies sometimes refer very specifically to some of these 'areas'. It is important, however, to realise that many of these 'areas' or 'approaches' cannot stand in isolation from some of the others, but are interdependent on them. For example, how a scene is staged will affect the audience's responses; how the tone and pace are controlled will be factors in establishing climaxes and resolutions of conflict; themes and characters sometimes cannot be separated.

11.6

A close look at the opening scene of a well-known play will reveal how some of these features emerge. Take, for example, the first scene of Shakespeare's *Richard III* (*Arden Shakespeare* text, ed. Antony Hammond, 1981):

Enter RICHARD, *Duke of Gloucester, souls.*

RICH.	Now is the winter of our discontent
	Made glorious summer by this son of York;
	And all the clouds that lour'd upon our House
	In the deep bosom of the ocean buried.

Now are our brows bound with victorious wreaths,   5
Our bruised arms hung up for monuments,
Our stern alarums chang'd to merry meetings,
Our dreadful marches to delightful measures.
Grim-visag'd War hath smooth'd his wrinkled front:
And now, instead of mounting barbed steeds   10
To fright the souls of fearful adversaries,
He capers nimbly in a lady's chamber,
To the lascivious pleasing of a lute.
But I, that am not shap'd for sportive tricks,   15
Nor made to court an amorous looking-glass;
I, that am rudely stamp'd, and want love's majesty
To strut before a wanton ambling nymph:
I, that am curtail'd of this fair proportion,
Cheated of feature by dissembling Nature,
Deform'd, unfinish'd, sent before my time   20
Into this breathing world scarce half made up –
And that so lamely and unfashionable
That dogs bark at me, as I halt by them –
Why, I, in this weak piping time of peace,
Have no delight to pass away the time,   25
Unless to spy my shadow in the sun,
And descant on mine own deformity.
And therefore, since I cannot prove a lover
To entertain these fair well-spoken days,
I am determined to prove a villain,   30
And hate the idle pleasures of these days.
Plots have I laid, inductions dangerous,
By drunken prophecies, libels, and dreams,
To set my brother Clarence and the King
In deadly hate, the one against the other: 35
And if King Edward be as true and just
As I am subtle, false, and treacherous,
This day should Clarence closely be mew'd up
About a prophecy, which says that 'G'
Of Edward's heirs the murderer shall be –   40
Dive, thoughts, down to my soul: here Clarence comes.

Enter CLARENCE *and* BRAKENBURY, *with a guard of* Men.

Brother, good day; what means this armed guard
That waits upon your Grace?

CLA.	His Majesty,
	Tend'ring my person's safety, hath appointed
	This conduct to convey me to the Tower. 45

RICH. Upon what cause?

CLA.   Because my name is George.

RICH. Alack, my lord, that fault is none of yours:
He should for that commit your godfathers.
O, belike his Majesty hath some intent
That you should be new-christen'd in the Tower.   50
But what's the matter, Clarence, may I know?

CLA. Yea, Richard, when I know: for I protest
As yet I do not. But, as I can learn,
He hearkens after prophecies and dreams,
And from the cross-row plucks the letter G;   55
And says a wizard told him that by 'G'
His issue disinherited should be.
And for my name of George begins with G,
It follows in his thought that I am he.
These, as I learn, and such like toys as these,   60
Have mov'd his Highness to commit me now.

RICH. Why, this it is, when men are rul'd by women:
'Tis not the King that sends you to the Tower;
My Lady Grey, his wife, Clarence, 'tis she
That tempers him to this extremity.   65
Was it not she, and that good man of worship,
Anthony Woodeville, her brother there,
That made him send Lord Hastings to the Tower,
From whence this present day he is deliver'd?
We are not safe, Clarence, we are not safe!   70

CLA. By heaven, I think there is no man secure,
But the Queen's kindred, and night-walking heralds
That trudge betwixt the King and Mistress Shore.
Heard you not what an humble suppliant
Lord Hastings was to her, for his delivery?   75

RICH. Humbly complaining to her deity
Got my Lord Chamberlain his liberty.
I'll tell you what: I think it is our way,
If we will keep in favour with the King,
To be her men, and wear her livery.   80
The jealous o'er-worn widow and herself,
Since that our brother dubb'd them gentlewomen,
Are mighty gossips in our monarchy.

BRAK. I beseech your Graces both to pardon me:
His Majesty hath straitly given in charge   85
That no man shall have private conference –
Of what degree soever – with his brother.

RICH. Even so; and please your worship, Brakenbury,
You may partake of any thing we say.
We speak no treason, man: we say the King   90
Is wise and virtuous, and his noble Queen
Well struck in years, fair, and not jealous.
We say that Shore's wife hath a pretty foot,
A cherry lip, a bonny eye, a passing pleasing tongue,

	And that the Queen's kindred are made gentlefolks.	95
	How say you, sir? Can you deny all this?	
BRAK.	With this, my lord, myself have nought to do.	
RICH.	Naught with Mistress Shore? I tell thee, fellow,	
	He that doth naught with her (excepting one)	
	Were best to do it secretly, alone.	100
BRAK.	What one, my lord?	
RICH.	Her husband, knave! Wouldst thou betray me?	
BRAK.	I do beseech your Grace to pardon me, and withal	
	Forbear your conference with the noble Duke.	
CLA.	We know thy charge, Brakenbury, and will obey.	105
RICH.	We are the Queen's abjects, and must obey.	
	Brother, farewell. I will unto the King,	
	And whatso'er you will employ me in –	
	Were it to call King Edward's widow 'sister' –	
	I will perform it to enfranchise you.	110
	Meantime, this deep disgrace in brotherhood	
	Touches me deeper than you can imagine.	

(*Embraces Clarence, weeping.*)

CLA.	I know it pleaseth neither of us well.	
RICH.	Well, your imprisonment shall not be long:	
	I will deliver you, or else lie for you.	115
	Meantime, have patience.	
CLA.	I must, perforce. Farewell.	

(*Exeunt Clarence, Brakenbury and guard*).

RICH.	Go, tread the path that thou shalt ne'er return;	
	Simple, plain Clarence, I do love thee so	
	That I will shortly send thy soul to Heaven –	
	If Heaven will take the present at our hands.	120
	But who comes here? The new-deliver'd Hastings?	

Enter LORD HASTINGS

HAST.	Good time of day unto my gracious lord.	
RICH.	As much unto my good Lord Chamberlain:	
	Well are you welcome to the open air.	125
	How hath your lordship brook'd imprisonment?	
HAST.	With patience, noble lord, as prisoners must;	
	But I shall live, my lord, to give them thanks	
	That were the cause of my imprisonment.	
RICH.	No doubt, no doubt; and so shall Clarence too:	130
	For they that were your enemies are his,	
	And have prevail'd as much on him, as you.	
HAST.	More pity that the eagles should be mew'd,	
	While kites and buzzards prey at liberty.	
RICH.	What news abroad?	
HAST.	No news so bad abroad, as this at home:	135
	The King is sickly, weak and melancholy,	
	And his physicians fear him mightily.	
RICH.	Now by Saint John, that news is bad indeed.	
	O, he hath kept an evil diet long,	

	And over-much consum'd his royal person:	140
	'Tis very grievous to be thought upon.	
	Where is he, in his bed?	
HAST.	He is.	
RICH.	Go you before, and I will follow you. *Exit Hastings.*	
	He cannot live, I hope, and must not die	145

He cannot live, I hope, and must not die   145
Till George be pack'd with post-horse up to Heaven.
I'll in to urge his hatred more to Clarence,
With lies well-steel'd with weighty arguments;
And if I fail not in my deep intent,
Clarence hath not another day to live: 150
Which done, God take King Edward to his mercy,
And leave the world for me to bustle in.
For then I'll marry Warwick's youngest daughter –
What though I kill'd her husband and her father?
The readiest way to make the wench amends   155
Is to become her husband, and her father:
The which will I, not all so much for love
As for another secret close intent,
By marrying her which I must reach unto.
But yet I run before my horse to market: 160
Clarence still breathes, Edward still lives and reigns;
When they are gone, then must I count my gains.   *Exit.*

Some notes on this scene to follow up:

1 *Main themes*
   Deformity, baseness contrasted with innocence and innocence with guile; ambition; usurpation (see the 'Tudor myth' idea of Shakespearean tragedy, pages 140–142).

2 *Characters*
   Richard is pivotal – the rest rotate round him; he knows himself ('subtle, false, treacherous') but others misjudge him; he 'lacks proportion' in more ways than one (an anti-Renaissance hero but a Machiavellian one); determined to be a villain with plots and dangerous inductions; able to dissimulate – compare the openness of his soliloquies with the *apparent* openness, but hidden guile of his dialogue.
   Clarence is contrasted with Richard (honesty/guile) and compared with Hastings (loyalty/deception/false accusation); gullible; angry; unable to judge character.
   Brakenbury is the loyal but oafish servant introduced to keep the plot going but also to humour and indicate a change of mood; he also 'points up' Richard's irony and guile.
   Edward IV is shown as weak and as putty in the hands of Lady Grey (and incidentally of Richard); barely worthy to be the king – he believes in magic and is sick.
   Edward, Lady Grey, and *Mistress Shore* are not introduced in this scene but their presence is felt – 'characterisation in absence', as it were.

3 *The language*

The language suggests **threat/menace** (winter/summer; 'lour'd', 'buried', etc.) reinforced by *imagery* ('grim-visaged', 'wan', becomes the beau and the lover; 'dogs'; 'shadows'; 'eagles'; 'kites'; 'buzzards') and *alliteration* (see how the plosive *b*'s of '*b*osom', *b*rowsbound', '*b*ruised' change to the soft labial '*m*'s' of '*m*onuments', '*m*erry *m*eetings', '*m*arches' and '*m*easures'); the *vocabulary* chosen adds to the feelings of threat: 'wanton', 'curtailed', 'rudely', 'dissembling','deform'd', 'unfinish'd', etc.; *breaks in sentences* (lines 21 and 23) as passion mounts or as Clarence's entry (line 40) demands a change of style; *rhetorical questions* (questions without answers!) are used to reassure Clarence; *irony* deceives ('that news is bad indeed') and reinforces the concept of double-dealing; *repetition* (*e.g.* 'patience' in line 116, 126) in different contexts provides verbal echoes to drive home irony, or prevailing mood; *puns* abound: sun/son, 'or else lie for you', etc., which again depend on double meanings. All these language devices are used to stress the main themes of threat and duplicity.

4 *Dramatic devices*

Soliloquys which always tell the truth (see page 148) are interjected to function as Prologue, comment on actions and characters, and publication of the future plot; they reveal character and provide contrasts between Richard and Clarence, Richard and Edward and between action and contemplation; *moments of tension* (entries of Clarence and Hastings); *commentaries on themes* (*e.g.* Edward's weaknesses barely make him a suitable king); *humour* (Brakenbury is seen as an oaf to be teased); *characters 'off'* are *referred to* so that the audience will recognise them; *the use of minor characters to advance the plot and provide commentary*; *variations in pace and tension*; *contrasts*.

5 *Progression of dramatic action*

The scene progresses from soliloquy to soliloquy, with a third, centrally placed, which allows the revelation of Richard's character and of the plot's future development to be clear to the audience; the Brakenbury incident provides a humorous interlude and lowers tension and sense of threat in order that it can be raised again at the end; a brooding violence which intensifies as the scene progresses, reinforced by images, language, characterisation, the scene is based on *contrasts and parallels* (Richard/ Edward; Clarence/Hastings, etc). The balance between openness and guile is held ironically in suspense, as the audience is clear about Richard's guile because of his openness with them and his duplicity with others.

6 *Dramatic effectiveness*

The scene does 'effectively' the work of the *exposition* (see pages 324–325); it establishes a context and major themes, introduces the major character(s), begins the action of the plot, and demonstrates the levels on which the language will operate throughout the play. Moreover, it has involved the audience (through the soliloquy), promised them future intrigue and suspense, and has at least two points where the focus of their interest and attention changes (the entrances of first Clarence and then Hastings); it is well integrated in theme, plot, action, and language.

11.7

These notes contain some of the points that candidates might have wished to develop, had this scene been set as a passage for commentary and analysis in an examination. They do not contain all that there is to say about the scene and do not remove from candidates the need to *go back in detail to the text*, to find the details they need to support their arguments, commentaries and analyses. They do, however, suggest the need to select ideas and to group them coherently, to give them the necessary focus to write relevantly. It is always of considerable help if they have as much practice as possible in breaking down texts into notes as they learn to read critically and in depth.

11.8

The construction of a set for this scene might be considered now. Laurence Olivier's portrayal of Richard of Gloucester as a twisted, limping hunchback with a leering sidelong glance, and a malevolent curl of the lip has become the norm for interpretations of the character. Any breaks from the tradition immediately invite comparisons and justifications.

The cast of the play is huge with fifty-two speaking parts, three more named but unspeaking parts, and several more not named specifically. Some of the characters are ghosts. No doubt actors doubled up the parts, but even so the costume-designer needs to work hard. The only essential parts of the set are two tents. There is little or no music and no mimed action.

In 1857, the Arden edition of the play points out, Charles Kean's production at the Princess Theatre had a cast of 121 and a funeral procession of monks with torches, priests with a golden cross and fifty-nine banner men. Richard's army had fifty-eight actors in it, all clothed in historically accurate costumes, as was the custom with the mid-nineteenth century's realistic approach.

As ritual is an important part of the play, and in the light of the large cast and the comparatively slight demands for properties or buildings, a symbolic setting might well be appropriate. The language of the play is rich in symbolism and a set which reflects the images of violence, darkness and distortion would enhance the effect and leave the actors room to move in an unencumbered manner. This is a play, however, which seems to demand an interpretation of the setting (with the language and the main tenor of the plot with its central dominating figure) embodying, as a very young Kenneth Tynan put it, 'Blake's conception of active, energetic evil, in all its wicked richness'. It is interesting to speculate how Blake, the poet-artist, would have seen the play visually in its distortion and maniac evil.

For *Questions* see Chapter Twelve.

12
Exercises on Commentary and Analysis

1.

This is the murder scene from the Victorian melodrama, *Maria Marten or The Murder in the Red Barn* (see pages 186, 218). The arch-villain Corder is afraid that Maria will tell the authorities that he has killed their baby and he decides to silence her. He arranges to meet her in the Red Barn from where they can both go to London to be married. Maria, disguised as a boy, goes to their rendezvous.

INSIDE THE RED BARN

CORDER *discovered digging a grave.* (*Villain's music*)

CORDER   All is complete, I await my victim. Will she come? Oh yes, a woman is fool enough to do anything for the man she loves. Hark, 'tis her footstep bounding across the fields! She comes, with hope in her heart, a song on her lips, little does she think that death is so near. (*He steps into a dark corner.*)

Enter MARIA. *The music turns soft and gentle*

MARIA   William not here, where can he be, what ails me? A weight is at my heart as if it told some evil, and this old Barn – how like a vault it looks! Fear steals upon me, I tremble in every limb, I will return to my home at once.

CORDER   (*advancing*).   Stay, Maria!

MARIA   I'm glad you are here, you don't know how frightened I've been.

CORDER   Did any one see you cross the fields?

MARIA   Not a soul, I remembered your instructions.

CORDER   That's good. Now, Maria, do you remember a few days ago threatening to betray me about the child to Constable Ayres? (*Tremolo fiddles.*)

MARIA   A girlish threat made in a heat of temper, because you refused to do justice to one you had wronged so greatly. Do not speak of that now, let us leave this place.

CORDER   Not yet Maria, you don't think my life is to be held at the bidding of a silly girl. *No*, look what I have made here! (*He drags her to the grave. Slow music.*)

MARIA   A grave. Oh William, what do you mean?

CORDER   To kill you, bury your body there. You are a clog upon my actions, a

	chain that keeps me from reaching ambitious height, you are to die.
MARIA	(*kneels*). But not by your hand, the hand that I have clasped in love and confidence. Oh! think, William, how much I have sacrificed for you, think of our little child above, now in heaven, pleads for its mother's life. Oh spare, oh spare me!
CORDER	'Tis useless, my mind's resolved, you die tonight. (*Thunder and lightning.*)
MARIA	Wretch!
	Since neither prayers nor tears will touch your stony heart, Heaven will surely nerve my arm to battle for my life. (*She seizes* CORDER.)
CORDER	Foolish girl, desist!
MARIA	Never with life! (*They struggle, he shoots her, she falls in his arms.*)
MARIA	(*soft music*)
	William, I am dying, your cruel hand has stilled
	The heart that beat in love alone for thee.
	Think not to escape the hand of justice, for
	When least expected it will mark you down;
	At that moment think of Maria's wrongs.
	Death claims me, and with my last breath I die blessing and forgiving thee. (*Dies*).
CORDER	Blessing and forgiveness! and for me, her (*loud music*) murderer! What have I done! Oh Maria, awake, awake, do not look so tenderly Upon me, let indignation lighten from your eyes and blast me! Oh may this crime for ever stand accurst, The last of murders, as it is the worst.

1   Discuss *two* different ways of staging this scene in order to achieve different effects.
2   Describe the methods used by the playwright to build up dramatic tension in this scene.
3   What elements of *melodrama* can you see in this extract?

2.

The following extract is the opening scene of *The Caucasian Chalk Circle*, written in 1944–5, by Bertolt Brecht. Read the account of Brecht's theories and work (pages 265–269) and then study the passage, bearing in mind that this is the beginning of the play.

THE STRUGGLE FOR THE VALLEY

Among the ruins of a destroyed Caucasian village the members of two kolchos villages are sitting in a circle, smoking and drinking wine. They consist mainly of women and old men, but there are also a few soldiers among them. With them is an expert of the Federal Reconstruction Commission from the capital.

A PEASANT WOMAN	(*left, pointing*) In those hills over there we stopped three Nazi tanks. But the apple orchard had already been destroyed.
AN OLD PEASANT	(*right*) Our beautiful dairy farm. All in ruins.

A GIRL TRACTOR DRIVER	(*left*) I set fire to it, Comrade. (*Pause.*)
THE EXPERT	Now listen to the report: the delegates of the goat-breeding kolchos 'Galinsk' have arrived in Nukha. When the Hitler armies were approaching, the kolchos had been ordered by the authorities to move its goat-herds further to the east. The kolchos now considers resettling in this valley. Its delegates have investigated the village and the grounds and found a high degree of destruction. (*The delegates on the right nod.*) The neighbouring fruit-growing kolchos 'Rosa Luxemburg' (*to the left*) moves that the former grazing land of the 'Galinsk' kolchos, a valley with scanty growth of grass, should be used for the replanting of orchards and vineyards. As an expert of the Reconstruction Commission, I request the two kolchos village to decide between themselves whether the 'Galinsk' kolchos shall return here or not.
AN OLD MAN	(*right*) First of all, I want to protest against the restriction of time for discussion. We of the 'Galinsk' kolchos have spent three days and three nights getting here. And now we are allowed a discussion of only half a day.
A WOUNDED SOLDIER	(*left*) Comrade, we no longer have as many villages and no longer as many working hands and no longer as much time.
THE GIRL TRACTOR DRIVER	(*left*) All pleasures have to be rationed. Tobacco is rationed, and wine and discussion, too.
THE OLD MAN	(*right, sighing*) Death to the Fascists! But I will come to the point and explain to you why we want to have our valley back. There are a great many reasons, but I want to begin with one of the simplest. Makinae Abakidze, unpack the goat cheese.
	A peasant woman, right, takes from a basket an enormous cheese wrapped in a cloth. Applause and laughter.
	Help yourselves, comrades. Start in.
AN OLD PEASANT	(*left, suspiciously*) Is this meant to influence us, perhaps?
THE OLD MAN	(*right, amidst laughter*) How could it be meant as an influence, Surab, you valley-thief? Everyone knows that you will take the cheese and the valley, too. (*Laughter.*) All I expect from you is an honest answer: Do you like the cheese?
THE OLD MAN	(*left*) The answer is yes.
THE OLD MAN	(*right*) Oh. (*Bitterly.*) I might have guessed you know nothing about cheese.
THE OLD MAN	(*left*) Why not? When I tell you I like it!
THE OLD MAN	(*right*) Because you can't like it. Because it's not what it was in the old days. And why isn't it? Because our

	goats don't like the new grass as they used to like the old. Cheese is not cheese because grass is not grass, that's it. Mind you put that in your report.
THE OLD MAN	(*left*) But your cheese is excellent.
THE OLD MAN	(*right*) It's not excellent. Barely decent. The new grazing land is no good, whatever the young people may say. I tell you, it's impossible to live there. It doesn't even smell of morning there in the morning.

Several people laugh.

THE EXPERT	Don't mind their laughter. They understand you all the same. Comrades, why does one love one's country? Because the bread tastes better there, the sky is higher, the air smells better, voices sound stronger, the ground is easier to walk on. Isn't that so?
THE OLD MAN	(*right*) The valley has belonged to us for centuries.
THE SOLDIER	(*left*) What does that mean – for centuries? Nothing belongs to anyone for centuries. When you were young you didn't even belong to yourself, but to Prince Kazbeki.
THE OLD MAN	(*right*) According to the law the valley belongs to us.
THE GIRL TRACTOR DRIVER	The laws will have to be re-examined in any case, to see whether they are still valid.
THE OLD MAN	(*right*) That's obvious. You mean to say it makes no difference what kind of tree stands beside the house where one was born? Or what kind of neighbour one has? Doesn't that make any difference? We want to go back just to have you as neighbours in our kolchos, you valley-thieves. Now you can laugh again.
THE OLD MAN	(*left, laughing*) Then why don't you listen to what your 'neighbour', Kato Wachtang, our agriculturist, has to say about the valley?
A PEASANT WOMAN	(*right*) We haven't said anywhere near all we have to say about our valley. Not all the houses are destroyed. At least the foundation wall of the dairy farm is still standing.
THE EXPERT	You can claim State support – both here and there. You know that.
A PEASANT WOMAN	(*right*) Comrade Expert, we're not trading now. I can't take your cap and hand you another, and say: 'This one's better.' The other one might be better, but you prefer yours.
THE GIRL TRACTOR DRIVER	A piece of land is not like a cap. Not in our country, comrade.
THE EXPERT	Don't get angry. It's true that we have to consider a piece of land as a tool with which one produces something useful. But it's also true that we must recognize the love for a particular piece of land. Before we continue the discussion I suggest that you explain to the comrades of the 'Galinsk' kolchos just what you intend to do with the disputed valley.

THE OLD MAN	(*right*) Agreed.
THE OLD MAN	(*left*) Yes, let Kato speak.
THE EXPERT	Comrade Agriculturist!
THE AGRICULTURIST	(*rising. She is in military uniform*) Last winter, Comrades, while we were fighting here in these hills as partisans, we discussed how after the expulsion of the Germans we could increase our orchards to ten times their former size. I have prepared the plan for an irrigation project. With the help of a coffer-dam on our mountain lake, three hundred hectares of unfertile land can be irrigated. Our kolchos could then grow not only more fruit, but wine as well. The project, however, would pay only if the disputed valley of the 'Galinsk' kolchos could also be included. Here are the calculations. (*She hands the expert a briefcase.*)
THE OLD MAN	(*right*) Write into the report that our kolchos plans to start a new stud farm.
THE GIRL TRACTOR DRIVER	Comrades, the project was conceived during the days and nights when we had to take cover in the mountains and often were without ammunition for our few rifles. Even to get a pencil was difficult.

Applause from both sides.

THE OLD MAN	(*right*) Our thanks to the comrades of the 'Rosa Luxemburg' kolchos and to all those who defended our country.

They shake hands and embrace.

THE PEASANT WOMAN	(*left*) Our thoughts were that our soldiers – both your men and our men – should return to a still more fertile homeland.
THE GIRL TRACTOR DRIVER	As the poet Mayakovski said: 'The home of the Soviet people shall also be the home of Reason!'

The delegates on the right (except the old man) have risen and, with the expert, study the agriculturist's plans. Exclamations such as: 'Why is there a fall of 66 feet?' – 'This rock here is to be dynamited!' – 'Actually, all they need is cement and dynamite!' – 'They force the water to come down here, that's clever!'

A VERY YOUNG WORKMAN	(*right, to the old man, right*) They are going to irrigate all the fields between the hills – look at that, Alleko.
THE OLD MAN	(*right*) I am not going to look at it. I knew the project would be good. I won't have a revolver pointed at my chest.
THE SOLDIER	But they are only pointing a pencil at your chest.

Laughter.

THE OLD MAN	(*right. He gets up gloomily and walks over to look at the drawings*) These valley-thieves know only too well that we can't resist machines and projects in this country.

THE PEASANT WOMAN	(*right*) Alleko Bereshvili, you yourself are the worst one at new projects. That is well known.
THE EXPERT	What about my report? May I write that in your kolchos you will support the transfer of your old valley for the project?
THE PEASANT WOMAN	(*right*) I will support it. What about you, Alleko?
THE OLD MAN	(*right, bent over the drawings*) I move that you give us copies of the drawings to take along.
THE PEASANT WOMAN	(*right*) Then we can sit down to eat. Once he has the drawings and is ready to discuss them, the affair is settled. I know him. And it will be the same with the rest of us.

The delegates embrace again amidst laughter.

THE OLD MAN	(*left*) Long live the 'Galinsk' kolchos and good luck to your new stud farm!
THE PEASANT WOMAN	(*left*) Comrades, in honour of the visit of the delegates from the 'Galinsk' kolchos and of the expert we have arranged a play featuring the singer Arkadi Tsheidse, which has some bearing on our problem.

Applause.

The girl tractor driver has gone off to fetch the singer.

THE PEASANT WOMAN	(*right*) Comrades, your play will have to be good. We're going to pay for it with a valley.
THE PEASANT WOMAN	(*left*) Arkadi Tsheidse knows 21,000 verses by heart.
THE OLD MAN	(*left*) We rehearsed the play under his direction. It is very difficult to get him, by the way. You and the Planning Commission should see to it that he comes north more often, comrade.
THE EXPERT	We are more concerned with economy.
THE OLD MAN	(*left, smiling*) You arrange the new distribution of grapevines and tractors. Why not of songs, too?

Enter the singer Arkadi Tsheidse, led by the girl tractor driver. He is a sturdy man of simple manners, accompanied by musicians with their instruments. The artistes are greeted with applause.

THE GIRL TRACTOR DRIVER	This is the comrade expert, Arkadi.

The singer greets those round him.

THE PEASANT WOMAN	(*right*) I am very honoured to make your acquaintance. I've heard about your songs ever since I was at school.
THE SINGER	This time it's a play with songs, and almost the whole kolchos takes part. We have brought along the old masks.
THE OLD MAN	(*right*) Is it going to be one of the old legends?
THE SINGER	A very old one. It is called 'The Chalk Circle' and is derived from the Chinese. But we will recite it in a

changed version. Yura, show the masks. Comrades, we consider it an honour to entertain you after such a difficult debate. We hope you will find that the voice of the old poet also sounds well in the shadow of the Soviet tractors. It may be mistaken to mix different wines, but old and new wisdom mix very well. Now I hope we will all be given something to eat before the recital begins. That usually helps.

VOICES   Of course. – Everyone into the club house.

All go cheerfully to the meal. While they begin to move off, the expert turns to the singer.

THE EXPERT   How long will the story take, Arkadi? I have to get back to Tiflis tonight.

THE SINGER   (*casually*) It is actually two stories. A few hours.

THE EXPERT   (*very confidentially*) Couldn't you make it shorter?

THE SINGER   No.

1   How effective do you consider this scene as the opening to a play?

2   Discuss the way this scene progresses dramatically, paying particular attention to any changes in its direction and to its overall unity.

3   What aspects of this scene would you try to bring out if you were directing it? What advice would you give to your cast in their approach to the characters they are playing? (Look carefully at Brecht's theories on *Verfremdungseffekte*, pages 267–268.)

3.

The following extract is from T. S. Eliot's *Murder in the Cathedral,* a verse-play written in 1935 for the Canterbury Festival in June of that year and subsequently revised. The main action of the play concerns the murder in the Cathedral of the Archbishop, Thomas à Becket, on December 2, 1170, by the Knights of Henry II.

Thomas's Priests have dragged him into the Cathedral in the vain belief that he would be safe there from the murderers coming for him:

(*In the cathedral.* THOMAS *and* PRIESTS.)

PRIESTS   Bar the door. Bar the door.
            The door is barred.
            We are safe. We are safe.
            They dare not break in.
            They cannot break in. They have not the force.
            We are safe. We are safe.

THOMAS   Unbar the doors! throw open the doors!
            I will not have the house of prayer, the church of
                Christ,
            The sanctuary, turned into a fortress.
            The Church shall protect her own, in her own way,
                not
            As oak and stone; stone and oak decay,
            Give no stay, but the Church shall endure.

The church shall be open, even to our enemies. Open
the door!

PRIEST My Lord! these are not men, these come not as men
come, but
Like maddened beasts. They come not like men, who
Respect the sanctuary, who kneel to the Body of Christ,
But like beasts. You would bar the door
Against the lion, the leopard, the wolf or the boar,
Why not more
Against beasts with the souls of damned men, against
men
Who would damn themselves to beasts. My Lord! My
Lord!

THOMAS You think me reckless, desperate and mad.
You argue by results, as this world does,
To settle if an act be good or bad.
You defer to the fact. For every life and every act
Consequence of good and evil can be shown.
And as in time results of many deeds are blended
So good and evil in the end become confounded.
It is not in time that my death shall be known;
It is out of time that my decision is taken
If you call that decision
To which my whole being gives entire consent.
I give my life
To the Law of God above the Law of Man.
Unbar the door! unbar the door!
We are not here to triumph by fighting, by stratagem,
or by resistance,
Not to fight with beasts as men. We have fought the
beast
And have conquered. We have only to conquer
Now, by suffering. This is the easier victory.
Now is the triumph of the Cross, now
Open the door! I command it. OPEN THE DOOR!

(*The door is opened. The* KNIGHTS *enter, slightly tipsy.*)

PRIESTS This way, my Lord! Quick. Up the stair. To the roof.
To the crypt. Quick. Come. Force him.

KNIGHTS Where is Becket, the traitor to the King?
Where is Becket, the meddling priest?
Come down Daniel to the lions' den,
Come down Daniel for the mark of the beast.
Are you washed in the blood of the Lamb?
Are you marked with the mark of the beast?
Come down Daniel to the lions' den,
Come down Daniel and join in the feast.
Where is Becket the Cheapside brat?
Where is Becket the faithless priest?
Come down Daniel to the lions' den,

	Come down Daniel and join in the feast.
THOMAS	It is the just man who
	Like a bold lion, should be without fear.
	I am here.
	No traitor to the King. I am a priest,
	A Christian, saved by the blood of Christ,
	Ready to suffer with my blood.
	This is the sign of the Church always,
	The sign of blood. Blood for blood.
	His blood given to buy my life.
	My blood given to pay for His death,
	My death for His death.
FIRST KNIGHT	Absolve all those you have excommunicated.
SECOND KNIGHT	Resign the powers you have arrogated.
THIRD KNIGHT	Restore to the King the money you appropriated.
FIRST KNIGHT	Renew the obedience you have violated.
THOMAS	For my Lord I am now ready to die,
	That His Church may have peace and liberty.
	Do with me as you will, to your hurt and shame;
	But none of my people, in God's name,
	Whether layman or clerk, shall you touch.
	This I forbid.
KNIGHTS	Traitor! traitor! traitor!
THOMAS	You, Reginald, three times traitor you:
	Traitor to me as my temporal vassal,
	Traitor to me as your spiritual lord,
	Traitor to God in desecrating His Church.
	No faith do I owe to a renegade,
	And what I owe shall now be paid.
THOMAS	Now to Almighty God, to the Blessed Mary ever
	Virgin, to the blessed John the Baptist, the holy apostles
	Peter and Paul, to the blessed martyr Denys, and to all
	the Saints, I commend my cause and that of the
	Church.

(*While the* KNIGHTS *kill him, we hear the* CHORUS)

Clear the air! clean the sky! wash the wind! take stone
    from stone and wash them.
The land is foul, the water is foul, our beasts and our-
    selves defiled with blood.
A rain of blood has blinded my eyes. Where is England?
    where is Kent? where is Canterbury?
O far far far far in the past; and I wander in a land of
    barren boughs: if I break them, they bleed; I
    wander in a land of dry stones: if I touch them
    they bleed.
How how can I ever return, to the soft quiet seasons?
Night stay with us, stop sun, hold season, let the day
    not come, let the spring not come.
Can I look again at the day and its common things, and

> see them all smeared with blood, through a cur-
> tain of falling blood?
> We did not wish anything to happen.
> We understood the private catastrophe,
> The personal loss, the general misery,
> Living and partly living;
> The terror by night that ends in daily action,
> The terror by day that ends in sleep;
> But the talk in the market-place, the hand on the broom,
> The night-time heaping of the ashes,
> The fuel laid on the fire at daybreak,
> These acts marked a limit to our suffering.
> Every horror had its definiton,
> Every sorrow had a kind of end:
> In life there is not time to grieve long.
> But this, this is out of life, this is out of time,
> An instant eternity of evil and wrong.
> We are soiled by a filth that we cannot clean, united to
> supernatural vermin,
> It is not we alone, it is not the house, it is not the city
> that is defiled,
> But the world that is wholly foul.
> Clear the air! clean the sky! wash the wind! take the
> stone from the stone, take the skin from the arm,
> take the muscle from the bone, and wash them.
> Wash the stone, wash the bone, wash the brain,
> wash the soul, wash them wash them!

1 What are the main dramatic features of this scene which you, as director, would try to bring out in a production?
2 Describe how you would try to portray Thomas in this scene *either* if you were playing the part *or* if you were directing another actor.
3 What problems *and/or* advantages does the verse form present (*a*) in the theatre, and (*b*) in a church setting?
4 Comment on the exchanges between Thomas and the other characters and on the commentary by the Chorus, in terms of how they might be directed to have a strong effect on an audience.

4.

The following extract is the opening of Chekhov's play *The Cherry Orchard*, first produced in 1904 (see pages 247–249 for some comments on Chekhov as a dramatist).

> *A room which is still known as the nursery. One of the doors leads to* ANYA's *room. Half-light, shortly before sunrise. It is May already, and the cherry trees are in blossom, but outside in the orchard it is cold, with a morning frost. The windows are closed.*
>
> *Enter* DUNYASHA *with a candle, and* LOPAKHIN *with a book in his hand.*

LOPAKHIN   God be praised, the train's arrived. What time is it?

DUNYASHA	Nearly two o'clock. (*Extinguishes the candle.*) It's light already.
LOPAKHIN	So the train's how late? Two hours, at least. (*Yawns and stretches.*) Fine one I am. Complete fool. Came all the way here to go and meet them at the station, and then just dropped off while I was sitting there. It's a shame. You might have woken me.
DUNYASHA	I thought you'd gone. (*Listens.*) That sounds like them now.
LOPAKHIN	(*listens*) No . . . Luggage to pick up, one thing and another . . .

Pause.

She's lived abroad for five years – I don't know what she'll be like now . . . She's a wonderful woman. Easy, straightforward. I remember, when I was a boy of fifteen or so, my father – he kept a shop then in the village here – dead now, of course – he hit me in the face with his fist, and the blood started to pour out of my nose . . . For some reason we'd come into the yard here together, and he was drunk, he was well away. She brought me in – and I can remember it so well, she was still a girl, a slim young girl – she brought me in and she took me to the washstand in this room, in the nursery. 'Don't cry,' She says. 'Brave little peasant, now. You'll live to dance at your wedding . . .'

Pause.

Brave little peasant . . . it's true, my father was a peasant – and here am I in a white waistcoat and yellow shoes. Like a pig in a pastry-cook's . . . I'm a rich man now, plenty of money, but look twice and I'm a peasant, a real peasant . . . (*Leafs through the book.*) I was reading this book. Couldn't understand a word. Fell asleep over it.

Pause.

DUNYASHA	And the dogs, they haven't slept all night. They can sense that the mistress is coming.
LOPAKHIN	What's the matter with you, Dunyasha?
DUNYASHA	My hands are all of a tremble. I'm going to faint.
LOPAKHIN	Very tender plant, aren't you, Dunyasha? Dress like a lady, do your hair like one, too. Not the way, is it? You want to remember who you are.

Enter YEPIKHODOV *with a bouquet. He is wearing a jacket and highly polished boots that squeak loudly. As he comes in he drops the bouquet.*

YEPIKHODOV	(*picks up the bouquet*). The gardener sent them. He says to put them in the dining-room. (*Gives the bouquet to* DUNYASHA.)
LOPAKHIN	And bring me some kvass.*
DUNYASHA	Right you are. (*Goes out.*)
YEPIKHODOV	Three degrees of frost this morning, and the cherry all in blossom. I can't give our climate my seal of approval. (*Sighs.*) Indeed I can't. It never knows how to lend a helping hand at the right moment. And I mean look at me – I bought myself these boots the day before yesterday, and they squeak so much, I mean it's quite

---

* rye-beer.

	impossible. I mean, put it like this – what should I grease them with?
LOPAKHIN	Leave off, will you? Pester, pester.
YEPIKHODOV	I don't know. Every day some disaster happens to me. Not that I complain. I'm used to it. I even smile.

Enter DUNYASHA. *She gives* LOPAKHIN *his kvass.*

YEPIKHODOV	I'll go, then. (*Stumbles against the table, which falls over.*) There you are . . . (*As if exulting in it.*) You see what I'm up against! I mean, it's simply amazing! (*Goes out.*)
DUNYASHA	To tell you the truth, he's proposed to me.
LOPAKHIN	Ah!
DUNYASHA	I don't know *what* to say . . . He's all right, he doesn't give any trouble, it's just sometimes when he starts to talk – you can't understand a word of it. It's very nice, and he puts a lot of feeling into it, only you can't understand it. I quite like him in a way, even. He's madly in love with me. He's the kind of person who never has any luck. Every day something happens. They tease him in our part of the house – they call him Disasters by the Dozen . . .
LOPAKHIN	(*listens*). I think they're coming.
DUNYASHA	They're coming! What's the matter with me? I've gone all cold.
LOPAKHIN	They are indeed coming. Let's go and meet them. Will she recognize me? Five years we haven't seen each other.
DUNYASHA	(*in agitation*). I'll faint this very minute . . . I will, I'll faint clean away!

Two carriages can be heard coming up to the house. LOPAKHIN *and* DUNYASHA *hurry out.*

The stage is empty. Then there is noise in the adjoining rooms. Across the stage, leaning on his stick, hurries FIRS, *who has gone to the station to meet the mistress. He is wearing ancient livery and a top hat. He is saying something to himself, but not a word of it can be made out. The noise offstage grows louder and louder.*

1 Chekhov called the play 'a comedy'; Stanislavski thought it was 'a tragedy'; Chekhov retorted that in places it was 'even a farce'. What would this opening scene lead you to expect? (Justify your comments and conclusions.)

2 Show how the non-verbal elements in this extract contribute to its dramatic effect.

3 Discuss the characters presented here and bring out their relationship to each other.

4 How effective do you consider this scene as an opening to a play?

5.

This is the opening of Samuel Beckett's *Waiting for Godot*, produced in London in 1955, which 'frankly jettisons everything by which we recognise theatre . . . A play, it asserts and proves, is basically a means of spending two hours in the dark without being bored'. (Kenneth Tynan).

Estragon, sitting on a low mound, is trying to take off his boot. He pulls at it with both hands, panting. He gives up, exhausted, rests, tries again. As before.

Enter Vladimir.

ESTRAGON   (*giving up again*).   Nothing to be done.

VLADIMIR   (*advancing with short, stiff strides, legs wide apart*).   I'm beginning to come round to that opinion. All my life I've tried to put it from me, saying, Vladimir, be reasonable, you haven't yet tried everything. And I resumed the struggle. (*He broods, musing on the struggle. Turning to Estragon.*)   So there you are again.

ESTRAGON   Am I?

VLADIMIR   I'm glad to see you back. I thought you were gone for ever.

ESTRAGON   Me too.

VLADIMIR   Together again at last! We'll have to celebrate this. But how? (*He reflects.*)   Get up till I embrace you.

ESTRAGON   (*irritably*).   Not now, not now.

VLADIMIR   (*hurt, coldly*).   May one enquire where His Highness spent the night?

ESTRAGON   In a ditch.

VLADIMIR   (*admiringly*).   A ditch! Where?

ESTRAGON   (*without gesture*).   Over there.

VLADIMIR   And they didn't beat you?

ESTRAGON   Beat me? Certainly they beat me.

VLADIMIR   The same lot as usual?

ESTRAGON   The same? I don't know.

VLADIMIR   When I think of it . . . all these years . . . but for me . . . where would you be . . . ?   (*Decisively.*)   You'd be nothing more than a little heap of bones at the present minute, no doubt about it.

ESTRAGON   And what of it?

VLADIMIR   (*gloomily*).   It's too much for one man. (*Pause. Cheerfully.*)   On the other hand what's the good of losing heart now, that's what I say. We should have thought of it a million years ago, in the nineties.

ESTRAGON   Ah stop blathering and help me off with this bloody thing.

VLADIMIR   Hand in hand from the top of the Eiffel Tower, among the first. We were presentable in those days. Now it's too late. They wouldn't even let us up. (*Estragon tears at his boot.*)   What are you doing?

ESTRAGON   Taking off my boot. Did that never happen to you?

VLADIMIR   Boots must be taken off every day, I'm tired telling you that. Why don't you listen to me?

ESTRAGON   (*feebly*).   Help me!

VLADIMAR   It hurts?

ESTRAGON   Hurts! He wants to know if it hurts!

VLADIMIR   (*angrily*).   No one ever suffers but you. I don't count. I'd like to hear what you'd say if you had what I have.

ESTRAGON   It hurts?

VLADIMIR   Hurts! He wants to know if it hurts!

ESTRAGON   (*pointing*).   You might button it all the same.

VLADIMIR   (*stooping*).   True. (*He buttons his fly*).   Never neglect the little things of life.

ESTRAGON   What do you expect, you always wait till the last moment.

VLADIMIR   (*musingly*).   The last moment . . . (*He meditates.*)   Hope deferred maketh the something sick, who said that?

ESTRAGON   Why don't you help me?

VLADIMIR   Sometimes I feel it coming all the same. Then I go all queer. (*He takes off his hat, peers inside it, feels about inside it, shakes it, puts it on again.*) How shall I say? Relieved and at the same time . . . (*he searches for the word*) . . . appalled. (*With emphasis.*) AP-PALLED. (*He takes off his hat again, peers inside it.*) Funny. (*He knocks on the crown as though to dislodge a foreign body, peers into it again, puts it on again.*) Nothing to be done. (*Estragon with a supreme effort succeeds in pulling off his boot. He looks inside it, feels about inside it, turns it upside down, shakes it, looks on the ground to see if anything has fallen out, finds nothing, feels inside it again, staring sightlessly before him.*) Well?

ESTRAGON   Nothing.

VLADIMIR   Show.

ESTRAGON   There's nothing to show.

VLADIMIR   Try and put it on again.

ESTRAGON   (*examining his foot.*) I'll air it for a bit.

VLADIMIR   There's man all over for you, blaming on his boots the faults of his feet. (*He takes off his hat again, peers inside it, feels about inside it, knocks on the crown, blows into it, puts it on again.*) This is getting alarming. (*Silence. Vladimir deep in thought, Estragon pulling at his toes.*) One of the thieves was saved. (*Pause.*) It's a reasonable percentage. (*Pause.*) Gogo.

ESTRAGON   What?

VLADIMIR   Suppose we repented.

ESTRAGON   Repented what?

VLADIMIR   Oh . . . (*He reflects.*) We wouldn't have to go into the details.

ESTRAGON   Our being born?

Vladimir breaks into a hearty laugh which he immediately stifles, his hand pressed to his pubis, his face contorted.

VLADIMIR   One daren't even laugh any more.

ESTRAGON   Dreadful privation.

VLADIMIR   Merely smile. (*He smiles suddenly from ear to ear, keeps smiling, ceases as suddenly.*) It's not the same thing. Nothing to be done. (*Pause.*) Gogo.

ESTRAGON   (*irritably*). What is it?

VLADIMIR   Did you ever read the Bible?

ESTRAGON   The Bible . . . (*He reflects.*) I must have taken a look at it.

VLADIMIR   Do you remember the Gospels?

ESTRAGON   I remember the maps of the Holy Land. Coloured they were. Very pretty. The Dead Sea was pale blue. The very look of it made me thirsty. That's where we'll go, I used to say, that's where we'll go for our honeymoon. We'll swim. We'll be happy.

VLADIMIR   You should have been a poet.

ESTRAGON   I was. (*Gesture towards his rags.*) Isn't that obvious.

Silence.

VLADIMIR   Where was I . . . How's your foot?

ESTRAGON   Swelling visibly.

VLADIMIR   Ah yes, the two thieves. Do you remember the story?

ESTRAGON	No.
VLADIMIR	Shall I tell it to you?
ESTRAGON	No.
VLADIMIR	It'll pass the time. (*Pause.*) Two thieves, crucified at the same time as our Saviour. One –
ESTRAGON	Our what?
VLADIMIR	Our Saviour. Two thieves. One is supposed to have been saved and the other . . . (*he searches for the contrary of saved*) . . . damned.
ESTRAGON	Saved from what?
VLADIMIR	Hell.
ESTRAGON	I'm going.

He does not move.

VLADIMIR	And yet . . . (*pause*) . . . how is it – this is not boring you I hope – how is it that of the four Evangelists only one speaks of a thief being saved. The four of them were there – or thereabouts – and only one speaks of a thief being saved. (*Pause.*) Come on, Gogo, return the ball, can't you , once in a way?
ESTRAGON	(*with exaggerated enthusiasm*). I find this really most extraordinarily interesting.
VLADIMIR	One out of four. Of the other three two don't mention any thieves at all and the third says that both of them abused him.
ESTRAGON	Who?
VLADIMIR	What?
ESTRAGON	What's all this about? Abused who?
VLADIMIR	The Saviour.
ESTRAGON	Why?
VLADIMIR	Because he wouldn't save them.
ESTRAGON	From hell?
VLADIMIR	Imbecile! From death.
ESTRAGON	I thought you said hell.
VLADIMIR	From death, from death.
ESTRAGON	Well what of it?
VLADIMIR	Then the two of them must have been damned.
ESTRAGON	And why not?
VLADIMIR	But one of the four says that one of the two was saved.
ESTRAGON	Well? They don't agree, and that's all there is to it.
VLADIMIR	But all four were there. And only one speaks of a thief being saved. Why believe him rather than the others?
ESTRAGON	Who believes him?
VLADIMIR	Everybody. It's the only version they know.
ESTRACON	People are bloody ignorant apes.

He rises painfully, goes limping to extreme left, halts, gazes into distance off with his hand screening his eyes, turns, goes to extreme right, gazes into distance. Vladimir watches him, then goes and picks up the boot peers into it, drops it hastily.

VLADIMIR	Pah!

He spits. Estragon moves to centre, halts with his back to auditorium.

ESTRAGON	Charming spot. (*He turns, advances to front, halts facing auditorium.*) Inspiring prospects. (*He turns to Vladimir.*) Let's go.
VLADIMIR	We can't.
ESTRAGON	Why not?
VLADIMIR	We're waiting for Godot.

1 Describe the relationship between the two characters as it emerges from this scene.
2 Show how the humour in this scene might emerge in a production.
3 Comment on (*i*) the language and (*ii*) the non-verbal effects in this scene.
4 Show how you would control the pace of this scene if you were directing it. What elements in the scene would you try to bring out for your audience?

6.

This is the closing scene of *The Spanish Tragedy*, written by Thomas Kyd and acted about 1589. It is a tragedy in the Senecan tradition (see pages 68–69).

Hieronimo, Marshal of Spain, has discovered that his son, Horatio, has been murdered by Lorenzo, the son of the Duke of Castile, and Balthazar, the son of the Vice-roy of Portugal, for having fallen in love with Bel-imperia, Lorenzo's sister, for political and personal reasons. Hieronimo and Bel-imperia put on a play (*cf. Hamlet*) to enact their revenge; Lorenzo and Balthazar are killed and Bel-imperia commits suicide. Hieronimo tries to hang himself but is prevented from doing so by the soldiers of the King of Spain, the brother of the Portuguese Vice-roy.

In this extract the King of Spain, the Vice-roy of Portugal, and the Duke of Castile have just prevented Hieronimo from committing suicide:

KING	O hearken, Viceroy! Hold, Hieronimo!
	Brother, my nephew and thy son are slain!
VIC.	We are betray'd; my Balthazar is slain!
	Break ope the doors; run, save Hieronimo.

(*They break in and hold* Hieronimo.)

	Hieronimo,
	Do but inform the king of these events;
	Upon mine honour, thou shalt have no harm.
HIER.	Viceroy, I will not trust thee with my life,
	Which I this day have offered to my son.
	Accursed wretch,
	Why stayest thou him that was resolv'd to die?
KING	Speak, traitor! damned, bloody murderer, speak!
	For now I have thee, I will make thee speak.
	Why hast thou done this undeserving deed?
VIC.	Why hast thou murdered my Balthazar?
CAST.	Why hast thou butchered both my children thus?
HIER.	O, good words!
	As dear to me was my Horatio,
	As yours, or yours, or yours, my lord, to you.

My guiltless son was by Lorenzo slain,
And by Lorenzo and that Balthazar
Am I at last revenged thoroughly,
Upon whose souls may heavens be yet avenged
With greater far than these afflictions.

CAST. But who were thy confederates in this?

VIC. That was thy daughter Bel-imperia;
For by her hand my Balthazar was slain:
I saw her stab him.

KING Why speakest thou not?

HIER. What lesser liberty can kings afford
Than harmless silence? then afford it me.
Sufficeth, I may not, nor I will not tell thee.

KING Fetch forth the tortures: traitor as thou art,
I'll make thee tell.

HIER. Indeed,
Thou mayest torment me, as his wretched son
Hath done in murd'ring my Horatio:
But never shalt thou force me to reveal
The thing which I have vow'd inviolate.
And therefore, in despite of all thy threats,
Pleas'd with their deaths, and eas'd with their revenge,
First take my tongue, and afterwards my heart.

(*He bites out his tongue.*)

KING O monstrous resolution of a wretch!
See, Viceroy, he hath bitten forth his tongue,
Rather than to reveal what we requir'd.

CAST. Yet can he write.

KING And if in this he satisfy us not,
We will devise th' extremest kind of death
That ever was invented for a wretch.

(*Then he makes signs for a knife to mend his pen.*)

CAST. O, he would have a knife to mend his pen.

VIC. Here, and advise thee that thou write the troth.

KING Look to my brother! save Hieronimo!

(*He with a knife stabs the Duke and himself.*)

What age hath ever heard such monstrous deeds?
My brother, and the whole succeeding hope
That Spain expected after my decease! –
Go, bear his body hence, that we may mourn
The loss of our beloved brother's death;
That he may be entomb'd, whate'er befall;
I am the next, the nearest, last of all.

VIC. And thou, Don Pedro, * do the like for us:

* The Vice-roy's brother.

> Take up our hapless son, untimely slain:
> Set me with him, and he with woeful me,
> Upon the main-mast of a ship unmann'd,
> And let the wind and tide haul me along
> To Scylla's barking and untamed gulf,
> Or to the loathsome pool of Acheron,
> To weep my want for my sweet Balthazar:
> Spain hath no refuge for a Portingal.
> *The trumpets sound a dead march; the* King of Spain *mourning after his brother's body, and the* King of Portingal *bearing the body of his son.*

1 The danger in presenting to a modern audience the last scene of a Revenge play (see above, pages 133–137, 193–194) is that the horror can, paradoxically, cause laughter in the theatre. How would you, as a director, avoid such a reaction in staging this scene?

2 Examine the relationships that emerge from the dialogue that exist between the King, the Vice-roy and the Duke in this scene.

3 Describe and comment on the use of blank-verse and other features of language in this extract.

7.

The following extract is taken from Christopher Marlowe's *The Tragical History of Doctor Faustus* (*c.* 1588).

Dr Faustus has made a contract with Lucifer to sell his soul for twenty-four years of life when, with the help of Mephistophilis, Lucifer's servant, he can have whatever he wishes. The play is a form of Morality play where different forces contend for Dr Faustus's soul. Here Dr Faustus conjures up the return of Helen of Troy by the black art of Mephistophilis:

Enter FAUSTUS *with two or three* SCHOLARS, *and* MEPHISTOPHILIS.

FIRST SCHOL. Master Doctor Faustus, since our conference about fair ladies, which was the beautifulest in all the world, we have determined with ourselves that Helen of Greece was the admirablest lady that ever lived: therefore, Master Doctor, if you will do us that favour, as to let us see that peerless dame of Greece, whom all the world admires for majesty, we should think ourselves much beholding unto you.

FAUST. Gentlemen,
For that I know your friendship is unfeign'd,
And Faustus' custom is not to deny
The just requests of those that wish him well,
You shall behold that peerless dame of Greece,
No otherways for pomp and majesty
Than when Sir Paris cross'd the seas with her,
And 'brought the spoils to rich Dardania.
Be silent, then, for danger is in words.

(*Music sounds, and Helen passeth over the stage.*)

SEC. SCHOL. Too simple is my wit to tell her praise,
Whom all the world admires for majesty.

THIRD SCHOL.	No marvel though the angry Greeks pursu'd
	With ten years' war the rape of such a queen,
	Whose heavenly beauty passeth all compare.
FIRST SCHOL.	Since we have seen the pride of Nature's works,
	And only paragon of excellence,
	Let us depart; and for this glorious deed
	Happy and blest be Faustus evermore!
FAUST.	Gentlemen, farewell: the same I wish to you.

[Exeunt Scholars.

Enter an Old Man.

OLD MAN.	Ah, Doctor Faustus, that I might prevail
	To guide thy steps unto the way of life,
	By which sweet path thou mayst attain the goal
	That shall conduct thee to celestial rest!
	Break heart, drop blood, and mingle it with tears,
	Tears falling from repentant heaviness
	Of thy most vile and loathsome filthiness,
	The stench whereof corrupts the inward soul
	With such flagitious crimes of heinous sin
	As no commiseration may expel,
	But mercy, Faustus, of thy Saviour sweet,
	Whose blood alone must wash away thy guilt.
FAUST.	Where art thou, Faustus? wretch, what hast thou done?
	Damn'd art thou, Faustus, damn'd; despair and die!
	Hell calls for right, and with a roaring voice
	Says, "Faustus, come; thine hour is almost come;"
	And Faustus now will come to do thee right.

[Mephistophilis gives him a dagger.

OLD MAN.	Ah, stay, good Faustus, stay thy desperate steps!
	I see an angel hovers o'er thy head,
	And, with a vial full of precious grace,
	Offers to pour the same into thy soul:
	Then call for mercy, and avoid despair.
FAUST.	Ah, my sweet friend, I feel
	Thy words to comfort my distressed soul!
	Leave me a while to ponder on my sins.
OLD MAN.	I go, sweet Faustus; but with heavy cheer,
	Fearing the ruin of thy hopeless soul.

[Exit.

FAUST.	Accursed Faustus, where is mercy now?
	I do repent; and yet I do despair:
	Hell strives with grace for conquest in my breast:
	What shall I do to shun the snares of death?
MEPH.	Thou traitor, Faustus, I arrest thy soul
	For disobedience to my sovereign lord:
	Revolt, or I'll in piece-meal tear thy flesh.
FAUST.	Sweet Mephistophilis, entreat thy lord
	To pardon my unjust presumption,
	And with my blood again I will confirm

	My former vow I made to Lucifer.
MEPH.	Do it, then, quickly, with unfeigned heart,
	Lest greater danger do attend thy drift.
FAUST.	Torment, sweet friend, that base and crooked age,
	That durst dissuade me from thy Lucifer,
	With greatest torments that our hell affords.
MEPH.	His faith is great; I cannot touch his soul;
	But what I may afflict his body with
	I will attempt, which is but little worth.
FAUST.	One thing, good servant, let me crave of thee,
	To glut the longing of my heart's desire,—
	That I might have unto my paramour
	That heavenly Helen which I saw of late,
	Whose sweet embracings may extinguish clean
	Those thoughts that do dissuade me from my vow,
	And keep mine oath I made to Lucifer.
MEPH.	Faustus, this, or what else thou shalt desire,
	Shall be perform'd in twinkling of an eye.

Re-enter HELEN.

FAUST.	Was this the face that launch'd a thousand ships,
	And burnt the topless towers of Ilium?—
	Sweet Helen, make me immortal with a kiss.—

[*Kisses her.*

Her lips suck forth my soul: see, where it flies!—
Come, Helen, come, give me my soul again.
Here will I dwell, for heaven is in these lips,
And all is dross that is not Helena.
I will be Paris, and for love of thee,
Instead of Troy, shall Wertenberg be sack'd;
And I will combat with weak Menelaus,
And wear thy colours on my plumed crest;
Yes, I will wound Achilles in the heel,
And then return to Helen for a kiss.
O, thou art fairer than the evening air
Clad in the beauty of a thousand stars;
Brighter art thou than flaming Jupiter
When he appear'd to hapless Semele;
More lovely than the monarch of the sky
In wanton Arethusa's azur'd arms;
And none but thou shalt be my paramour!

[*Exeunt.*

1. Describe and comment on the dramatic development in this passage with particular reference to Faustus's character and the language of the extract.
2. Show how Marlowe reveals the dramatic conflict within Dr. Faustus here.
3. Design a set for this scene and show how you would harmonise its dramatic elements with the set you plan.
4. Describe the main features of the poetry in this extract and comment on their effectiveness as dramatic verse.

8.

The following is the opening of Bernard Shaw's *Androcles and the Lion* (1915). Later the lion of this scene confronts Androcles, the Christian, who is about to be martyred for his faith in Rome's Coliseum; out of gratitude for Androcles's help in the scene below, the lion refuses to attack him and the Roman emperor has to re-think his own position:

PROLOGUE

Overture: forest sounds, roaring of lions, Christian hymn faintly.

A jungle path. A lion's roar, a melancholy suffering roar, comes from the jungle. It is repeated nearer. The lion limps from the jungle on three legs, holding up his right forepaw, in which a huge thorn sticks. He sits down and contemplates it. He licks it. He shakes it. He tries to extract it by scraping it along the ground, and hurts himself worse. He roars piteously. He licks it again. Tears drop from his eyes. He limps painfully off the path and lies down under the trees, exhausted with pain. Heaving a long sigh, like wind in a trombone, he goes to sleep.

Androcles and his wife Megaera come along the path. He is a small, thin, ridiculous little man who might be any age from thirty to fifty-five. He has sandy hair, watery compassionate blue eyes, sensitive nostrils, and a very presentable forehead: but his good points go no further: his arms and legs and back, though wiry of their kind, look shrivelled and starved. He carries a big bundle, is very poorly clad, and seems tired and hungry.

His wife is a rather handsome pampered slattern, well fed and in the prime of life. She has nothing to carry, and has a stout stick to help her along.

MEGAERA	[*suddenly throwing down her stick*] I wont go another step.
ANDROCLES	[*pleading wearily*] Oh, not again, dear. Whats the good of stopping every two miles and saying you wont go another step? We must get on to the next village before night. There are wild beasts in this wood: lions, they say.
MEGAERA.	I dont believe a word of it. You are always threatening me with wild beasts to make me walk the very soul out of my body when I can hardly drag one foot before another. We havnt seen a single lion yet.
ANDROCLES.	Well, dear, do you want to see one?
MEGAERA.	[*tearing the bundle from his back*] You cruel brute, you dont care how tired I am, or what becomes of me [*she throws the bundle on the ground*]: always thinking of yourself. Self! self! self! always yourself! [*She sits down on the bundle*].
ANDROCLES.	[*sitting down sadly on the ground with his elbows on his knees and his head in his hands*] We all have to think of ourselves occasionally, dear.
MEGAERA.	A man ought to think of his wife sometimes.
ANDROCLES.	He cant always help it, dear. You make me think of you a good deal. Not that I blame you.
MEGAERA.	Blame me! I should think not indeed. Is it my fault that I'm married to you?
ANDROCLES.	No, dear: that is my fault.
MEGAERA.	Thats a nice thing to say to me. Arnt you happy with me?
ANDROCLES.	I dont complain, my love.
MEGAERA.	You ought to be ashamed of yourself.
ANDROCLES.	I am, my dear.
MEGAERA.	Youre not: you glory in it.
ANDROCLES.	what, darling?

MEGAERA. In everything. In making me a slave, and making yourself a laughing-stock. It's not fair. You get me the name of being a shrew with your meek ways, always talking as if butter wouldnt melt in your mouth. And just because I look a big strong woman, and because I'm goodhearted and a bit hasty, and because youre always driving me to do things I'm sorry for afterwards, people say "Poor man: what a life his wife leads him!" Oh, if they only knew! And you think I dont know. But I do, I do, [*screaming*] I do.

ANDROCLES. Yes, my dear: I know you do.

MEGAERA. Then why dont you treat me properly and be a good husband to me?

ANDROCLES. What can I do, my dear?

MEGAERA. What can you do! You can return to your duty, and come back to your home and your friends, and sacrifice to the gods as all respectable people do, instead of having us hunted out of house and home for being dirty disreputable blaspheming atheists.

ANDROCLES. I'm not an atheist, dear: I am a Christian.

MEGAERA. Well, isnt that the same thing, only ten times worse? Everybody knows that the Christians are the very lowest of the low.

ANDROCLES. Just like us, dear.

MEGAERA. Speak for yourself. Dont you dare to compare me to common people. My father owned his own public-house; and sorrowful was the day for me when you first came drinking in our bar.

ANDROCLES. I confess I was addicted to it, dear. But I gave it up when I became a Christian.

MEGAERA. Youd much better have remained a drunkard. I can forgive a man being addicted to drink: it's only natural; and I dont deny I like a drop myself sometimes. What I cant stand is your being addicted to Christianity. And whats worse again, your being addicted to animals. How is any woman to keep her house clean when you bring in every stray cat and lost cur and lame duck in the whole countryside? You took the bread out of my mouth to feed them: you know you did: dont attempt to deny it.

ANDROCLES. Only when they were hungry and you were getting too stout, dearie.

MEGAERA. Yes: insult me, do. [*Rising*] Oh! I wont bear it another moment. You used to sit and talk to those dumb brute beasts for hours, when you hadnt a word for me.

ANDROCLES. They never answered back, darling. [*He rises and again shoulders the bundle*].

MEGAERA. Well, if youre fonder of animals than of your own wife, you can live with them here in the jungle. Ive had enough of them and enough of you. I'm going back. I'm going home.

ANDROCLES. [*barring the way back*] No, dearie: dont take on like that. We cant go back. Weve sold everything: we should starve; and I should be sent to Rome and thrown to the lions—

MEGAERA. Serve you right! I wish the lions joy of you. [*Screaming*] Are you going to get out of my way and let me go home?

ANDROCLES. No, dear—

MEGAERA. Then I'll make my way through the forest; and when I'm eaten by the wild beasts youll know what a wife youve lost. [*She dashes into the jungle and nearly falls over the sleeping lion*]. Oh! Oh! Andy! Andy! [*She totters back and collapses into the arms of Androcles, who, crushed by her weight, falls on his bundle*].

ANDROCLES. [*extracting himself from beneath her and slapping her hands in great anxiety*] What is it, my precious, my pet? Whats the matter? [*He raises her head. Speechless with terror, she points in the direction of the sleeping lion. He steals cautiously towards the spot indicated by Megaera. She rises with an effort and totters after him*].

MEGAERA. No, Andy: youll be killed. Come back.

The lion utters a long snoring sigh. Androcles sees the lion, and recoils fainting into the arms of Megaera, who falls back on the bundle. They roll apart and lie staring in terror at one another. The lion is heard groaning heavily in the jungle.

ANDROCLES. [*whispering*] Did you see? A lion.

MEGAERA. [*despairing*] The gods have sent him to punish us because youre a Christian. Take me away, Andy. Save me.

ANDROCLES. [*rising*] Meggy: theres one chance for you. Itll take him pretty nigh twenty minutes to eat me (I'm rather stringy and tough) and you can escape in less time than that.

MEGAERA. Oh, dont talk about eating. [*The lion rises with a great groan and limps towards them*]. Oh! [*She faints*].

ANDROCLES. [*quaking, but keeping between the lion and Megaera*] Dont you come near my wife, do you hear? [*The lion groans. Androcles can hardly stand for trembling*]. Meggy: run. Run for your life. If I take my eye off him, it's all up. [*The lion holds up his wounded paw and flaps it piteously before Androcles*]. Oh, he's lame, poor old chap! He's got a thorn in his paw. A frightfully big thorn. [*Full of sympathy*] Oh, poor old man! Did um get an awful thorn into um's tootsums wootsums? Has it made um too sick to eat a nice little Christian man for um's breakfast? Oh, a nice little Christian man will get um's thorn out for um; and then um shall eat the nice Christian man and the nice Christian man's nice big tender wifey pifey. [*The lion responds by moans of self-pity*]. Yes, yes, yes, yes, yes. Now, now [*taking the paw in his hand*], um is not to bite and not to scratch, not even if it hurts a very very little. Now make velvet paws. Thats right. [*He pulls gingerly at the thorn. The lion, with an angry yell of pain, jerks back his paw so abruptly that Androcles is thrown on his back*]. Steadeee! Oh, did the nasty cruel little Christian man hurt the sore paw? [*The lion moans assentingly but apologetically*]. Well, one more little pull and it will be all over. Just one little, little, leetle pull; and then um will live happily ever after. [*He gives the thorn another pull. The lion roars and snaps his jaws with a terrifying clash*]. Oh, mustnt frighten um's good kind doctor, um's affectionate nursey. That didnt hurt at all: not a bit. Just one more. Just to shew how the brave big lion can bear pain, not like the little crybaby Christian man. Oopsh! [*The thorn comes out. The lion yells with pain, and shakes his paw wildly*]. Thats it! [*Holding up the thorn*]. Now it's out. Now lick um's paw to take away the nasty inflammation. See? [*He licks his own hand. The lion nods intelligently and licks his paw industriously*]. Clever little liony-piony! Understands um's dear old friend Andy Wandy. [*The lion licks his face*]. Yes, kissums Andy Wandy. [*The lion wagging his tail violently, rises on his hind legs, and embraces Androcles, who makes a wry face and cries*]

Velvet paws! Velvet paws! [*The lion draws in his claws*]. Thats right. [*He embraces the lion, who finally takes the end of his tail in one paw, places that tight round Androcles' waist, resting it on his hip. Androcles takes the other paw in his hand, stretches out his arm, and the two waltz rapturously round and round and finally away through the jungle*].

MEGAERA. [*who has revived during the waltz*] Oh, you coward, you havnt danced with me for years: and now you go off dancing with a great brute beast that you havnt known for ten minutes and that wants to eat your own wife. Coward. Coward! Coward! [*She rushes off after them into the jungle*].

1. Shaw was very careful to give full stage-directions to his plays. If you were directing a production of this scene show how you would use (or depart from) them.
2. What advice, as a director, would you give to the members of the case playing Androcles and Magaera to bring out the humour in this scene?
3. Imagine that you are Megaera, writing up the day's events in your diary. Write an account of what happens in this scene, expressing your thoughts and feelings as you do so, as your diary entry.
4. What do you consider are the main dramatic elements in this scene? How would you bring them out in a production you were directing?

9.

Compare and contrast the following two passages as openings to plays. The first is from Pirandello's *Six Characters in Search of an Author* (first produced in 1921) and the second from Dylan Thomas's *Under Milk Wood* (written just before the poet's death in 1953).

Passage One

When the audience enters, the curtain is already up and the stage is just as it would be during the day. There is no set; it is empty, in almost total darkness. This is so that from the beginning the audience will have the feeling of being present, not at a performance of a properly rehearsed play, but at a performance of a play that happens spontaneously. Two small sets of steps, one on the right and one on the left, lead up to the stage from the auditorium. On the stage, the top is off the PROMPTER'S *box and is lying next to it. Downstage, there is a small table and a chair with arms for the* PRODUCER: *it is turned with its back to the audience.*

Also downstage there are two small tables, one a little bigger than the other, and several chairs, ready for the rehearsal if needed. There are more chairs scattered on both left and right for the ACTORS: *to one side at the back and nearly hidden is a piano.*

When the houselights go down the STAGE HAND *comes on through the back door. He is in blue overalls and carries a tool bag. He brings some pieces of wood on, comes to the front, kneels down and starts to nail them together.*

The STAGE MANAGER *rushes on from the wings.*

STAGE MANAGER Hey! What are you doing?
STAGE HAND What do you think I'm doing? I'm banging nails in.
STAGE MANAGER Now? (*He looks at his watch.*) It's half-past ten already. The Producer will be here in a moment to rehearse.
STAGE HAND I've got to do my work some time, you know.

STAGE MANAGER	Right – but not now.
STAGE HAND	When?
STAGE MANAGER	When the rehearsal's finished. Come on, get all this out of the way and let me set for the second act of '*The Game As He Played It*'.

The STAGE HAND *picks up his tools and wood and goes off, grumbling and muttering. The* ACTORS *of the company come in through the door, men and women, first one then another, then two together and so on: there will be nine or ten, enough for the parts for the rehearsal of a play by Pirandello,* 'The Rules of the Game', *today's rehearsal. They come in, say their 'Good-mornings' to the* STAGE MANAGER *and each other. Some go off to the dressing-rooms; others, among them the* PROMPTER *with the text rolled up under his arm, scatter about the stage waiting for the* PRODUCER *to start the rehearsal. Meanwhile, sitting or standing in groups, they chat together; some smoke, one complains about his part, another one loudly reads something from* 'The Stage'. *It would be as well if the* ACTORS *and* ACTRESSES *were dressed in colourful clothes, and this first scene should be improvised naturally and vivaciously. After a while somebody might sit down at the piano and play a song; the younger* ACTORS *and* ACTRESSES *start dancing.*

STAGE MANAGER	(*clapping his hands to call their attention*). Come on everybody! Quiet please. The Producer's here.

The piano and the dancing both stop. The ACTORS *turn to look out into the theatre and through the door at the back comes the* PRODUCER; *he walks down the gangway between the seats and, calling 'Good-morning' to the* ACTORS, *climbs up one of the sets of stairs onto the stage. The* SECRETARY *gives him the post, a few magazines, a script. The* ACTORS *move to one side of the stage.*

PRODUCER	Any letters?
SECRETARY	No. That's all the post there is. (*Giving him the script.*)
PRODUCER	Put it in the office. (*Then looking round and turning to the* STAGE MANAGER.) I can't see a thing here. Let's have some lights please.
STAGE MANAGER	Right. (*Calling.*) Workers please!

In a few seconds the side of the stage where the ACTORS *are standing is brilliantly lit with white light. The* PROMPTER *has gone into his box and spread out his script.*

PRODUCER	Good. (*Clapping hands.*) Well then, let's get started. Anybody missing?
STAGE MANAGER	(*heavily ironic*). Our leading lady.
PRODUCER	Not again! (*Looking at his watch.*) We're ten minutes late already. Send her a note to come and see me. It might teach her to be on time for rehearsals. (*Almost before he has finished, the* LEADING ACTRESS'S *voice is heard from the auditorium.*)
LEADING ACTRESS	Morning everybody. Sorry I'm late. (*She is very expensively dressed and is carrying a lap-dog. She comes down the aisle and goes up on to the stage.*)

PRODUCER	You're determined to keep us waiting, aren't you?
LEADING ACTRESS	I'm sorry. I just couldn't find a taxi anywhere. But you haven't started yet and I'm not on at the opening anyhow. (*Calling the* STAGE MANAGER, *she gives him the dog.*) Shut him in my dressing-room for me will you?
PRODUCER	And she's even brought her lap-dog with her! As if we haven't enough lap-dogs here already. (*Clapping his hands and turning to the* PROMPTER.) Right then, the second act of '*The Game As He Played It*'. (*Sits in his arm-chair.*) Quiet please! Who's on?

The ACTORS *clear from the front of the stage and sit to one side, except for three who are ready to start the scene and the* LEADING ACTRESS. *She has ignored the* PRODUCER *and is sitting at one of the little tables.*

PRODUCER	Are you in this scene, then?
LEADING ACTRESS	No – I've just told you.
PRODUCER	(*annoyed*). Then get off, for God's sake. (*The* LEADING ACTRESS *goes and sits with the others. To the* PROMPTER.) Come on then, let's get going.
PROMPTER	(*reading his script*). 'The house of Leone Gala. A peculiar room, both dining-room and study.' . . . .

Passage Two

(*Silence*)
FIRST VOICE (*Very softly*)

To begin at the beginning:

It is spring, moonless night in the small town, starless and bible-black, the cobblestreets silent and the hunched, courters'-and-rabbits' wood limping invisible down to the sloeblack, slow, black, crowblack, fishingboat-bobbing sea. The houses are blind as moles (though moles see fine to-night in the snouting, velvet dingles) or blind as Captain Cat there in the muffled middle by the pump and the town clock, the shops in mourning, the Welfare Hall in widows' weeds. And all the people of the lulled and dumbfound town are sleeping now.

Hush, the babies are sleeping, the farmers, the fishers, the tradesmen and pensioners, cobbler, schoolteacher, postman and publican, the undertaker and the fancy woman, drunkard, dressmaker, preacher, policeman, the webfoot cockle-women and the tidy wives. Young girls lie bedded soft or glide in their dreams, with rings and trousseaux, bridesmaided by glowworms down the aisles of the organplaying wood. The boys are dreaming wicked or of the bucking ranches of the night and the jollyrodgered sea. And the anthracite statues of the horses sleep in the fields, and the cows in the byres, and the dogs in the wetnosed yards; and the cats nap in the slant corners or lope sly, streaking and needling, on the one cloud of the roofs.

You can hear the dew falling, and the hushed town breathing. Only *your eyes* are unclosed to see the black and folded town fast, and slow, asleep. And you alone can hear the invisible starfall, the darkest-before-dawn minutely dewgrazed stir of the black, dab-filled sea where the *Arethusa*, the *Curlew* and the *Skylark*, *Zanzibar*, *Rhiannon*, the *Rover*, the *Cormorant*, and the *Star of Wales* tilt and ride.

Listen. It is night moving in the streets, the processional salt slow musical wind in Coronation Street and Cockle Row, it is the grass growing on Llaregyb Hill, dewfall, starfall, the sleep of birds in Milk Wood.

Listen. It is night in the chill, squat chapel, hymning in bonnet and brooch and bombazine black, butterfly choker and bootlace bow, coughing like nannygoats, sucking mintoes, fortywinking hallelujah; night in the four-ale, quiet as a domino; in Ocky Milkman's lofts like a mouse with gloves; in Dai Bread's bakery flying like black flour. It is to-night in Donkey Street, trotting silent, with seaweed on its hooves, along the cockled cobbles, past curtained fernpot, text and trinket, harmonium, holy dresser, watercolours done by hand, china dog and rosy tin teacaddy. It is night neddying among the snuggeries of babies.

Look. It is night, dumbly, royally winding through the Coronation cherry trees; going through the graveyard of Bethesda with winds gloved and folded, and dew doffed; tumbling by the Sailors Arms.

Time passes. Listen. Time passes.

Come closer now.

Only you can hear the houses sleeping in the streets in the slow deep salt and silent black, bandaged night. Only you can see, in the blinded bedrooms, the coms. and petticoats over the chairs, the jugs and basins, the glasses of teeth, Thou Shalt Not on the wall, and the yellowing dickybird-watching pictures of the dead. Only you can hear and see, behind the eyes of the sleepers, the movements and countries and mazes and colours and dismays and rainbows and tunes and wishes and flight and fall and despairs and big seas of their dreams.

From where you are, you can hear their dreams.

10.

The following extract is the final part of the closing scene of R. C. Sherriff's play about the 1914–18 World War, *Journey's End* (1928). [In the first production a very young Laurence Olivier played the part of Stanhope.]

The scene depicts a dug-out in the British front line in France. Stanhope is the commanding officer and Raleigh is a young lieutenant, an ex-public-schoolboy, who has just recently joined the forward group. An enemy attack is under way:

> *A dark figure stands out against the pale sky; comes hurrying down the steps* – a PRIVATE SOLDIER, *out of breath and excited.*

STANHOPE   Yes?

SOLDIER   Message from Mr. Trotter, sir. Shells falling mostly behind support line. Minnies along front line.

STANHOPE   Who's just been hit?

SOLDIER   Corporal Ross, I think it was, sir. Minnie dropped in the trench at the corner – just as I come away.

> *The* SERGEANT-MAJOR *comes down the steps, very much out of breath.*

STANHOPE   (*to the* SOLDIER)   All right, thanks.

> *The* SOLDIER *salutes, and goes up the steps slower than he came.*

S.-M.   Beginning to get 'ot, sir.

STANHOPE	Corporal Ross hit?
S.-M.	Yessir.
STANHOPE	Badly?
S.-M.	Pretty badly, sir.
STANHOPE	Most of the shelling's going over, isn't it?
S.-M.	Most of the *shells* is be'ind, sir, but there's Minnies and rifle grenades along the front line. Pretty 'ot it's getting, sir. They're attacking down south – there's rifle fire.
STANHOPE	All right, sergeant-major; thanks.
S.-M.	What I come to ask, sir – what about the wounded – getting 'em down, sir? The shelling's pretty thick over Lancer's Alley.
STANHOPE	What about Fosse Way?
S.-M.	Pretty bad there, too, sir.
STANHOPE	Don't try then. Take anyone badly hit down into the big dug-out on the right. Let the stretcher-bearers do what they can there.
S.-M.	Very good, sir.
STANHOPE	Only Corporal Ross hit?
S.-M.	That's all, sir—

Again there comes the drawn-out call – several times as it is passed from man to man: "Stretcher bear-ers!"

The SERGEANT-MAJOR'S *eyes meet* STANHOPE'S. *He turns and goes up the steps.*

STANHOPE *is alone. Flying fragments of shell whistle and hiss and moan overhead. The sharp "crack" of the rifle grenades, the thud of the shells, and the boom of the Minenverfer mingle together in a muffled roar.* STANHOPE *takes his belt from the table and buckles it on, puts his revolver lanyard round his neck, and drops his flask and sandwiches into his pocket.*

The SERGEANT-MAJOR *reappears and comes hurrying down the steps.*

STANHOPE	(*turning quickly*) What is it, sergeant-major?
S.-M.	Mr. Raleigh, sir—
STANHOPE	What!
S.-M.	Mr. Raleigh's been 'it, sir. Bit of shell's got 'im in the back.
STANHOPE	Badly?
S.-M.	Fraid it's broke 'is spine, sir; can't move 'is legs.
STANHOPE	Bring him down here.
S.-M.	Down 'ere, sir?
STANHOPE	(*shouting*) Yes! Down here – quickly!

The SERGEANT-MAJOR *hurries up the steps. A shell screams and bursts very near. The* SERGEANT-MAJOR *shrinks back and throws his hands across his face, as though a human hand could ward off the hot flying pieces. He stumbles on again into the trench, and hurriedly away.*

STANHOPE *is by* OSBORNE'S *bed, fumbling a blanket over it. He takes a trench coat off the wall and rolls it for a pillow. He goes to his own bed, takes up his blanket, and turns as the* SERGEANT-MAJOR *comes carefully down the steps carrying* RALEIGH *like a child in his huge arms.*

(*With blanket ready.*) Lay him down there.

S.-M.	'E's fainted, sir. 'E was conscious when I picked 'im up.

The SERGEANT-MAJOR *lays the boy gently on the bed; he draws away his hands, looks furtively at the palms, and wipes the blood on the sides of his trousers.* STANHOPE *covers* RALEIGH *with his blanket, looks intently at the boy, and turns to the* SERGEANT-MAJOR.

STANHOPE   Have they dressed the wound?
S.-M.   They've just put a pad on it, sir. Can't do no more.
STANHOPE   Go at once and bring two men with a stretcher.
S.-M.   We'll never get 'im down, sir, with them shells falling on Lancer's Alley.
STANHOPE   Did you hear what I said? Go and get two men with a stretcher.
S.-M.   (*after a moment's hesitation*)   Very good, sir.

The SERGEANT-MAJOR *goes slowly away.*

STANHOPE *turns to* RALEIGH *once more, then goes to the table, pushes his handkerchief into the water-jug, and brings it, wringing wet, to* RALEIGH'S *bed. He bathes the boy's face. Presently* RALEIGH *gives a little moan, opens his eyes, and turns his head.*

RALEIGH   Hullo – Dennis—
STANHOPE   Well, Jimmy – (*he smiles*) – you got one quickly.

There is silence for a while. STANHOPE *is sitting on a box beside* RALEIGH. *Presently* RALEIGH *speaks again – in a wondering voice.*

RALEIGH   Why – how did I get down here?
STANHOPE   Sergeant-major brought you down.

RALEIGH *speaks again, vaguely, trying to recollect.*

RALEIGH   Something – hit me in the back – knocked me clean over – sort of – winded me—I'm all right now.   (*He tries to rise.*)
STANHOPE   Steady, old boy. Just lie there quietly for a bit.
RALEIGH   I'll be better if I get up and walk about. It happened once before – I got kicked in just the same place at Rugger; it – it soon wore off. It – it just numbs you for a bit.   (*There is a pause.*)   What's that rumbling noise?
STANHOPE   The guns are making a bit of a row.
RALEIGH   Our guns?
STANHOPE   No.   Mostly theirs.

Again there is silence in the dug-out. A very faint rose light is beginning to glow in the dawn sky. RALEIGH *speaks again – uneasily.*

RALEIGH   I say – Dennis—
STANHOPE   Yes, old boy?
RALEIGH   It – it hasn't gone through, has it? It only just hit me. – and knocked me down?
STANHOPE   It's just gone through a bit, Jimmy.
RALEIGH   I won't have to – go on lying here?
STANHOPE   I'm going to have you taken away.
RALEIGH   Away?   Where?
STANHOPE   Down   to   the   dressing-station – then   hospital – then   home.   (*He smiles.*)   You've got a Blighty one,* Jimmy.

---

* Blighty one – Blighty meant England, and a Blighty one was a wound which would require hospital treatment in England. It was considered a piece of luck.

RALEIGH But I – I can't go home just for – for a knock in the back. (*He stirs restlessly.*) I'm certain I'll be better if – if I get up. (*He tries to raise himself, and gives a sudden cry.*) Oh – God! It does hurt!

STANHOPE It's bound to hurt, Jimmy.

RALEIGH What's – on my legs? Something holding them down—

STANHOPE It's all right, old chap; it's just the shock – numbed them.

Again there is a pause. When RALEIGH *speaks, there is a different note in his voice.*

RALEIGH It's awfully decent of you to bother, Dennis. I feel rotten lying here – everybody else – up there.

STANHOPE It's not your fault, Jimmy.

RALEIGH So – damn – silly – getting hit. (*Pause.*) Is there – just a drop of water?

STANHOPE (*rising quickly*) Sure. I've got some here.

He pours some water into the mug and brings it to RALEIGH. (*Cheerfully.*) Got some tea-leaves in it. D' you mind?

RALEIGH No. That's all right – thanks—

STANHOPE *holds the mug to* RALEIGH'S *lips, and the boy drinks.*

I say, Dennis, don't you wait – if – if you want to be getting on.

STANHOPE It's quite all right, Jimmy.

RALEIGH Can you stay for a bit?

STANHOPE Of course I can.

RALEIGH (*faintly*) Thanks awfully.

There is quiet in the dug-out for a long time. STANHOPE *sits with one hand on* RALEIGH'S *arm, and* RALEIGH *lies very still. Presently he speaks again – hardly above a whisper.*

Dennis—

STANHOPE Yes, old boy?

RALEIGH Could we have a light? It's – it's so frightfully dark and cold.

STANHOPE (*rising*) Sure! I'll bring a candle and get another blanket.

STANHOPE *goes to the left-hand dug-out, and* RALEIGH *is alone, very still and quiet, on* OSBORNE'S *bed. The faint rosy glow of the dawn is deepening to an angry red. The grey night sky is dissolving, and the stars begin to go. A tiny sound comes from where* RALEIGH *is lying – something between a sob and a moan.* STANHOPE *comes back with a blanket. He takes a candle from the table and carries it to* RALEIGH'S *bed. He puts it on the box beside* RALEIGH *and speaks cheerfully.*

Is that better, Jimmy? (RALEIGH *makes no sign.*) Jimmy—

Still RALEIGH *is quiet.* STANHOPE *gently takes his hand. There is a long silence.* STANHOPE *lowers* RALEIGH'S *hand to the bed, rises, and takes the candle back to the table. He sits on the bench behind the table with his back to the wall, and stares listlessly across at the boy on the bed. The solitary candle-flame throws up the lines on his pale, drawn face, and the dark shadows under his tired eyes. The thudding of the shells rises and falls like an angry sea.*

A PRIVATE SOLDIER *comes scrambling down the steps, his round, red face wet with perspiration, his chest heaving for breath.*

SOLDIER   Message from Mr. Trotter, sir – will you come at once.

STANHOPE gazes round at the SOLDIER – *and makes no other sign.*

Mr. Trotter, sir – says will you come at once!

STANHOPE rises stiffly and takes his helmet from the table.

STANHOPE   All right, Broughton, I'm coming.

The SOLDIER *turns and goes away.*

STANHOPE pauses for a moment by the bed and lightly runs his fingers over RALEIGH'S *tousled hair. He goes stiffly up the steps, his tall figure black against the dawn sky.*

The shelling has risen to a great fury. The solitary candle burns with a steady flame, and RALEIGH *lies in the shadows. The whine of a shell rises to a shriek and bursts on the dug-out roof. The shock stabs out the candle-flame; the timber props of the door cave slowly in, sandbags fall and block the passage to the open air.*

There is darkness in the dug-out. Here and there the red dawn glows through the jagged holes of the broken doorway.

Very faintly there comes the dull rattle of machine-guns and the fevered spatter of rifle fire.

1   Show how the pathos in the scene carefully emerges as it proceeds.
2   Imagine that you were Stanhope and you were writing up the events of this scene in your private journal later the same night. What would you say and what feelings would you try to express?
3   What advice as a director, would you give to the actors playing the Sergeant-Major, Raleigh and Stanhope in this scene, if you intended your production of the whole play to be a statement about the waste and futility of war?

Selected Bibliography

The 'Revels' History of Drama in English, 8 vols., 1975–83.

G. E. Bentley, *The Jacobean and Caroline Stage,* 7 vols., 1941–68.

M. C. Bradbrook, *History of Elizabethan Drama,* 6 vols., 1979.
    Shakespeare: the Poet and his World, 1978.

E. K. Chambers, *The Medieval Stage,* 2 vols., 1903.
    The Elizabethan Stage, 4 vols., 1932.

E. Crompton, *A Handbook of the Theatre,* second edition, 1973.

J. Elsom, *Post-war British Theatre,* 1979.

J. Elsom and N. Tomalin, *The History of the National Theatre,* 1979.

M. Esslin, *The Theatre of the Absurd,* third edition, 1974.

U. Ellis-Fermor, *The Jacobean Drama,* fifth edition, 1965.

P. Hartnoll, *The Oxford Companion to the Theatre,* fourth edition, 1983.

S. Josephs, *The Story of the Playhouse in England,* 1963.

H. D. Kitto, *Greek Tragedy,* 1961.

L. C. Knights, *Drama and Society in the Age of Jonson,* 1957.

Allardyce Nicoll, *History of English Drama,* 1600–1900, 6 vols., 1952–9.
    British Drama, sixth edition, revised J. C. Trewin, 1978.

I. Ribner, *The English History Play in the Age of Shakespeare,* revised edition, 1965.

R. Southern, *The Staging of Plays before Shakespeare,* 1973.

J. L. Styan, *Modern Drama in Theatre and Practice,* 3 vols., 1981.

J. Russell Taylor, *Anger and after: a Guide to the New British Drama,* second edition, 1977.

K. Tynan, *Curtains: a Critic's View of Plays, Players and Theatrical Events,* 1950–60, 1961.

Index

Main entries in **bold** type